BIBLIOGRAPHIES OF WRITINGS BY AMERICAN AND BRITISH WOMEN TO 1900

VOLUME 3

Bibliographies of writings by American and British women to 1900

Volumes published

Volume 1   Personal writings by women to 1900
Volume 2   Poetry by women to 1900
Volume 3   Drama by women to 1900

DRAMA BY WOMEN
TO 1900

A BIBLIOGRAPHY OF AMERICAN AND BRITISH WRITERS

COMPILED BY GWENN DAVIS AND BEVERLY A. JOYCE

MANSELL

6003636137

First published 1992 by
Mansell Publishing Limited, *A Cassell Imprint*
Villiers House, 41/47 Strand, London WC2N 5JE, England

© Gwenn Davis and Beverly A. Joyce 1992

British Library Cataloguing in Publication Data
Davis, Gwenn
 Drama by women to 1900: a bibliography of American
 and British writers.
 I. Title   II. Joyce, Beverly A.
 016.822089287

 ISBN 0–7201–2102–7

Printed and bound in Great Britain at Bookcraft (Bath) Ltd., Avon

CONTENTS

Introduction   vii

Selected sources   xxii
    General   xxii
    Specialized   xxiii

List of abbreviations of sources   xxvii

The Bibliography   1

Appendices   167
    Chronological listing   167
    List of actresses   173

Subject index   175

Index of adaptions and translations   181

INTRODUCTION

Drama by Women to 1900: A Bibliography of American and British Writers is the third volume in a series designed to make accessible literary works by well known and neglected writers in order to reestablish the range and variety of printed books published by women from 1475–1900. Other volumes in the series cover personal writing, poetry, short fiction, long fiction, and juvenile literature. A dictionary of pseudonyms and alternative names will be the final volume. Each bibliography presents the writers in alphabetical order. An appendix places them in order of publication date; an index to types of works and topics appropriate to the genre under consideration further defines the subject of each volume. The entries for the whole series were developed from a complete reading of *The National Union Catalog, Pre-1956 Imprints* (NUC) and the catalog of the British Museum (now the British Library), Department of Printed Books, *General Catalogue of Printed Books* (BL), supplemented by the data base of the Online Computer Library Center (OCLC), other standard bibliographies and biographical dictionaries, and inspection of many of the works. The individual volumes are intended to be useful on their own as guides to particular literary forms. Taken together as a series, they permit their users to compare an individual author's work to others in a given genre and by consulting the other volumes to discover the full range of that writer's literary publications.

Establishing the record of women's contributions is in some ways more difficult for *Drama* than for any of the other genres. The catalogs that form the base files for this series, BL, NUC, and OCLC, do not provide the same coverage they do for other forms. BL, for example, lists the British publisher, Thomas H. Lacy, who with Samuel French in New York published thousands of acting editions, but does not catalog all the individual plays that it holds. In order to present as complete a listing of works as possible, we have, therefore, relied more heavily than we usually do on other reference materials. Certain of these sources, Nicoll and Mullin, for example, include works that are now known only through records of performances. Other works, especially those mentioned in the early sources such as Baker's *Biographia Dramatica*, may yet be rediscovered as Elizabeth Polwhele's *The Frolicks* was in the 1970s. Close to 20 percent of the entries on this bibliography are found only in secondary sources and are not presently known or available in print. The catalogs remain, however, the major source of entries. About 40 percent of the entries here are derived exclusively from BL, NUC or OCLC and are not mentioned in any other source. The remaining 40 percent may be found in both the catalogs and in other sources. Although in other volumes we cite important bibliographies, such as Matthews' and Ponsonby's standard works in *Personal Writings*, the number of entries in those works represent only a tiny fraction of the total. We have had to design certain parameters for the inclusion of references to the large number of heterogeneous sources for *Drama*.

These sources range from standard histories and bibliographies (Booth's *The Revel's History of Drama in English* or Carl Stratman's *Bibliography of English Printed Tragedy 1565–1900*) to compendiums of documents relating to the stage (Arnott and Robinson), lists of performances (Mullin, Wearing) and publishers' lists of acting series. They vary greatly in format and in the attention they pay to pseudonyms and alternative names. Some, such as Ellis, Donohue and Zak provide indexes of women writers and of pseudonyms. Others, such as Mullin, trace a few pseudonyms but overlook others such as 'George Villars' [Mrs Randolph Clay] or 'Ross Neil', the name under which Isabella Harwood fooled nearly every critic and reviewer of her time. In general, those drawn from playbills provide the least information on authorship. We have attempted to trace the full legal name of each author and provide for this volume our usual set of cross-references to all alternative forms of it as well as to all pseudonyms used for drama. The most standard and readily available sources we have used, Allardyce Nicoll's *A History of Drama 1660–1900* or Ellis, Donohue and Zak's *English Drama of the Nineteenth Century: an Index and Finding Guide*, for example, are listed by an abbreviation in the entries; other less comprehensive sources from which we have derived limited amounts of information are cited in the notes. As the list of Specialized Sources indicates, to note every reference work in which the entries may occur would overwhelm the entries themselves.

The more central issue, what constitutes a published dramatic work, is difficult to resolve. Original plays issued in collected works published before 1900 or included in the acting editions published by French, Lacy or W. H. Baker obviously fit our standard guidelines. To confine ourselves to these would, however, present only a portion of women's dramatic writings, Plays for the public theatre may have been performed and revised many times before they were published; some dramatic poems and closet dramas were never presented. Quite a number of plays were performed in the nineteenth century but not published either in a commercial acting edition or in the author's collected works until the twentieth century. Lucy (Lane) Clifford, for example, had several comedies produced in West End theatres in the 1890s; Nicoll and Mullin mention a production of *A Honeymoon Tragedy* in 1896 and an acting edition, but the catalogs cite an edition by Samuel French in 1904. We have included, in addition to works cited in the major supplementary sources, works in the catalogs that were produced before 1900. Translations and adaptations of classic plays or popular novels for the stage may so alter the original works that they constitute an entirely new work. We did not collect translations when the base file for this series was established, but we do include those that are covered in the additional sources and have supplied the information when they are contained in NUC, BL or

OCLC. We also include a number of translations that were published in collections listed in the *Poetry* volume. Pageants, tableaux, and charades, when fully scripted and developed, are the equivalent of a one or two act play. Prologues, epilogues, and interludes, brief though they are, are forms through which women established themselves in the public theatre. These works, whether published separately or in collections, are included. Only the broadest definitions of form and of time frame can accommodate women's dramatic writings.

The resources available to students of drama also differ from those for other genres. The series of microprint editions of dramatic literature published by Readex make available materials that were never published in their own time or that are today extremely rare. The Readex collection of Bergquist's *Three Centuries of English and American Plays*, is based on and incorporates all but 150 of the works covered by Nicoll, Frank Hill's *American Plays Printed, 1714–1830*, W. W. Greg's *A Bibliography of English Printed Drama to the Restoration*, and Woodward and McManaway's *A Checklist of English Plays, 1641–1700*. These works and other bibliographical guides—Bergquist, Ellis, Donohue and Zak, and Wells—are cited in the entries. The Larpent manuscripts (McMillan) are now being included in this series. Though we do not list manuscripts in the other volumes, we do so here in order to include works that were performed before 1900 and to assist users who have access to the Readex series.

This volume includes a few works that are cited in other volumes, as for example, collected works that combine plays and short fiction or juvenile literature. This has been done so that each bibliography may be used independently. The relationship to the *Poetry* volume is more complex. Plays in verse published as separate works such as Aphra Behn's *The Amorous Prince* are cited only in *Drama*. Collections of poetry that include plays in verse such as Sally Caulfield's *The Innocents, a sacred drama. Ocean; and The Earthquake at Aleppo; Poems* appear in both volumes. The index to *Poetry* lists works that contain dramatic poems and poems for recitation, while the index to *Drama* covers plays written in verse as well as dramatic poems and recitations. This will eliminate extensive duplication, yet enable the reader to trace the extent of each form. A number of the works included here were intended for family entertainment and contain a large number of parts for children. Those that appeal to adults as well as to children, burlesques, fairy plays and pantomimes meant for a broad audience, for example, are cited here. Plays written exclusively for performance by and entertainment of children are cited only in the bibliography of *Juvenile Literature*. Further information on the indexes may be found in the section on scope and arrangement below.

The inclusion of dramatic poems and poems for recitation indicates something of the breadth of our definition of dramatic literature. We include plays that enjoyed popular acclaim on the public stage and works for amateurs, such as those published in Lacy's Home Entertainments series, closet drama, and extravaganzas. If the work was considered by its author to be in dramatic form, we include it here. A number of writers of dramatic poems were ambivalent about their work. Harriet Downing, for example, thought her work, *The Bride of Sicily. A Dramatic Poem* (1830) would never be produced, but included stage directions just in case. Clearly she had in mind classical drama when she wrote it, and she hoped it would be appreciated in that context. We also include any work intended for performance whether in commercial theatres or private entertainments. Pageants, tableaux or drills that rely purely on visual effects are excluded, but those that contain speaking parts or narration are recorded here.

This volume departs in another respect from the others. We have included here some works that are known today only through records of performances and some printed books published after 1900 when they contain plays that were performed and circulated in printed texts before then. A performance is not precisely equivalent to publication, but it does suggest that the work was made available to an audience, even if a limited one. Some plays survive if only in manuscript or prompt copies. Others that were suppressed are still available. For example, *The Art of Management; or, Tragedy expelled*, Charlotte (Cibber) Charke's satire on Charles Fleetwood,

manager of the Theatre Royal, Drury Lane, and no admirer of her acting, was produced only once. According to William Chetwood, 'It was printed in 1735, with a Humourous Dedication to Mr. *Fleetwood*, who endeavoured to smother it, by purchasing the whole impression; however some escaped the Flames, and crept into the world.' (*The British Theatre*, p. 186.) Ironically, Charke's other works, a comedy called *The Carnival; or, Harlequin blunderer* and a medley, *Tit for tat; or, The comedy and the tragedy of war*, are now known only because Nicoll records their performance. Plays, from Shakespeare's time on, were performed and revised many times before they were published. A collection such as Charlotte Mary Sanford Barnes' *Plays, Prose and Poetry* (1848) includes work in its most polished form. One of the plays, *Octavia Brigaldi*, was first produced in 1837 though it may have been written earlier. The other, *The Forest Princess*, was probably not acted. We include all three types, plays performed but not printed, plays performed and revised, and closet drama.

Women published in every field of letters, not just in those covered by this series. They wrote biographies, histories, volumes of essays and controversial pamphlets. They were some of the first translators and were early and prolific contributors to periodicals. Their work in these fields is beyond our scope. Our purpose is to show that they published a considerable number of printed books in the major literary genres. Although *Drama* is the shortest volume in these bibliographies and includes some works that were never published, it confirms the impressive record of women's participation in the literary marketplace that this series is designed to reveal. If one considers that women did not write for the public stage until the Restoration and that published plays in the nineteenth century represent a relatively small percentage of total literary publication, then this volume shows as the others do a consistent record of writing and publication. It should open the way for fresh consideration of women's achievements.

There is much to be done in reevaluating women dramatists. Current critical and scholarly resources do not cover the range of their activities. Twentieth century theatre, especially feminist theatre, and dramatic literature up to the middle of the eighteenth century is receiving a good bit of attention. There are few considerations of nineteenth century women dramatists. Chinoy and Jenkins' sourcebook, *Women in American Theatre*, includes articles on Mercy Otis Warren, on early actresses, and on Jane Addams' establishment of an art theatre at Hull House. Robinson, Roberts, and Barranger include a few early figures in their biographical dictionary, *Notable Women in the American Theatre*. The earliest women playwrights have so far received the most scholarly and critical attention. Two recent studies, Nancy Cotton's *Women Playwrights in England c1363–1750* and Jacqueline Pearson's *The Prostituted Muse: Images of Women and Women Dramatists, 1642–1737*, examine the careers of these writers, their works and the themes that distinguish them from their male contemporaries. Aphra Behn's work in all genres has recently been studied; some of the most famous and prominent of the British dramatists, Cowley, Centilivre, and Inchbald, continue to hold a place in the dramatic canon. American women are less well known. The standard histories mention only Mercy (Otis) Warren and Anna Cora Mowatt Ritchie. Daniel Havens gives Mowatt Ritchie's *Fashion* full treatment as the comedy that truly established American comic form. Others, usually actresses or members of theatrical families, are mentioned in passing. Fanny Kemble, Marie (Wilton) Bancroft, and Mary (Anderson) De Novello, who are remembered, were stars who left autobiographies as well as a record of writing for the stage. Given the continuing fascination with stage personalities, it is not surprising that the dramatic poets, like other women poets, have been almost entirely neglected. Home theatre and private productions which are considered a minor art are also little studied even though the writers, Katherine Lacy, Olivia Wilson, or Mary Seymour, for example, may have been best sellers in their own time. The materials in this bibliography should make a reconsideration of the full range of women's dramatic writings possible.

Unlike the early poets whose work quickly went out of print, early dramatists were read, produced, and enjoyed throughout the eighteenth and early nineteenth centuries. John Bell, a London publisher and book seller who maintained a circulating library lists 50,000 volumes in his 1777 catalog. Among these are the plays of the Duchess of Newcastle (2 vols.), Mrs Behn (3 vols.), Susanna Centilivre (3 vols.), and the poems of Mary Leapor, including her *The unhappy father, A tragedy*; the appendix contains *Inflexible Captives, A tragedy* by 'Miss Hannah Moore.' Mrs Inchbald's works became standard, not only from their success on the stage, but because she compiled two important collections, *The British Theatre* in 25 volumes and *The Modern Theatre* in 10 volumes. She had a place in many country libraries, and her plays were produced everywhere. Her *Lover's Vows* is the play performed in Jane Austen's *Mansfield Park*. In the mid-nineteenth century, inexpensive acting editions and collections of 'possible plays' for amateur actors, such as those by Katherine Lacy and Mary Seymour continue this tradition. They brought women playwrights a large circulation outside the theatre centers.

Several eighteenth century dramatists became standards in repertory companies. This may have given them a greater prominence than is now recognized. Joseph Donohue notes in *Theatre in the Age of Kean* that only 14 percent of the plays produced in the season 1794–95 were new main pieces. Revivals were the staple of nineteenth century theatrical offerings. Mrs Inchbald remained a favorite. Six of her works were revived: *Animal Magnetism* in 1841 and 1845; *To Marry or Not to Marry* in the 1840s; *Everyone Has His Fault, The Wedding Day*, and *Wives as They Were and Maids as They Are* four times each in the 1840s and 50s; *The Midnight Hour* in 1838 and again in 1868. Hannah Cowley's *A Bold Stroke for a Husband* was revived only once, at Sadler's Wells in 1850, but her comedy, *The Belle's Stratagem*, was produced eleven times from 1838 to 1881. The earliest of these writers, Susanna Centilivre, delighted audiences until the end of the nineteenth century. A version of *A Bold Stroke for a Wife, The Guardians off their Guard*, played at the Olympic in 1840. *The Busy Body*, first produced in 1709 was revived six times in the 1840s and 50s, and the most popular of all, *The Wonder: A Woman Keeps a Secret* was presented a dozen times from 1837 to 1868. Although little known today, they enjoyed a long run.

Dramatic literature by women falls essentially into three types: closet drama, including dramatic poetry and translations of great dramatists, practised primarily by aristocrats and other educated women in private life; professional theatre written—and frequently acted—by women from all levels of the middle and working classes; and amateur or home entertainment written by middle class women for their families and friends or by professional writers. Overall, the dramatists come from ordinary backgrounds; only 39 are titled, 36 Englishwomen and three North Americans. The largest identifiable group is the 15 percent who were actresses or members of theatrical families. Many playwrights also published in other genres, poetry, juvenile literature, and especially fiction. Something of the writers' backgrounds and interests can be established through the kinds of drama they wrote, and the patterns of development in drama over time should be seen in the light of the three types of plays.

The overall demographic patterns for the dramatic writers resemble those for other genres. The great majority of writers date from the latter half of the nineteenth century; women's rate of publication increases exponentially over time. Yet *Drama* includes an exceptional number of writers before 1800. Twenty percent of the British women here wrote during the late seventeenth and eighteenth centuries. Americans are more sparsely represented in that period than in other genres, perhaps because of the resistance to the theatre in Quaker Philadelphia and Puritan Boston, the early literacy centers of the United States. Mercy (Otis) Warren, Susanna (Haswell) Rowson and Judith (Sargent) Stevens Murray established their careers before the turn of the nineteenth century. Margaretta (Bleeker) Faugeres' *Belisarius, A Tragedy* published in 1795, was probably never produced, but Mrs Marriott's farce, *The Chimera; or, Effusions of Fancy* played in Philadelphia in 1794. In total numbers, the British writers comprise 60 percent of the dramatists listed in this bibliography and the North Americans 40 percent. The additional sources we

have used account for part of this. One might expect more British women to publish before the 1830s when North American publishing centers were well established and problems of book distribution had been solved. For the later periods, record keeping was better in England. Productions on the London stage are better documented than those in the United States which has never had an established theatre or one geographic center for it.

The issue of nationality is complicated by the number of trans-Atlantic careers. Fanny Lily Gipsy Davenport, for example, was born in London, made her debut in Boston, and established herself as a major actress as a member of Augustin Daly's troupe at the Fifth Avenue Theatre in New York. Ettie Henderson, educated in a convent in Cincinnati, toured London and the provinces as Fanchon. Laura Keene, the great theatrical manager who opened her theatre in New York in the 1850s was born in England and first established her reputation at Mme Vestris' theatre, the Lyceum. Throughout the nineteenth century writers and plays enjoyed success on both sides of the Atlantic. *Uncle Tom's Cabin* was so popular in the States that in 1859 fifty 'Tom Shows' were on the road performing in tents around the country (Hughes). It also went through nine separate adaptations and productions on the London stage from 1852 to 1896. Although there were a few commercial genres that did not travel well, minstrel shows or Christmas pantomimes, the best known dramatists and performers enjoyed fame and influence on both sides of the ocean.

The three types of drama do reveal some differences in authorship. Closet drama was, at the beginning, primarily an aristocratic pursuit. The works of Viscountess Falkland, the Countesses of Pembroke and Winchelsea, the Duchess of Newcastle, and Queen Elizabeth I established the genre and defined its characteristics for the less exalted writers who followed. Closet drama is generally in verse, it deals with serious subjects, tragic or historical events, encompasses translations of classical dramatists, and most important, it is meant to be read in private, savored for the elegance of its writing. The common characteristic of these writers is their learning. After 1750, only two titled women, the Countess of Strathmore and Princess Troubetzkey published closet work, but the literary aristocracy is well represented: Joanna Baillie, Katherine Bradley and Edith Cooper, Elizabeth (Barrett) Browning, George Eliot, Mrs Hemans, Emma Lazarus, Mary Russell Mitford, Frances Fuller Victor, and Constance Woolson, to cite only a few. Perhaps half the closet works appear in larger collections of verse. These dramatists were well educated, serious writers who saw themselves primarily as poets.

Private theatricals, like closet drama, had aristocratic origins, but became a general pursuit. Queen Henrietta Maria devised pastorals and masques, and other women of the court probably also shaped these productions. Elizabeth Craven during her second marriage to the Margrave of Anspach revived the form in the late eighteenth and early nineteenth centuries. Only a few of the works she wrote and presented at Brandenburgh House survive, including two translations and two works that were presented on the legitimate stage, *The Princess of Georgia*, an opera, and *The Miniature Picture*, a comedy. Lady Georgiana (Russell) Peel and her sister, Lady Victoria Russell, published a limited edition of the masque they wrote and staged for their brother's twenty-first birthday in 1858. A few other coterie works were printed, but the majority of the home theatricals were written for a general audience by women from diverse backgrounds. Lady Bell and Lady Cadogan published collections for the home theatre and also saw their works produced in the public theatre. Other women who are now obscure, Gabrielle De Nottbeck, Florence Gailey, Jean Ingraham, Frances Peard, Winnie Rover, to cite a few at random, published plays or collections of charades. Bell's *Chamber Comedies* were published by Longmans Green; other British collections were brought out by major houses, Sampson Low or Rivingtons. In the United States, Walter H. Baker of Boston was the major publisher of comediettas, farces and amateur pieces, but two publishers in Ohio, Eldridge in Franklin and Ames in Clyde, developed long lists of comedies and entertainments. This suggests that there was a substantial market for such work in both Britain and North America.

The circulation of these publishers argues that amateur theatre was indeed thriving outside the major theatre centers.

The professional theatre from the period of the Restoration offered women employment, celebrity, and an outlet for their talent and drew women from all layers of the middle and working classes. Unlike the lyric and dramatic poets who circulated their work among their friends seeking recognition primarily from that intimate and sophisticated audience, dramatists who wrote for the public stage required the test of production and the affirmation of applause. Before it was possible to earn a living by writing poetry or fiction, a career on the stage offered both fame and financial reward even while it placed these women in an ambiguous social position. That ambiguity has led to the assumption that most of the early actresses were from poor, even unsavory backgrounds. Nell Gwynne, the cockney daughter of a prostitute, epitomizes the early actress raised from the slums to the uncertain rank of King's mistress. Her contemporaries in Thomas Killigrew's company at Drury Lane refute this. Ann and Rebecca Marshall were the daughters of a Presbyterian minister; Elizabeth Barry's father was a lawyer and Anne Bracegirdle's a country gentleman.

The playwrights, too, were primarily middle class, despite the famous exceptions often considered the norm. Like the writers of closet drama, they recognized the ancient and serious character of drama. Aphra Behn, a thorough professional, a spy, actress, and a colonial may have been outside the recognized social order. Jane (Holt) Wiseman who wrote one tragedy, *Antiochus the Great; or The Fatal Relapse*, while employed as a servant and set up a tavern with her husband on the proceeds represents the lower end of the scale. The majority of the other writers were middle class women. Quite a few had connections with the guilds, the landed gentry and the church. Mary (Griffith) Pix, the daughter of a minister, married a merchant tailor; Mary Davys was the widow of a clergyman; and Catherine (Trotter) Cockburn, daughter of Scottish gentleman and wife of a minister, aspired to the highest level of education, teaching herself Latin, Greek, and French. Professionals also wrote, and developed for themselves larger parts than they found in others' work. Of the eighty-three women listed in Baker's *Biographia Dramatica*, which covers the stage from the reign of Elizabeth I to 1814, at least sixteen were actresses including Anna (Ross) Brunton, Susanna Centilivre, Kitty Clive, Eliza Haywood, Marie Therese Kemble, and Frances (Chamberlaine) Sheridan as well as the lesser known Teresa Cornelys, Phillipina (Burton) Hill, Miss Pope and Mrs Robertson. At least two, Mrs Kemble and Mrs Sheridan, married into theatrical dynasties.

Writing for the professional theatre in the late eighteenth and early nineteenth centuries was not a disreputable pastime. Garrick and other managers were deluged with scripts by amateurs. Some of the most persistent ultimately saw their works performed, but others had recourse to alternative publication. John Galt's periodical, *The Rejected Theatre*, was established to print works that were not produced. Anne (Hamilton) M'Taggart's attempts to find an audience give some insight into the aspirations of a dramatist. She sent her work to John Kemble who did not return it, then applied to Galt. Her first play, *Valville*, written in 1790, was criticized by the friends who read it, but later works were widely circulated, even read in manuscript by Queen Charlotte and Princess Elizabeth who complained of M'Taggart's handwriting. Ultimately she brought out two editions of her work in the 1820s and 30s, the first volume anonymously and the second under her own name. In the preface she states that she began writing to experiment with the form of blank verse, then developed her own idea of what drama should be. 'My idea of a good play was, that it should be interesting without sacrificing sense and probability. . . . I preferred describing beings more like myself.' In this she anticipates the increasingly close connection between drama and the novel, the direction many women playwrights would take. Other ordinary women in this period also sought to associate themselves with the stage and perhaps to derive some of its glamour. Mary Julia Young brought out in 1792 a limited edition of her *Genius and Fancy*, a dialogue between these deities on the actors and actresses of the day. She then published an expanded edition with other poems,

hoping 'the candour of an indulgent Public will make allowance for the changes that have taken place in the Dramatic World.' Young, like M'Taggart, sought to link herself to the professionals.

The commercial stage in the mid-Victorian age did retain something of the unsavory reputation of the Restoration theatre. The ambiguous social position of the actress may have discouraged some from going on the stage or writing for it, but it continued to attract women for financial reward and for the outlet of their talents. Anna Mowatt [Ritchie] took pains in her autobiography to defend the moral character and the industry of her fellow players. Mowatt was born into a prosperous family and turned to the theatre to support herself when their fortunes suffered. Her contemporary, Anna Katherine (Green) Rohlfs, the daughter of a lawyer, married a tragedian. When his career waned, he became a furniture designer; she published thrillers and wrote plays to help support them. Money could provide opportunity, too. John Scott who had made a fortune in laundry soap, bought the Sans Pareil theatre in London for his daughter, Jane. Some records of the musicals she produced survive, along with one published work, *The Old Oak Chest; or, The Smuggler's Son and the Robber's Daughter*. Talented and ambitious women sought theatrical careers.

Other professionals, notably those from theatrical families, the Cibbers, the Kembles, and the Sheridans were admired and received almost everywhere. Although none of them wrote plays, Adams mentions nineteen actresses who married titles. There are others who did write, Lady Moncton and Marie Wilton, wife of the theatrical knight, Squire Bancroft. In addition to Mowatt and Wilton, seven other actresses published both theatrical pieces and autobiographies: Charlotte (Cibber) Charke, Fanny (Wright) D'Arusmont, Mary (Anderson) De Navarro, Phillipina (Burton) Hill, Mrs Inchbald, Dorothea (Bland) Jordan, and Olive Logan. Most of the plays by actresses were never published, though Mary Anderson's adaptations of Shakespeare survive. Other women from theatrical families were better known for their fiction. Sydney (Owenson), Lady Morgan's father was an actor in the Dublin theatre. Although her reputation rests on her novels, she wrote a comic opera, *The First Attempt*, which ran only a few nights and *Dramatic Scenes from Real Life*, a novel in dramatic form.

The largest group of professional writers to turn to the stage in the later nineteenth century were novelists. Many adapted their own works, and often the dramatic versions became far more famous than the originals. *East Lynne* in Mrs Humphrey Ward's version and in others held the stage long into the twentieth century when her novel was out of print. Frances (Hodgson) Burnett adapted two of her works for the stage, *A Lady of Quality* and *Little Lord Fauntleroy*. The latter, which is still being revived, was so popular in the 1880s that she called her first stage version 'The Real Little Lord Fauntleroy' to distinguish it from unauthorized adaptations. Louisa May Alcott, Lucie Ayres, Pearl Craigie, Mary Eleanor (Wilkins) Freeman, Anna Maria (Fielding) Hall, Mary St. Leger Harrison, Florence (Price) James, Florence (Marryat) Lean, and Henrietta Stannard, to cite only a few, were all better known for their fiction than their theatrical pieces.

Though some may have been put off by the reputation of the commercial stage, the esteem in which the best known actresses were held and the number of successful novelists who adapted their work to the stage, suggests that by the end of the nineteenth century, dramatic literature had regained the standing it lost in the Romantic age. The entries in this bibliography suggest that talented women were always interested in the theatre. Even Victorian modesty did not confine them to closet drama or cause them to avoid identification. The majority in all periods published under their own names. Closet drama, considered a form of literature rather than theatre, was published with a half dozen exceptions (Amica Religionis, Ephelia, A L[ady] o[f] E[ngland], An Officer's Wife, Philanthea, Margaret Russell), under the writers' own names. Of the eighty pseudonyms here, only eighteen are male and another nine are neuter. Of the eighteen, only 'Michael Field' [Bradley and Cooper] and 'Ross Neil' [Isabella Harwood] were designed to fool the dramatic critics. The majority of the others were first used for fiction or other genres and served as much for advertisement as disguise:

'John Oliver Hobbes' [Craigie], for example, or 'Lucas Malet' [Harrison]; 'Harley St. John' [Ellen Pollock], 'Charles Marlowe' [Harriet Jay] or 'Peter Sparks, Gentleman' [S. Howell]. Some women published and remain anonymous. For example, one work *The Sultan; or A Peep into the Seraglio*, in John Bell's *Supplement to Bell's British Theatre*, may well be by a woman. The dramatic focus is on the heroine, and English captive, and her part is unusually full. Some will never be traced. Nonetheless, there is a consistent record of women writing for the public theatre as well as for private reading or acting. The professionals were the most visible, but women from a variety of backgrounds wrote plays and sought both profit and recognition from them.

The patterns of publication of drama follow the trend in other genres in that the number of women writers increases greatly over time, but there are some major differences. Most striking is the increase in numbers of works in the final quarter of the nineteenth century. Fifty percent of the writers in this volume published and produced their plays during that time. This is not due to an increase in the works now known only by records of performance. Mullin lists 136 women writers whose work was presented on the London stage in this period, but that constitutes 20 percent of the total, about the same percentage as these works represent in the entire bibliography. More probably this phenomenal growth is due to an increase in the number of theatres, especially in North America, and to an increase in the audience for plays both on the public stage and in amateur performance. Closet drama has nearly disappeared. Dramatic poems in collections and plays written for reading comprise less than 1 percent of the works in this period. The overwhelming majority of works are fully scripted and arranged for the stage.

Among the earlier playwrights, the patterns of publication are closest to women's record in other genres and mirror the literary interests of their times. Although more women before 1750 published dramatic literature than published printed volumes of poetry, they are still a tiny number, less than 10 percent of the writers listed here. In the second half of the eighteenth century, 11 percent of the writers here published or produced their work. During the Romantic age, the first half of the nineteenth century, dramatic literature is less prominent. Eight percent of the writers were active from 1800 to 1824 and another 8 percent from 1825 to 1850. As might be expected, this is the age of the dramatic poem and of the closet tragedy. Fourteen percent of the closet works were published from 1750–1800, 17 percent appeared in the first quarter of the nineteenth century, and 35 percent in the second quarter. In the period from mid-century to 1875 dramatic activity increased, but not radically. The percentage of closet works drops off to 13 percent in this quarter century before it virtually disappears. The number of writers increases, but only to 14 percent of all authors here. Again, there is probably no single explanation for this fluctuation in the number of writers and works. Volumes of poetry roughly double for each quarter of the nineteenth century; drama goes out of fashion and returns in the last thirty years in record proportions. In part this is a function of the increase in the number of theatres, the increase in audience and in audience demand for novelty, as well as the renewed interest in home acting as a wholesome form of entertainment. It is also an indication of the shift of taste away from Romanticism, the developments in drama, especially melodrama and its allied forms, domestic and temperance drama, and in the relationship between popular fiction and the stage.

Comedy in all its forms, comedy, comedietta, farce, is the dominant form here, it accounts for 40 to 45 percent of the works. Drama and melodrama come next at 28 percent, and together with historical drama constitute 37 percent of all the works. Tragedies comprise only 10 percent of all works. Musical forms, operas, minstrel shows, ballad operas and other spectacular forms, charades, burlesques and pageants account for the rest, and most of these should be considered comic. Another 10 percent of the works are adaptations and translations, including closet translations of Classical writers, translations of continental dramatists for English language productions, and adaptations of fiction and verse for the stage.

The choice of genre correlates, in general, with the three types, closet, private and public drama, and with the period in which the works were written. Comedy is the universal form. It had the greatest success on the commercial stage and was the overwhelming choice for amateur production. As already noted, the works of Mrs Inchbald, Susanna Centilivre, and Hannah Cowley that remained in the nineteenth century repertoire were their comedies. Their tragedies, however, *The Cruel Gift* or *The Fate of Sparta*, were not revived. Restoration comedy was universally loved. A number of collections for home performance includes comedies set in the Civil War and the eighteenth century, as for example, Netta Parker's *For the Honour of the House*, a royalist romance, or her *In Danger's Hour* and *My Lady of Levenmore*. Annie (Frost) Shield's *Wooing under Difficulties* is an American variation set in the war of 1812.

Comedy assumed all forms, farce, burlesques, comic sketch and monologue. The more extensive and most sophisticated mirrored the wit of the Restoration or the 'sprightliness' of thee French, though without the indelicacy. Only one comedy appears in a collection, Sarah Anne Curzon's *The Sweet Girl Graduate* in the volume titled for her historical drama, *Laura Secord, the Heroine of 1812*. These works were intended for performance. Parody and satire were also comic modes and illustrate the audience's familiarity with dramatic literature and dramatic conventions. Clara Sherwood wrote *The Cable Car. A Howellian Burlesque*. 'Polly Pritchard' [Delia Heywood] included a spoof of temperance drama, *The Perils of Moderate Drinking* in her collection for amateurs, *Choice Dialogues*. Another amateur play, Annie (Frost) Shield's *Dramatic*, ridicules an aspiring actor and the bombastic delivery of nineteenth century tragedians.

Tragedy is primarily a closet form, but a few plays were produced, the greatest concentration of them in the last half of the eighteenth century. Two thirds of the tragedies from that time were acted or prepared for the stage. Sophia Lee's *Almeyda, Queen of Granada* was presented at Drury Lane in 1796; Ann Yearsley's *Earl Goodwin, An Historical Play* in Bath in 1789. Miss R. Roberts gives full stage directions for *Malcolm* (1779), though no productions are recorded. Hannah Brand starred in her own play, *Huniades*. While Elizabeth Griffith's comedies were popular at Drury Lane and Covent Garden, her tragedy, *Amana*, is a dramatic poem. The number of productions drops off drastically until the last quarter of the nineteenth century at which point about half the tragedies written were intended for the stage.

The Romantic emphasis on character and motivation was not theatrical, especially in an era of spectacle, tableaux, equestrian and water drama. Joanna Baillie's work was not a success on stage, but she was widely read in Britain and North America. Sarah Richardson, widow of the proprietor of Drury Lane published two stage works, *Ethelred* and *Gertrude*, Isabel Hill's *The Poet's Child* played Covent Garden in 1829, but the majority of these works were for reading: Miss H. St. A. Kitching's *The Fate of Ivan* (1832), Caroline Hentz's *De Lara; or, The Moorish Bride* (1843) or Eliza Dana's *Iona* (1864). Dramatic form was used for effect. Harriet Skidmore's allegorical drama, *The Ransomed Captive*, was never intended for the stage. Verse tragedy was generally beyond the skill of amateur performers. Only one tragedy was published in a collection of short plays, Caro Dugan's *The King's Jester*. Those who wished to perform more serious work could, of course, turn to the famous tragic dramatists. Gabrielle De Nottbeck's adaptation of scenes from Shakespeare and Fanny Kemble's translation and adaptation of Schiller's *Mary Stuart* were widely available.

The prevalence of historical topics links these works to the form most popular after comedy, historical drama. Both forms rely primarily on the remote past, perhaps because it is hard to discern heroic stature in one's contemporaries. The Middle Ages and antiquity were the most important settings, but there are some patterns in the subjects that exemplify women's interests. Many deal with heroines, and many deal with the theme of bondage and deliverance. Although few are directly concerned with abolition, the most influential of those works were, like *Uncle Tom's Cabin*, melodramas, some of them do meet these issues head on. Sara Groenvelt's *Otille the Octoroon* explores the tragic situation of a woman of mixed blood, and Mary Autry Greer looked at the establishment of the Ku Klux Klan in *Reconstruction in the South (A Tragedy Founded on Fact)*. Mary Putnam's two verse dramas, *Tragedy of Errors* (1861) and its sequel, *Tragedy of Success* (1862) deal explicitly with slavery in the United States.

The heroines of the historical plays are generally tragic figures, the wives of Henry VIII, Joan of Arc, or Biblical: Ruth and Esther were especially popular. Some were strong figures, Emilia Gowing's *Boadicea* (1899), for example, or Pocohontas in Charlotte Barnes' *The Forest Princess*. Others exemplified the virtues of a loyal wife as in Constance Barry's *Brutus' Portia*. More often, though they are figures of passion, Heloise in Emily De Lesdernier's dramatic poem or Medea in Harriette Read's. The anti-heroine was Sappho, the subject of a number of poems and plays. Some of these were translations of Grillparzer, but not Estelle Anna Lewis's *Sappho of Lesbos; or Love that Kills* (1868). All these works play on the idea that women are the emotional sex, but two of the most important, Mary Queen of Scots and Lady Jane Grey offer a religious dimension. Lady Jane is a Protestant martyr; Mary, a womanly woman in contrast to the powerful Elizabeth I, is a Roman Catholic martyr. Comedy is preoccupied with the formation of marriage, and is certainly the mode for expressing the social ideal for women. The tragedies and histories debated the same issues. Those written for production also offered splendid parts for the actresses.

The other genres, opera and musical drama, spectacles, ballets, involved women to a limited extent as professional writers and to a considerable extent as amateurs. Although the Laura Keenes and the Jane Scotts had the resources to mount commercial productions, the majority of these works are occasional and were written for amateur performance, Sarah Dawes' *The Braxton Minute Men. A Centennial Drama*, for example, or Florine McCray's *Columbus*. Mrs Cresswell combined several genres and effects in her play on the English Civil War, *The King's Banner; or Aimez Loyaute: An Original Semi-historical Drama, in Four Acts and Several Tableaux*. Women composed few operas, though they translated quite a few libretti. They wrote quite a few shorter pieces, largely for amateur production. Some of these were also presented as interludes or curtain raisers, as Ellen Lancaster-Wallis pieces were. Rosina Fillipi's street scenes and slices of life, *An Idyll of New Year's Eve* and *In the Italian Quarter* were performed at the Vaudeville and published as 'Carpet Plays' for those who did not tread the boards professionally.

The importance of amateur theatre and the seriousness of its dramatists should not be dismissed. It met a variety of needs and had the highest social sanction. Queen Victoria's enjoyment of the theatre—she reintroduced the office of Master of the Revels and had plays staged at Windsor—lent respectability. Touring companies could not satisfy the theatrical appetite of people in English provincial towns, let alone the more scattered communities of North America. Chatauquas brought education and entertainment to smaller settlements and involved the local talent. Sarah Pratt's *Penelope's Symposium; a Dialogue Illustrating Life in Ancient Greece. Containing Full Directions for Presentations*, had nine female parts and was written for a Chautauqua women's meeting. Moreover, plays could support local causes. Effie Merriman's *Socials* gives full instructions on fund raising as well as a play. There were commercial possibilities, too. Thomas Lacy advertized a full range of properties, costumes and stage sets in copies of the acting series.

Women were particulary active in writing for home performance. It was a role that began early. In the preface to a collection of plays for children, Frances Callow notes that it is the job of the eldest daughter to keep the younger children 'busy, merry, and happy' on their holidays and that putting on plays is one of the most wholesome ways to accomplish that task. The majority of their works are comediettas, brief melodramas, fairy plays, sketches and charade plays, but that is not an indication that they were meant merely as skits or that the authors had no larger literary ambitions. The casts are small, the properties minimal, and the stage directions copious. Clearly the writers knew the resources of those who would produce these works. Yet, as Sarah Annie (Frost) Shields suggests in the preface to *Parlor Charades*, one of a best selling series of works for home performance, these writers also hoped to demonstrate some dramatic sophistication and literary skill. Her plays 'are intended solely for perform-

ance by small circles of friends, in private parlors or saloons, and require but little trouble or expense to make them effective. The plots are simple and intelligible, although sometimes a striking dramatic situation, or strong contrast of character, has been attempted.' Her work is for amateur players; she was not an amateur playwright.

Anne Bowman traced the origin of the charade: 'these spirited entertainments were originally borrowed from our sprightly neighbors, the French.' She criticizes the British practice which develops the plot and character of each element and neglects dramatic unity: 'the charade thus hastily arranged, is but a series of isolated scenes, having no connecting link. This, however, is not the original and genuine Charade, of which the ideas or scenes employed to suggest the several syllables and the complete word should naturally arise one out of the other, and thus give harmony and point to the whole.' For Bowman wit and artistic integrity are necessary to a good charade. These works might not take their place as great literature—amateurs who wished to perform Shakespeare could and often did mount such productions—but the women who specialized in writing light comedy and dramatic sketches saw them as a vehicle for artistic expression as well as a wholesome entertainment. They illustrate the taste of the period and the importance of drama in ordinary peoples' lives.

The theatre involved women as actresses, managers, producers, and as dramatists. If being on the public stage placed actresses in an ambiguous social position, it also offered recognition and a livelihood for the ambitious and talented. Civic and private stages offered other women similar outlets and applause. Drama was an important genre for women writers in other ways because they discerned its power to instruct. Hannah More's *Sacred Dramas* were written for the improvement of young ladies; Mrs Short's *Dramas for the Use of Young Ladies* (1792) taught elocution, decorum, and wifely virtues.

The theatre was, especially in the nineteenth century, a conservative forum; it reinforces the social order. Audiences loved happy endings, the marriages of comedy, the perils narrowly averted of melodrama, the remote sacrifices of historical tragedy. It was not a place for advocacy, but women writers did use it to express their major concerns. Abolition was addressed in tragedy and melodrama. Temperance, the other major cause of nineteenth century women also lent itself to the stage. Both men and women wrote temperance melodrama, but women invented new settings and hybridized forms. Nellie Bradley and others wrote dialogues, Laura Arnold a drama and a commedietta, and Ida Buxton a temperance cantata. Suffrage was most often mocked. The bluestocking was a stock character along with the maiden aunt. Victoria Woodhull's daughter, Zula Maud, did write a dialogue, *The Proposal*, in which a woman convinces her suitor of the subjugation of women in marriage. It is hard to see how this could have been produced in such an era or form.

Even though drama was not the most important literary forum for women's causes and concerns, it certainly occupied an important place in their lives and in their culture. The three types of drama covered in this bibliography show the full range of women's involvement, as writers of poetic and other closet dramas, as writers, players and producers of commercial theatre, and as amateur playwrights and actresses. Their record is more extensive than has been recognized, and we hope that the works listed here and the apparatus of the bibliography will make a fresh evaluation of women's contribution possible.

SCOPE AND ARRANGEMENT

The entries for this series of bibliographies were first developed by a complete reading of NUC and BL because they represent the most complete collections of works in English by American and British authors, and they offer the further advantage of guiding the reader to locations where the works may be seen. OCLC and the other standard bibliographical and biographical sources were used to establish the most complete list possible. We have consulted other general sources, a selected list of which is supplied, to help in identifying and characterizing the works and to provide biographical background for the authors. The most important of these are included is the list of selected General Sources. As mentioned in the general preface above, the number of specialized

sources is large. The key sources, those that cite works never published, produced or now lost, are cited in the main entries in abbreviated form, together with other bibliographies that guide readers to the Readex microprint editions of plays—Bergquist, Ellis, Greg, Hixon, Nicoll, and Wells. A list of abbreviations is provided, with full bibliographical details to be found in the list of Selected Sources, together with other works consulted. Finally, we examined many of the works included here in order to be sure they fit the parameters of this volume; we also examined others that were excluded.

In reading the catalogs to develop the materials for this series of bibliographies, we established only a few guidelines for exclusion. We chose to end our collection with the nineteenth century, as more work has been done and more resources are available for twentieth century writers. Of course, some works by earlier writers were not published until the twentieth century and some women who began writing in the nineteenth century continued to publish into the next, but the volume of information was so large, that we chose to confine ourselves to works that were available to readers before 1900. We have for this volume made an exception for plays produced before 1900, but we do not trace the entire twentieth century career of writers who first published before the turn of the century. We looked for original literary works, not scholarly or practical ones, manuscripts, materials in translation, or periodical publications unless they were later collected in a book. Again, *Drama* differs somewhat from the other volumes in the series. We do include manuscripts, translations, and plays that were produced but not printed if they are cited in at least one of the specialized sources. This was done because of the special characteristics of the genre and so that we might present as full a picture as possible of women's dramatic writings.

Having collected this information for all the genres in the series this way, we separated it into the constituent volumes in several ways, using reference works such as the ones listed in our bibliographies, library classifications, publishers' descriptions and advertisements, biographies and literary criticism. We also read a large number of the works themselves. NUC, BL and OCLC doubtless do not hold every book ever printed and tired eyes have undoubtedly missed some works, but we hope we have provided as full a listing within these guidelines as possible. This is not intended to be an analytic or descriptive bibliography. The scope of the entire series is too great to permit full annotation of each entry. Instead brief notes intended to clarify the character of the work if that is not made evident by its full title and subtitle are provided. Our focus throughout the series is on the women writers and their published imaginative work. Again because of the special characteristics of the drama, we do list dates of first production of plays. Those who wish more information on the precise dates, the theatre companies, etc., may refer to the specialized sources listed in the entries and in the list of Selected Sources. We have also listed publisher's series such as French's Acting Editions, Baker's Novelties or Ames' Standard Drama where possible as these indicate something of the nature of the work and the audiences for which it was intended.

The entries in *Drama* supply for each author the following information: her name, following the way it is listed in NUC; her husband's name; nationality; birth and death dates where known or century; alternative forms of her legal name under which she published or was known; and pseudonyms under which she published dramatic works. Birth names are placed in parentheses. Where a birth name is known and the husband's name is not, the title, Mrs, is omitted. Where the birth name is not clear, we do not supply the title Mrs. In cases where the woman is identified only by initials which may be either hers or her husband's, we also include the title, Mrs. We list all known forms of a woman's legal name(s) as alternative names. For example, Judith (Sargent) Stevens Murray who was known by her birth name and two married names is listed as:

MURRAY, Judith (Sargent) Stevens, Mrs. John Murray [Am. 1751–1820] ALT: Sargent, Judith; Stevens, Mrs. John; Stevens, Judith PSEUD: Constantia

She is cross-referenced under both Stevens, Mrs John and Stevens, Judith because she may be found in some sources each way. She is also cross-referenced under both her birth name and her pseudonym. Pseudonyms used for *Drama* but not those used in other literary genres are listed in this volume. In the *Dictionary of Pseudonyms and Alternative Names* volume, authors will be listed under all forms of their real names and cross-references from all pseudonyms will be supplied. We follow NUC form for names, and include alternative spellings found in other sources, for example, Elizabeth Ryves is listed as: ALT: Ryes, Elizabeth, even though that is probably a typographical error in one source.

As our main focus is on the women writers themselves, memorial volumes are listed under the subject's name as the primary entry even though they may appear under the editor's or compiler's name in NUC and BL. Editors and compilers are cross-referenced for all works. In the case of multiple authorship, works are listed under the name of the woman who appears first on the title page of the book and cross-references are given from all known forms of the names of the co-author(s).

For each work we list the title, the name or pseudonym under which it was written where this differs from the author entry, co-authors, place, publisher, date of first publication, page numbers, catalog(s) and major sources in which it was found. Information from multiple sources is merged to form the most complete entry possible. We give only the first edition of a work. When new editions contain substantial revisions, they are generally covered in the annotation to the first edition. Works that have been completely revised and really constitute a new work are given separate entries.

In order to provide a full listing of dramatic works which appear in collected editions of an author's works or in compilations of plays such as Eliza Keating's *Dramas for the Drawing Room* or publishers' series such as Phineas Garrett's *Dramatic Leaflets*, we enter the collections in alphabetical order at the beginning of the writer's entry and provide full bibliographic details there. The works are then listed in alphabetical order and the collection in which they appear is cited but without repeating the publication information or the list of sources. If a play was published separately as well as in a collection, full publication information is supplied for the work and the collection is cited in the note. So, for example, under Mary Russell Mitford the first entries are to collections:

Dramatic scenes, sonnets, and other poems.
L: Geo. B. Whittaker, 1827. 392p. NUC BL E N

————The dramatic works of Mary Russell Mitford.
L: Hurst & Blackett, 1854. 2v. NUC BL OCLC T

Later entries include:

————The fawn.
In: Dramatic scenes . . . .
[1 scene.]

————The Foscari. A tragedy in five acts.
L: G.B. Whittaker, 1826. 78p. NUC BL OCLC E N
[Verse. Prod. Covent Garden, 1826. Also in Dramatic works.]

We try whenever we can to present the information in its fullest possible form. Any omissions within the entries indicate that the information was not available. We print, in most cases, the full title, as this often gives the character and flavor of the work. We do omit information not relevant to the primary work, as, for example, notices of other works by the same author or lists of appendices. We list compilers and editors, but not illustrators or composers. Cross-references are also supplied from all known forms of the legal name for all co-authors, editors, and compilers. Wherever possible we give full names rather than initials in both entries and cross-references. We do use a few standard abbreviations (L for London, NY for New York, and U.S. for United States) within the entries. We also supply standard abbreviations of U.S. states as part of the place of publication, except for cities (Philadelphia or Chicago, for example) whose location is well known.

APPENDICES

The chronological appendix sets the writers into their appropriate general time frame. The list is divided by century to 1700, by half century for the eighteenth and by quarter century for the nineteenth century. Writers are listed in each period in which they published or saw their work performed. Where dates of performance or publication are not known, we use date of death in assigning a writer to a given period. Exact dates of publication and precise dates of birth and death where known may be found in the main entries.

A second appendix lists the names of actresses, performers and theatre managers. An index has also been provided for the writers whose work has been translated or adapted by the women listed in this bibliography. Any works listed as adaptations in the main index have not been traced to their source. The first authors are listed as they appear in the works. For example, a story by Ouida is listed under Ouida, pseud. with her real name, [Louise de la Ramee] in brackets. The authors of the original works are not cross-referenced in the main bibliography.

SUBJECT INDEX

The subject index to this volume is intended as a general guide to forms, genres, and subject matter as well as to issues of particular concern to women. This index covers traditional dramatic forms: Comedy, Tragedy, Farce, Pastoral, etc.; forms popular in the eighteenth and nineteenth centuries: Fairy plays, Melodrama, Tableaux, Extravaganzas; and other types of dramatic work: Monologues, Duologues, etc. Sketches are essentially dramatized anecdotes. Where indicated by the author, we have listed these as Comic or Dramatic sketches. Otherwise, they are listed only as Sketches. Commedietta refers to comedies in one act or less. We try to eliminate duplication in the index to genres, so a play listed under English History will not be listed again under Historical drama.

Three types of works may appear in two or more categories in the index. The musical forms, Cantata, Opera, Operetta, Musical Comedy indicate the genre of the work. The general category, Musical, refers to works that do not fall into those genres but which include songs or supply musical scores. So, for example, a Pastoral play or a Melodrama may be listed under that generic class and again under Musical, but an Operetta will not. Dramatic poems were published separately or in volumes of poetry and are listed only there.

The general category, Verse, indicates a play written partly or entirely in verse and does not include any works listed under Dramatic Poems. Plays for amateur or home performance may be found under several categories. The index covers two classes: Amateur Productions refers to those works written for public presentation, pageants or community theatre, for instance; Home Entertainment covers works intended for private production and so designated by the authors. These designations follow the authors' titles or statements in the prefaces. These works may also be found under their generic categories, Commedietta, Sketch, Monologue, etc. As mentioned above, quite a few works were performed on the public stage and also by amateur actors, so the designations Amateur and Home Entertainment do not incorporate all works for non-professionals. Certain genres should also be considered as evidence of works for home performance, most notably Charades and Proverb plays.

Women writers were particularly concerned with writing for and about other women. Several classifications in the index flag these concerns. Biblical Heroines and Heroines identify dramas and tragedies with female protagonists. Central historical women about whom a number of plays were written, Mary, Queen of Scots, Lady Jane Grey, and Sappho, are also indexed. Female Characters indicates plays with female parts only. These, too, are primarily for amateurs or for home performance and may be found in the index both ways.

A few special categories have been set up to distinguish within broader categories. Biblical themes refers to fully developed plays based on characters or incidents in the Bible. Mystery Plays are short works covering major events in the Old Testament or in the life of Christ. Classical Themes covers plays based on mythological characters and events, while Greek and Roman History refer to actual persons or incidents. Abolition, Temperance and Suffrage cover plays about three of women's traditional concerns. While the index cannot begin to cover the diverse works in the bibliography, we hope it will give a general sense of the most popular dramatic forms and themes.

Some of these index terms will be found in other volumes in the series. Abolition, Juvenile Authors, Memorial Volumes, for example, are indexed for each genre. We have not tried to indicate any other literary activities of these authors, as they will be covered in the appropriate volume. We hope that this volume will stand on its own as a resource for the study of dramatic literature by women. Taken together with the others in the series, it will enable users to trace an individual woman's career, to compare the frequency of memorial volumes or works on Biblical Heroines, and to gain an overview of the publications of women before 1900.

ACKNOWLEDGEMENTS

Finally, we would like to thank some people whose help has been invaluable. Jan Valouch for her dedication to the project which exceeds even her remarkable skill in entering and maintaining the data base and in editing it. Kristy Wallisch and Alison Circle for research assistance, and Wayne Joyce for research and moral support. Martha Burris for her skill in setting up the earliest files. George Economou for his unfailing support of the project.

We thank especially the National Endowment for the Humanities for the generous research grant which gave us the time and the research support to make this volume possible and the Endowment staff for its concern and assistance.

The librarians and staff of the Library of Congress and the British Library have given valuable help. We should also like to thank for their special assistance the librarians of: Boston Public Library, Brown University, Buffalo and Erie County Public Library, Case Western Reserve University Library, Cornell University, Duke University, The Houghton and Harvard College Libraries of Harvard University, Huntington Library, Newberry Library, New York Public Library, Princeton University Library, Rutgers University Library, University of British Columbia Library, University of Kansas Libraries, University of Texas Libraries, University of Virginia Library and Yale University Library.

Gwenn Davis
Norman, Oklahoma
1991

SELECTED SOURCES

GENERAL

ADAMS, Elmer C. *Heroines of Modern Progress*. New York: Sturgis & Walton Co., 1918.

ADAMS, Oscar. *A Dictionary of American Authors*. 6th ed. Boston: Houghton Mifflin, 1904. Repr. Detroit, MI: Gale, 1969.

ADELMAN, Joseph. *Famous Women*. New York: Ellis Lonow Co., 1926.

ALEXANDER, William. *The History of Women From the Earliest Antiquity; Giving Some Account of Almost Every Interesting Particular Concerning That Sex, Among All Nations Ancient and Modern*. 2 vols. London: W. Strahan & T. Cadell, 1779.

ALLIBONE, S. Austin. *A Critical Dictionary of English Literature and British Authors*. 3 vols. Philadelphia: J.B. Lippincott, 1899.

American Authors 1600–1900. Ed. Stanley J. Kunitz and Howard Haycraft. New York: The H.W. Wilson Co., 1938.

American Women Writers: A Critical Reference Guide from Colonial Times to the Present. Ed. Lina Mainiero. 4 vols. New York: Frederick Ungar Pub. Co., 1979.

American Writers Before 1800: A Biographical and Critical Dictionary. Ed. James A. Levernier & Douglas R. Wilmas. Westport, CT: Greenwood Press, 1983.

AMORY, Thomas. *Memoirs of Several Ladies of Great Britain*. 2 vols. London: Pr. for John Noon, 1775.

BALLARD, George. *Memoirs of British Ladies, Who Have Been Celebrated for Their Writings or Skill in the Learned Languages, Arts and Sciences*. London: Pr. for J. Evans, 1775.

BETHAM, Mary Matilda. *A Biographical Dictionary of the Celebrated Women of Every Age and Country*. London: B. Crosby & Co., 1804.

The Biographical Cyclopaedia of American Women. Comp. Mabel Ward Cameron and Erma Conckling Lee. New York: Halvord Pub. Co., 1924.

Biographium Femineum. The Female Worthies: Or Memoirs of the Most Illustrious Ladies of All Ages and Nations. 2 vols. London: S. Crowder, 1766.

Black American Writers, Past and Present: A Bio-graphical and Bibliographical Dictionary. Ed. Theresa Gunnels Rush, Carol Fairbanks Myers, and Esther Spring Arata, 2 vols. Metuchen, NJ: Scarecrow, 1975.

Black American Writers, 1773–1949: A Bibliography and Union List. Comp. Geraldine O. Matthews, et al. Boston: Hall, 1975.

BLANCK, Jacob Nathaniel. *Bibliography of American Literature*. New Haven: Yale University Press, 1955.

BOASE, Frederic. *Modern English Biography, Containing . . . Many Concise Memoirs of Persons Who Have Died Since . . . the Year 1850 . . . With an Index of the Most Interesting Matter*. 6 vols. Truro: Netherton & Worth, 1892–1921.

British Authors Before 1800; A Biographical Dictionary. Ed. Stanley J. Kunitz and Howard Haycraft. New York: Wilson, 1952.

British Authors of the Nineteenth Century. Ed. Stanley Kunitz and Howard Haycraft. New York: Wilson, 1936.

British Museum. Department of Printed Books. *General Catalogue of Printed Books*. Photolithographic edition to 1955. London: Trustees, 1959–66.

The Cambridge History of American Literature. Ed. William Peterfield Trent, John Erskine, Stuart P. Sherman and Carl Van Doren. New York: The McMillan Co., 1944.

The Cambridge History of English Literature. Ed. A.W. Ward and A.R. Waller. New York & London: G.P. Putnam's sons, 1907–17.

CAMERON, M.W. *The Biographical Encyclopaedia of Women*. New York: Halvord, 1924.

CASEY, Elizabeth. *Illustrious Irishwomen*. 2 vols. London: Tinsley bros., 1887.

CHAMBERS, Robert. *A Biographical Dictionary of Eminent Scotsmen*. New Ed. Rev. by Thomas Tomson. 3 vols. London: Blackie and son, 1870.

CRONE, John S. *A Concise Dictionary of Irish Biography*. Dublin: The Talbot Press, 1928.

Dictionary of American Biography. Ed. Allen Johnson et al. 11 vols. New York: Scribner, 1946–58.

Dictionary of National Biography Ed. Sir Leslie Stephen and Sir Sidney Lee. 22 vols. London: Oxford University Press, 1921–22.

Dictionary of Welsh Biography Down to 1940. London: The Honourable Society of Cymmrodorion, 1959.

Eighteenth-Century Short-Title Catalogue: The British Library Collections. 113 microfiche. London: British Library, 1990.

The Europa Biographical Dictionary of British Women. Ed. Anne Crawford, Tony Hayter, Ann Hughes, Frank Prochaska, Pauline Stafford, Elizabeth Vallance. Detroit, MI: Gale Research Co., 1983.

EVANS, Charles. *American Bibliography: A Chronological Dictionary of All Books, Pamphlets and Periodical Publications Printed in the United States of America from the Genesis of Printing in 1639 down to and including the year 1820, with Bibliographical and Biographical Notes*. 14 vols. Chicago: Blakely, for Evans, 1903–34; Worcester, MA: American Antiquarian Society, 1955–59.

The General Biographical Dictionary. Ed. Alexander Chalmers. 32 vols. London: Pr. for J. Nichols, 1812–17.

HAYS, Mary. *Female Biography; or, Memoirs of Illustrious and Celebrated Women of All Ages and Countries*. 3 vols. London: R. Phillips, 1803.

The International Dictionary of Women's Biography. Comp. and Ed. Jennifer S. Uglow. New York: Continuum Pub. Co., 1982.

JAMES, Edward T., et al. *Notable American Women: A Biographical Dictionary*. 3 vols. Cambridge, MA: Belknap Press of Harvard University Press, 1971.

MACMURCHY, A. *Handbook of Canadian Literature*. Toronto: William Briggs, 1906.

MATTHEWS, Geraldine O. and the African-American Materials Project Staff School of Library Science, North Carolina Central University, comp. *Black American Writers, 1773–1949: A Bibliography and Union List*. Boston: Hall, 1975.

NADEL, Ira Bruce. *Jewish Writers of North America*. Detroit, MI: Gale, 1981.

National Union Catalog. Pre-1956 Imprints. London: Mansell, 1968–1981.

New Cambridge Bibliography of English Literature. Ed. George Watson. 4 vols. and index. Cambridge: Cambridge University Press, 1969–76.

OCLC (Online Computer Library Center). Dublin, OH; 1967–   .

POLLARD, Alfred W. and Gilbert R. Redgrave. *A Short-Title Catalogue of Books Printed in England, Scotland, and Ireland and of English Books Printed Abroad 1475–1640*. London: Bibliographical Soc., 1926; Repr. London: Oxford University Press, 1969, 1985.

SIMS, Janet. *The Progress of Afro-American Women: A Selected Bibliography and Resource Guide*. Westport, CT: Greenwood Press, 1980.

TODD, Janet, ed. *A Dictionary of British and American Women Writers 1600–1800*. Totowa, NJ: Rowman & Allanheld, 1985.

WING, Donald, ed. *Short-Title Catalogue of Books Printed in England, Ireland, Wales, and British America and of English Books Printed in Other Countries 1641–1700*. 2d ed. New York: Modern Language Association, 1972.

SPECIALIZED

ADAMS, William D. *A Dictionary of the Drama: A Guide to the Plays, Playwrights, Players and Playhouses of the United Kingdom and America from the Earliest Times to the Present*. Philadelphia: J.B. Lippincott Co., 1904.

The American Theatre: A Sum of its Parts. New York: Samuel French, 1971.

ARATA, Esther S. and Nicholas J. Rotoli, eds. *Black American Playwrights, 1800 to the Present: A Bibliography*. Metuchen, NJ: Scarecrow, 1976.

ARNOTT, William D. and John W. Robinson. *English Theatrical Literature, 1559–1900: A Bibliography Incorporating Robert W. Lowe's A Bibliographical Account of English Theatrical Literature* [1888]. London: Society for Theatre Research, 1970.

BAKER, Blanch Merritt. *Dramatic Bibliography*. New York: H.W. Wilson, 1933.

BAKER, David Erskine, Isaac Reed, and Stephen Jones. *Biographia Dramatica; or, A Companion to the Playhouse: Containing Historical and Critical Memoirs, and Original Anecdotes of British and Irish Dramatic Writers, from the Commencement of Our Theatrical Exhibitions ... Originally Compiled, to the Year 1704, by David Erskine Baker. Continued thence to 1782, by Isaac Reed, and Brought Down to the End of November 1811, with Very Considerable Additions and Improvements Throughout, By Stephen Jones*. London: Longman, et al., 1812. 3 vols. Repr. New York: AMS Press, 1966.

BATES, Katherine Lee and Lydia Boker Godfrey. *English Drama: A Working Basis*. Boston: S.G. Robinson, 1896.

BELL, John. *A New Catalogue of Bell's Circulating Library*. London: John Bell, 1777.

BELL, John. *Supplement to Bell's British Theatre, Consisting of the Most Esteemed Farces and Entertainments Now Performing on the British Stage*. 4 vols. London: John Bell, 1784.

BENTLEY, Gerald Eades. *The Jacobean and Caroline Stage*. Oxford: Clarendon Press, 1941–68.

BERGQUIST, G. William. *Three Centuries of English and American Plays: A Checklist, England 1500–1800; United States: 1714–1830.* New York: Readex, 1963.

BEVIS, Richard, W. *English Drama: Restoration and Eighteenth Century, 1660–1789.* London: Longman, 1988.

BOOTH, Michael R. *English Plays of the Nineteenth Century.* 2 vols. Oxford: Clarendon Press, 1969–76.

BOOTH, Michael R., et al. *The Revels History of Drama in English.* London: Methuen, 1975–83.

BRADBY, David, Louis James, and Bernard Sharratt, eds. *Performance and Politics in Popular Drama: Aspects of Popular Entertainment in Theatre, Film and Television, 1800–1976.* Cambridge: Cambridge University Press, 1980.

BRANDWEIN, Pearl J. *Mary Queen of Scots in Nineteenth and Twentieth Century Drama. Poetic License with History.* New York: Peter Lang, 1989.

BROWN, Thomas Allston. *History of the American Stage.* New York: Dick and Fitzgerald, 1870.

BRYAN, George B. *Stage Lives: A Bibliography and Index to Theatrical Biographies in English.* Westport, CT: Greenwood Press, 1985.

CHAMBERS, E.K. *The Elizabethan Stage.* Oxford: Clarendon Press, 1923.

CHETWOOD, William Rufus. *The British Theatre. Containing the Lives of the English Dramatic Poets With an Account of all their Plays. Together With the Lives of Most of the Principal Actors as well as Poets. To which Is Prefixed a Short View of the Rise and Progress of the English Stage.* Dublin: Peter Wilson, 1750.

CHINOY, Helen Krick and Linda Walsh Jenkins. *Women in American Theatre: Careers, Images, Movements. An Illustrated Sourcebook.* Rev. and Expanded ed. New York: Theatre Communications Group, 1987.

CLARK, B.H., gen. ed. *America's Lost Plays.* Princeton, NJ: Princeton University Press, 1940.

CLARK, William Smith. *The Early Irish Stage: The Beginnings to 1720.* Oxford: Oxford University Press, 1955.

COLLIER, John Payne. *The History of English Dramatic Poetry to the Time of Shakespeare and Annals of the Stage to the Restoration.* 3 vols. London: John Murray, 1831. New ed. London: G. Bell & sons, 1879.

CONOLLY, L.W. and J.P. Wearing. *English Drama and Theatre, 1800–1900: A Guide to Information Sources.* Detroit, MI: Gale, 1978.

COTTON, Nancy. *Women Playwrights in England c. 1363–1750.* Lewisburg, PA: Bucknell University Press, 1980.

CULLEN, Rosemary L. *The Civil War in American Drama Before 1900: Catalog of an Exhibition, November, 1982.* Providence, RI: Brown University Press. 1982.

CUMBERLAND, John. *Cumberland's British Theatre.* London: J. Cumberland, 1829–

DONOHUE, Joseph W. *Dramatic Character in the English Romantic Age.* Princeton: Princeton University Press, 1970.

DONOHUE, Joseph W. *Theatre in the Age of Kean* Totowa, NJ: Rowman and Littlefield, 1975.

DUNCOMBE, J. *Duncombe's Edition of the British Theatre.* London: J. Duncombe, 18--?

ELDREDGE, H.J. [Reginald Clarence, pseud.], comp. *'The Stage' Cyclopaedia; A Bibliography of Plays.* London: 'The Stage', 1909.

ELLIS, James, Joseph Donohue, and Louise Allen Zak, eds. *English Drama of the Nineteenth Century: An Index and Finding Guide.* New Canaan, CT: Readex Books, 1985.

EMELJANOW, Victor. *Victorian Popular Dramatists.* Boston: Twayne, 1987.

FISHER, Judith L. and Stephen Watt. *When They Weren't Doing Shakespeare. Essays on Nineteenth-Century British and American Theatre.* Athens, GA: University of Georgia Press, 1989.

FREEDLEY, George and Allardyce Nicoll. *English and American Plays of the Nineteenth Century.* New York: Readex Microprint, 1965–   .

GALT, John, ed. *The New British Theatre.* 4 vols. London: Henry Colburn, 1814.

GENEST, John. *Some Account of the English Stage from the Restoration in 1660 to 1830.* 10 vols. Bath: Pr. H.E. Carrington, 1832.

GREG, Walter Wilson. *A Bibliography of the English Printed Drama to the Restoration.* 4 vols. London: Oxford University Press, for the Bibliographical Society, 1939–59; Repr. 1970.

HALLIWELL, James O. *Dictionary of Old English Plays.* London: John Russell Smith, 1860.

HARBAGE, Alfred. *Annals of English Drama, 975–1700: An Analytical Record of All Plays, Extant or Lost, Chronologically Arranged and Indexed by Authors, Titles, Dramatic Companies, etc.* Rev. by Samuel Schoenbaum. London: Methuen, 1964.

HARTMAN, John Geoffrey. *The Development of American Social Comedy from 1787 to 1936.* Philadelphia: University of Pennsylvania Press, 1939.

HATCH, James V. *Black Image on the American*

Stage: A Bibliography of Plays and Musicals, 1770–1970. New York: DBS Publications, 1970.

HATCH, James V. and Omanii Abdullah, ed. *Black Playwrights, 1823–1977: An Annotated Bibliography of Plays*. New York: Bowker, 1977.

HAVENS, Daniel F. *The Columbian Muse of Comedy. The Development of a Native Tradition in Early American Comedy, 1787–1845*. Carbondale, IL: Southern Illinois University Press, 1973.

HEMLOW, Joyce. *The History of Fanny Burney*. Oxford: Clarendon Press, 1958.

HIGHFILL, Philip H., Jr., Kalman A. Burnim, Edward A. Langhans, ed. *A Biographical Dictionary of Actors, Actresses, Musicians, Dancers, Managers and Other Stage Personnel in London, 1660–1800*. Carbondale, IL: Southern Illinois University Press, 1973.

HILL, Frank Pierce. *American Plays Printed, 1714–1830; A Bibliographic Record*. Stanford, CA: Stanford University Press; London: Oxford University Press, 1934.

HIXON, Donald L. and Don A. Henessee, eds. *Nineteenth-Century American Drama: A Finding Guide*. Metuchen, NJ: Scarecrow, 1977.

HUBERMAN, Jeffrey H. *Late Victorian Farce*. Ann Arbor, MI: U.M.I. Research Press, 1986.

HUGHES, Glenn. *A History of the American Theatre, 1700–1950*. New York: Samuel French, 1951.

HUTTON, Laurence. *Curiosities of the American Stage*. New York: Harper & Bros., 1891.

HUTTON, Laurence. *Plays and Players*. New York: Hurd & Houghton, 1875.

INCHBALD, Elizabeth Simpson, ed. *The British Theatre; or A Collection of Plays . . . acted at the Theatres Royal . . . printed . . . from the Prompt Books*. 25 vols. London: Longman, Hurst, Rees and Orme, 1808.

INCHBALD, Elizabeth Simpson, ed. *The Modern Theatre; A Collection of Successful Modern Plays . . . Printed from the Prompt Books*. 10 vols. London: Longman, Hurst, Rees, Orme and Brown, 1811.

INGLIS, Ralston. *The Dramatic Writers of Scotland*. Glasgow: G.D. Mackellar, 1868.

LINK, Frederick M., ed. *English Drama, 1660–1800: A Guide to Information Sources*. Detroit, MI: Gale, 1975.

LONGE, Francis. *[Collection of Plays.] 1607–1812*. [Title supplied and original collection of 325 volumes owned by Library of Congress.]

LOWENBERG, Alfred, ed. *A Bibliography of the Theatres of the British Isles (Excluding London)*. London: Society for Theatre Research, 1950.

MACQUEEN-POPE, W. *Ladies First. The Story of Woman's Conquest of the British Stage*. London: W.H. Allen, 1952.

MAYER, David. *Harlequin in His Element: The English Pantomime 1806–1836*. Cambridge, MA: Harvard University Press, 1969.

McMILLAN, Dougald. *Catalogue of the Larpent Plays in the Huntington Library*. San Marino, CA: Huntington Library, 1939.

MCCONACHIE, Bruce A. and Daniel Friedman, eds. *Theater for Working-Class Audiences in the United States, 1830–1980*. Westport, CT: Greenwood, 1985.

MESERVE, Walter J. *American Drama to 1900: A Guide to Information Sources*. Detroit, MI: Gale, 1980.

MESERVE, Walter J. *An Emerging Entertainment: The Drama of the American People to 1928*. Bloominton, IN: Indiana University Press, 1977.

MOYER, Ronald L. *American Actors, 1861–1910: An Annotated Bibliography of Books Published in the United States in English from 1861 Through 1976*. Troy, NY: Whitston Publishing Co., 1979.

MULLIN, Donald, comp. *Victorian Actors and Actresses in Review: A Dictionary of Contemporary Views of Representative British and American Actors and Actresses, 1837–1901*. Westport, CT: Greenwood Press, 1983.

MULLIN, Donald, comp. *Victorian Plays. A Record of Significant Productions on the London Stage, 1837–1901*. Westport, CT: Greenwood Press, 1987.

NICOLL, Allardyce. *A History of English Drama 1660–1900*. 6 vols. Cambridge: Cambridge University Press, 1952–59.

ODELL, George C.D. *Annals of the New York Stage*. 15 vols. New York: Columbia University Press, 1927.

OULTON, Walley Chamberlain, Comp. *The Drama Recorded; or Barker's List of Plays, Alphabetically arranged, Exhibiting at One View, the Title, Size, Date, and Author, With their Various Alterations, From the Earliest Period to 1814; To Which Are Added, Notitia Dramatica, or A Chronological Account of Events Relative to the English Stage*. London: James Barker, 1814.

PASCOE, Charles E. *Our Actors and Actresses. The Dramatic List: A Record of the Performances of Living Actors and Actresses of the British Stage*. 2d ed. 1880; Repr. New York: Benjamin Blom, 1969.

PEARSON, Jacqueline. *The Prostituted Muse: Images of Women and Women Dramatists, 1642–1737*. New York: St Martin's Press, 1988.

PETERSON, Bernard L., Jr. *Early Black American Playwrights and Dramatic Writers: A Biographical Directory and Catalog of Plays, Films, and Broadcasting Scripts*. New York: Greenwood Press, 1990.

QUINN, Arthur Hobson. *A History of American Drama From the Civil War to the Present Day*. New York: F.S. Crofts & Co., 1936.

REYNOLDS, Ernest. *Early Victorian Drama, 1830–1870*. Cambridge: W. Heffer & sons, 1936; Repr. New York: Benjamin Blom, 1965.

RICHARDS, Kenneth and Peter Thomson, eds. *Essays on Nineteenth-Century British Theatre*. London: Methuen, 1971.

ROBINSON, Alice M., Vera Mowry Roberts, and Milly S. Barranger. *Notable Women in the American Theatre: A Biographical Dictionary*. New York and Westport, CT: Greenwood Press, 1989.

RODEN, Robert F. *Later American Plays, 1831–1900; Being a Compilation of the Titles of Plays By American Authors Published and Performed in America since 1831*. New York: Dunlap Society, 1900.

ROWELL, George. *The Victorian Theatre 1792–1914. A Survey*. 2d. ed. Cambridge: Cambridge University Press, 1978.

SCHELLING, Felix E. *Elizabethan Drama, 1558–1642*. 2 vols. Boston: Houghton Mifflin, 1908.

SHERBO, Arthur. *English Sentimental Drama*. East Lansing, MI: Michigan State University Press, 1957.

STRATMAN, Carl Joseph. *Bibliography of English Printed Tragedy, 1565–1900*. Carbondale, IL: Southern Illinois University Press, 1966.

STRATMAN, Carl Joseph. *Bibliography of the American Theater, Excluding New York City*. Chicago: Loyola University Press, 1965.

SULLIVAN, Victoria and James Hatch, eds. *Plays By and About Women*. New York: Random House [Vintage Books], 1973.

SUMMERS, Montague. *A Bibliography of the Restoration Drama*. London: Fortune Press, 1934; Repr. New York: Russell & Russell, 1970.

TAYLOR, George. *Players and Performances in the Victorian Theatre*. Manchester: Manchester University Press, 1989.

THOMPSON, Lawrence S., ed. *Nineteenth and Twentieth Century Drama: A Selective Bibliography of English Language Works*. Boston: Hall, 1975.

VAN LENNEP, William Emmett L. Avery, Arthur Scouten, George W. Stone and C. Beecher Hogan, eds. *The London Stage, 1660–1880: A Calendar of Plays, Entertainments & Afterpieces, Together with Casts, Box-Receipts, and Contemporary Comment, Compiled from the Playbills, Newspapers and Theatrical Diaries of the Period*. 11 vols. Carbondale, IL: Southern Illinois University Press, 1965–69.

VAUGHN, Jack A. *Early American Dramatists: From the Beginning to 1900*. New York: Ungar, 1981.

WAGENKNECHT, Edward. *Seven Daughters of the Theatre*. Norman, OK: University of Oklahoma Press, 1964.

WAGNER, Anton, ed. *Canada's Lost Plays*. Volume II: Women Pioneers. Toronto: Canadian Theatre Review Publications, 1979.

WATSON, Ernest Bradlee. *Sheridan to Robertson: A Study of the Nineteenth Century London Stage*. Cambridge, MA: Harvard University Press, 1926.

WEARING, J.P. *American and British Theatrical Biography: A Directory*. Metuchen, NJ: Scarecrow Press, 1979.

WEARING, J.P. *The London Stage 1890–1899: A Calendar of Plays and Players*. Metuchen, NJ: Scarecrow Press, 1976.

WELLS, Henry Willis. *Chronological List of Extant Plays Produced in or about London, 1581–1642*. New York: Columbia University Press, 1940.

WELLS, Henry Willis. *Three Centuries of Drama: American and English, 1500–1800*. New York: Readex Microprint, 1952.

WILEY, Autrey Nell, ed. *Rare Prologues and Epilogues, 1642–1700*. London: G. Allen & Unwin, 1940.

WILKANDER, Matthew H. *The Play of Truth and State: Historical Drama from Shakespeare to Brecht*. Baltimore: Johns Hopkins University Press, 1986.

WILMETH, Don B. *American Entertainment: A Guide to Information Sources*. Detroit, MI: Gale, 1980.

WOODWARD, Gertrude L. and James G. McManaway. *A Checklist of English Plays, 1641–1700*. Chicago: Newberry Library, 1945. Supplement by Fredson Bowers, 1949.

ABBREVIATIONS OF SOURCES

For full bibliographical details see *Selected Sources*

Adams   Adams, William D. *A Dictionary of the Drama*.

B   Bergquist, G. William. *Three Centuries of English and American Plays*.

BioD   Baker, David Erskine, Isaac Reed and Stephen Jones. *Biographia Dramatica; or, A Companion to the Playhouse*.

BL   British Museum. Department of Books. *General Catalogue of Printed Books*.

C   Cullen, Rosemary L. *The Civil War in American Drama Before 1900*.

E   Ellis, James, Joseph Donohue and Louise Allen Zak. *English Drama of the Nineteenth Century*.

Greg   Greg, Walter Wilson. *A Bibliography of the English Printed Drama to the Restoration*.

H   Hixon, Donald L. and Don A. Henessee, eds. *Nineteenth Century American Drama: A Finding Guide*.

Har   Harbage, Alfred. *Annals of English Drama, 975–1700*.

Hatch   Hatch, James V. *Black Image on the American Stage*.

Longe   Longe, Francis. *[Collection of Plays]*.

M   Mullin, Donald, comp. *Victorian Plays. A Record of Significant Productions on the London Stage, 1837–1901*.

N   Nicoll, Allardyce. *A History of English Drama, 1660–1900*.

NUC   *National Union Catalog. Pre–1956 Imprints*.

OCLC   Online Computer Library Center, Ohio.

R   Roden, Robert F. *Later American Plays, 1831–1900*.

S   Summers, Montague. *A Bibliography of the Restoration Drama*.

T   Thompson, Lawrence S., ed. *Nineteenth and Twentieth Century Drama: A Selective Bibliography of English Language Works*.

Wells   Wells, Henry Willis. *Three Centuries of Drama*.

Wiley   Wiley, Autrey Nell. *Rare Prologues and Epilogues 1642–1700*.

WM   Woodward, Gertrude L. and James G. McManaway. *A Checklist of English Plays, 1641–1700*.

THE BIBLIOGRAPHY

A. see SHORE, Arabella

1. ACHURCH, Janet [Br. 1864-1916]
ALT: Charrington, Mrs. Charles;
Sharp, Janet Achurch
Frou-Frou. With Charles Charrington.
1886. N
[Drama. Prod. in Manchester, 1886.]

2. ACKERMAN, Irene [Am. d. 1916]
The gold mine. A play in 5 acts.
NY: J. Polhemus, 1881. 52p. NUC BL

3. -----Inez. A drama in 3 acts.
NY: C.H. Bauer, 1882. 62p. NUC BL

ACTON, Mrs. Adams see ADAMS-ACTON,
Marion Hamilton

ACTON, Jeanie Hering, see ADAMS-
ACTON, Marion Hamilton

ADAMS, Miss see BARRYMORE, Mrs.
William

ADAMS, Annie see FIELDS, Annie
(Adams)

4. ADAMS, Catherine [Br. 19/20c]
Feminine strategy. A musical duologue
in 1 act.
L: J. Williams, 1899. 15p. BL E N
[Prod. in Basingstoke, 1893.]

5. ADAMS, E., Mrs. [Am. 19c]
Love and remorse. A drama taken from
facts in my own life.
Cleveland, OH: Kennedy & Doty, 1885.
19 1. NUC

6. ADAMS, Mrs. Edward [Br. 19c]
Don Pedro. An operetta.
1892. N

7. ADAMS, Florence Davenport [19c]
The three fairy gifts.
In: Children's plays, no. 1-12.
L & NY: S. French, 1900? NUC BL N
[Comic drama. Prod. in Worthing,
1896. Her other work is for
children. N lists with adult
theater.]

ADAMS, L.B., Miss see SWANWICK,
Catherine

8. ADAMS, Sarah Fuller (Flower), Mrs.
William Bridges Adams [Br. 1805-1848]
ALT: Flower, Sarah Fuller
Vivia perpetua: a dramatic poem. In
five acts.
L: Charles Fox, 1841. 200p. NUC BL
OCLC E N

ADAMS, Mrs. William Bridges see
ADAMS, Sarah Fuller (Flower)

9. ADAMS-ACTON, Marion Hamilton [Br.
1846-1928] ALT: Acton, Mrs. Adams;
Acton, Jeanie Hering; Hering, Jeanie
The darkest hour.
1895. N
[Drama. Amateur prod. at St. John's
Wood, 1895.]

10. -----Dulvery dotty. A farce.
1894. N M
[Farce, 1 act. Prod. Terry's, & by
amateurs at St. John's Wood, 1894.]

11. -----The triple bill.
1894. N
[Entertainment. Amateur prod. at St.
John's Wood, 1894.]

12. -----Who's married? A farce.
1893. N
[Farce. Prod. Bijou, 1893.]

13. -----The woman in black. A farce.
1895. N
[Farce. Amateur prod. at St. John's
Wood, 1895.]

14. -----Woman's wit.
1893. N
[Comic drama. Prod. 1893.]

15. ADDISON, Julia de Wolf (Gibbs)
[Am. b. 1866]
Blighted buds; a farce in one act.
Boston: Walter H. Baker & co., c1896.
24p. NUC OCLC
[Baker's Edition of plays]

16. ADDITON, Mrs. J.H. [Am. 19c]
The operetta of Carlotta.
Rockland, ME: n.p., 1870. 16p. R
[5 acts. Music by James Wright.]

ALCOTT, Anna Bronson, co-author see
ALCOTT, Louisa May

17. ALCOTT, Louisa May [Am. 1832-
1888] PSEUD: Jo
Comic tragedies: written by "Jo" and
"Meg" [Anna Bronson (Alcott) Pratt].
Acted by the "little women".
Boston: Roberts bros., 1893. 317p.
NUC BL OCLC H

18. -----Bianca; an operatic tragedy.
In: Comic tragedies ... .

19. -----The captive of Castile; or,
The Moorish maiden's vow.
In: Comic tragedies ... .

20. -----The Greek slave.
In: Comic tragedies ... .

21. -----Ion. In: Comic tragedies ...
.

22. -----Norna; or, The witch's
curse.
In: Comic tragedies ... .

23. -----The unloved wife; or,
Woman's faith.
In: Comic tragedies ... .

ALDERSON, Miss see OPIE, Amelia
(Alderson)

ALDERSON, Amelia see OPIE, Amelia
(Alderson)

24. ALDRICH, Mildred [Am. 1853-1928]
Nance Oldfield, a play in one act,
arranged from Charles Reade's story,
"Art, a dramatic tale".
Boston: W.H. Baker & co., 1894. 22p.
NUC OCLC H

25. ALLEN, A. M., Miss [Br. 19/20c]
The madcap prince.
1894. N
[Drama, amateur prod. at Folkstone,
1894.]

26. ALLEN, Annie, Mrs. [Br. d. 1893]
Mercy's conquest. A play in one act.
L: Burns and Oates, 1882. BL

27. ALLEN, Charlotte H. [Am. 19c]
Marriage dramas.
Philadelphia: Levy type co., 1895. 9
l. NUC
[Tableaux. Incl. "Jewish wedding"]

ALLEN, Frank, co-author see DOREMUS,
Elizabeth Johnson (Ward)

28. ALLEN, Lucy [Am. 19c]
Debutantes in the culinary art; or, A
frolic in the cooking class.
NY: Roxbury, 1899. 23p. H

29. ALLEN, Marie Townsend [Am. 19c]
Bobs and nabobs. A domestic drama in
four acts.
St. Louis, MO: Q.I. Jones & co.,
1882. 73p. NUC

30. -----Ceramics, a summer idyl. An
original comedy in 5 acts.
St. Louis, MO: Nixon-Jones pr. co.,
1884. 62p. NUC

31. -----The Foresters; or Robin
Hood. Libretto for romantic opera.

St. Louis, MO: Nixon-Jones pr. co.,
1888. 37p. NUC

32. ALLEN, Maud [Am. 19c]
The summer boarder. A play in four
acts.
Cincinnati, OH: R. Clarke & co.,
1894. 36p. NUC OCLC

ALLEN, MRS. FAIRCHILD, pseud. see
MCINTYRE, Anna E., Mrs.

33. ALLEYN, Annie [Br. 1860-1896]
ALT: Bernard, Mrs. Charles
Woman's love.
1881. N
[Drama, prod. in Manchester, 1881.]

34. ALMA-TADEMA, Laurence, Miss [Br.
d. 1940] ALT: Tadema, Laurence Alma-
Four plays.
L: "The green sheaf," 1905. 143p. NUC
BL OCLC
[Incl: "The unseen helmsman;" "Childe
Vyet; or, The brothers;" "The
merciful soul;" "New wrecks upon old
shores."]

35. -----One way of love. A play.
Edinburgh: Priv. pr. by R. & R.
Clark, 1893. 32p. NUC BL OCLC N

36. -----The unseen helmsman.
In: Four Plays.
1897. N
[Prod. Comedy 1901; entered with Lord
Chamberlain, 1897.

AMERICAN LADY, AN, pseud. see CHILD,
Lydia Maria (Francis)

AMICA RELIGIONIS, pseud. see DODGE,
H.M., Mrs.

37. AMORY, Esmerie [Am. 19c]
The epistolary flirt. In four
exposures.
Chicago: Way & Williams, 1896. 100p.
NUC OCLC H

ANDERSON, Mary see DE NAVARRO, Mary
(Anderson)

38. ANDREWS, Frances Hester [Br. 19c]
May-Day in the last century! A
charade.
Birmingham: J. Upton, 1881. 20p. BL

ANNA MATILDA, pseud. see COWLEY,
Hannah (Parkhouse)

ANSPACH, H.S.H., the Margravine of
see CRAVEN, Elizabeth (Berkeley)

ANSPACHER, Mrs. Louis Kauffman see
KIDDER, Kathryn

39. ANSTRUTHER, Hon. Eva Isabella
Henrietta [Br. 1869-1935]
A secret of state.
1898. N
[Drama. Prod. St. Cuthbert's Hall,
1898.]

APPLETON, Sophia Louise see BRADBURY,
Sophia Louise (Appleton)

ARBLAY, Mrs. Alexander d' see ARBLAY,
Frances (Burney) d'

40. ARBLAY, Frances (Burney) d', Mrs.
Alexander d'Arblay [Br. 1752-1840]
ALT: Burney, Fanny; D'Arblay, Mrs.
Alexander; D'Arblay, Frances Burney A
busy day.
1800.
[Comedy, unpublished. MS. NY
Library. Berg Collection.]

41. -----The East Indian.
1782. B
[Supposed author. Larpent MS. #596]

42. -----Edwy and Elgiva.
1795. N
[Tragedy of Edwy, King of England, d.
959. Prod. Drury Lane, 1795,
afterward withdrawn for editing by
author. MS. NY Public Library Berg
Collection.]

43. -----Elberta.
[MS. NY Public Library, Berg
Collection]

44. -----Hubert de Vere.
[MS. NY Public Library, Berg
Collection.]

45. -----Love and fashion.
1798.
[Comedy. Never produced because of
her father, Dr. Burney's objections.
MS. NY Public Library, Berg
Collection.]

46. -----The siege of Pevensey.
[MS. NY Public Library, Berg
Collection.]

47. -----The Witlings.
1779.
[Satire on literary ladies, (i.e.
Mrs. Montagu) never performed;
suppressed by author to protect her
literary reputation & future. MS. NY
Public Library, Berg Collection.]

48. -----The woman hater.
[MS. NY Public Library, Berg
Collection.]

49. ARCHER, Miss [Br. 19c]
My life.
L: 1882. N M
[Drama, 4 acts. Prod. Gaiety, 1882.]

50. ARCHER, Frances Elizabeth, Mrs.
William Archer [Br. 19c]
The lady from the sea. Trans. of
Henrik Ibsen.
In: Ibsen's prose dramas. Ed. William
Archer.
NY: Scribner & Welford, 1890; L:
Walter Scott, 1904. 5v. NUC BL OCLC E

51. -----The wild duck. Trans. of
Henrik Ibsen.
In: Ibsen's prose dramas.

ARCHER, Mrs. William see ARCHER,
Frances Elizabeth

ARCHER, William, ed. see ARCHER,
Frances Elizabeth
ARGENT-LONERGAU, Mrs. E. see
LONERGAN, Mrs. E. Argent

ARGYLL, Anna (Mackenzie) Lindsay
Campbell, Countess of see CAMPBELL,
Anna (Mackenzie) Lindsay, Countess of
Argyll

52. ARIA, Eliza Davis [Br. b. 1866]
The Runaways.
1898. N M
[Farce. Prod. Criterion, 1898.
Entered with Lord Chamberlain as:
"The baby and the bachelor."]

53. ARIADNE, pseud. [Br. 17c] PSEUD:
Young lady, A
She ventures and he wins. "Written
by a young lady."
L: Hen. Rhodes, J. Harris & Samuel
Briscoe, 1696. 44p. NUC BL OCLC Har
[Comedy, written for Betterton's, &
prod. at Lincoln's Inn Fields, 1696.]

54. -----Unnatural mother, the scene
in the kingdom of Siam. "Written by a
young lady."
L: R. Basset, 1698. 52p. NUC OCLC Har
[Tragedy, written for Betterton's.
Prod. at Lincoln's Inn Fields, 1697.
Based on Elkanah Settle's "Distress'd
innocence."]

55. ARMITAGE, Ethel [Br. 19c]
Archibald Danvers, M.D. With Gertrude
Southam.
1893. N

[Comedietta. Prod. Southport, 1893.]

56. ARMSTRONG, L. M. C. [Am. 19c]
Gertrude Mason, M.D.; or, The lady
doctor. A farce in one act for
female characters only.
NY: Dick & Fitzgerald, 1898. 14p. NUC
OCLC H

57. ARNOLD, Laura C., Mrs. [Am. 19c]
Harry Delmar; or, "The road to ruin."
A temperance drama, in four acts,
founded on incidents in real life.
Columbus, IN: Democrat print, 1880.
24p. NUC

58. -----"Sauce for the goose": a
temperance comedietta in one act.
Columbus, IN: Democrat office, 1880.
12p. NUC

59. ASCHER, Mrs. Isidore Gordon F.
[Br. 19c]
Circumstances alter cases.
L & NY: S. French, 1888. 20p. NUC BL
OCLC N
[Comedietta. First prod. 1888.
French's & Lacy's Acting Edition.]

60. -----The horn of plenty.
1897. N
[Comedietta. Prod. in Acton, 1897.]

61. ASHLEY, Evelyn Unsworth, Mrs.
J.B. Ashley [Br. 19c] ALT: Unsworth,
Evelyn
For queen and country.
1890. N
[Prod. in Neath, 1890.]

ASHLEY, Mrs. J.B. see ASHLEY, Evelyn
(Unsworth)

ATTENBOROUGH, F.G. see ATTENBOROUGH,
Florence Gertrude

62. ATTENBOROUGH, Florence Gertrude
[Br. 19/20c] ALT: Attenborough, F. G.
PSEUD: Crystabel
Poppies in the corn; pastoral
cantata. Music by Alex S. Beaumont.
Words by F.G. Attenborough
(Crystabel).
New & enl. ed. L: C. Woolhouse, 1900.
NUC OCLC
[No info. on 1st ed. Two 20c works:
"Alfred the Great, a drama, a ballad
of Dundee, and other poems." L: W.
Reeves, 1902. 90p. BL; "Atalanta in
Arcady, a pastoral play." L: Musical
News, 1903. 26p. BL. No information
on earlier productions available.]

63. -----Won by wit.

1895. N
[Operetta. Prod. in Islington.]

64. ATTERSOLL, Mrs. [Br. 19c]
Peter the cruel, King of Castile and
Leon, an historical play in five
acts.
Angers: T. Pavie, 1818. 88p. BL
[Tragedy, in verse]

65. AUBERT, Mrs. [Br. 18c] ALT:
Aubert, Isabella
Harlequin-Hydaspes: or, the
Greshamite. A mock-opera.
L: J. Roberts, 1719. 55p. NUC BL OCLC
B N
[Attr. to her. Burlesque. 3 acts,
verse & prose. Perf. Lincoln's Inn
Fields, 1719.]

AUBERT, Isabella see AUBERT, Mrs.

66. AUBIN, Penelope, Mrs. [Br. 1679-
1731]
The merry masqueraders; or, the
humorous cuckold.
1730. L: T. Astley, 1732. 64p. N
[Comedy. Perf. Haymarket, 1730. Also
pub. as: "The humours of the
masqueraders." L: T. Reynolds, 1733.
64p. Longe, V. 76, no. 1.]

AUGUSTA, Clara see JONES, Clara
Augusta

67. AUSTEN, Jane [Br. 1775-1817]
Charades, etc. written a hundred
years ago.
L: Spottiswoode, 189-. NUC BL OCLC
[3 charades by Jane Austen, others by
her family]

AUSTIN, H., co-author see WADE,
Florence
AVELING, Eleanor see MARX, Eleanor

AVELING, Mrs. Edward see MARX,
Eleanor

68. AVERY-STUTTLE, Lilla Dale, Mrs.
[Am. 19/20c]
Poems of the Christ life, arranged in
a series of recitations for use in
Sabbath school entertainments.
Lansing, MI: Beacon pub. co., 1893.
48p. NUC
[Poems arranged chronologically, to
be used with suitable music, not for
children only.]

69. AYER, Harriet (Hubbard), Mrs.
Herbert Copeland Ayer [Am. 1849/54-
1903]
The widow. A comedy in three acts.

NY: DeWitt, 1877. 29p. NUC BL H
[DeWitt's acting plays, no. 213.
Based on "La veuve" by Henri Meilhac
& Ludovic Halevy.]

AYER, Mrs. Herbert Copeland see AYER,
Harriet (Hubbard)

70. AYLMER, Mrs. John [Br. 19c]
The charlatan.
1889. N
[Drama, prod. in Torquay.]

71. AYRES, Lucie Leveque [Am. 19/20c]
PSEUD: Cameron, Rhoda
Great Jupiter. A comic opera in
three acts.
NY: Rooney & Otten pr. co., c1900.
69p. NUC

72. AYRES, Lucie Leveque
Lafitte, a play in prologue and four
acts. By Rhoda Cameron. With Lucile
Rutland.
NY: Goerck art press, 1899. 96p. NUC

B., A. see BEHN, Aphra

B., E.B. see BROWNING, Elizabeth
(Barrett)

B., J. see BAILLIE, Joanna

73. BACON, Delia Salter [Am. 1811-
1859]
The bride of Fort Edward, founded on
an incident of the Revolution.
NY: S. Coleman, 1839. 174p. NUC BL
OCLC R
[Author says not intended for
representation. Scenes are intended
to refer to impressions for the
reader. 6 parts: I. The Crisis and
its victim. II. Love. III. Fate.
IV. Fulfillment. V. Fulfillment. VI.
Reconciliation.]

74. BAILLIE, Joanna [Br. 1762-1851]
ALT: B., J.
Dramas.
L: Longman & co., 1836. 3v. NUC BL
OCLC E N
[Author states that all these plays
are new to the public except "The
Martyr" and "The Bride" which are
suitable for gifts to youthful
readers. The rest are a continuation
of plays on the stronger passions of
the mind.]

75. -----The dramatic and poetical
works of Joanna Baillie, complete in
one volume.
L: Longman, Brown, Green & Longmans,
1851. 847p. NUC BL OCLC
[3 divisions: Plays on the Passions,
Miscellaneous Plays (incl. all her
other plays) and Poetry (incl. some
short poems never before published.)
Author made corrections & additions
herself. Incl. life of author.]

76. -----Miscellaneous plays.
L: Longman, Hurst, Rees & Orme, 1804
[1805 E]. 438p. NUC E
[Preface indicates this is first
publication of those plays.]

77. -----A series of plays: in which
it is attempted to delineate the
stronger passions of the mind, each
passion being the subject of a
tragedy and a comedy.
L: T. Cadell & W. Davies, 1798-1812.
3v. NUC BL OCLC B E N R
[Pub. as: Plays on the passions.
Philadelphia: M. Carey, 1811. 208p.;
NY: Longworths, 1812.]

78. -----The alienated manor. A
comedy in 5 acts.
In: Dramas.

79. -----The beacon: a serious
musical drama, in two acts.
In: A series of plays.

80. -----The bride, a drama. In
three acts.
In: Dramas.
[In verse. Also pub.: L: H. Diggens;
Henry Colburn; Philadelphia: C. Neal,
1828.]

81. -----Constantine Paleologus: or,
The last of the Caesars. A tragedy.
In: Miscellaneous plays.

82. -----Count Basil: a tragedy, in
five acts.
In: A series of plays.
[Verse; set in Italy. Title in first
Am. ed.: "Basil, a tragedy."]

83. -----The country inn; a comedy.
In: Miscellaneous plays.

84. -----De Montfort: a tragedy in
five acts.
In: A series of plays.
[Also pub.: NY: David Longworth,
1809. 84p. L: Longman & co., 1823.
95p., German settings. Prod. Drury
Lane, 1800.]

85. -----The dream; a tragedy in prose, in three acts.
In: A series of plays.

86. -----The election: a comedy, in five acts.
In: A series of plays.
[Prod. English Opera House, 1817.]

87. -----Enthusiasm: a comedy.
In: Dramas.
[3 acts.]

88. -----Ethwald.
In: A series of plays.
[5 acts, in verse.]

89. -----The family legend: a tragedy.
Edinburgh: J. Ballantyne & co., 1810. 152p. NUC BL OCLC E N
[In verse. Prod. Edinburgh, 1815. Orig. title: "The lady of the rock."]

90. -----Henriquez.
In: Dramas.
[Tragedy, 5 acts.]

91. -----The homicide. A tragedy.
In: Dramas.
[Tragedy, 5 acts, verse & prose. Prod. Drury Lane, 1836.]

92. -----The martyr: a drama, in three acts.
In: Dramas.
[In verse.]

93. -----The match: a comedy, in three acts.
In: Dramas.

94. -----Orra: a tragedy.
In: A series of plays.
[5 acts.]

95. -----The phantom: A musical drama.
In: Dramas.
[2 acts.]

96. -----Rayner, a tragedy.
In: Miscellaneous plays.
[5 acts]

97. -----Romiero, a tragedy.
In: Dramas. [5 acts]

98. -----The second marriage.
In: A series of plays.
[5 acts.]

99. -----The separation. A tragedy.
In: Dramas.

[5 acts, verse. Prod. Covent Garden, 1836.]

100. -----The siege: a comedy, in five acts.
In: A series of plays.

101. -----The stripling. A tragedy.
In: Dramas.
[5 acts, prose. Based on an event in Scotland.]

102. -----The tryal: a comedy.
In: A series of plays.
[5 acts, English setting. Also in B.]

103. -----Witchcraft. A tragedy.
In: Dramas.
[5 acts, prose.]

104. BAKER, Delphine Paris [Am. 19c]
ALT: Delphine
Solon; or, The rebellion of '61. A domestic and political tragedy. By Delphine.
Chicago: S.P. Rounds, 1862. 74p. H

BAKER, George M., co-author see GALE, Rachel E. (Baker)

BAKER, Rachel E. see GALE, Rachel E. (Baker)

BAKER, Robert Melville, co-author see GALE, Rachel E. (Baker)

BALFOUR, CLARA, pseud. see HEMANS, Felicia Dorothea (Browne)

105. BALFOUR, Mary Devens [Br. 19c]
Kathleen O'Neil. A grand national melodrama. As performed at the Belfast Theater.
Belfast: Archbold and Dugan, pr., 1814. 54p. BL E N
[3 acts, prose. Prod. Belfast, 1814.]

106. BANCROFT, Marie Effie (Wilton), Lady [Br. 1839-1921] ALT: Bancroft, Mrs. Squire Bancroft; Wilton, Marie
My daughter.
1892. N M
[Drama, 1 act, adapted from German. Prod. Garrick, 1892.]

107. -----A riverside story.
1890. N M
[Play, 2 acts. Prod. Haymarket, 1890.]

BANCROFT, Mrs. Squire Bancroft see BANCROFT, Marie Effie (Wilton), Lady

108. BANNAN, Martha Ridgway [Am. 19c]
The fisher maiden. A vaudeville
written for the Court at Weimar [and]
The lover's caprice. A pastoral play
in verse. (From the German of Johann
Wolfgang Von Goethe).
Philadelphia: John C. Yorston pub.
co., 1899. 116p. NUC OCLC H
[The fisher maiden was also suggested
by Goethe's "Die Fischerein."]

109. BARING, Stephanie [Br. 19c]
Snatched from death. With Walter
Beaumont.
1896. M
[Drama, 1 act. Prod. Novelty, 1896.]

110. BARKER, A. E., Miss [Br. 19c]
Lady Barbara's birthday. A
comedietta.
In: Layinella and other drawing-room
plays. Comp. Edward Litt Laman
Blanchard.
L: G. Routledge & sons, 1883. 127p.
BL N
[Prod. Brighton, 1872.]

111. BARMBY, Beatrice Helen [Br. 19c]
Gisli Snisson: a drama; Ballads and
poems of the old Norse days and some
translations.
L & Westminster: Archibald Constable,
1900. 206p. NUC BL OCLC E

112. BARNES, Charlotte Mary Sanford,
Mrs. E.S. Conner Barnes [Am. 1818-
1863]
Plays, prose and poetry.
Philadelphia: E.H. Butler, 1848.
489p. NUC BL OCLC N R

113. -----The forest princess: or,
two centuries ago. An historical
play, in three parts.
In: Plays, prose and poetry.
[In verse. On Pocahontas, in 2
parts: First period, 1607; second
period, 1617. Prod. Liverpool, 1844;
Philadelphia, 1848. N]

114. -----Octavia Bragaldi: or, The
confession. A tragedy founded on
facts.
In: Plays, prose and poetry.
[5 acts, verse. 1st prod. in NY,
1837. Prod. Surrey Theatre, 1844. N
Based on an incident in Frankfort,
KY, 1825.]

BARNES, Mrs. E.S. Conner see BARNES,
Charlotte Mary Sanford

BARON-WILSON, Mrs. Cornwell see
WILSON, Margaret (Harries) Baron

115. BARRELL, Maria [Br. 18c]
The captive.
L: n.p., 1790. 31p. NUC BL N
[Drama]

BARRETT, Elizabeth see BROWNING,
Elizabeth (Barrett)

BARRETT, George C., co-author see
BARRETT, Gertrude F.

116. BARRETT, Gertrude F. [Am. 19c]
The watchword. A comedy in five
acts. With George C. Barrett.
NY: n.p., 1876. 105p. NUC OCLC

BARRITT, Frances see VICTOR, Frances
Auretta (Fuller) Barritt

BARRITT, Mrs. Jackson see VICTOR,
Frances Auretta (Fuller) Barritt

117. BARROW, Grace M. [Br. 19c]
Lady Jane Grey. A tragedy, in five
acts.
L: Grellier, 1881. 32p. BL
[verse]

118. BARRY, Constance E. [Am. 19c]
Brutus' Portia. An historical drama
in four acts.
San Francisco: n.p., 1890. 24p. NUC

119. BARRY, Helen [Br. d. 1904] ALT:
Rolls, Mrs. Alexander
A night's frolic. With Arthur Thomas.
L: 1891. N M
[Farce, adapted from German of Gustav
von Moser. Prod. Strand, 1891.]

120. BARRYMORE, Mrs. William [Br. d.
1862] ALT: Adams, Miss
Evening revels.
1823. N
[Prod. Drury Lane, 1823.]

121. BARSTOW, Ellen M. [Am. 19c]
The mission of the fairies.
Portland, ME: S. Berry, pr., 1869.
24p. NUC OCLC
[Fairies remind mortals of youthful
dreams and loves. Not juvenile.]

122. BARTHOLOMEW, Anne Charlotte
(Fayermann) Turnbull, Mrs. Valentine
Bartholomew [Br. 19c] ALT: Turnbull,
Anne Charlotte; Turnbull, Mrs. Walter
It's only my aunt! A comic interlude,
in one act.
L: n.p., 1850. BL

123. -----The ring, or the farmer's
daughter. A domestic drama, in two
acts. By Mrs. Walter Turnbull.

L: n.p., 1845. NUC BL
[NUC & BL copies, pp. 93-108,
detached from a larger work.]

BARTHOLOMEW, Mrs. Valentine see
BARTHOLOMEW, Anne Charlotte
(Fayermann) Turnbull

BARTLETT, George B., comp. see BELL,
Lucia Chase
BARTLETT, George B., comp. see
GRAHAM, Mary

BARTLETT, George B., comp. see
JOHNSON, Fannie M.

BASING, S. Herberte-, co-author see
BESSLE, Elizabeth

BATEMAN, Mrs. H.L. see BATEMAN,
Sidney Frances (Cowell)

124. BATEMAN, Isabel Emilie [Am./Br.
1854-1934]
The courtship of Morrice Buckler.
With A[lfred] E[dward] W[oodley]
Mason.
8th ed. L & NY: Macmillan, 1896.
373p. NUC OCLC N M
[Adaptation of Mason's novel. Play,
4 acts. Prod. Grand, 1897.]

125. BATEMAN, L. M. Beal, Mrs. [Am.
19c] PSEUD: Glenn, Grace
The prohibition speaker, a collection
of readings, recitations, dialogues,
tableaux and songs. By Grace Glenn.
Cincinnati, OH: Fillmore bros., 1889.
80p. NUC

126. BATEMAN, Sidney Frances
(Cowell), Mrs. H.L. Bateman [Am.
1823-1881] ALT: Cowell, Sidney
Frances
The dead secret: a drama adapted by
permission of the author from the
novel of Wilkie Collins, especially
for the Lyceum Theatre.
L: Pr. E.S. Boot, 1877. 40p. NUC
[Comedy, 3 acts]

127. -----Fanchette: or, The will o'
the wisp.
Edinburgh: 1871. M N
[Drama, 4 acts. Adapted from German
dramatization of a novel by George
Sand [Amandine Aurore Lucie Dupin].
Prod. Lyceum, 1871.]

128. -----Geraldine: or, Love's
victory.
1859. M N
[Tragedy. Prod. as: "Geraldine; or,
The master passion," Adelphi, 1865.]

129. -----The golden calf; or,
Marriage a la mode.
St. Louis, MO: Pr. at the Mo.
Republican office, 1857. 63p. NUC
OCLC
[Comedy, 3 acts]

130. -----Self: an original comedy.
NY: S. French, 1856. 46p. NUC BL OCLC
R
[3 acts. NY society play. French's
standard drama, no. 163.]

131. BATES, Ella Skinner [Am. 19c]
The convention of the Muses, a
classical play for parlor and school,
for nine females.
Boston: W.H. Baker & co.; NY: E.S.
Werner, c1891. 8p. NUC
[Baker's edition of plays.]

132. BATES, Margret Holmes
(Ernsperger) [Am. 1844-1927] ALT:
Holmes, Margaret Dialogues for
Christmas.
Indianapolis, IN: De-Witt, Bates,
1887. 118p. NUC OCLC

133. BATES, Rosa [Am. 19c]
Recalled to life. A play in four
acts, dramatized and adapted ....
from the celebrated novel, "A tale of
two cities" [by Charles Dickens].
NY: n.p., 1876. NUC

134. BAUM, Rosemary [Am. 19c]
Love in a lighthouse; a farce in one
act.
Boston: Walter H. Baker & co., c1896.
18p. NUC OCLC H
[Baker's edition of plays.]

135. -----That box of cigarettes; a
farce in three acts.
Boston: Walter H. Baker & co., c1892.
25p. NUC OCLC H
[Baker's edition of plays]

136. BAYLESS, Bell [Am. 19c]
Left in charge. Farce in one act.
Philadelphia: Penn pub. co., 1908.
23p. NUC OCLC H
[Earlier copyright: 1897]

137. BAYLIFF, R. L. and C.M.A. [Br.
19c]
Our hated rival.
In: Home acting for amateurs. 2d
series. By Nella Parker.
13 pts. L: F. Warne & co., 1892. NUC
BL N
[Duologue. Prod. Richmond, 1891.]

BEAUCHAMPS, Emily see MORLAND,
Charlotte E.

138. BEAUCHAMPS, Emily [Br. 19c]
The anti-matrimonial society.
1876. N
[Comedietta. Prod. Gaiety, Dublin,
1876.]

139. -----The matrimonial agency.
1896. M N
[Comedy, 1 act. Prod. Strand,
1896/1897.]

140. -----Yes or no.
1877. M N
[Comedy, 3 acts. Prod. Dublin 1877;
prod. Strand, 1897]

BEAUMONT, Walter, co-author see
BARING, Stephanie

141. BECKETT, Mrs. Harry [Br. 19c]
Jack.
L: 1886. M N
[Comedy, 4 acts. Prod. Royalty,
1886.]

142. BEERBOHM, Constance [Br. 19c]
A little book of plays for
professional and amateur actors.
Adapted from the French by C.
Beerbohm. L: George Newnes, 1897.
127p. BL E

143. -----An April shower: a little
comedy in one act. From the French
of [Ernest] Grenet-Dancourt.
In: A little book ... .
[Monologue for a female character]

144. -----Charity begins at home.
From the French of C. D'Epinay. In: A
little book ... .
[Duologue]

145. -----The chatterbox. From the
French of Ernest D'Hervilly.
In: A little book ... .
[Duologue, 2 scenes, for 2 female
characters]

146. -----He and she. From the
French of Abraham Dreyfus.
In: A little book ... .
[Duologue]

147. -----A little surprise. From
the French of Abraham Dreyfus.
In: A little book ... .
[Comedietta]

148. -----A secret.
In: A little book ... .
1888. M N
[Duologue for 2 women, adapted from
French. Prod. St. George Hall, 1888.
Comedietta.]

BEHN, A. see BEHN, Aphra

149. BEHN, Aphra [Br. 1640-1689] ALT:
B., A.; Behn, A.
The dramatic works of Mrs. Behn.
Complete in two volumes.
L: Collected [probably by James
Pullham] in the year 1820. NUC

150. -----The plays, histories, and
novels.
L: Pearson,1871. 6v. NUC BL OCLC

151. -----Abdelazer, or The Moor's
revenge. A tragedy.
L: J. Magnes & R. Bentley, 1677. NUC
B M N W S
[Prod. Dorset Garden, 1676. An
adaptation of "Lust's dominion, or
The lascivious queen," 1657,
erroneously attr. to Christopher
Marlowe.]

152. -----The amorous prince; or the
curious husband. A comedy.
L: J.M. for Thomas Dring, 1671. 82p.
NUC BL B N S WM
[Comedy, in verse. Perf. Lincoln's
Inn Fields & Dorset Garden, 1671.]

153. -----The city-heiress: or, Sir
Timothy Treat-all. A comedy.
L: D. Brown, T. Benskin & H. Rhodes,
1682. 61p. NUC BL OCLC B S WM
[Perf. Dorset Garden, 1681/2.]

154. -----The counterfeit bridegroom:
or, The defeated widow.
L: Langley Curtiss, 1677. B Har N WM
[Perf. Dorset Garden, 1677. Attr. to
Behn & to Thomas Betterton. N lists
with her work.]

155. -----The debauchee: or, The
credulous cuckold. A comedy.
L: John Amery, 1677. 63p. NUC BL B N
S WM
[Adapted from Richard Brome's "Mad
couple well match't." Perf. Dorset
Garden, 1676/7.]

156. -----The Dutch lover: a comedy.
L: Thomas Dring, 1673. 98p. NUC BL
OCLC B N S WM
[Perf. Dorset Garden, 1672/7]

157. -----The emperor of the Moon: a
farce.
L: Pr. by R. Holt, for Joseph Knight
& Francis Saunders, 1687 [1688
NUC][1678 B]. 76p. NUC OCLC B N S WM
[3 acts. Perf. Dorset Garden,
1686/7. Also in: Plays ...]

158. -----The fair jilt: or, The history of the Prince Tarquin and Miranda. L: R. Holt, for Will. Canning, 1688. 120p. NUC BL [Caption title: "The fair hypocrite."]

159. -----The false count; or, A new way to play an old game. L: Pr. by M. Flesher, for Jacob Tonson, 1682. 65p. NUC BL OCLC B N WM S [Also in: Plays. Farce, 5 acts. Prod. Dorset Garden, 1681.]

160. -----The feign'd curtizans, or a night's intrigue. A comedy. L: Jacob Tonson, 1679. 71p. NUC BL OCLC B N S WM [5 acts. Perf. Dorset Garden, 1678/79. Also in: Plays ...]

161. -----The forced marriage; or, the jealous bridegroom. A tragi-comedy. L: H.L. & R.B. for James Magnus, 1671. 89p. NUC BL OCLC B N S WM [5 acts, in verse. Perf. Lincoln's Inn Fields, 1670. Also in: Plays ...]

162. -----The history of the nun: or, The fair vow-breaker. L: A. Baskerville, 1689. 148p. NUC BL [Title: "The nun: or, The perjured beauty," in Plays ...]

163. -----The lady's looking-glass, to dress herself by: or, The whole art of charming. L: W. Onley for S. Briscoe, 1697. 24p. NUC BL [Dramatic piece. Some poetry included.]

164. -----Like father, like son; or, The mistaken brothers. 1682. Har N S [Perf. Dorset Garden, 1682. Only the prologue and epilogue survive. Adaptation of Thomas Randolph's "The Jealous Lovers." N lists with Behn. Prologue in Wiley, pp. 97-99 from a broadside, 1682. Also pub. in: Behn's Miscellany, 1685.]

165. -----The luckey chance, or an alderman's bargain. A comedy. L: Pr. by R.H. for W. Canning, 1687. 69p. NUC OCLC B N S WM [5 acts. Perf. Drury Lane, 1686. Entered in Stationer's Register, 1686, as: "The disappointed marriage; or, Ye generous mistress." Also in Plays.]

166. -----Miscellany, being a collection of poems by several hands. Together with Reflections on morality, or Senecca unmasqued. L: J. Hindmarsh, 1685. 301-82p. NUC BL [The dedicatory epistle signed: A. Behn.]

167. -----Prologue and epilogue to: Anon., Romulus and Hersilia. L: Pr. for J.V.; Pr. Nath. Thompson, 1682. [In Wiley, pp. 132-134. From a broadside, 1682.]

168. -----Prologue to: John Wilmot, Earl of Rochester's Valentinian. 1685. [In Wiley, pp. 249-50]

169. -----The revenge; or, a match in Newgate. L: W. Cademan, 1680. B Har N WM [Comedy. Perf. Dorset Garden, 1680. Note on Narcissus Luttrell's copy of play attr. to Behn. N lists as hers; WM lists under Thomas Betterton. Adaptation of John Marston's "Dutch Courtesan."]

170. -----The roundheads; or, The good old cause. A comedy. L: D. Brown, Benskin & H. Rhodes, 1682. 56p. NUC BL OCLC B N S WM [5 acts, mostly prose. Perf. Dorset Garden, 1881.]

171. -----The rover; or, The banish't cavaliers. A comedy by Aphra Behn. The first part. L: John Amery, 1677. 85p. NUC BL OCLC B S [5 acts. Perf. Dorset Garden, 1676/7. Also in: Dramatic works.]

172. -----The second part of the rover. L: Jacob Tonson, 1681. 85p. NUC BL OCLC B N S WM [5 acts. Command perf. before royalty, April 4, 1680/1. Also in: Dramatic works.]

173. -----Sir Patient Fancy: a comedy. L: E. Flesher for Richard Tonson & Jacob Tonson, 1678. 91p. NUC BL B N S WM [5 acts. Perf. Dorset Garden, 1677/8. Also in: Plays.]

174. -----The town-fopp: or Sir Timothy Tawdrey. A comedy.

L: Pr. by T.N. for James Magnes &
Richard Bentley, 1677. 66p. NUC BL
OCLC B N S WM
[5 acts. Perf. Dorset Garden, 1676.
Also in: Plays.]

175. -----The Widdow Ranter, or, the
history of Bacon in Virginia. A
tragi-comedy.
L: James Knapton, 1690. 56p. NUC BL
OCLC B N S WM
[5 acts. Perf. Drury Lane, 1689.
Also in: Plays.]

176. -----The young King: or, the
mistake.
L: D. Brown, T. Benskin & H. Rhodes,
1683. 63p. NUC OCLC B Har N S WM
[5 acts. Perf. Dorset Garden, 1679.
Also in: Plays ... .]

177. -----The younger brother; or,
The amorous jilt. A comedy.
L: J. Harris, sold by R. Baldwin,
1696. 52p. NUC BL OCLC B N S WM
[5 acts. Perf. Drury Lane, 1695/6.
Also in: Plays.]

BELASCO, Mme. Isaac Dolaro see
DOLARO, Selina

178. BELL, Florence Eveleen Eleanore
(Olliffe), Lady [Br. 1851-1930] ALT:
Bell, Mrs. Hugh
Chamber comedies. A collection of
plays and monologues for the drawing
room. By Mrs. Hugh Bell.
L & NY: Longmans, Green, & co., 1890.
321p. NUC BL OCLC E N
[Incl. 3 plays for children and a 1-
act play in French]

179. -----Alan's wife. A dramatic
study in three scenes. With Elizabeth
Robins.
L & NY: Longmans, Green, 1890. 321p.
L: Henry & co., 1893. 54p. NUC BL
OCLC E M N
[3 acts. Perf. Terry's, 1893.
Independent Theatre Series of plays,
No. 2. Founded on a story by Elin
Ameen]

180. -----Between the posts. By Mrs.
Hugh Bell.
L: Samuel French; NY: Henry French,
1887. 16p. NUC BL E
[Comedietta, one act. First
performed 1887. French's Acting Ed.]

181. -----The bicycle.
1896. N
[Dramatic sketch. Prod. Comedy,
1896.]

182. -----Blue or green?
1896. M N
[Comedietta. Perf. Comedy, 1896.]

183. -----A chance interview.
In: Chamber Comedies.
1889. N
[Comic duologue, 1 act. Prod. St.
George Hall, 1889.]

184. -----Cross questions and crooked
answers. A duologue. With Frances
Bell.
L & NY: French, 1899. 8p. BL NUC E
[Duologue. French's acting edition.]

185. ------The crossing sweeper. In:
Chamber Comedies.
[Monologue]

186. -----Giving him away.
In: Dialogues of the day. Ed. Oswald
Crawfurd.
L: Chapman & Hall, 1895. 13p. OCLC E

187. -----The great illusion.
1895. N
[Comedietta. Prod. Albert Hall,
1895.]

188. -----A hard day's work.
In: Chamber Comedies.
[Monologue]

189. -----In a first-class waiting-
room.
In: Chamber Comedies.
[Comedy, 1 act.]

190. -----In a telegraph office.
1893. N
[Comedietta. Prod. in Sloane Square,
1893.]

191. -----Jerry-Builder Solness.
1893. N
[Parody of Ibsen. Prod. St. George,
1893.]

192. -----A joint household. A
comedietta in one act.
L & NY: French, 1891. 14p. NUC BL
OCLC E M N
[Perf. Steinway Hall, 1891; Grand,
1892. French's Acting Edition. Also
in: Chamber Comedies.]

193. -----Karin.
1892. N M
[Drama, 2 acts. From Swedish of
Alfhild Agrell. Perf. Vaudeville,
1892.]

194. -----L'Indecis.

1887. M N
[Comedietta. Also prod. as: "Between
the Posts," 1887. An adaptation by
G.W. Godfrey, prod. as: "The man that
hesitates," Royalty, 1887.]

195. -----Last words.
In: Chamber Comedies.
[1 act.]

196. -----A lost thread.
1890. N
[Dramatic sketch. Prod. Prince of
Wales, 1890.]

197. -----The masterpiece.
1893. M N
[Comedietta. Perf. Royalty, 1893.]

198. -----Miss Flipper's holiday.
With Harrie Bell.
L & NY: S. French, 1900. 8p. E
[Lacy's Acting ed.]

199. -----A modern Locusta.
In: Chamber Comedies.
[1 act.]

200. -----Nicholson's niece.
1892. M N
[Farce, 3 acts. Perf. Terry's,
1892.]

201. -----Not to be forwarded.
In: Chamber Comedies.
[Monologue]

202. -----Oh, no! In: Chamber
Comedies.
[Monologue]

203. -----The public prosecutor.
In: Chamber Comedies.
[1 act.]

204. -----The reliquary.
In: Chamber comedies.
[Monologue]

205. -----A sixpenny telegram.
Comedietta in one act.
L & NY: French, 1887. 20p. NUC BL
OCLC E N
[French's Acting Ed., v. 126]

206. -----A superflous lady.
1891. N
[Comedietta. Prod. Lyric, 1888.]

207. -----The "Swiss Times." In:
Chamber comedies.
[Comedy, 1 act.]

208. -----Time is money. With Arthur
Cecil [Blunt].

1890. E N M
[Comedietta. Perf. in Newcastle,
1890; Comedy, 1892. BL: French's
acting ed., 1905. 27p.]

209. -----An underground journey.
With Charles H.E. Brookfield.
1893. N M
[Comedietta. Perf. Comedy, 1893.]

210. -----An unpublished MS.
In: Chamber Comedies.
[Comedy, 1 act.]

211. -----The viceroy's wedding.
In: Chamber Comedies. [Monologue]

212. -----The waterproof.
In: Chamber Comedies.
[Monologue]

213. -----A woman of courage.
In: Chamber Comedies.
[Monologue.]

214. -----A woman of culture.
In: Chamber Comedies.
[Comedy, 1 act.]

215. -----The wrong poet.
In: Chamber Comedies.
[1 act]

BELL, Frances, co-author see BELL,
Florence Eveleen Eleanore (Olliffe)

BELL, Harrie, co-author see BELL,
Florence Eveleen Eleanore (Olliffe)

BELL, Mrs. Hugh see BELL, Florence
Eveleen Eleanore (Olliffe), Lady

216. BELL, Lucia Chase [Am. 19c]
Buoyant. A Dickens charade in three
scenes.
In: A dream of the centuries and
other entertainments for parlor and
hall. Comp. George B. Bartlett
Boston: W.H. Baker, 1889. 43p. NUC
OCLC H
[Baker's novelties.]

217. BELL, Minnie [Br. 19c]
The gavotte.
1890. N
[Dramatic sketch. Prod. Steinway
Hall, 1890.]

218. -----Is Madame at home?
1887. N
[Comedietta. Prod. Prince of Wales,
1887.]

219. -----Lady Browne's diary.

1892. N M
[Comedy, adapted from French of
Octave Feuillet, "La Crise." Perf.
Strand, 1892.]

BENHAM, Arthur, co-author see BURNEY,
Estelle

220. BENNETT, Anna R. (Gladstone)
[Br. 19c]
Iphigenia in Tauris. From the German
of [Johann Wolfgang von] Goethe.
With original poems.
Liverpool: Priv. pr., 1851. 200p. BL

221. BENNETT, Emelie [Br. 19c]
Among the Amalekites.
L: 1889. N
[comedy]

222. BERESFORD, Isabel [Br. 19c]
Until the day break.
1898. N
[Comic drama. Prod. Bijou, 1898.]

223. BERINGER, Aimée Danielle, Mrs.
Oscar Beringer [Br. 1856-1936]
The agitator.
NY: Rosefield, 1897. NUC
[Play, 1 act. Prod. Hick Theatre,
London, 1917.]

224. -----Bess.
1891. N M
[Drama, 3 acts. Perf. St. James,
1893.]

225. -----A bit of old Chelsea. A
play in one act. By Mrs. Oscar
Beringer.
L & NY: French, 1905. 25p. E N M
[Prod. Court Theatre, 1897 & 3 other
theatres through January 1898.
French's acting ed.]

226. -----The holly tree inn. Play
in one act ... adapted ... from ...
Charles Dickens' Christmas story,
"The holly tree."
NY & L: French, 1891. 32p. NUC BL E N
M
[Prod. Terry's, 1891. French's
acting ed., v. 153.]

227. -----My lady's orchard. With
George P. Hawtrey.
1877. N M
[Play, 1 act. Perf. Avenue, 1897.]

228. -----The plot of his story.
1899. N M
[Play, 1 act. From a story by Morley
Roberts. Perf. St. James, 1899.]

229. -----The prince and the pauper.
1890. N M
[Play, 4 acts, adapted from Mark
Twain [Samuel L. Clemmens]. Perf.
Gaiety, 1890.]

230. -----Salve.
1895. N
[Dramatic sketch. Prod. Opera
Comique, 1895.]

231. -----Tares.
1888. N M
[Drama, 3 acts. Perf. Prince of
Wales, 1888, & Opera Comique, 1889.]

232. -----That girl. With Henry
Hamilton.
1890. N
[Comedy. Prod. Haymarket, 1890.]

BERINGER, Mrs. Oscar see BERINGER,
Aimée Danielle

233. BERNARD, Caroline Richings [Am.
19c]
The Huguenots; grand opera in five
acts. By Giacomo Meyerbeer. Trans.
and adapted by Caroline Richings
Bernard.
Philadelphia: Ledger job pr. off.,
1870. 35p. NUC

BERNARD, Mrs. Charles see ALLEYN,
Annie

234. BERNHARDT-FISHER, Mrs. [Br. 19c]
ALT: Fisher, Mrs. Bernhardt
Claire.
1887. N
[Drama. Prod. New Cross, 1887.]

235. BERRIE, E., Miss [Br. 19c]
Captain Smith: a farce in one act.
NY & Clyde, OH: Ames, 1870? 14p. L:
Lacy, 1871. 19p. BL
[First performed April 4, 1870. Ames
Standard & Minor Drama; Lacy's Acting
Ed.]

236. BERRY, Mary [Br. 1763-1852]
The fashionable friends; a comedy, in
five acts.
L: J. Ridgway, 1802. 85p. NUC BL OCLC
B E
[Perf. at Strawberry Hill, 1801.
Longe, v. 264, no. 5]

237. BESSLE, Elizabeth [Br. d. 1906]
The electric spark.
1889. N M
[Comedy from French of Edouard
Pailleron. Perf. Olympic, 1889 &
Trafalgar Square, 1894.]

238. -----Gringoire. With S.
Herberte-Basing.
1890. N
[Drama.   Prod. in Battersea & Oxford,
1890.]

239. -----The tinted Venus.
1889. N
[Comedietta.   Prod. at Wandsworth
Common, 1889.]

240. -----The understudy.
1892. N
[Duologue.   Prod. Opera Comique,
1892.]

241. BEVINGTON, Louisa Sarah [Br. b.
1845] ALT: Guggenberger, Louisa Sarah
(Bevington)
Chiefly a dialogue.   Concerning some
difficulties of a dunce.
L: "Freedom" Office, 1895. 15p. NUC
OCLC
[Imaginary conversation on
anarchism.]

242. BIDALLES, Adelaide Helen [Br.
19c]
Amy Lawrence, the Freemason's
daughter.
1851. N
[Drama.   Entered with Lord
Chamberlain, 1851.]

243. BIGG, Louisa [Br. 19c]
A splendid lie. A new and original
drama in five acts.
L: J. Bale & sons, 1893. 44p. NUC BL

BIGOT, Mme. Charles see BIGOT, Marie
(Healy)

244. BIGOT, Marie (Healy), Mme.
Charles Bigot [Br. b. 1843] ALT:
Healy, Marie
The home theatre.
L: Sampson, Low, Marston, Low &
Searle, 1871. 292p. NUC OCLC

245. -----A flirtation.
In: The home theatre.
[Comedy, 1 act.]

246. -----A lost game.
In: The home theatre.
[Drama, 4 acts]

247. -----The skeleton in the closet.
In: The home theatre.
[Dramatic sketch, 1 act.]

248. -----An unexpected guest.
In: The home theatre.
[Comedy, 2 acts.]

249. -----Weather-bound.
In: The home theatre.
[Comedietta, 1 act.]

250. -----"Yes or no?"
In: The home theatre.
[Comedietta, 1 act.]

BINISTEAD, Mary (Openshaw) see
OPENSHAW, Mary

251. BINNS, Gertrude [Br. 19c]
The school for husbands. With J.
Halford.
1897. N
[Dramatic sketch.   Prod. Mount View
Hall, 1897.]

BISGOOD, J.J., co-author see
LAWRENCE, Ewceretta, Miss

BLACKWOOD, Helen Selina (Sheridan),
Baroness Dufferin see DUFFERIN and
CLANDEBOYE, Helen Selina (Sheridan)
Blackwood, Baroness

BLAKE, Emilia see GOWING, Emilia
Julia (Blake) Aylmer

252. BLANCHARD, Amy Ella [Am. 1856-
1926]
Hearts and clubs.   Comedy in three
acts.
Philadelphia: Penn pub. co., [1910
OCLC] 1913. 21p. NUC OCLC H
[Earlier copyright: 1896.]

BLANCHARD, Edward, comp. see BARKER,
A.E., Miss

BLAND, Dorothy see JORDAN, Dorothy
(Bland)

253. BLANDIN, Isabella Margaret
Elizabeth (John) [Am. 19/20c]
From Gonzales to San Jacinto.   A
historical drama of the Texas
revolution.
NY: n.p.; Houston, TX: Dealy & Baker,
1897. 18p. NUC OCLC

BLEECKER, Margaretta see FAUGERES,
Margaretta Van Wyck (Bleecker)

BLEECKER, Peggy see FAUGERES,
Margaretta Van Wyck (Bleecker)

254. BLEVIN, Mary Ann [Am. b. 1834]
Maphine, of the true lovers; a
romantic drama, representing New
England scenes of thirty or forty
years ago.   Five acts, 18 scenes.
Hope Valley, RI: 1898.

255. BLOEDE, Gertrude [Am. 1845-1905]
PSEUD: Sterne, S.; Sterne, Stuart
Makaria. A play in five acts. By S.
Sterne.
St. Louis, MO: 1876-78. NUC
[A detached copy from The Western: a
journal of literature, education and
art.]

BLOOD, Gertrude Elizabeth see
CAMPBELL, Gertrude Elizabeth (Blood)

256. BLOOMFIELD, Helen [Br. 19c]
The Euston Hotel.
1845. N
[Farce. Entered with Lord
Chamberlain.]

BLUNT, Arthur Cecil, co-author see
BELL, Florence Eveleen Eleanore
(Olliffe)

257. BOADEN, Caroline [Br. 19c]
Don Pedro the cruel and Don Manuel
the cobbler! or, the corregidor of
Seville! A comic drama, in two
acts... Adapted from the French.
L: J. Duncombe, 1838. 33p. NUC BL E
[Duncombe, V.30]

258. -----A duel in Richelieu's time.
1832. N
[Drama. Prod. Haymarket, 1832.]

259. -----Fatality: a drama, in one
act.
L: J. Cumberland, 1829. 28p. NUC BL E
M N
[Acc. The Dramatic magazine, Oct. 1,
1829, a trans. from Fr. M says
farce, 1 act. Prod. Haymarket, 1829;
Olympic, 1847. Cumberland's British
Theatre, V.23, No. 3.]

260. -----The first of April: a farce
in two acts.
L: J. Cumberland, 1830. 36p. NUC E
[Cumberland's British Theatre]

261. -----Quite correct.
1825. N
[Comedy. Prod. Haymarket, 1825.]

262. -----The two Thompsons; or,
stagecoach adventure! A farce, in
two acts.
Philadelphia: C. Neal, 1833. 27p. NUC

263. -----William Thompson; or which
is he? a farce, in two acts. L: J.
Cumberland, 1829. 32p. NUC BL OCLC E
N
[Prod. Haymarket, 1829. Cumberland's
British Theatre, v. 23.]

BOADEN, James, ed. see INCHBALD,
Elizabeth (Simpson)

264. BOOTH, Mrs. [Br. 18c]
The little French lawyer...A farce.
Taken from [Francis] Beaumont and
[John] Fletcher.
L: J. Bell, 1778. 40p. NUC B N
[Farce. Prod. Covent Garden, 1778.]

265. BOOTH, Helen [Am. 19c]
After twenty years.
In: Dramatic leaflets.
Philadelphia: Phineas Garrett, c1877.
1 vol. in 20 pts. NUC OCLC H
[Romantic comedy, 1 act.]

266. -----At the Red Lion.
In: Dramatic Leaflets.
[Romantic comedy, 1 act.]

267. -----An electric episode.
In: Dramatic leaflets.
[Romantic comedy, 1 act.]

268. -----A fifty-dollar milliner's
bill.
In: Dramatic leaflets.
[Comedy, 1 act.]

269. -----Pepita, the gipsey girl of
Andalusia.
In: Dramatic leaflets.

270. BOOTH, Mrs. Otto Von [Br. 19c]
Corinne. 1885. M
[Drama from her novel. Prod.
Standard, 1885. No further
information available.]

271. BOOTHBY, Frances [Br. 17c]
Marcella; or, The treacherous friend.
A tragi-comedy.
L: For Will. Cademan & Giles
Widdowes, 1670. 95p. NUC BL OCLC B N
S WM
[Perf. Theatre Royal in Bridges St.,
1669.]

BOTHAM, Mary see HOWITT, Mary
(Botham)

BOULDING, James Winsett, co-author
see LANCASTER-WALLIS, Ellen

BOWERS, Mrs. D.P. see BOWERS,
Elizabeth (Crocker)

272. BOWERS, Elizabeth (Crocker),
Mrs. D.P. Bowers [Am. 1830-1895]
The black agate; or, Old foes with
new faces. Five acts.
Philadelphia: Pr. for the author by
U.S. steam-power bk. & job pr., 1859.
30p. NUC H

[From Charles Kingsley's novel,
"Hypatia."]

BOWES, Mary Eleanor Lyon, Countess of
Strathmore see STRATHMORE, Mary
Eleanor (Bowes) Lyon, Countess of

273. BOWMAN, Anne [Br. 19c]
Charade dramas for the drawing room.
L: G. Routledge & co., 1855. [1856
NUC] 114p. NUC BL
[7 charades; each three scenes, 15p.]

274. BOYD, Elizabeth [Br. 18c] PSEUD:
Louisa
Don Sancho: or, the student's whim, a
ballad opera of two acts, with
Minerva's triumph, a masque.
L: C. Corbet; the Booksellers of
London & Westminster, 1739. 20p. NUC
BL B N
[Longe, v. 59, no. 1. Not
performed.]

275. BOYLE, Mary Louisa [Br. 1810-
1890]
The bridal of Melcha; a dramatic
sketch.
L: Henry Colburn, 1844. 133p. NUC BL
[4 acts, verse. Based on an Irish
legend.]

BOYNE, William, co-author see
CORBETT, Elizabeth Burgoyne

276. BOYNTON, Mary May [Am. 19/20c]
Aunt Nancy's account of a fashionable
parlor recital.
n.p.: Franklin, OH 190-?. 4p. NUC

277. -----Aunt Nancy's account of
their family reunion.
Franklin, OH: Eldridge entertainment
house, 1898. 4p. NUC OCLC
[Monologue]

278. -----A rural theft. Franklin,
OH: Eldridge, 1898. 3 l. NUC OCLC
[Monologue]

279. -----A vocal courtship.
Franklin, OH: Eldridge entertainment
house, 1898? 4p. NUC OCLC

280. -----The ward of the king.
Franklin, OH: Eldridge, n.d. 8p. NUC
[Eldridge popular monologues]

BRACKLEY, Lady Elizabeth (Cavendish),
co-author see CAVENDISH, Lady Jane

281. BRADBURY, Louise A. [Am. 19c]
Game of dominance. Comedy in one
act.

Boston: W.H. Baker, 1885. 28p. NUC
OCLC H
[From French of Louis-Emile Dubry.
1905 ed.: "The masqueraders; or, A
game of dominos."]

282. BRADBURY, Sophia Louise
(Appleton) [Am. 19c] ALT: Appleton,
Sophia Louise
My Country.
In: Easy entertainments for young
people. Comp. Margaret Cameron
Kilvert Smith.
Philadelphia: Penn pub. co., 1892.
NUC OCLC

283. -----The pirate. A serio-comic
opera. In three acts.
Cambridge, MA: Pr. for the author by
Welch, Bigelow, 1865. 55p. NUC BL H
[In verse. First performed 1833 in
Philadelphia]

BRADDON, Mary Elizabeth see MAXWELL,
Mary Elizabeth (Braddon)

284. BRADLEY, Katherine Harris [Br.
1848-1904] PSEUD: Field, Michael
[with Edith Emma Cooper; 1862-1913];
Leigh, Arran
Anna Ruina. By Michael Field.
L: D. Nutt, 1899. 101p. NUC BL OCLC E
N
[Drama, in verse]

285. -----Attila, my Attila. By
Michael Field.
L: Elkin Mathews, 1896. [1895 OCLC]
107p. NUC BL OCLC E N
[Drama]

286. -----Bellerophon, by Arran and
Isla Leigh [Edith Emma Cooper].
L: C. Kegan Paul, 1881. 180p. NUC BL
E
[Classical myth, in verse.]

287. -----Brutus Ultor. By Michael
Field.
L: George Bell & sons; Clifton: J.
Baker & son, 1886. 78p. NUC BL OCLC E
N
[Tragedy; in verse]

288. -----Callirhoe. Fair Rosamund.
By Michael Field. L: G. Bell & sons;
Clifton: C. Baker & sons; NY: H. Holt
& co., 1884. 206p. NUC BL OCLC E N
[Callirhoe: classical setting in
verse, 3 acts.]

289. -----Canute the great. The cup
of water.
L: G. Bell; Clifton: C. Baker & sons,
1887. 170p. NUC BL OCLC E N

[Dramas in verse & prose]

290. -----The cup of water.
In: Canute ... .

291. -----Fair Rosamund.
In: Callirhoe ... .
[English historical drama, 2 acts,
verse.]

292. -----The father's tragedy.
William Rufus. Loyalty or love?
L: G. Bell, 1885. 312p. NUC BL OCLC E
N
[Drama in verse & prose]

293. -----Loyalty or love? In: The
father's tragedy ... .

294. -----Noontide branches. A small
sylvan drama interspersed with songs
and invocations. By Michael Field.
Oxford: pr. by H. Daniel, 1899. 44p.
NUC BL OCLC E N

295. -----A question of memory. A
play in four acts. By Michael Field.
L: Elkin Mathews & John Lane, 1893.
48p. NUC BL OCLC E M N
[Drama, 4 acts. Prod. Opera Comique,
1893, by Independent Theatre Soc.]

296. -----Stephania; a trialogue. By
Michael Field.
L: E. Mathews & J. Lane, 1892. 100p.
NUC BL OCLC E N

297. -----The tragic Mary. By
Michael Field.
L: G. Bell & sons, 1890. 261p. NUC BL
OCLC E N
[Tragedy of Mary, Queen of Scots,
verse & prose]

298. -----William Rufus.
In: The father's tragedy ... .

299. -----The world at auction. By
Michael Field.
L: Hacon & Ricketts, 1898. NUC BL
OCLC
[Drama, verse]

BRADLEY, Margaret Louisa see WOODS,
Margaret Louisa (Bradley)

300. BRADLEY, Nellie H. [Am. 19c]
The first glass: or, the power of
woman's influence. And the young
teetotaler; or, Saved at last.
Rockland, ME: Z.P. Vose & co., 1868.
35p. NUC [At head of title: New
temperance dialogues.]

301. -----An hour with Mother Goose
and her temperance family.
NY: National temperance soc. & pub.
house, 1887. 32p. NUC
[Incl. music]

302. -----Marry no man if he drinks;
or, Laura's plan, and how it
succeeded.
Rockland, ME: Z. Pope Vose, 1868.
24p. OCLC
[At head of title: New temperance
dialogues.]

303. -----New temperance dialogues.
Rockland, ME: Z. Pope Vose, 1868.
24p. OCLC
[Bound in a vol., VTZ, v. 37, nos. 21
& 22]

304. -----Reclaimed: or, the danger
of moderate drinking.
Rockland, ME: Z.P. Vose & co., 1868.
23p. OCLC
[At head of title: New temperance
dialogues.
In: VTZ v. 37, no. 20]

305. -----The stumbling block, or why
the deacon gave up his wine.
Rockland, ME: 1871. 33p. NUC
[At head of title: New temperance
dialogues]

306. -----A temperance picnic with
the old woman who lived in a shoe.
In: VTZ p.v. 66, no. 18.
NY: National temperance soc. & pub.
house, 1888. 45p. NUC
[Operetta in 2 acts.]

307. -----Wine as a medicine; or,
Abbie's experience.
Rockland, ME: Z.P. Vose & co., 1871.
22p. NUC
[On cover: New temperance dialogues.
In: VTZ p. v. 65, no. 16]

BRADSHAW, Mrs. Albert see BRADSHAW,
Annie M. (Tree)

308. BRADSHAW, Annie M. (Tree), Mrs.
Albert Bradshaw [Br. 19/20c] ALT:
Tree, Annie M.; Tree, Ann Marie
"A debt of honour," and other
recitations.
L: Capper & Newton, 1893. 27p. BL
[Lynn's "One at a time" series, no.
8.]

309. -----The skyward guide. With
Mark Melford.
L: 1895. M N
[Drama, 4 acts. Prod. Royalty,
1895.]

BRAND, Barbarina Ogle Wilmot,
Baroness Dacre see WILMOT, Barbarina,
Baroness Dacre

310. BRAND, Hannah [Br. d. 1821]
Plays and poems.
L: F. & C. Rivington; Norwich:
Beatniffe & Payne; F. & C. Rivington,
1798. 424p. NUC BL OCLC B N

311. -----Adelinda; a comedy.
In: Plays and poems.
[5 acts. Altered from "La Force du
Natural" by Philippe Nericault
Destouches]

312. -----The conflict; or, Love,
honour and pride: a heroic comedy.
In: Plays and poems.
[5 acts, verse. Altered from "Don
Sanche d'Aragon," by Pierre
Corneille]

313. -----Huniades; or, The siege of
Belgrade: a tragedy.
In: Plays and poems.
[5 acts, verse. Perf. Haymarket,
1792, under this title, & as:
"Agmunda." She made her debut as
Agmunda. BioD.]

BRANDENBURG, Anspach and Bayreath,
H.S.H., the Margravine of see CRAVEN,
Elizabeth (Berkeley)

BRAZZA-SAVORGNAN, Cora Ann (Slocomb),
Countess of see SAVORGNAN, Cora Ann
(Slocomb) Brazza-, Contesa di

314. BREWSTER, Emma E. [Am. 19/20c]
Parlor varieties, plays, pantomimes
and charades.
Boston: Lee & Shepard, 1881-1887. 3v.
NY: C.T. Dillingham, 1880. 261p. NUC
OCLC
[Part 1 by Brewster; Part 2 with
Lizzie B. Scribner; Part 3, pub.
1887, by Olivia Lovell Wilson. Also
incl. a pantomime and one charade
play for children.]

315. -----Aunt Mehetible's scientific
experiment, a farce in one act for
female characters only. With Lizzie
B. Scribner.
Boston: Baker, c1878. 11p. NUC OCLC H
[Baker's Ed. of Plays. Also in:
Parlor Varieties.]

316. -----Beresford benevolent
society. Farce in one act.
Boston: W.H. Baker, 1906. 22p. NUC
OCLC H
[Baker's Ed. of Plays. Earlier
copyright: 1885.]

317. -----Cent-any-all. Centennial.
Charade in three acts.
Boston: Lee, 1881. 8p. NUC
[Also in: Parlor varieties.]

318. -----A bunch of buttercups.
In: Parlor varieties.
[Musical entertainment. All parts
sung to Gilbert & Sullivan.]

319. -----The Christmas box: parlor
theatrical in two acts.
Boston: Lee & Shepard, 1881. 20p. NUC
OCLC
[Pub. in 1887 in Kaye's Christmas
entertainments for school & home.
Also in: Parlor varieties.]

320. -----A dog that will fetch will
carry; a farce in two scenes, for
female characters only.
Boston: Walter H. Baker & co., c1880.
37p. NUC OCLC
[Baker's Ed. of Plays. Also in:
Parlor varieties.]

321. -----The don's stratagem.
In: Parlor varieties ... .
[3 acts]

322. -----Eliza's bona-fide offer; a
farce in one act, for female
characters only.
Boston: W.H. Baker, c1880. 12p. NUC
OCLC
[Pub. Boston: Baker's edition of
plays, 1901. 12p. Also in: Parlor
varieties]

323. -----Elizabeth Carisbrooke with
a "P." In: Parlor varieties ... .
[3 acts]

324. -----The free ward.
In: Parlor varieties ... .
[1 act]

325. -----How the colonel proposed, a
farce in three scenes.
Boston: W.H. Baker, 1880. 19p. NUC
OCLC
[Also in: Parlor varieties]

326. -----Jane's legacy.
In: Parlor varieties ... .
[1 act]

327. -----My sister's husband.
In: Parlor varieties ... .
[2 acts]

328. -----Poor Peter. A farce in one
act.
Boston: Lee, 1881. p. [93]-112. NUC

[Caption title: Parlor varieties, etc.]

329. -----A pretty piece of property. In: Parlor varieties ... . [3 acts]

330. -----Zerubbabel's second wife, a farce in one act. Boston: Walter H. Baker & co., 1880. 15p. NUC OCLC [Date on cover, 1899. Baker's edition of plays. Also in: Parlor Varieties.]

331. BRIDGES, Eloise [Am. 19c] Our cause; or, The female rebel. 1862. C [Pro-Confederate]

BRIGHT, Mrs. Augustus see BRIGHT, Kate C.

332. BRIGHT, Eva [Br. 19c] Love's young dream. 1891. M N [Play, 1 act. Prod. Strand, 1891.]

333. -----Tabitha's courtship. With Florence Bright. 1890. N [Comedietta. Prod. Comedy, 1890.]

BRIGHT, Florence, co-author see BRIGHT, Eva

334. BRIGHT, Florence [Br. 19/20c] Caught out. 1888. M N [Comedietta, adapted from German of Pfahl ["Die Kunstreiterin"]. Prod. St. George Hall, 1888.]

335. BRIGHT, Kate C., Mrs. Augustus Bright [Br. d. 1906] ALT: Pitt, Kate Bracken Hollow. 1878. N [Drama. Prod. in Sheffield, 1878.]

336. -----Dane's dyke. 1881. N [Drama. Prod. in Sheffield, 1881.]

337. -----Naomi's sin; or, where are you going to, my pretty maid? 1879. N [Drama. Prod. in Sheffield, 1879.]

338. -----Noblesse oblige, a comedy-drama in a prologue and three acts. By Mrs. Augustus Bright. L & NY: S. French, 1880. 34p. NUC BL OCLC E N [Prod. in Exeter, 1878. Lacy's Acting Ed.]

339. -----Not false, but fickle. A new and original comedy-drama in one act. Sheffield: Pawson & Brailsford, 1878. 20p. L & NY: S. French, 1878? 12p. NUC BL OCLC N [Prod. in Sheffield, 1878. French's Acting Ed., v. 115]

BROOKE, Frances (Moore) see BROKE, Frances (More)

340. BROOKE, Frances (More [Moore NUC]), Mrs. John Brooke [Br./Can. 1724-1789] Marian, a comic opera in 2 acts. L: T.N. Longman & O. Rees, 1800. 31p. NUC BL OCLC B N [Prod. Covent Garden, 1788.]

341. -----Rosina, a comic opera, in two acts. L: T. Cadell, 1783. 46p. NUC BL OCLC B E N [Prod. Covent Garden, 1782.]

342. -----The siege of Sinope, a tragedy. L: T. Caddell, 1781. 71p. Dublin: Sam Price, etc., 1781. 61p. NUC BL OCLC B N [5 acts, verse. Prod. Covent Garden, 1781. Classical themes.]

343. -----Virginia, a tragedy. With odes, pastorals and translations. By Mrs. Brooke. L: Pr. for the Author, sold by A. Millar, 1756. 159p. NUC BL OCLC N [5-acts, verse. Based on story of Appius & Virginia. Pastorals, dialogues, pp. 131-38.]

BROOKE, Mrs. John see BROOKE, Frances (More)

BROOKFIELD, Charles H.E., co-author see BELL, Florence Eveleen Eleanor (Olliffe)

BROOKS, F.M., co-author see SCUDDER, Vida Dutton

344. BROWN, Abbie Farwell [Am. 1871-1927] Quits. Comedy in one act. Boston: W.H. Baker, 1896. 21p. NUC OCLC H [Baker's ed. of plays]

345. BROWN, Catherine [Am. 1800?-1823] PSEUD: Lady, A The converted Cherokee; a missionary drama, founded on fact. Written by a lady.

New Haven, CT: S. Converse, 1819.
27p. NUC OCLC Hill Wells
[Hill & Wells list only under pseud.
and give title as: "Catherine Brown,
the converted Cherokee."]

BROWN, M. Frances see BROWN, Minnie
Frances

346. BROWN, Minnie Frances [Am.
19/20c] ALT: Brown, M. Frances
A glimpse of grammarland: a farce.
Syracuse, NY: C.W. Bardeen, 1894.
16p. NUC

347. -----The harvest rune, a thanksgiving entertainment; original verse
and prose.
Chicago: A. Flanagan, 1899. 61p. NUC
OCLC
[Pub. in special issue of "The
teacher's helper."]

BROWN, W. Heron, co-author see COOK,
Mabel (Collins)

BROWNE, Felicia Dorothea see HEMANS,
Felicia Dorothea (Browne)

348. BROWNE, Frances Elizabeth [Br.
1816-1879]
Ruth: a sacred drama, and original
lyrical poems.
NY: Wynkoop & Hallenbeck, 1871. 121p.
NUC

BROWNE, Isaac Hawkins, ed. see
LEAPOR, Mary, Mrs.
 BROWNING, E.B. see BROWNING,
Elizabeth (Barrett)

BROWNING, Mrs. Robert see BROWNING,
Elizabeth (Barrett)

349. BROWNING, Elizabeth (Barrett),
Mrs. Robert Browning [Br. 1806-1861]
ALT: B., E. B.; Barrett, Elizabeth;
Browning, E. B.
Prometheus bound and other poems.
L: A.J. Valpy, 1833. 163p. NUC BL
OCLC E
[Trans. of Aeschylus pub. with other
poems by Browning.]

350. -----Psyche apocalypte: a
lyrical drama. Projected by E.B.
Browning and R.H. Horne. Repr. St.
James's Magazine and United Empire
Review for February, 1876.
L & Aylesbury: Pr. by Hazell, Watson
& Viney, 1876. 19p. NUC BL
[Drafts & correspondence concerning
the play]

351. BRUNNER, Mme. [Br. 19c]
Our lodgers.
1868. N
[Farce. Prod. Sunderland, 1868.]

352. BRUNTON, Anna (Ross), Mrs. John
Brunton [Br. b. 1773] ALT: Brunton,
Annie; Ross, Anna PSEUD: Dee, L.S.
The cottagers; a comic opera in two
acts. Music by William Shield. By
Anna Ross.
L: The author, 1788. NUC BL B N
[In prose with songs. Written at age
15. Comic actress at Covent Garden,
BioD.]

353. -----The family ghost.
1881. N
[Comedietta. Prod. at Hanley, 1881.]

354. -----The queen of diamonds.
1882. N
[Comic drama. Prod. at Coatbridge,
1882.]

355. -----Won by honours.
1882. M
[Comedy, 4 acts. Prod. Comedy,
1882.]

BRUNTON, Annie see BRUNTON, Anna
(Ross)

BRUNTON, Mrs. John see BRUNTON, Anna
(Ross)

BUCHANAN, Robert William, co-author
see JAY, Harriett

BUCHANAN, Mrs. Robert William see
JAY, Harriett

BUELL, Sarah Josepha see HALE, Sarah
Josepha (Buell)

356. BULL, Lucy Catlin [Am. 19c] ALT:
Robinson, Lucy Catlin (Bull)
A child's poems from October to
October, 1870-1871. By Lucy Catlin
Bull.
Hartford, CT: Case, Lockwood &
Brainard, priv. pr., 1872. 171p. NUC
OCLC
[10 yr.-old author. Incl. 3 verse
dramas, 5 acts each: "Rolling stone;"
"Spilled milk;" "Victor."]

357. BULLOCK, Cynthia [Am. b. 1821]
Washington and other poems.
NY: Pub. for author by Reid &
Cunningham, 1847. 108p. NUC OCLC H
[Incl.: "Dialogue. Poet and
musician," dramatic poem, pp. 71-73]

358. BURGESS, Mrs. [Br. 18c]
The oaks, or the beauties of
Canterbury. A comedy.
Canterbury: Simmons & Kirkby, 1780.
7, 63p. NUC BL N
[Operatic farce. Prod. Canterbury,
1780.]

359. BURKE, Miss [Br. 18c]
Songs, duets, choruses, etc.
In: The ward of the castle. A comic
opera, in two acts.
L: T. Cadell, 1793. 22p. BL B N
[Prod. Covent Garden, 1793. Larpent
Ms. #992.]

360. BURNETT, Frances Eliza
(Hodgson), Mrs. Swan M. Burnett [Br.
1849-1924]
Editha's burglar. With Stephen
Townsend.
1890. N
[Prod. in Neath, 1890.]

361. -----Esmerelda, a comedy drama
in four acts. With William H.
Gillette.
NY: S. French, 1881. 59p. NUC OCLC M
N
[French's International Ed. of the
Best Authors. Prod. Madison Square,
1881. Also prod. in England under
title: "Young folks' ways," St.
James, 1883.]

362. -----A lady of quality. With
Stephen Townsend.
1899. NUC OCLC M N
[Drama, 5 acts, adapted from her
novel. NY: Grosset & Dunlap, 1896.
363p. Leipzig: B. Tauchnitz, 1896.
2v. L: Frederick Warne & co., 1896.
368p. 1899. Prod. Comedy, 1899.
Copyrt. 1896; 3 prod. 1899.]

363. -----Little Lord Fauntleroy. A
drama in three acts founded on the
story of the same name.
NY: Samuel French; L: Lacy's acting
ed., 1889. 60p. NUC BL OCLC M
[Her own adaptation of her novel.
Prod. at Princess's, 1889, and as
"The real little Lord Fauntleroy" at
Terry's & Comedy, 1888. Another
adaptation by E.V. Seebohn, prod.
Prince of Wales, 1888, & Terry's,
1888. French's International
Copyright Ed. of the Works of the
Best Authors, no. 42.]

364. -----Nixie. With Stephen
Townsend.
1890. M N
[Play, 3 acts. Prod. Terry's, 1890,
& Globe, 1890]

365. -----Phyllis.
1889. M N
[Play, 4 acts. Prod. Globe, 1889.]

366. -----The showman's daughter.
1892. M
[Comedy, 3 acts. Prod. Royalty,
1892.]

BURNETT, Mrs. Swan M. see BURNETT,
Frances Eliza (Hodgson)

367. BURNEY, Estelle [Br. 19c]
The county. With Arthur Benham.
1892. M N
[Play, 4 acts. Prod. Terry's, 1892.]

368. -----An idyll of the closing
century.
L & NY: French, 1896. 10p. 1898. 16p.
NUC BL OCLC E M
[Duologue. Prod. Lyceum, 1896.
Lacy's Acting Ed.]

369. -----The ordeal of the
honeymoon.
1899. N
[Duologue. Prod. Prince of Wales,
1899.]

370. -----Settled out of court.
1897. M N
[Comedy, 4 acts. Prod. Globe, 1897.]

BURNEY, Fanny see ARBLAY, Frances
(Burney) d'

BURNEY, Fanny see BURNEY, Frances

371. BURNEY, Frances [Br. d. 1828]
ALT: Burney, Fanny
Tragic dramas; chiefly intended for
representation in private families:
to which is added Aristodemas, a
tragedy from the Italian of Vincenzo
Monti.
L: Pr. for the author, 1818. 191p.
NUC BL N
[Niece of Frances (Burney) D'Arblay,
N attr. to D'Arblay.]

372. -----Aristodemus, or, The
spectre.
In: Tragic dramas ... .
[5 acts, trans. of Aristodemo by
Abate Vincenzo Montí.]

373. -----Fitzormond, or Cherished
resentment.
In: Tragic dramas ... .
[3 acts, iambic pentameter.]

374. -----Malek Adhel, the champion
of the crescent.

In: Tragic dramas ... .
[3 acts, iambic pentameter, adapted
from Mathilde by Madame Cittin.]

375. BURRELL, Lady Sophia Raymond
[Br. 1750?-1802] ALT: Clay, Mrs.
William Maximian, a tragedy. Taken
from [Pierre] Corneille.
L: Pr. by Luke Hansard, sold by Leigh
& Sotheby, 1800. 98p. BL OCLC B N
[5 acts. In verse. Longe, v. 295,
no. 1]

376. -----Poems.
L: Leigh & Sotheby; J. Cooper, 1793.
2v. NUC BL OCLC B N
[Incl.: Comala; a dramatic poem in
three acts.]

377. -----A search after perfection.
A comedy in five acts.
L: n.p., 1814. NUC OCLC
[In: Galt, John, ed. The new British
theatre. L: n.p., 1814. v.3, pp. 33-
94]

378. -----Theodora; or, the Spanish
daughter: a tragedy.
L: Pr. Luke Hansard, 1800. 100p. NUC
BL OCLC B N
[Five acts, verse]

379. BURTON, Mrs. [Br. 19c]
The repentance of King Aethelred the
Unready.
1887. N
[Operetta. Prod. in Shrewsbury,
1887.]

380. BURTON, Mrs. Henry S. [Am. 19c]
Don Quixote de la Mancha. A comedy,
in five acts, taken from [Miguel de]
Cervantes' novel of that name.
San Francisco: Pr. J.H. Carmany &
co., 1876. 63p. NUC OCLC

BURTON, Philippina see HILL,
Philippina (Burton)

BUTE, Marchioness of, ed. see
HASTINGS, Lady Flora

BUTLER, Frances Anne (Kemble) see
KEMBLE, Frances Anne

BUTLER, Mrs. Pierce see KEMBLE,
Frances Anne

381. BUXTON, Ida M. [Am. 19c]
Carnival [Festival OCLC] of days.
Clyde, OH: A.D. Ames, 1888. 10p. NUC
OCLC RLIN
[Ames' Standard & Minor Drama. no.
250. Verse drama. On cover: Festival
of days.]

382. -----Cousin John's album. A
pantomime.
Clyde, OH: Ames, 1888. 7p. OCLC
[Ames' Standard & Minor Drama. No.
260.]

383. -----How she has her own way.
An interlude in one scene.
Clyde, OH: Ames, 18--? 5p. H
[Ames' Standard & Minor Drama, no.
50]

384. -----Matrimonial bliss, a scene
from real life.
Clyde, OH: A.D. Ames, 1884. 6p. NUC
OCLC
[Ames' Standard & Minor Drama, no.
139.]

385. -----On to victory; a temperance
cantata, in one scene.
Clyde, OH: A.D. Ames, c1886. 13p. NUC
OCLC
[Ames' Standard & Minor Drama, no.
215.]

386. -----Our awful aunt.
Clyde, OH: A.D. Ames, 1885. 12p. NUC
OCLC
[Comic drama. Ames' Standard & Minor
Drama, no. 146.]

387. -----A sewing circle of the
period, an original farce, in one
act.
Clyde, OH: A.D. Ames, 1884. 7p. NUC
[Ames' Standard & Minor Drama, no.
138.]

388. -----Taking the census.
Original farce in one act.
Clyde, OH: A.D. Ames, 1883. 6p. NUC
OCLC
[Ames' Standard & Minor Drama, no.
137]

389. -----Tit for tat, an original
sketch, in one scene.
Clyde, OH: A.D. Ames, 1884. 8p. NUC
OCLC
[Ames' Standard & Minor Drama, no.
142]

390. -----Why they joined the
Rebeccas. An original farce in one
act.
Clyde, OH: A.D. Ames, 1885. 5p. NUC
[Ames' Standard & Minor Drama, no.
155.]

BYRON, Mrs. G.F. see BYRON, May
Clarissa (Gillington)

391. BYRON, May Clarissa
(Gillington), Mrs. G.F. Byron [Br. d.
1936] ALT: Gillington, May Clarissa
The jewel maiden. Music by Florian
Pascal, pseud. [Lionel Elliot].
L: Joseph Williams, n.d. 31p. NY:
Schuberth, 1898. 101p. OCLC E
[Libretto]

392. -----Masque of May. Music by
Florian Pascal, pseud. [Lionel
Elliot].
L: J. Williams, c1899. 11p. NUC OCLC

393. -----The patient: musical farce
in one act from "Deux vielles
gardes." Music by Leo Delibes.
L: J. Williams, 18--? 15p. OCLC

394. -----The wedding guest: a
musical sketch for three characters.
Music by Franz Schubert.
L: Joseph Williams, 188-? 31p. OCLC

395. BYRON, Medora Gordon [Br. 19c]
ALT: Gordon, Medora
Zameo; or the white warrior! An
operatic romance... By Medora Gordon.
L: J. Duncombe, 1834. [40p. E] 14p.
NUC BL E
[Duncombe's ed. of the British
Theatre, V. 15. Attr. to: C.P.
Thompson.]

C., A.B., pseud. see LAWRENCE, Sarah,
Miss

C., C. see COCKBURN, Catherine
(Trotter)

C., E. see FALKLAND, Elizabeth
(Tanfield) Carew, Viscountess

C., L.M. see CHILD, Lydia Maria
(Francis)

C., M. see CLEPHANE, Anna Jane
Douglas Maclean

396. CADOGAN, Adelaide, Lady [Br.
1820-1890]
Drawing-room plays; selected and
adapted from the French.
L: Sampson Low, Marston, Searle &
Rivington, 1888. 126p. NUC
[No French sources cited. Preface
indicates a desire "to express French
wit and sparkle in an English
dress."]

397. -----Bric-a-brac.

In: Drawing-room plays ... .
[Comedy, 1 act.]

398. -----Caught at last.
L: n.p., 1889. M N
[Comedietta. Prod. Comedy, 1886, &
Avenue, 1889. Also in: Drawing-room
plays. Adapted from French of Armand
des Roseux.]

399. -----Crocodile tears.
In: Drawing-room plays ... .
[Comedy, 1 act.]

400. -----Exchange no robbery.
In: Drawing-room plays ... .
[Romantic comedy, 1 act.]

401. -----How happy could I be with
either! In: Drawing-room plays ... .
[Comedy, 1 act.]

402. -----Tit for tat.
In: Drawing-room plays ... .
[Comedy, 1 act.]

403. -----Well matched after all.
In: Drawing-room plays ... .
[Comedy, 1 act.]

404. CALVERT, Adelaide Helen
(Biddles), Mrs. Charles Calvert [Br.
1837-1921]
Can he forgive her?
1891. N
[Comedy. Prod. in Manchester, 1891]

405. -----Trotty Veck.
1872. M N
[Drama, 2 acts. Prod. Gaiety, 1872.]

CALVERT, Mrs. Charles see CALVERT,
Adelaide Helen (Biddles)

406. CAMERON, Kate [Br. 19c]
Fatality.
1898. N
[Domestic drama. Prod. in Bishop
Aukland, 1898.]

CAMERON, RHODA, pseud. see AYRES,
Lucie Leveque

407. CAMPBELL, Amelia Pringle [Am.
19c]
The great house; or, Varities of
American life.
NY: Edward O. Jenkins, 1882. 56p. NUC
H

408. CAMPBELL, Anna (Mackenzie)
Lindsay, Countess of Argyll [Br. 19c]
ALT: Argyll, Anna Mackenzie) Lindsay
Campbell, Countess of; Lindsay, Lady;

Lindsay, Anna Mackenzie), Countess of Balcarres
Forget-me-not; a play in two short acts. By Lady Lindsay.
L: Bradbury, Agnew & co., 1875. 24p. NUC

409. -----Runa; a sketch. By Lady Lindsay.
L: Bradbury, Agnew & co., 1875. 14p. NUC

410. -----A tangled web.
L: n.p., 1894. NUC

411. -----Three girls; a comedietta, in one act. By Lady Lindsay.
L: Bradbury, Agnew & co., 1875. 20p. NUC

412. -----A weak plot; a comedietta, in one act. By Lady Lindsay.
L: Bradbury, Agnew & co., 1875. 18p. NUC

CAMPBELL, Lady Archibald see CAMPBELL, Janey Sevilla (Callander)

CAMPBELL, Lady Colin see CAMPBELL, Gertrude Elizabeth (Blood)

413. CAMPBELL, Gertrude Elizabeth (Blood), Lady Colin Campbell [Br. 1857-1911] ALT: Blood, Gertrude Elizabeth
Bud and blossom.
L: 1893. M N
[Farce, 1 act. Prod. Terry's, 1893.]

414. CAMPBELL, Harriette [Br. 1817-1841]
The days of the merry monarch. With Rev. G.R. Gleig. 1840. Inglis
[Prod. Chelsea Hospital Theatre, 1840. Inglis: a Christmas entertainment for the benefit of the Chelsea Hospital. Play deals with Nell Gwynne's gift of the site for the hospital.]

415. CAMPBELL, Janey Sevilla (Callander), Lady Archibald Campbell [Br. b. 1846]
Tamlin.
1899. N
[Drama. Prod. in Edinburgh, 1899.]

416. CAMPBELL, Jean (Morison) [Br. 19/20c] ALT: Morison, Jean; Morison, Jeanie
Pontius Pilate, a drama. And other poems.
L: Daldy Ibister & co., 1878. NUC BL

417. CAMPBELL, Josephine Elizabeth, Mrs. Vere Campbell [Br. 19c]
The king's password.
1894. N
[Play. Also prod. as: "Trelawney," in Folkstone, 1894.]

418. -----The maid of yesterday.
1896. N
[Duologue. Prod. in S. Kensington & at Garrick, 1896.]

419. -----Rizpah misery.
1894. N
[Drama. Prod. Glasgow, 1894, & Garrick, 1896.]

420. CAMPBELL, Marian D. [Am. 19c]
A Chinese dummy, a farce in one act. For female characters only.
Boston: Walter H. Baker & co., c1899. 17p. NUC OCLC
[Baker's edition of plays]

421. -----An open secret, a farce in two acts.
Boston: W.H. Baker & co., 1898. 16p. NUC OCLC
[Earlier copyrt. 1872? For 10 female characters. Orig. presented at Radcliffe. Baker's edition of plays]

422. -----Sunbonnets; a farce-comedy in two acts.
Boston: W.H. Baker & co., 1900. 36p. NUC OCLC
[Baker's edition of plays]

CAMPBELL, Mrs. Vere see CAMPBELL, Janey Sevilla (Callander)

423. CARD, Evelyn Gray (Whiting) [Am. 19c] ALT: Whiting, Evelyn Gray
A confidence game. Comedy in two acts. By Evelyn G. Whiting.
Boston: W.H. Baker, 1900. 26p. NUC OCLC H
[Baker's ed. of plays. Orig. produced under title: "Vacation days."]

424. CAREO, Zella [Am. 19c]
The hidden treasures; or, Martha's triumph. A drama in a prologue and four acts.
Clyde, OH: Ames, c1883. 15p. NUC
[Ames' Standard & Minor Drama, no. 141.]

CAREW, Elizabeth (Tanfield), Viscontess Falkland see FALKLAND, Elizabeth (Tanfield) Carew, Viscountess

425. CAREY, Miss
A bow with two strings.
Manchester: A. Heywood & sons, c1899.
[2 females]

CAREY, H.M. see CAREY, Harriet Mary

426. CAREY, Harriet Mary, Mrs. Tom
Carey [Br. d. 1868] ALT: Carey, H. M.
Merry evenings for merry people; or,
proverbs arranged for drawing room
acting.
L: Hall, Virtue & Co., 1859. 129p. BL

CAREY, Mrs. Tom see CAREY, Harriet
Mary

427. CARLYLE, Rita [Br. 19c]
Falsely accused.
L: 1897. M N
[Drama, 4 acts. Prod. Pavillion,
1897.]

CARR, Mrs. see CLARKE, Mary Carr

428. CARR, Alice Van Sittart
(Strettell), Mrs. J. Comyns Carr [Br.
b. 1850]
The butterfly.
1879. N
[Comic drama. Prod. Glasgow, 1879.]

CARR, Mrs. J. Comyns see CARR, Alice
Van Sittart (Strettell)

CARRINGTON, Charles, co-author see
ACHURCH, Janet

CARRINGTON, Mrs. Charles see ACHURCH,
Janet

CARROLL, Mary Teresa Austin, Mother
see CARROLL, Mary Theresa Austin,
Mother

429. CARROLL, Mary Theresa [Teresa
OCLC] Austin, Mother [Am. d. 1909]
The Tudor sisters, an historical
drama.
New Orleans, LA: T. Fitzwilliam &
co., 1883. 32p. NUC OCLC

CARROLL, Susanna (Freeman) see
CENTLIVRE, Susanna Freeman

CARY, Constance see HARRISON,
Constance (Cary)

CARY, Elizabeth see FALKLAND,
Elizabeth (Tanfield) Carew,
Viscountess

430. CASE, Laura V. [Am. 19c]
May court in Greenwood.

In: Dramatic leaflets.
Philadelphia: Phineas Garrett, 1877.
1 v. in 20 pts. NUC BL OCLC H
[Dramatic poem, 1 scene.]

431. -----The veiled priestess.
In: Dramatic leaflets.
[Dramatic poem, 5 scenes. Love vies
with justice for sinner's soul.]

432. CASSILIS, Ina Leon [Br. 19c]
Duologues.
L: Griffith, Farran & co., 1892.
124p. BL

433. -----At bay. With Charles
Lander.
1896. M N
[Drama, 4 acts. Prod. Ladbrooke
Hall, 1888; Novelty, 1896.]

434. -----Cash for coronets.
1894. N
[Comedy. Prod. in Dalston, 1894, and
as: Claire; or, Cash for coronets in
Acton, 1894.]

435. -----"Charlie." In: Duologues.
[Female characters]

436. -----Cheerful and musical;
duologue.
L & NY: Samuel French, 1891. 11p. NUC
BL OCLC E N
[Prod. Jersey, 1891. Lacy's Acting
Ed., no. 2011.]

437. -----Demon Darrell. With Frank
H. Morland.
1898. M N
[Drama, 5 acts. Prod. Britannia,
1898.]

438. -----"Hearts or diamonds?" In:
Duologues.
1891. N
[Prod. Steinway Hall, 1891.]

439. -----A hidden foe.
1892. N
[Melodrama. Prod. at Greenwich,
1892.]

440. -----Interviewed.
In: Duologues.

441. -----A lesson in courtship.
In: Duologues.

442. -----The light of Pengarth.
1891. M N [Play, 1 act. Prod. Opera
Comique, 1891.]

443. -----"Love's old sweet song."
In: Duologues.

[Play, 1 act, 3 characters]

444. -----Michael Dane's grandson.
1896. N
[Prod. in Hammersmith, 1896.]

445. -----A noble atonement.
1892. M N
[Drama, 4 acts. Prod. Opera Comique,
1892.]

446. -----Psychical research.
In: Duologues.

447. -----Rational chess.
In: Duologues.

448. -----"A sensational case." In:
Duologues.
[Female characters]

449. -----"A superior person";
duologue.
L & NY: S. French, c1891. 9p. NUC BL
OCLC
[Lacy's acting ed. no. 2003.]

450. -----Those landladies! Duologue
in one act.
L & NY: Samuel French, 1894. 11p. NUC
BL E N
[Lacy's acting ed., v. 2050]

451. -----The two Misses Ibbetson. A
play in one act.
L: Lacy, 1900. 8p. NY: S. French,
1900. 8p. NUC BL OCLC E
[Lacy's Acting Ed. The minor drama,
no. 391]

452. -----The unfinished story.
1891. N
[Duologue. Prod. St. James, 1891.]

453. -----Vida. With Charles Lander.
1891. M N
[Drama, 4 acts. Copyrt. & 2 prods.
1891. Prod. Prince of Wales, 1892.]

454. -----The wrong door.
1890. M N
[Farce. Prod. Comedy, 1890.]

455. CASTLE, Harriet Davenport [Am.
b. 1843]
The courting of Mother Goose. An
entertainment.
Chicago: Dramatic pub. co., n.d. 27p.
H
[Philadelphia: Penn pub. co., 1923.
85p. NUC]

CAULFEILD, Mrs. Edwin Toby see
CAULFEILD, Frances Sally

456. CAULFEILD, Frances Sally, Mrs.
Edwin Toby Caulfeild [Br. 19c]
The innocents; a sacred drama.
Ocean; and the earthquake at Aleppo;
poems.
Bath: S. Simms, 1824. 63p. NUC BL

CAVAZZA, Elisabeth (Jones) see
PULLEN, Elisabeth (Jones) Cavazza

457. CAVENDISH, LADY CLARA, pseud.
[Br. 19c]
The woman of the world, a drama in
two acts.
L: T.H. Lacy, 1859. 52p. NUC BL OCLC
E M N
[Prod. Queen's, 1858. Lacy's Acting
Ed.]

458. CAVENDISH, Lady Jane [Br. 1621-
1669]
Concealed fancies. With Lady
Elizabeth (Cavendish) Brackley
[c1623-1663].
1645. NUC Har DNB
[Closet comedy. Ms. in Bodleian
Library NUC]

459. -----A pastoral.
1645. Har DNB
[Closet pastoral dialogue.]

CAVENDISH, Margaret (Lucas), Duchess
of Newcastle see NEWCASTLE, Margaret
(Lucas) Cavendish, Duchess of

CECIL, ARTHUR, pseud., co-author see
BELL, Florence Eveleen Eleanore
(Olliffe)

460. CELESIA, Dorothea (Mallet) [Br.
1738-1790] PSEUD: Lady, A
Almida, a tragedy. By a lady.
L: T. Becket & co., 1771. 66p. NUC
OCLC B N
[Adapted from Francois Marie Arouet
de Voltaire's "Lancrede." Some
additions by David Garrick. Prod.
Drury Lane, 1771. Longe, v. 41, no.
2.]

CENTLIVRE, Mrs. Joseph E. see
CENTLIVRE, Susanna (Freeman)

461. CENTLIVRE, Susanna (Freeman),
Mrs. Joseph E. Centlivre [Br. 1667-
1723] ALT: Carroll, Susanna (Freeman)
The dramatic works of the celebrated
Mrs. Centilivre with a new account of
her life.
L: J. Knapton, 1760-61. 3v. L: John
Pearson, 1872. NUC BL OCLC

462. -----The artifice. A comedy, in
five acts.

L: T. Payne, 1723. 106p. NUC BL OCLC
B N
[Comedy. Prod. Drury Lane, 1722.]

463. -----The basset-table. A comedy
in five acts.
L: W. Turner, 1706. 64p. 2d ed. L:
Jonas Browne; S. Chapman, 1706. 69p.
NUC BL OCLC B N
[Comedy. Prod. Drury Lane, 1705.]

464. -----The beau's duel; or, a
soldier for the ladies. A comedy.
L: D. Brown & N. Cox, 1702. 55p. NUC
BL OCLC B N
[Comedy, 5 acts, prose. Prod.
Lincoln's Inn, 1702. No record of
original prod. N]

465. -----A Bickerstaff's burying;
or, Work for the upholders. A farce,
in one act.
L: Bernard Lintott, 1710. 23p. NUC BL
OCLC B N
[Farce. Prod. Drury Lane, 1710.
Afterwards revived under title: "The
custom of the country."]

466. -----A bold strike for a wife: a
comedy in five acts.
L: W. Mars, J. Browne & F. Clay,
1718. 68p. NUC BL OCLC B E N
[Comedy. Prod. Lincoln's Inn,
1717/8. Revived in 1840 as: "The
guardians off their guard."]

467. -----The busie body. A comedy
in five acts.
L: Bernard Lintot, 1709? 72p. NUC BL
OCLC B E N
[Comedy. Prod. Drury Lane, 1709.
The sequel, "Mar-Plot," pub. 1711.]

468. -----The cruel gift; a tragedy
in five acts.
L: E. Curl; A. Bettesworth, 1717.
65p. NUC BL OCLC B
[Tragedy. Prod. Drury Lane, 1716.
Running title: "The cruel gift; or,
The royal resentment."]

469. -----The gamester: a comedy.
L: Wm. Turner & Wm. Davis, 1705. 70p.
NUC BL OCLC B N
[Comedy, 5 acts, prose. Prod.
Lincoln's Inn, 1704/5. Based on "Le
Joueur" of Jean Francois Regnard]

470. -----The ghost. A comedy of two
acts.
L: J. Williams, 1767. 27p. NUC BL
OCLC
[Short version of "The man's
bewitched."]

471. -----The Gotham election, a
farce in one act.
L: S. Keimer, 1715. 72p. NUC BL OCLC
B N
[Later pub. as: "The humours of
elections."]

472. -----Love at a venture, a comedy
in five acts.
L: John Chantry, 1706. 54p. NUC BL
OCLC B N
[Comedy. Prod. New Theatre, Bath, by
Duke of Grafton's men.]

473. -----Love's contrivance, or, Le
Medecin malgre lui. A comedy in five
acts.
L: Bernard Lintott, 1703. 67p. NUC BL
OCLC B N
[Comedy. Prod. Drury Lane, 1703.
Some scenes from Moliere. Dedication
signed R.M.]

474. -----The man's bewitch'd; or,
The Devil to do about her. A comedy
in five acts.
L: Bernard Lintott, 1710. 68p. NUC BL
OCLC B N
[Comedy. Prod. Haymarket, 1709.]

475. -----Mar-plot; or, The second
part of the busy body. Five acts.
L: Jacob & R. Tonson, 1711. 62p. NUC
OCLC B N
[Comedy. Prod. Drury Lane, 1710.]

476. -----The perjur'd husband: or,
The adventures of Venice. A tragedy.
By S. Carroll.
L: Bennet Banbury, 1700. 40p. NUC BL
OCLC B N WM
[Verse & prose, 5 acts. No records
of perf. N.]

477. -----The perplex'd lovers. A
comedy in five acts.
L: Owen Lloyd, 1712. 60p. NUC BL OCLC
B N
[Comedy. Prod. Drury Lane, 1711/12.]

478. -----The platonick lady. A
comedy.
L: J. Knapton & Egbert Sanger, 1707.
72p. NUC BL OCLC B N
[Comedy, 5 acts. Prod. Haymarket,
1706.]

479. -----The stolen heiress; or the
Salamanca doctor out-plotted, a
comedy.
L: W. Turner & John Nutt, 1703. 69p.
NUC OCLC B N
[Comedy, 5 acts: based on Thomas
May's "The heir." Prod. Lincoln's

Inn, 1702. Also acted as: "The heiress."]

480. -----A wife well manag'd. A farce.
L: S. Keimer, 1715. 21p. NUC B N
[Farce, 1 act. Prod. Drury Lane, 1715. Pub. anon., but with portrait of Centlivre. A ballad opera based on this, "The disappointment," appeared 1732.]

481. -----The wonder: a woman keeps a secret. A comedy in five acts.
L: E. Curll; A. Bettesworth, 1714. 79p. NUC BL OCLC B E N
[Comedy. Prod. Drury Lane, 1714.]

482. CHAMBERS, Marianne [Br. 18/19c]
Ourselves, a comedy in five acts.
L: J. Barker, 1811. 91p. NUC BL OCLC E N
[Comedy. Prod. Lyceum, 1811.]

483. -----The school for friends, a comedy in five acts.
L: Barker & son, 1805. 93p. NUC BL OCLC E N
[Comedy. Prod. Drury Lane, 1805.]

484. CHANDLER, Miss B. [Br. 19c]
Powder and shot.
1896. N
[Farce. Prod. in Basingstoke, 1896.]

485. CHANDOS, Alice [Br. 19c] PSEUD: Livondals, A.V.; Livandais, A.
Jealous of the past.
1885. N
[Comedietta. Prod. New Cross, 1885. Entered with Lord Chamberlain as: "Green-eyed; or, Jealous of the past."]

486. -----Philanthropy.
1888. M N
[Prod. Princess', 1888.]

487. CHANEY, Caroline I., Mrs. George L. Chaney [Am. 19c]
William Henry.
Boston: J.R. Osgood, c1874, 1875. 74p. NUC OCLC H
[Dramatized from Abby (Morton) Diaz's books, "William Henry Letters" and "William Henry and His Friends."]

CHANEY, Mrs. George L. see CHANEY, Caroline I.

CHANLER, Amélie Rives see TROUBETZKOY, Amelie (Rives)

488. CHAPIN, Alice [Am./Br. d. 1934]

Dresden china. With E.H.C. Oliphant.
1892. N
[Extravaganza. Prod. Vaudeville, 1892.]

489. -----Shame. With E.H.C. Oliphant.
1892. M N
[Drama, 1 act. Prod. Vaudeville, 1892.]

490. -----Sorrowful Satan; or, Lucifer's match.
1897. N
[Duologue. Prod. in Kentish Town, 1897.]

491. -----A woman's sacrifice.
1899. M N
[Drama. Prod. St. George's Hall, 1899. Adapt. from French of Victor Hugo.]

492. -----The wrong legs.
1896. N
[Comedietta. Prod. at Ilkeston, 1896.]

493. CHAPIN, Anna Alice [Am. 1880-1920]
The spring song; a play.
NY: n.p., n.d. 7 l. NUC
[Typescript]

494. CHAPMAN, Jane Frances [Br. 19c]
King Rene's daughter. Translated from Henrick Hertz.
L: Smith, Elder, 1845. 87p. BL OCLC E
[Danish lyric drama]

495. CHARKE, Charlotte (Cibber), Mrs. Richard Charke [Br. 1713-1760]
The art of management; or, tragedy expell'd.
L: W. Rayner 1735. 47p. NUC BL B N
[Farce. Prod. York Buildings, 1735. Satire on theatre manager who fired her as an actress from Drury Lane. He attempted to destroy all copies of play.]

496. -----The Carnival; or, Harlequin blunderer.
1735. N
[Comedy. Prod. Lincoln's Inn, 1735; now lost.]

497. -----Tit for tat; or, The comedy and tragedy of war.
1743. N
[Medley. Prod. James-street Theatre, 1749; not published, now lost.]

CHARKE, Mrs. John see CHARKE, Charlotte (Cibber)

CHATTERTON, Georgiana, Lady see
CHATTERTON, Henrietta Georgiana
Marcia Lascelles (Iremonger), Lady

498. CHATTERTON, Henrietta Georgiana
Marcia Lascelles (Iremonger), Lady
[Br. 1806-1876] ALT: Chatterton,
Georgiana, Lady
Oswald of Deira: a drama by
Georgiana, Lady Chatterton.
L: Longmans, Green & co., 1867. 155p.
NUC BL OCLC E
[In verse]

CHENEY, Miss see GARDNER, (Cheney)

499. CHEZY, Wilhelmine Christiane Von
[Br. 1783-1856]
Euryanthe; a grand romantic opera in
three acts. Music by Von Weber.
L: A. Schloss, 18--? 51p. NUC BL OCLC
T
[In English & German]

CHILD, Mrs. David see CHILD, Lydia
Maria (Francis)

500. CHILD, Lydia Maria (Francis),
Mrs. David Child [Am. 1802-1880] ALT:
C., L. M.; Francis, Lydia Maria
PSEUD: American lady, An
Evenings in New England. Intended
for juvenile amusement and
instruction. By an American lady.
Boston: Cummings, Hilliard & co.,
1824. 181p. NUC OCLC Hill Wells
[Contains: General Lee, a drama. pp.
14-27. The triumphal arch, a drama.
pp. 62-67]

501. -----The stars and stripes.
In: The Liberty Bell.
Boston: Nat. anti-slavery bazaar,
1858. pp. 122-185. NUC OCLC C
[Minstrel show, but with abolitionist
character. No record of
performance.]

502. CHILDE-PEMBERTON, Harriet Louisa
[Br. 19/20c] ALT: Pemberton, Harriet
Louisa Childe
Dead letters, and other narrative and
dramatic pieces.
L: Ward, Lock & co., 1896. 125p. BL
OCLC
[Based on well known stories,
designed for recitation. Incl. 9
poems.]

503. -----Original readings and
recitations. "Prince," a story of
the American War, and other ...
poems.
L: Ward & co., 1883. 79p. BL

[9 narrative poems based on well
known stories written and/or adapted
for recitation. "Prince" has running
title at top: "Original Readings and
Recitations."]

504. -----"Twenty minutes" drawing
room duologues.
L & Sidney: Griffith, Farran & co.,
1891. 128p. BL
[Incl. some works not also pub.
separately.]

505. -----A backward child. A
duologue. Farce for two females.
L: Lacy's acting ed., No. 143, 1899.
10p. NUC BL E
[Also in: Twenty Minutes.]

506. -----Chatterboxes. Comedietta
in one act.
Chicago & NY: Dramatic pub. co., n.d.
13p. NUC BL OCLC E
[Sergel's Acting Drama, #388. Also
in: Twenty Minutes ...]

507. -----The deuce of clubs.
In: Dead letters ... .
[Duologue]

508. -----A figure of speech. A
comedietta, in one act.
NY: DeWitt pub. house, 189? 18p. NUC
OCLC E
[DeWitt's acting plays, no. 392.
First pub. in London. Also in:
Twenty Minutes.]

509. -----Geese.
In: Original readings ... .
[Duologue]

510. -----He, she, and the poker: a
duologue, and other dramatic pieces.
L: Griffith, Farran & co., 1900. 83p.
BL

511. -----I and my father-in-law.
In: Twenty minutes ... .
[Monologue]

512. -----My missing spectacles.
In: Twenty minutes ... .
[Monologue]

513. -----Nicknames: a comedietta in
one act.
Chicago: Dramatic pub. co., 18--?
16p. NUC OCLC E T
[Sergel's Acting Drama, #394. Also
in: Twenty Minutes.]

514. -----The science of
advertisement. A comedy, in one act.

NY: DeWitt, 1870-1877. 30p. NUC OCLC
[Also in: Twenty Minutes. DeWitt's
Acting Plays, no. 395.]

515. -----Shattered nerves. A
duologue. L: Lacy, 1899. 10p. BL E
[Also in: Twenty minutes. Lacy's
Acting Ed., no. 143.]

516. -----Smoke.
In: Dead letters ... .
[Monologue]

517. -----Sunbeams at home.
In: Dead letters ... .
[Fairy play]

518. -----The train de luxe from
Cannes, a comedietta, in one act.
NY: DeWitt pub. house, 18-? 15p. NUC
[Also in Twenty Minutes. DeWitt's
acting plays, 390.]

CHI-LO-SA, pseud. see HOSMER, Harriet
Goodhue

519. CHIPPENDALE, Mary Jane
(Snowden), Mrs. William Henry
Chippendale [Br. 1837?-1888]
Mamma.
1876. N
[Comedy. Prod. Dublin, 1876.]

CHIPPENDALE, Mrs. William Henry see
CHIPPENDALE, Mary Jane (Snowden)

CHRISTIAN, Mrs. Thomas see PENNY,
Anne (Hughes) Christian

CHURCH, Mrs. Ross see LEAN, Florence
(Marryat) Church

520. CIBBER, Susanna Maria (Arne),
Mrs. Theophilus Cibber [Br. 1714-
1766]
The oracle. A comedy of one act.
L: J. Roberts; R. Dodsley, 1752. 46p.
BL OCLC B N
[Masque. Prod. Covent Garden, 1752.
Adaption of Germain Francois Poullain
de St. Foix, "L'Oracle."]

CIBBER, Mrs. Theophilus see CIBBER,
Susanna Maria (Arne)

CLARA AUGUSTA see JONES, Clara
Augusta

CLARK, Clara Savile- see CLARKE,
Clara Savile-

521. CLARK, Jeannette R. [Am. 19c]
ALT: Nettie
Nettie's poems, and a farce: Old fogy
and young America.

Cincinnati, OH: 1880. 78, 24p. NUC
OCLC
[44 misc. poems & 2-act play designed
for home entertainment.]

522. CLARKE, Clara Savile [Br. 19c]
ALT: Clark, Clara Savile-
Choosing a ball dress.
In: Dialogues of the day. Ed. Oswald
Crawfurd.
L: Chapman & Hall, 1895. 8p. NUC BL
OCLC E

523. -----A human sacrifice.
In: Dialogues of the day.

524. -----A point of honour.
In: Dialogues of the day.

525. -----A woman's vengeance; or, a
cruel alternative.
1892. N
[Duologue. Prod. St. George's, 1892,
& as: "A cruel alternative," 1893.]

CLARKE, Eliza see COBBOLD, Elizabeth
(Knipe)

CLARKE, Helen Archibald, co-author
see PORTER, Charlotte Endymion

526. CLARKE, Mary Carr [Am. 19c] ALT:
Carr, Mrs.
The benevolent lawyers, or, villainy
detected.
Philadelphia: n.p., 1823. 77p. NUC
OCLC B H
[Comedy, 5 acts]

527. -----The fair Americans. By
Mrs. Carr.
Philadelphia: Mrs. Carr, 1815. 44p.
NUC OCLC Hill Wells
[Comedy, 5 acts. Patriotic play set
during War of 1812.]

528. -----Sarah Maria Cornell, or the
Fall River murder, a domestic drama
in three acts.
NY: n.p., 1833. 48p. NUC

529. CLARKE, Olivia, Lady [Br. 19c]
The Irishwoman. A comedy in five
acts.
Dublin & L: Henry Colburn, 1819. 82p.
NUC BL OCLC N
[Comedy. Prod. Crow-Street, Dublin,
1819.]

CLARKE, Mrs. William see COBBOLD,
Elizabeth (Knipe)

530. CLAY, Mrs. Randolph [Br. 19c]
PSEUD: Villars, George

Lady Lovington, or "A soiree dramatique;" comedietta in one act. "Only a cushion," duologue. "A first performance," monologue.
L: R. Buckenham, 1899. 24p. NUC M N
[Prod. Athenaeum Ladbrooke Hall, 1888 & St. George Hall, 1894. Both M & N list under pseudonymn.]

CLAY, Mrs. Raymond see BURRELL, Lady Sophia (Raymond)

531. CLAYTON, Eliza [Br. 19c]
The red lamp; or, The dark dens of the city.
1863. M
[Drama, 2 acts. Prod. Grecian, 1863.]

532. CLAYTON, Estelle [Am. 1867-1917]
"Favette;" the story of a waif; a comedy drama in four acts.
NY: n.p., 1885. 75p. NUC OCLC
[Adams lists another play, "A gentle savage."]

533. -----A sad coquette: a modern comedy of error, in four acts. NY: H.A. Richardson, 1887. NUC

534. -----The Viking. Comic opera in two acts.
NY: Springer & Welty, 1893. 46p. NY: G.M. Abbey, 1895. NUC H
[Music by E.T. Darling & E.R. Steiner]

535. CLEAVER, Mary [Br. 19c]
The ballybaggerty bequest.
1852. N
[Interlude. Prod. in Edinburgh, 1852.]

536. -----The Erl King's daughter; or, the fairy reformed.
1851. N
[Interlude. Entered with Lord Chamberlain 1851.]

537. CLEPHANE, Anna Jane Douglas Maclean [Br. 19c] ALT: C., M.
Plays and poems. By M.C.
Northampton: Priv. pr. Stanton & son, 1864. 40p. BL OCLC
[Pub. as memorial.]

538. -----Carberry hill, or, Mary, Queen of Scots, an historical tragedy.
In: Plays and poems, pp. 1-86.
[5 acts, verse.]

539. -----Godfrey; or, The vassal. A tragedy.

In: Plays and poems, pp. 87-174.
[Verse, 5 acts.]

540. -----The last Earl of Gowrie, an historical tragedy.
In: Plays and poems, pp. 175-281.
[Verse, 5 acts.]

CLERGYMAN'S WIFE, A, pseud. see HART, Fanny (Wheeler)

541. CLEVEDON, Alice [Br. 19c]
The worship of Plutus; or, Poses.
1888. N
[Copyright 1888.]

CLIFFORD, Elizabeth Lydia Rosabelle (Bonham) De La Pasture, Lady see DE LA PASTURE, Elizabeth Lydia Rosabelle (Bonham)

542. CLIFFORD, Lucy (Lane), Mrs. William Kingdon Clifford [Br. 1853-1929] ALT: Clifford, Mrs. W. K.
A honeymoon tragedy. A comedy in one act.
L & NY: French, 1904. 14p. NUC BL OCLC E
[Comedy. Prod. Comedy, 1896. Lacy's Acting Ed. 1896. M N]

543. -----An interlude. With Walter H. Pollock.
1893. M N
[Play, 1 act. Prod. Terry's, 1893.]

544. -----The likeness of the night. A modern play in four acts. By Mrs. W.K. Clifford.
L: Adam & Charles Black, 1900. 146p. NY: Macmillan co., 1900. 90p. NUC BL OCLC E

545. -----A supreme moment.
L: n.p., 1899. 19p. NUC
[1-act play. Detached from The nineteenth century, v. 46, 1899. No. 7 in vol. lettered "Modern Plays."]

546. -----A long duel; a serious comedy in four acts. By Mrs. W.K. Clifford.
L & NY: John Lane, 1901. 151p. NUC BL
[Adapted from her short story, "The last touches," written 1892. No info. on performances. Listed in Adams along with another play, "The search light," 1902.]

CLIFFORD, Mrs. W.K. see CLIFFORD, Lucy (Lane)

CLIFFORD, Mrs. William Kingdon see CLIFFORD, Lucy (Lane)

547. CLIFTON, Mary A. Delano [Am. 19c]
Der two subprises. Farce in one act.
Clyde, OH: Ames, n.d.; 191-? 7p. NUC OCLC H
[Ames' Standard & Minor Drama, no. 49]

548. -----Schnapps. A farce in one act.
Clyde, OH: Ames, 188-? 6p. NUC OCLC H
[Ames' Standard & Minor Drama, no. 48]

549. -----The wrong box. An Ethiopian farce in one act.
Clyde, OH: Ames, n.d. 6p. NUC OCLC H
[Ames' Standard & Minor Drama, no. 47. on t.p. as: "In the wrong box."]

CLIVE, Catherine (Rafton) see CLIVE, Catherine (Raftor)

550. CLIVE, Catherine (Rafton), Mrs. George Clive [Br. 1711-1785] ALT: Clive, Kitty
Every woman in her humour.
1760. NUC B N
[Farce. Prod. Drury Lane. Larpent MS. #174.]

551. -----The faithful Irishwoman.
1765. NUC B N
[Farce. Prod. Drury Lane. Larpent MS. #247.]

552. -----The island of slaves.
1761. N
[Farce. Prod. Drury Lane, 1761. Trans. of Pierre Carlet de Chamblainde Marivaux, "Isle des Esclaves."]

553. -----The rehearsal; or, Bays in petticoats. A comedy in two acts. L: R. Dodsley, 1753. 43p. NUC BL OCLC N
[Prod. Drury Lane, 1750. Music composed by Dr. Boyce.]

554. -----The sketch of a fine lady's return from a rout.
1763. NUC B N
[Farce. Prod. Drury Lane. Larpent MS. #220.]

CLIVE, Mrs. George see CLIVE, Catherine (Raftor)

CLIVE, Kitty see CLIVE, Catherine (Raftor)

555. COBB, Josephine H. [Am. 19c]
The Oxford affair. Comedy in three acts. With Jennie E. Paine.

Philadelphia: Penn pub. co., c1896. 31p. NUC OCLC H
[For 8 female characters. Dramatic library, vol. 1, no. 109.]

556. COBB, Mary L. [Am. 19c]
Poetical dramas for home and school.
Boston: Lee & Shepard, 1873. 189p. NY: Lee, Shepard & Dillingham, NUC OCLC H R
[In NUC as comp. Amateur theatricals.]

557. COBBOLD, Elizabeth (Knipe), Mrs. John Cobbold [Br. 1767-1824] ALT: Clarke, Eliza; Clarke, Mrs. William; Knipe, Eliza PSEUD: Lady, A
Poems.
Ipswich: J. Raw, 1825. 383p. NUC BL OCLC E

558. -----The brave's task.
In: Poems.
[Fragment]

559. -----The Roman mutiny.
In: Poems.

COBBOLD, Mrs. John see COBBOLD, Elizabeth (Knipe)

560. COCKBURN, Catherine (Trotter), Mrs. Patrick Cockburn [Br. 1679-1749] ALT: C., C.; Trotter, Catherine PSEUD: Young lady, A
The works of Mrs. Catherine Cockburn, theological, moral, dramatic, and poetical. Several of them now first printed. By Thomas Birch.
L: J. & P. Knapton, 1751. 2v. NUC BL OCLC
[Vol 1. incl. essays, letters & biography which mentions a comedy, "Love and a bottle," acted 1698.]

561. -----Agnes de Castro, a tragedy ... written by a young lady.
L: H. Rhodes, R. Parker & S. Briscoe, 1696. 47p. NUC BL OCLC B N S WM
[Tragedy. Acted at Theatre Royal in 1695 when she was 17.]

562. -----Fatal friendship. A tragedy.
L: Francis Saunders, 1698. 56p. NUC BL OCLC B N S WM
[Five acts, verse. Perf. New Theatre, Lincoln's Inn, 1698.]

563. -----Love at a loss; or most votes carry it. A comedy.
L: W. Turner, 1701. 56p. NUC BL OCLC B N S
[Verse, 5 acts. Prod. Drury Lane, 1700; Theatre Royal, 1701. Revised

version, "The honourable deceivers; or, All right at the last," not produced. Longe, v. 194, no. 5.]

564. -----The revolution of Sweden. A tragedy.
L: J. Knapton & co., 1706. 71p. NUC BL OCLC B N S
[Verse. Acted Queen's Theatre, Haymarket, 1705/06. Longe, v. 113. no. 6]

565. -----The unhappy penitent; a tragedy.
L: William Turner & John Nutt, 1701. 48p. NUC BL OCLC B N S
[Five acts, verse. Prod. Drury Lane, Theatre Royal, 1701. Longe, v. 294, no. 3]

COCKBURN, Mrs. Patrick see COCKBURN, Catherine (Trotter)

566. COCKBURN, T., Mrs. [Br. 19c]
Princess Verita.
1896. N
[Operetta. Prod. in Newcastle, 1896.]

567. COFFIN, Emily [Br. 19c]
My Jack.
1887. M N
[Comedietta. Prod. Princess', 1887.]

568. -----No credit.
1892. M N
[Comedietta. Prod. Strand, 1892.]

569. -----Run wild.
1888. M N
[Comedy, 3 acts. Prod. Strand, 1888. Entered with Lord Chamberlain as: "Uncle John."]

570. COLBURN, Carrie W. [Am. 19/20c]
His last chance; or, The little joker; a comedy in three acts.
Boston: W.H. Baker, 1895. 63p. NUC OCLC
[Baker's edition]

COLCLEUGH, Emma Shaw see COLCLOUGH, Emma Shaw

571. COLCLOUGH, Emma Shaw [Am. 1847-1940] ALT: Colcleugh, Emma Shaw
An object lesson in history. An historical exercise for school exhibitions.
NY & Chicago: E.L. Kellogg, 1896. 24p. NUC OCLC H

572. COLEMAN, Mrs. Wilmot Bouton [Am. 19c]

Maud Stanley; or, Life scenes and life lessons. Domestic drama; five acts. NY: n.p., 1874. 241 l. NUC H
[Promptbook in mss. Adapted from Elvira L. Mills' novel, "Maud Stanley."]

573. COLLET, Rose [Br. 19c]
The gambler's wife; or, She was tempted sorely. An original melodrama in three acts.
Liverpool?: n.p., 1883. 43p. BL

574. COLLETTE, Mary [Br. 19c]
Cousin's courtship.
1892. N
[Sketch. Prod. Lyric, 1892 & at Shaftsbury.]

COLLING, Mabel see COOK, Mabel (Colling)

575. COLMAN, Julia [Am. 1828-1909]
An evening with Robinson Crusoe.
NY: Nat. Temperance Soc. & pub. house, 1891. 16p. NUC
[Temperance recitations. Adapted from Daniel Defoe.]

576. -----No king in America. A patriotic temperance program in three parts.
NY: Nat. temp. soc. & pub. house, 1888. 31p. NUC H

577. -----Our cider entertainment. A concert exercise. With tableaux vivants.
Enl. & rev. ed. NY: National Woman's Christian temperance union, 189-? 29p. NUC

578. COLQUHOUN, Katherine [de (St. Vitalis) Lady] [Br. 19c]
Alias, a farce in one act.
L: Harrison & sons, 1859. 22p. NUC BL
[In verse]

579. -----The emigre. A drama, in two acts.
Paddington: Pr. for priv. circ.; L: Chapman, pr., 1858. 46p. NUC BL

580. -----The old hall. A drama, in one act.
Paddington: Pr. for priv. circ.; L: Chapman, pr., 1860? 24p. NUC BL

581. -----The sham widow. A farce in one act.
L: Pr. Harrison & sons for priv. circ., 1858. 23p. NUC

COLVIL, EDWARD, pseud. see PUTNAM, Mary Traill Spence (Lowell)

582. COMPTON, Mrs. Charles G. [Br. 19c]
A vacant place.
L: 1899. N
[duologue]

CONHEIM, Mrs. Herman see MORTON, Martha

CONKLING, Mrs. Albert Steele see CONKLING, Margaret Cockburn

583. CONKLING, Margaret Cockburn, Mrs. Albert Steele Conkling [Am. 1814-1890]
The widower's stratagem; or, a circle within a circle. A drama in 5 acts. Racine, WI: Sanford & Tapley, 1860. 39p. NUC OCLC

584. CONNELLY, Celia (Logan) Kellogg [Am. 1837-1904]
An American marriage. A play in four acts.
n.p.: n.p., 1883. 51 l. NUC

585. -----"Maryland" an original drama in four acts.
n.p.: n.p., 1884. 46 l. NUC

586. -----"A sailor's heart" a domestic drama in three acts.
n.p.: n.p., 1884. 40 l. NUC

587. -----"Vassar," or girl graduates. An original opera.
n.p.: n.p., 1884. 22 l. NUC

CONQUEST, George, co-author see TINSLEY, Lily

CONSTANTIA, pseud. see MURRAY, Julia (Sargent) Stevens

588. COOK, Eliza [Am. 1818-1889]
Guy Fawkes; or, A match for a king. In: Massey's exhibition reciter, and drawing room entertainments. Comp. Charles Massey.
NY: S. French, 1856. 186p. OCLC H

589. -----Little Jim.
In: Massey's exhibition ... .

590. -----The mourners.
In: Massey's exhibition ... .

COOK, Mrs. Keningate Robert see COOK, Mabel (Collins)

591. COOK, Mabel (Collins), Mrs. Keningate Robert Cook [Br. 1851-1937]
ALT: Collins, Mabel
A modern Hypatia: A drama of today.

1894. N M
[Drama. Prod. Bijou, 1894; Terry's, 1895.]

592. -----Suggestion; or, the hypnotist. With W. Heron Brown. N
[Drama. Prod. Lyric, Hammersmith, 1891. Adaptation of her novel of the same name, pub. 1891.]

COOPER, Edith Emma, co-author see BRADLEY, Katherine Harris

593. COOPER, Elizabeth [Br. 18c] The Nobleman; or, the family quarrel. 1736. N
[Comedy. Prod. Haymarket, 1736. Play has been lost.]

594. -----The rival widows; or, The fair libertine. A comedy.
L: T. Woodward, 1735. 124p. BL B N
[Prod. Covent Garden, 1734/5.]

595. COOPER, Emily [Br. 19c]
Tales and conversations.
L: Charles Fox, 1833. 186p. BL
[Incl.: "Queen Margaret: a drama."]

596. CORBET, Miss [Br. 19c]
Aloyse.
1828. Inglis
[Drama. Prod. Theatre Royal, Edinburgh, 1828. Inglis.]

597. -----The odd volume.
Edinburgh: D. Lizars, 1826-7; Vol. II L: Longmans. OCLC Inglis
[Incl.: "Guzzle," a dramatic fragment and "The babbling barber," from the Danish of Ludvig, Baron Holberg. Inglis. "By the Misses Corbet." Halkett & Lang.]

598. -----Tales and legends.
Edinburgh: n.p., 1828. 3v. Inglis
[Vol. 2 incl.: "Lorenzo, a dramatic fragment."]

599. -----A week at Holyrood; or, The merry days of James the Sixth.
1829. Inglis
[With her sister. Prod. in Edinburgh 1829-30.]

CORBETT, E.B. see CORBETT, Elizabeth (Burgoyne)

600. CORBETT, Elizabeth (Burgoyne), Mrs. George Corbett [Br. b. 1846]
ALT: Corbett, E. B.
A bit of human nature.
1899. M N

[Drama, 1 act. Prod. Terry's, 1899.]

601. -----The war correspondent. With
William Boyne.
1898. N
[Drama. Prod. Surrey Theatre, 1898.]

CORBETT, Mrs. George see CORBETT,
Elizabeth (Burgoyne)

CORDER, Frederick, co-author see
CORDER, Henrietta Louisa (Walford)

CORDER, Mrs. Frederick see CORDER,
Henrietta Louisa (Walford)

602. CORDER, Henrietta Louisa
(Walford), Mrs. Frederick Corder [Br.
19c] ALT: Walford, Miss H. L.;
Walford, Henrietta Louisa Ambition.
1870. N
[Drama. Prod. Gallery of
Illustration, 1870.]

603. -----Der Ring des Nibelingen.
Music by Richard Wagner.
Magence: B. Schott's sohne, 1882.
678p. BL OCLC
[Tr. with Frederick Corder.]

604. -----Die Meistersinger von
Nurnberg. Music by Richard Wagner.
Magence: B. Schott, 189-? 135p. NUC
BL OCLC
[Libretto trans. with Frederick
Corder.]

605. -----Edwin and Angelina; or, the
children of mystery. By Miss H.L.
Walford.
1871. N
[Burlesque. Amateur prod. 1871,
Gallery of Illustration.]

606. -----Impeached. By Miss H.L.
Walford.
1873. M N
[Drama. Entered with Lord
Chamberlain as: A life lost. Amateur
prod., 1870.]

607. -----Lohengrin. Music by
Richard Wagner.
Leipzig: Breitkopf & Hartel, 1889.
63p. BL OCLC

608. -----Lord Fitzharris. By Miss
H.L. Walford.
1873. N
[Comedietta. Prod. Gallery of
Illustration.]

609. -----A lost life. By Miss H.L.
Walford.

1870. M N
[Drama. Entered with Lord
Chamberlain as: "A life lost."
Amateur prod., 1870.]

610. -----The noble savage. With
Frederick Corder.
1885. N
[Comic opera. Prod. Brighton, 1885.]

611. -----Parsifal. Music by Richard
Wagner.
Magence: B. Schott's sohne, 1879?
62p. NUC BL OCLC
[Translated. with Frederick Corder.]

612. -----A storm in a teacup.
1882. N
[Operetta. Prod. at Brighton &
Gaiety, 1882.]

613. -----Tristan and Isolda. Music
by Richard Wagner.
Leipzig & NY: Greitkopf & Hartel,
1882? 96p. BL OCLC
[Translated with Frederick Corder.]

614. -----The veiled prophet of
Korassan; or, the Maniac, the mystery
and the malediction. By Miss H.L.
Walford.
1870. N [Burlesque. Amateur prod.,
1870, Gallery of Illustration.]

615. -----Weeds. By Miss H.L.
Walford.
1871. N
[Comedy. Amateur prod., 1871,
Gallery of Illustration.]

CORDOVA, Rudolph de, co-author see
RAMSAY, Alicia

616. CORNELYS, Teresa Imer [Br. 1723-
1797]
The deceptions.
1781. N
[Comedy. She appeared in the prod.,
Dublin, 1781.]

617. CORRIE, Jessie Elizabeth [Br. b.
1855]
An obstinate woman. Comedietta in
one act.
L & NY: S. French, n.d. 12p. NUC BL
OCLC E
[Lacy's Acting Ed. No. 2225.]

618. CORWIN, Jane Hudson [Am. 1809-
1881]
The harp of home; or, The medley.
Cincinnati, OH: Moore, Wilstack,
Keys, 1858. 382p. NUC OCLC H

[Incl.: A dialogue between Mr. Native and Mrs. Foreigner, on literary subjects, pp. 15-32]

619. COSTELLO, Miss [Br. 19c]
A bad quarter of an hour.
1896. N
[Comedietta. Prod. in Dublin & Cheltenham, 1896.]

620. -----The plebeian.
1891. N
[Comedy. Prod. Vaudeville, 1891.]

621. COTE, Marie [Am. 19c]
The witch of bramble hollow. Four acts.
NY: Wm. H. Young, 1899. 62p. NUC OCLC H

622. COURTENAY, Edith [Br. 19c]
Sisters.
1893. N
[Comedy. Prod. in Addlestone, 1893; in Balham, 1895.]

COWELL, Sidney Frances see BATEMAN, Sidney Frances (Cowell)

623. COWEN, Miss [Br. 19c]
Neither of them. A comedietta in one act.
NY & L: Samuel French, 1899. 18p. NUC BL E
[French's acting ed. v. 145]

624. COWEN, Henrietta [Br. 19c]
A quiet pipe. With S.M. Samuel.
1880. M N
[Comedy, 1 act. Prod. Folly, 1880.]

625. COWLEY, Hannah (Parkhouse) [Br. 1743-1809] PSEUD: Anna Matilda
Works; drama and poems.
L: Wilkie & Robinson, 1810, 1813. 3v. NUC BL OCLC
[V. 1-2 Dramas. V. 3 Poems.]

626. -----Albina, Countess Raimond; a tragedy ... .
L: J. Dodsley, 1779. 84p. NUC BL OCLC B N
[Tragedy, 5 acts. Written 1776. Prod. Haymarket, 1779. Also in: Works. Larpent Ms. #486]

627. -----The belle's stratagem: a comedy, of five acts ... .
Dublin: Pr. T. Bathe, 1781. 79p. NUC BL OCLC B E N
[Comedy. Prod. Covent Garden, 1780. Also in: Works.]

628. -----A bold stroke for a husband, a comedy in five acts.

Dublin: Pr. by all the booksellers, 1783. 52p. L: T. Evans, 1784. 87p. NUC BL OCLC B N
[Comedy, 5 acts. Prod. Covent Garden, 1783. Also in: Works; Longe, v.92, no. 3]

629. -----A day in Turkey, or the Russian slaves. A comedy.
L: G.G.J. & J. Robinson, 1792. 86p. NUC BL OCLC B N
[Comedy. First pub. 1791. Prod. Covent Garden, 1792. Also in: Works; Longe, v. 217, no. 2]

630. -----The fate of Sparta; or, the rival kings. A tragedy.
L: G.G.J. & J. Robinson, 1788. 85p. NUC BL OCLC B N
[5 acts, verse. Prod. Drury Lane, 1788. Also in: Works; Longe, v. 110, no. 5.]

631. -----More ways than one, a comedy.
2d ed. L: T. Evans, 1784. 97p. NUC BL OCLC B N
[Comedy, 5 acts. Prod. Covent Garden, 1783. Satire, on medical profession. Also in: Works; Longe, v. 94, no. 3.]

632. -----The runaway, a comedy.
L: Pr. for the author, 1776. 72p. NUC BL OCLC B N
[5 acts. Acted Drury Lane, 1776. Also in: Works; Longe, v. 86, no. 3. Last play produced by David Garrick, incl. epilogue by him.]

633. -----The school for eloquence.
1780. N
[Interlude. Prod. Drury Lane.]

634. -----A school for graybeards; or, the mourning bride: a comedy, in five acts.
L: G.G.J. & J. Robinson, 1786. 74p. NUC BL OCLC B N
[In part adapted from Aphra Behn's "The lucky chance." Prod. Drury Lane, 1786. Also in: Works.]

635. -----The town before you; a comedy ... .
2d ed. L: T.N. Longman, 1795. 103p. Dublin: P. Wogan, 1795. 82p. NUC BL OCLC B N
[First pub. 1791. Prod. Covent Garden, 1795. Also in: Works; Longe, v. 229, no. 5]

636. -----Which is the man? A comedy.

2d ed. L: C. Dilly, 1783. 54p.
Dublin: Pr. J. Brady, 1783. 74p. NUC
BL OCLC B E N
[5 acts. Prod. Covent Garden, 1782.
Also in: Works; Longe, v. 90, no. 3]

637. -----Who's the dupe? A farce in
two acts.
L: J. Dodsley, 1779. 6, 26p. NUC BL
OCLC B E N
[Acted Drury Lane, 1779. Also in:
Works.]

638. -----The world as it goes; or, A
party at Montpellier.
1781. OCLC N
[Comedy. Prod. Covent Garden.
Another version: "Second thoughts are
best," also prod. Covent Garden,
1781.]

639. COX, Mrs. Douglas [Br. 19c]
The pink letter.
1898. N
[Comedietta. Prod. at Maidenhead,
1898.]

640. COX, Eleanor Rogers [Am. 1867-
1931]
A duel at dawn.
NY: P.J. Kenedy, Excelsior pub.
house, 1894. 45p. H
[Kenedy's new series of plays. One
act, tragedy.]

641. CRACKANTHORPE, Blanche Alethea
Elizabeth (Holt), Mrs. Hubert
Montague Crackanthorpe [Br. 19c]
Other people's shoes.
In: Dialogues of the day. Ed. Oswald
Crawfurd.
L: Chapman & Hall, 1895. 12p. NUC BL
OCLC E

CRACKANTHORPE, Mrs. Hubert Montague
see CRACKANTHORPE, Blanche Alethea
Elizabeth (Holt)

CRAIG, Isa se KNOX, Isa (Craig)

642. CRAIGIE, Pearl Mary Teresa
(Richards), Mrs. Reginald Walpole
Craigie [Br. 1867-1906] PSEUD:
Hobbes, John Oliver
The ambassador: a comedy, in four
acts. By John Oliver Hobbes.
L: T.F. Unwin, 1898. 152p. NY:
Frederick A. Stokes, 1898. 173p. NUC
BL OCLC M N
[Comedy. Prod. St. James, 1898.]

643. -----The fool's hour. The first
act of a comedy. By John Oliver
Hobbes and George Moore.

In: The yellow book.
L: n.p., 1894. pp. 253-272. NUC

644. -----Journeys end in lovers'
meeting. With George Moore.
1894. N [Proverb drama. Prod.
Daly's, 1894.]

645. -----Osbern and Ursyne. A drama
in three acts.
L & NY: J. Lane, 1899. 94p. NUC BL E
N

646. -----A repentance: an original
drama in one act. By John Oliver
Hobbes.
L: Chiswick, 1899. 26p. NUC OCLC N
[Prod. St. James, 1899.]

647. -----The school for saints. By
John Oliver Hobbes.
NY: Century co.; L: T.F. Unwin, 1896.
86p. NUC BL OCLC E N
[Drama, 3 acts. Prod. Lyceum, 1896.]

648. -----The wisdom of the wise; a
comedy in three acts. By John Oliver
Hobbs.
NY: F.A. Stokes co., 1900. 136p. L:
T.F. Unwin, 1901. 151p. NUC BL OCLC E

CRAIGIE, Mrs. Reginald Walpole see
CRAIGIE, Pearl Mary Teresa (Richards)

649. CRANE, Eleanor Maud [Am. 19/20c]
"Just for fun;" an up-to-date society
comedy in three acts.
NY: Dick & Fitzgerald pub. co., 1899.
52p. NUC OCLC

650. -----A regular flirt ... comedy,
3 acts.
NY: Dick & Fitzgerald, 18-? 72p. NUC

651. CRANE, Elizabeth Green [Am.
19/20c]
Berquin; a drama in five acts.
NY: C. Scribner's sons, 1891. 110p.
NUC OCLC

CRAVEN, Baroness see CRAVEN,
Elizabeth (Berkeley)

652. CRAVEN, Elizabeth (Berkeley),
Baroness Craven [Br. 1750-1828] ALT:
Anspach, H. S. H., the Margravine of;
Brandenburg, Anspach and Bayreath,
H.S.H. the Margravine of
Airs and chorusses in The Princess of
Georgia, an opera.
n.p.: n.p., 1799. 15p. NUC BL OCLC N
[Performed at Brandenburgh-House
Theatre, 1798; Covent Garden, 1799.
Larpent Ms. #1251. Also pub. as:
"The Georgian Princess."]

653. -----The arcadian pastoral.
1782. N
[Interlude. Prod. privately,
Burlington Gardens.]

654. -----Love in a convent.
1805. N
[Comedy. Prod. privately,
Brandenburgh House.]

655. -----Love rewarded.
1799. N [Pastoral. In English &
Italian.]

656. -----The miniature picture: a
comedy in three acts.
L: G. Riley, 1781. 87p. NUC BL OCLC B
N
[Prod. privately at Newberry; Drury
Lane, 1780. Longe, v. 163, no. 2.]

657. -----Nicodemus in despair.
1803. N
[Farce. Prod. Haymarket, 1803. Also
acted as: "Poor Tony," at Brandenburg
House, 1803.]

658. -----Nourgad.
1803. N
[Interlude. Prod. privately,
Brandenburgh House.]

659. -----Le philosophe moderne.
Comedie en trois actes.
L: n.p., 1790. 84p. BL N
[Comedy. In French.]

660. -----The princess of Georgia.
1799. N
[Opera. Prod. privately,
Brandenburgh House; Covent Garden,
1799.]

661. -----Puss in boots.
1799. N
[Pantomime. Prod. privately,
Brandenburgh House.]

662. -----The robbers; a tragedy in
five acts. Trans. and altered from
the German of Johann [Christoph
Friedrich von] Schiller. Preface,
prologue and epilogue by Her Serene
Highness the Margravine of Anspach.
L: W. Wigstead, 1799. NUC BL
[Longe, v. 284, no. 6]

663. -----The silver tankard; or, The
point at Portsmouth.
n.p.: n.p., 1781. NUC B N
[Operatic farce. Prod. Haymarket,
1781. MS. Larpent Coll. #564.]

664. -----The sleep-walker ...
translated from the French.

Strawberry Hill: T. Kirgate, 1778.
NUC BL B N
[Comedy. Prod. privately, Newberry.]

665. -----The statue feast.
1782. N
[Comedy. Prod. privately, Benham
House.]

666. -----The Yorkshire ghost.
1794. N
[Comedy. Prod. privately,
Brandenburgh House.]

CRAWFURD, Oswald, ed. see BELL,
Florence Eveleen Eleanore (Olliffe)

CRAWFURD, Oswald, ed. see CLARKE,
Clara Savile

CRAWFURD, Oswald, ed. see
CRACKANTHORPE, Blanche Alethea
Elizabeth (Holt)

CRAWFURD, Oswald, ed. see DIXON,
Marion Hepworth

CRAWFURD, Oswald, ed. see ELLIOT,
Silvia Fogg

CRAWFURD, Oswald, ed. see HUNT,
Margaret (Raine)

CRAWFURD, Oswald, ed. see HUNT,
Violet

CRAWFURD, Oswald, ed. see L'EVERSON,
Mrs. Ernest

667. CREIGHTON, Bertha [Am. 19c]
The copper lion. A play of New
England in four acts.
n.p.: n.p., 1895. 82 l. NUC

CRESSWELL, Mrs. George see CRESSWELL,
I.S.

668. CRESSWELL, I. S., Mrs. George
Cresswell [Br. 19c]
The king's banner; or, Aimez loyaute:
an original semi-historical drama, in
four acts and several tableaux.
L & Dublin: Henry S. King & co.,
1873. 87p. NUC BL N
[Prod. Dublin, 1872. Set in the
Civil War, 1648-1660.]

669. CREWE, Annabel [Br. 19c]
The next generation. A farce.
L: Provost & co., 1879. 19p. NUC BL

CROSBY, Fanny see CROSBY, Frances
Jane

670. CROSBY, Frances Jane [Am. 1820–1915] ALT: Crosby, Fanny; Van Alstyne, Mrs. Alexander; Van Alstyne, Frances Jane (Crosby)
The flower queen; or, The coronation of the rose. A cantata in two parts.
NY: Mason bros., 1852. 15p. NUC H
[Prod. 1854. Music by George F. Root]

671. -----Zanie, an operetta.
Libretto by Fanny Crosby, music by H.P. Danks.
Cincinnati, OH: J. Church co., 1887. 64p. NUC

CROSS, Mrs. J.W. see EVANS, Marian

CROSS, Marian (Evans) see EVANS, Marian

672. CROWE, Catherine (Stevens), Mrs. John Crowe [Br. 1800–1876] ALT: Stevens, Catherine
Aristodemus: a tragedy.
Edinburgh: William Tait; L: Simpkin, Marshall & co.; Dublin: John Cumming, 1838. 98p. NUC BL OCLC E
[In verse]

673. -----The cruel kindness. A romantic play, in five acts.
L: George Routledge & co., 1853. 64p. NUC BL OCLC E M N
[Comedy. Prod. Haymarket, 1853. Entered with Lord Chamberlain as: "The Physician's Daughter"]

CROWE, Mrs. John see CROWE, Catherine (Stevens)

674. CRUMPTON, M. Nataline [Am. 1857–1911]
Ceres, a mythological play for parlor and school.
Boston: W.H. Baker & Co., 1890. 17p. NUC
[3 acts for 2 males & 12 females]

675. -----Pandora, a classical play for parlor and school.
Boston: W.H. Baker & Co., 1890. 11p. NUC
[3 acts for 4 males & 3 females]

676. -----Theseus, a mythological play for parlor and school.
NY: E.S. Warner, 1892. 29p. NUC
[5 acts]

CRYSTABEL, pseud. see ATTENBOROUGH, Florence Gertrude

677. CULBRETH, Amy [Am. 19c]

Love and death.
San Francisco: n.p., 1896. 164 l. NUC
[Drama, 6 acts]

678. -----Love eternal; or, united in death. A drama.
San Francisco: n.p., 1895. 20p. NUC

679. CULLUM, Mrs. [Br. 18c]
Charlotte; or, one thousand seven hundred and seventy-three. A play.
L: Baker & Galabin, 1775. 67p. NUC BL OCLC B N
[Longe, v. 8, no. 4]

680. CUMMINGS, Minnie [Am. 19c]
Suspected.
1879. Hatch
[Source: Black images on the American stage.]

CUNNINGHAM, Mrs. P.C. see CUNNINGHAM, Virginia Juhan

681. CUNNINGHAM, Virginia Juhan, Mrs. P.C. Cunningham [Am. 1834–1874]
Madelaine, the belle of the Faubourg.
Boston: William V. Spencer, 1856. 40p. NUC OCLC
[Drama, 3 acts. Spencer's Boston Theatre, no. 49.]

682. -----Maid of Florence; or, a woman's vengeance. A pseudo-historical drama. Charleston, SC: Miller, 1839. 92p. L: S. Low, Marston, Low & Searle; Toronto: Copp, Clark & co., 1874. 128p. NUC OCLC
[5 acts; tragedy]

683. CURRIE, Mary Montgomerie (Lamb) Singleton, Baroness [Br. 1843–1905] ALT: Lamb, Mary Montgomery; Singleton, Mary Montgomerie (Lamb)
PSEUD: Fane, Violet
Anthony Babington. A drama. By Violet Fane.
L: Chapman & Hall, 1877. 180p. NUC BL E
[5 acts; verse & prose]

684. CURTIS, Ariana Randolph (Wormeley), Mrs. Daniel Sargent Curtis [Am. 1833–1922] ALT: Curtis, Mrs. D. S.
The spirit of seventy-six; or, The coming woman; a prophetic drama; followed by A change of pace, and Doctor Mondschein. With Daniel Sargent Curtis.
Boston: Little, Brown & co., 1868. 141p. NUC BL OCLC R T
[3 plays intended for amateur or drawing-room performance. Spirit of

'76 is a   1-act satire on women's
emancipation.]

685. -----A change of pace.
In: The spirit of '76.
[Comedy, 1 act.]

686. -----Doctor Mondschein.
In: The spirit of '76.
[Comedy, 1 act.]

687. CURTIS, Austice [Am. 19c]
One question.
NY & Chicago: Brentanos, 1889. 122p.
NUC
[Dramatic poem, 2 acts.]

CURTIS, Mrs. D.S. see CURTIS, Ariana
Randolph (Wormeley)

CURTIS, Daniel Sargent, co-author see
CURTIS, Ariana Randolph (Wormeley)

CURTIS, Mrs. Daniel Sargent see
CURTIS, Ariana Randolph (Wormeley)

CURZON, Mrs. Robert see CURZON, Sarah
Anne

688. CURZON, Sarah Anne, Mrs. Robert
Curzon [Can. 1833-1898]
Laura Secord, the heroine of 1812: a
drama.   And other poems.
Toronto: C. Blackett Robinson, 1887.
215p. NUC BL OCLC
[3 act historical play. Incl. misc.
poems & fables, orig. & from the
French.]

689. -----The sweet girl graduate.
In: Laura Secord.
[Comedy, 4 acts.]

690. CUSACK, Sister Mary Frances
Clare [Am. 1829/30-1899] Tim Carty's
trial; or, Whistling at landlords.
NY: S. Mearns, pr., 1886. 57p. NUC
OCLC H

691. CUSHING, Eliza Lanesford
(Foster) [Am. b. 1794]
Esther, a sacred drama: with Judith,
a poem.
Boston: Joseph Dowe, 1840. 118p. NUC
BL
[Esther, 3-act verse drama, pp. 1-
103]

692. CUTHBERTSON, Catherine [Br. 19c]
Anna.
1793. B N
[Comedy. Prod. Haymarket, 1793.
Larpent Ms. #969.]

693. CUTHELL, Edith [Br. 19c]
The wrong envelope.
1887. M N
[Comedy. Prod. Strand, 1887;
Novelty, 1888.]

D., F.I. see DUNCAN, Florence I.

DACRE, Barbarina (Ogle) Brand,
Baroness see WILMOT, Barbarina,
Baroness Dacre

694. D'AGUILAR, Rose, Miss [Br. 18c]
Götz von Berlichingen.
1799. BioD
[Trans. of Johann Wolfgang von
Goethe.]

695. DALLAS, Mary Kyle [Am. 1830-
1899]
Aroused at last, a comedy in one act.
Chicago: The Dramatic pub. co.,
c1892. 22p. NUC OCLC
[Sergel's acting drama, no. 440]

696. -----Original character
sketches. With George Kyle.
NY: E.S. Werner, 1891. 186p. NUC OCLC
[Werner's readings and recitations,
no. 3.]

697. -----Our Aunt Robertina: a
comedietta in one act.
NY: Edgar S. Werner, 1891. 12p. NUC

698. DALRYMPLE, Lina [Br. 19c]
Tricked.
1884. N
[Comedietta. Prod. at Athlone,
1884.]

699. DALY, Julia [Br. 1833-1887] ALT:
Edgarton, Mrs. Warren; Olwine, Mrs.
Wayne
In and out of place.
1872. M
[Farce. Prod. Princess's, 1872. She
played 6 character parts in it.]

700. DANA, Eliza A. (Fuller) [Am.
19c] ALT: Dana, Elizabeth A. (Fuller)
Gathered leaves.
Cambridge, MA: Priv. pr. H.O.
Houghton, 1864. 160p. NUC OCLC H R
[Incl.: "Iona. An Indian tragedy."
Verse]

DANA, Elizabeth A. (Fuller) see DANA,
Eliza A. (Fuller)

D'ARBLAY, Mrs. Alexander see ARBLAY,
Frances (Burney) d'

D'ARBLAY, Frances (Burney) see
ARBLAY, Frances (Burney) d'

DARLING, Adam, Jr., co-author see
ELDREDGE, Ruth

701. DARLING, Isabella Fleming [Br.
1861-1903]
Whispering hope.
Edinburgh & Glasgow: John Menzies; L:
Simpkin & Marshall, 1893. 240p. NUC
BL E
[Incl.: "Woman's rights: a dialogue,"
in verse, pp. 154-167.]

DARMESTER, Mrs. James see DUCLAUX,
Agnes Mary Frances (Robinson)

702. D'ARUSMONT, Frances (Wright),
Mme. William Phiquepal-D'Arusmont
[Br. 1795-1852] ALT: Wright, Fanny;
Wright, Frances
Altorf, a tragedy.
Philadelphia: M. Carey & son, 1819.
83p. NUC BL OCLC B Hill Wells
[In verse]

D'ARUSMONT, Mme. William Phiquepal-
see D'ARUSMONT, Frances (Wright)

703. DAVENPORT, Fanny Lily Gypsy [Am.
1850-1898] ALT: Price, Mrs. Edwin H.;
MacDowell, Mrs. William Melbourne
Olivia. Vicar of Wakefield.
NY: n.p., 1878. 209p. H
[Mss. prompt book. Adapted from play
by William Gorman Wills & from Oliver
Goldsmith's novel.]

704. -----La Tosca.
n.p.: n.p., 1888. 115 l. H
[Based on play by Victorien Sardou.]

705. DAVIDSON, Frances A., Mrs. [Br.
19c]
Don Cesar de Bazan: a drama.
Translated from French of [Philippe
Francois Piner] Dumanoir and [Adolph
Philippe] Dennery.
L: Davidson, 1848. NUC BL
[Perf. at Theatres Royal.]

706. -----Giralda; or, Which is my
husband?
L: G.H. Davidson, n.d. 38p. NY: S.
French, 188-? 45p. NUC BL OCLC E N
[Comic drama, 3 acts. Prod. Grecian
Saloon, 1850. Adaptation of
"Giralda" by Augustin Eugene Scribe.]

707. -----Gustave III. Music by
Auber.
L: G.H. Davidson, 185-? 40p. NUC BL
OCLC E

[Libretto. Davidson's illustrated
libretto books.]

708. DAVIES, Blanche [Br. 19c]
Octavia; or, The bride of St. Agnes.
A tragedy, in five acts.
Doncaster: Brooke & co.; C. White,
1832. 62p. NUC BL E
[In verse]

709. DAVIS, Helen [Br. 19c]
A life policy.
1894. M N
[Drama, adapted from her novel: "For
so little." Prod. Terry's, and as
"Lawrence Maber," at Ladbrooke Hall,
1894.]

710. DAVIS, Lillie [Br. 19c]
Another engagement. A comedietta in
one act.
Manchester: A. Heywood & son, c1899.
12p. NUC

711. -----Aunt Madge. A comedietta
in one act.
Manchester: Abel Heywood & son; L: F.
Pitman, 1898. 15p. NUC BL E
[Abel Heywood & sons' series of
copyrt. plays for the use of
amateurs, 6.]

712. -----Difficult to please. A
dramatic sketch in one act for three
female characters.
Manchester: Abel Heywood & son; L: F.
Pitman, 1896. 21p. BL E
[Abel Heywood & son's series of
original dramas, dialogues &
readings. Adapted for amateur
entertainments. #162.]

713. -----Don't jump at conclusions.
Comedietta.
Manchester: Abel Heywood & son; L: F.
Pitman, 1894. 11p. NUC BL E
[Abel Heywood & son's series of
copyrt. plays for the use of
amateurs, #2.]

714. -----Dorothy's victory. A
dramatic sketch in one act for two
female characters.
Manchester: Abel Heywood & son; L: F.
Pitman, 1895. 12p. NUC BL E
[Abel Heywood & son's series of
original dramas, dialogues &
readings. Adapted for amateur
entertainments, 159.]

715. -----The little performers. A
dialogue.
Manchester: Abel Heywood & son; L: F.
Pitman, n.d. 12p. NUC

716. -----My lost golosh. Female monologue.
Manchester: A. Heywood & sons, c1899.
E

717. -----Rival relatives; a short, easy dialogue.
Manchester: Abel Heywood & son; L: F. Pitman, 189-? 16p. NUC

718. -----The two Georges. A comedietta in one act.
Manchester: Abel Heywood & son; L: F. Pitman, 1895. 16p. BL E
[Abel Heywood & son's series of copyrt. plays for the use of amateurs, 3.]

719. -----Which got the best of it? A comedietta in one act.
Manchester: Abel Heywood & son; L: F. Pitman, 1894. 12p. BL E
[Abel Heywood & son's series of original dramas, dialogues & readings. Adapted for amateur entertainments, 155.]

DAVIS, M.E.M. see DAVIS, Mary Evelyn (Moore)

720. DAVIS, Mary Evelyn (Moore), Mrs. Thomas E. Davis [Am. 1844/1852-1904/09] ALT: Davis, M. E. M.; Moore, Mary Evelyn; Moore, Mollie E.
A bunch of roses. A romantic comedy.
NY: E.S. Werner, 1899. 24p. NUC H

721. -----Christmas boxes.
NY: E.S. Werner, 1907. H
[Earlier copyright: 1899.]

722. -----A Christmas masque of St. Roch, Pere Dagobert, and Throwing the wanga.
Chicago: A.C. McClurg & co., 1896. 58p. NUC OCLC

723. -----A dress rehearsal.
NY: E.S. Werner, 1899. 68p. NUC OCLC H T

724. -----The new system. Comedy.
NY: E.S. Werner, 1907. NUC OCLC H
[Earlier copyright: 1899]

725. -----Queen Anne cottages. Romantic comedy.
NY: E.S. Werner, 1907. NUC OCLC H
[Earlier copyright: 1899]

726. DAVIS, Mrs. Maxwell [Br. 19c]
Pamela's prejudice. Comedietta.
L: S. French; NY: T. Henry French, 1899. 9p. NUC BL OCLC E

DAVIS, Mrs. Thomas E. see DAVIS, Mary Evelyn (Moore)

727. DAVYS, Mary, Mrs. Peter Davys [Br. 1674-1731]
The works of Mrs. Davys: consisting of, plays, novels, poems, and familiar letters.
L: Pr. H. Woodfall for the author, 1725. 2v. NUC BL OCLC B N
[First publication of most of the works]

728. -----The merry wanderer.
In: Works ... .

729. -----The modern poet.
In: Works ... .

730. -----The northern heiress; or, The humours of York. A comedy.
L: A. Bettesworth, J. Browne & W. Mears, 1716. 72p. NUC BL OCLC B N
[Comedy. Prod. Lincoln's Inn, 1716. Also known by the subtitle.]

731. -----The self-rival: a comedy.
In: Works.
N
[5 acts]

DAVYS, Mrs. Peter see DAVYS, Mary

732. DAWES, Sarah Elizabeth, Mrs. [Am. b. 1832]
The Braxton minute-men. A centennial drama.
Boston: J. B. & N. Niles, 1876. 34p. NUC OCLC

733. -----Hiring help; a farce in one act.
Boston: W.H. Baker & co., c1886. 10p. NUC

DE CAMP, Marie Therese see KEMBLE, Marie-Therese (DeCamp)

DEE, L.S., pseud. see BRUNTON, Anna (Ross)

DE HAN, RICHARD, pseud. see GRAVES, Clotilda Inez Mary

734. DE HUMBOLDT, Charlotte [Br. 19c]
ALT: Humboldt, Charlotte de Corinth, a tragedy; and other poems.
L: Ellerton, 1821. 111p. NUC BL OCLC E
[5 act dramatic poem on the fall of Periander. Expanded ed. L: Longman, Orme, Brown, Green & Longman, 1838. 188p.]

735. DELAFIELD, Emily Prime [Am. 19c]
Alice in wonderland; a play compiled
from Lewis Carroll's stories.
NY: Dodd, Mead & co., 1898. 89p. OCLC
[7 acts. From both "Alice" &
"Through the Looking Glass."
Presented March 14, 1897, at the
anniversary of the opening of the
Waldorf with a cast of 60 children.]

736. DELANOY, Mary Frances (Hanford)
[Am. 19c] PSEUD: Eddy, Marion
The outcast's daughter. A drama in
four acts. By Marion Eddy.
Chicago: The Dramatic pub. co.,
c1899. 32p. NUC OCLC H T
[Sergel's Acting Drama.]

737. DE LA PASTURE, Elizabeth Lydia
Rosabelle (Bonham), Mrs. Henry De La
Pasture [Br. 1866-1945] ALT:
Clifford, Elizabeth Lydia Rosabelle
(Bonham) De La Pasture, Lady The
modern craze.
1899. M N
[Comedy. Prod. St. George Hall,
1899.]

738. -----Poverty.
Brighton: Priv. pr., n.d. N
[Comedy]

DE LA PASTURE, Mrs. Henry see DE LA
PASTURE, Elizabeth Lydia Rosabelle
(Bonham)

739. DE LESDERNIER, Emily Pierpont,
Mrs. [Br. 19c] ALT: Lesdernier, Emily
P.
Voices of life. By Mrs. Emily P.
Lesdernier.
Paris: E. Briere, 1862. 104p. NY:
Cornish, Lamport & co., 1853. 38p.
NUC BL OCLC
[Incl.: "Heloise, a drama of the
passions, in 4 acts." Blank verse.]

DELILLE, Mrs. Henry S. see LOGAN,
Olive

DELPHINE, see BAKER, Delphine Paris

DEMILLE, Beatrice M., co-author see
FORD, Harriet

DE NAVARRO, Mrs. Antonio F. see DE
NAVARRO, Mary (Anderson)

740. DE NAVARRO, Mary (Anderson),
Mrs. Antonio F. de Navarro [Am. 1859-
1940] ALT: Anderson, Mary
As you like it. Arrangement of
Shakespeare's play.
L & N Y: S. French, n.d. 72p. E

741. -----Romeo and Juliet.
Arrangement of Shakespeare's play.
L: W.S. Johnson, 1884. 72p. E

742. -----The winter's tale.
Arrangement of Shakespeare's play.
L: W.S. Johnson, 1888. 66p. BL E

DENHAM, Sir John, co-author see
PHILIPS, Katherine (Fowler)

743. DENING, Christina, Mrs. [Br.
19c]
An awful experience.
1893. N
[Duologue. Amateur prod. Somerville
Club, 1893.]

744. -----Justice.
1893. N
[Drama. Amateur prod. in
Westminster, 1893.]

745. -----Mistakes.
1893. N
[Comedy. Amateur prod., Pioneer
Club, 1893.]

746. -----Olympus. 1893. N
[Melodrama. Amateur prod. Somerville
Club, 1893.]

747. -----Training a husband.
1893. N
[Duologue. Amateur prod. Somerville
Club, 1893.]

748. DE NOTTBECK, Gabrielle [Am. 19c]
Heroines of France: an historic
tragedy. Arranged with quoted parts
from Shakespeare's plays, and
original parts by the writer. NY:
n.p., 1877. 51p. NUC

DENTON, Clara J. see DENTON, Clara
Janetta (Fort)

749. DENTON, Clara Janetta (Fort)
[Am. 19/20c] ALT: Denton, Clara J.
All is fair in love. A drama in
three scenes.
Boston: W.H. Baker, c1890, 1897. 19p.
NUC OCLC
[Baker's edition of plays]

750. -----A change of color; a drama
in one act.
Boston: W.H. Baker & co., 1897. 12p.
NUC OCLC
[Baker's edition of plays]

751. -----The man who went to Europe;
a comedy in one act.
Boston: W.H. Baker & co., 1897. 12p.
NUC OCLC

[Baker's edition of plays]

752. -----Sorry for Billy.
Franklin, OH: Eldridge entertainment
house, n.d. 3p. NUC OCLC
[Clara J. Denton monologues]

753. -----Surprised, a comedy in one
act.
Philadelphia: Penn pub. co., 1898.
11p. NUC
[c1892]

754. -----To meet Mr. Thompson; a
farce in one act.
Boston: Walter H. Baker & co., 1890.
9p. NUC
[Baker's edition of plays]

755. -----Uncle Peter and the widow.
Franklin, OH: Eldridge entertainment
house, 189-? 6p. NUC OCLC
[Clara J. Denton monologues]

756. -----"W.H."; a farce in one act.
Boston: Walter H. Baker & co., 1897.
14p. NUC OCLC
[Baker's edition]

757. -----Waiting for Oscar.
Franklin, OH: Eldridge entertainment
house, 189-? 8p. NUC OCLC
[Clara J. Denton monologues]

758. DENTON, Mrs. Oscar [Am. 19c]
Mammy Crittie and Baby Sugon, negro
dialect monologue for a woman.
NY: E.S. Werner, c1896. 4p. NUC OCLC

759. DENVIL, Mrs. [Br. 19c]
Faust and Margurite.
1854. M
[Adapt. from French of Miguel Cané.
Prod. Princess's, 1854.]

760. DE RETAN, Daphne [Br. 19c] ALT:
DeRohan, Daphne
Oh! my wife!
1897. N
[Musical comedy, prod. in Ealing,
1897.]

DE ROHAN, Daphne see DE RETAN, Daphne

DERWENT, Clarence, co-author see
DERWENT, Elfrida

761. DERWENT, Elfrida [Br. d. 1958]
The family failing, in three acts, by
Elfrida and Clarence Derwent.
NY: Rialto mimeo. & typing service
bureau, n.d. 118 l. NUC

762. -----His Easter bride; a comedy
of English life, by Elfrida and
Clarence Derwent.
NY?: n.p., n.d. 1v. NUC

763. -----Our swan song, by Elfrida
and Clarence Derwent.
NY: n.p., n.d. 28 l. NUC

DE SMART, Mrs. Alec see SMART, Mrs.
Alec

764. DE VERE, Florence [Br. 19c]
Eugenie; or, the Spanish bride.
L: Ward & Lock, 1856. 302p. BL N
[Eugenie: tragedy, 5 acts, verse.]

765. -----The lady and the lawyers;
or, Honesty is the best policy.
In: Eugenie.
[Satiric comedy, 4 acts, prose.]

766. DEVERELL, Mary, Mrs. [Br. b.
1737?] PSEUD: Philanthea
Mary, Queen of Scots; an historical
tragedy, or, dramatic poem.
L: Pr. & sold by author, 1792. 116p.
NUC BL OCLC B N
[Blank verse, 5 acts]

767. DEVINE, Alice L. {De Vine} [Am.
19c]
A dramatization of [Henry Wadsforth]
Longfellow's Hiawatha.
St. Paul, MN: n.p., c1894. NUC BL
[6 acts]

DEVOT, Gertrude (Price) Jones see
JONES, Gertrude (Price)

768. DE WITT, Emilie [Br. 19c] The
guilty shadows.
1885. N
[Drama. Prod. Imperial, 1885.]

769. DEWITT, Jennie Dowling [Am. 19c]
Original dialogues; or conversations.
Designed for the use of schools and
the family circle.
Cincinnati, OH: 1858. 200p. 1v. 2nd
ed. Cincinnati, OH: R. Clarke; W.B.
Smith, 1859. 200p. NUC BL OCLC

DEYONGE, ANNEMINA, pseud. see WATSON,
A., Miss

770. DICKENS, Fanny [Br. d. 1895]
A living lie; or, sowing and reaping.
1863. N
[Drama. Prod. at Blackburn, 1883.]

771. DICKINSON, Anna, Miss [Br. 1842-
1932] ALT: Dickinson, Anna Elizabeth
An American girl.

1880. Quinn
[MS. Prod. Haverley's Fifth Ave.
Theatre; Sept. 20, 1880.]

772. -----Anna Boleyn.
n.p.: n.p., 1877. N
[drama]

773. -----Mary Tudor.
n.p.: n.p., 1876. N
[drama]

DICKINSON, Anna Elizabeth see
DICKINSON, Anna, Miss

774. DICKINSON, Eva Lyle [Am. 19c]
A Thanksgiving lesson.
NY: E.S. Werner, 1899. pp. 153-161.
H
[In: Werner's Magazine, vol. 24]

DIDDEAR, Harriett see FAUCIT,
Harriett Elizabeth (Diddear)

775. DIEHL, Anna T. (Randall) [Am.
19/20c] ALT: Randall-Diehl, Anna T.
The bride of Ischia. A monologue.
NY: E.S. Werner pub. & supply co.,
1899. 7p. NUC

776. -----Elocutionary studies and
new recitations.
NY: E.S. Werner, 1887. 200p. NUC OCLC
[Contains 2 prose pieces by Diehl,
poetry & prose by other authors]

777. DIETZ, Linda [Am. d. 1920]
Lessons in harmony.
1875. N
[Comedietta. Prod. St. George Hall,
1875.]

778. -----Wild love; or, Eagle Wally.
1881. N
[Drama. Prod. in Bristol and other
provincial theaters, with Dietz in
the lead, 1881. Adams]

779. DILLAYE, Ina [Am. 19c]
Ramona; a play in five acts, adapted
from Helen Hunt Jackson's Indian
novel.
Syracuse, NY: F. Le C. Dillaye, 1887.
40p. NUC OCLC

DILLEY, Joseph J., co-author see
ROWSELL, Mary Catherine

780. DILLON, Clara [Br. 1843?-1898]
His own enemy.
1898. N
[Melodrama. Prod. in Aldershot,
1898.]

781. DIX, Beulah Marie [Am. 1876-
1970]
Cicely's cavalier, a comedy in one
act.
Boston: W.H. Baker & co., 1897. [1896
OCLC]. 19p. NUC OCLC
[Baker's edition of plays. On British
civil war, 1642-49]

782. DIXEY, Kate [Br. 19c]
A girl's freak. With Lillian
Feltheimer.
1899. M N
[Farce comedy, 2 acts. Prod. St.
George Hall, 1899.]

783. DIXIE, Lady Florence Caroline
(Douglas) [Br. 1857-1905] ALT:
Douglas, Lady Florence Caroline
Abel avenged; a dramatic tragedy.
L: E. Moxon, 1877. 122p. NUC BL
[3 acts, verse]

784. DIXON, Marion Hepworth [Br. 19c]
Truth will out.
In: Dialogues of the day. Ed. Oswald
Crawfurd.
L: Chapman & Hall, 1895. 7p. NUC BL
OCLC E

785. DODGE, H. M., Mrs. [Am. 19c]
PSEUD: Amica Religionis
Heselrigge; or, The death of Lady
Wallace; with other poems. By Amica
Religionis.
Utica, NY: Hastings & Tracy, 1827.
[40p. Wells] 158p. NUC OCLC B Hill
Wells
[5-act tragedy in verse; Based on
Scottish history]

DODSON, Mrs. J.E. see IRISH, Annie

786. DOLARO, Selina [Br. 1849-1889]
ALT: Belasco, Mme Isaac Dolaro
In the fashion.
1887. N
[Comedy. Prod. Ladbrooke Hall, 1887.
Copyright Ms. "Fashion: a play,"
listed in NUC]

787. DON, Laura [Am. 19c]
A daughter of the Nile. A play in
five acts.
NY: n.p., 1881. 108 l. NUC

788. DONNELL, Florence T. [Am. 19c]
Drackkov. Russian drama in five
acts.
NY: W.R. Jenkins, 1890. 66p. NUC

789. DONNELL, Florence T.
Moneymaking and matchmaking; or, New
York in 1890. Comedy in five acts.

NY: Wm. R. Jenkins, 1891. 115p. NUC
OCLC

790. DONNELL, Florence T.
A revolutionary marriage; drama in
five acts.
NY: W.R. Jenkins, 1890. 82p. NUC OCLC

791. DORAN, Marie [Am. 19c]
Carmen, a romantic play, adapted from
[Prosper] Merimée and [the opera by
Georges] Bizet. By Marie Doran and
Mollie Revel.
Boston: n.p., 1896. NUC OCLC
[Playbill for performance in Boston,
April, 1896. NUC copyrt. 1905.]

792. -----Dorothy's neighbors.
NY: S. French, 1899? DLC
[Comedy, 4 acts. NUC & OCLC date
1917.]

793. -----The new co-ed.
NY: S. French, 1899? DLC
[Comedy, 4 acts. NUC & OCLC date
1915.]

794. -----Tempest and sunshine: a
southern comedy-drama, 4 acts.
NY: S. French, 189-? DLC
[NUC & OCLC date 1913.]

DOREMUS, Mrs. Charles A. see DOREMUS,
Elizabeth Johnson (Ward)

795. DOREMUS, Elizabeth Johnson
(Ward), Mrs. Charles A. Doremus [Am.
19/20c]
Grif; a play in one act by Mrs.
Charles A. Doremus and Frank Allen.
n.p.: n.p., n.d. NUC
[Typewritten]

796. -----Mock trial for breach of
promise, by Mrs. C.A. Doremus and
Miss H.E. Manchester.
NY: T.H. French, 18--? 22p. OCLC
[French's minor drama. The acting
edition no. 333]

797. DORISI, Lisa [Br. 19c]
A Japanese lamp.
L: Doremi & co., 1896. 35p. NUC OCLC
N [Musical comedy in 1 act. Prod. in
Tiverton, 1897.]

798. -----Preciosita; operetta in one
act.
L: Doremi & co., 1893. 16p. BL E N
[In prose with songs. Prod. St.
George Hall, 1893.]

DOUGLAS, Lady Florence Caroline see
DIXIE, Lady Florence Caroline
(Douglas)

799. DOUGLAS, Johnstone, Miss [Br.
19c]
Pamela.
1898. N
[Comedy. Prod. at Falkirk, 1898.]

800. DOUGLASS, Amy (Steinberg), Mrs.
John Douglass [Br. 19c] ALT:
Steinberg, Amy
My mother. By Amy Steinberg.
1890. M N
[Farce, 3 acts. Prod. Toole's,
1890.]

801. -----My uncle. By Amy
Steinberg.
1889. M N
[Farce, 3 acts. Prod. Terry's,
1889.]

DOUGLASS, Mrs. John see DOUGLASS, Amy
(Steinberg)

802. DOWLING, Mildred T. [Br. 19c]
Dangerfield '95.
1898. N
[Drama. Prod. Garrick, 1898.]

803. DOWNING, Harriet [Br. 19c]
The bride of Sicily, a dramatic poem.
L: Hurst, Chance & co., 1830. 167p.
NUC BL
[Incl. stage directions]

804. -----Satan in love: a dramatic
poem.
L: n.p., 1840. NUC BL

805. DOWNING, Laura Case [Am. 19c]
Defending the flag; or, The message
boy. A drama in five acts.
Clyde, OH: Ames, 1894. 34p. NUC OCLC
[Ames' Standard & Minor Drama. no.
342.]

806. DOWNSHIRE, Dowager Marchioness
of [Br. 19c]
The ferry girl. Music by Lady Arthur
Hill.
1890. N
[Operetta. Prod. Savoy, 1890.]

DOWSON, Mrs. H.M. see FILIPPI, Rosina

DOWSON, Rosina (Filippi) see FILIPPI,
Rosina

DRAKE, Frank C., co-author see
LITTLETON, Mary L., Mrs.

807. DUBOIS, Lady Dorothea Annesley
[Br. 1728-1774]
All the world's a stage; a farce.
L: T. Becket, 1771. 29p. NUC OCLC

[OCLC attributes this to Isaac Jackman, 1777.]

808. -----The divorce. A musical entertainment.
L: J. Whele [Wheble B], 1771. 18p.
NUC OCLC B N
[Musical. Prod. Marylebone Gardens, 1771. Longe, v. 184, no. 7. OCLC attr. Isaac Jackman]

809. -----The haunted grove.
1773. N
[Comic opera. Prod. Crow-Street, Dublin.]

810. -----The magnet. A musical entertainment.
L: T. Becket, 1771. 29p. OCLC B N
[Prod. Marylebone Gardens, 1771.]

811. DUCKWORTH, Mary G. [Br. 19c]
The tragedy of Blue Beard; a Greek play.
L: J.S. Forsaith, 1896. 20p. NUC

812. DUCLAUX, Agnes Mary Frances (Robinson) [Br. 1856-1944] ALT: Robinson, A. Mary F.; Darmesteter, Mrs. James
Songs, ballads and a garden play. By A. Mary F. Robinson.
L: T.F. Unwin, 1888. 142p. NUC BL OCLC E
["Our Lady of the broken heart," 1 act, set in a garden.]

DUER, Alice Maude, co-author see DUER, Caroline King

813. DUER, Caroline King [Am. 1865-1956]
Poems. With Alice Maud Duer [Miller, 1874-1942].
NY: Geo. H. Richmond & co., 1896. 62v. NUC BL OCLC H
[Incl.: "A dialogue" and "Overheard in a conservatory," by Caroline.]

DUFFERIN and AVA, The Marquess of, ed. see DUFFERIN and CLANDEBOYE, Helen Selina (Sheridan) Blackwood, Baroness

814. DUFFERIN and CLANDEBOYE, Helen Selina (Sheridan) Blackwood, Baroness [Br. 1807-1867] ALT: Blackwood, Helen Selina (Sheridan), Baroness Dufferin; Gifford, Helen Selina (Sheridan) Blackwood Hay, Countess of; Hay, Helen Selina (Sheridan) Blackwood, Countess of Gifford
Songs, poems and verses. By Helen, Lady Dufferin ... . Ed. with a

memoir, and some account of the Sheridan family, by her son, the Marquess of Dufferin and Ava.
2d ed. L: John Murray, 1894. 429p.
NUC BL OCLC M N
[Incl: "Finesse; or, A busy day in Messina. A comedy in 3 acts." A farce written for Mr. Wigan's talent of playing a Frenchman speaking broken English. Prod. Haymarket, 1863, as: "Finesse; or, Spy and counter spy."]

815. DUGAN, Caro Atherton [Am. 19c]
Collected works.
Boston & NY: Houghton, Mifflin, 1899. 364p. H

816. -----The king's jester, and other short plays.
Boston & NY: Houghton, Mifflin & co., 1899. 364p. NUC OCLC
[The title play is a tragedy, 4 acts. Contains music. Also in: Collected works.]

817. -----The apple of discord.
In: Collected works.
[2 acts, based on the classical legend. Also in: The king's jester.]

818. -----Cinderella.
In: Collected works.
[3 acts. Also in: The king's jester.]

819. -----The flight of the sun goddess.
In: Collected works.
[A legend of old Japan. 3 acts. Also in: The king's jester.]

820. -----The gift of Aphrodite.
In: Collected works.
[Retelling of Pygmalion & Galatea legend, 3 acts. Also in: The king's jester.]

821. -----The gypsy girl of Hungary.
In: Collected works.
[4 acts. Also in: The king's jester.]

822. -----Nino's revenge.
In: Collected works.
[Romance, 4 acts. Also in: The king's jester.]

823. -----Pandora.
In: Collected works.
[2 acts. Also in: The king's jester.]

824. -----The queen's coffer.

In: Collected works.
[2 acts. Set in 15th c. Scotland.]

825. -----The sleeping beauty.
In: Collected works.
[3 acts. Also in: The king's
jester.]

826. -----Undine. Five acts.
In: Collected works.
[Retells classical legend. Also in:
The king's jester.]

827. DUNCAN, Florence I. [Am. 19c]
ALT: D., F. I.
Ye last sweet thing in corners, being
ye faithful drama of ye artists'
vendetta. By F.I.D. Philadelphia:
Duncan & Hall, 1880 [1881 R]. 66p.
NUC OCLC R
[3 acts. Satire on art critics &
collectors]

828. DUNNE, Norah [Am. 19c]
Miss tom boy. Comedy in one act.
Chicago & NY: Dramatic pub. co.,
1899. 15p. H
[Sergel's acting drama, no. 539]

829. -----Mrs. Plodding's nieces; or,
Domestic accomplishments. A comedy in
one act for young ladies.
Chicago: The Dramatic pub. co.,
c1899. 22p. NUC OCLC
[Sergel's acting drama; no. 453]

830. DUQUETTE, S. Nettie [Am. 19c]
Aunt Dinah's husking bee. A very
popular new entertainment suitable
for church or social societies.
Lockport, NY: Pilot print, 1890. 16p.
NUC

831. DURANT, Heloise [Br. 19c] ALT:
Rose, Heloise Durant
Dante: a dramatic poem.
L: Kegan Paul, Trench & co., 1889.
136p. NUC BL OCLC E
[In three acts & a prologue. Ends
with dying Dante's vision of
Beatrice.]

832. -----Our family motto; or,
Noblesse oblige.
1889. N
[Comedietta. Prod. Queen's Gate,
1889.]

833. DUVAL, Mary Virginia [Am. b.
1850]
The queen of the South, a drama.
Pulaski, TN: The Citizen Print, 1899.
23p. NUC OCLC

834. DYER, Elizabeth [Am. 19c]
A tangled skein, in three knots.
Providence: J.A. & R.A. Reid, 1881.
31p. H

E., A. see TRUMBULL, Annie Eliot

E., A.L.O., pseud. see TUCKER,
Charlotte Maria

E., C. see ELLIOTT, Charlotte

E., E.F. see ELLET, Elizabeth Fries
(Lummis)

835. EASTMAN, Charlotte Whitney [Am.
19c]
One hundred entertainments, ...
designed especially for parlor use.
Chicago: T.S. Denison, c1898. 119p.
NUC

EBSWORTH, Mrs. Joseph see EBSWORTH,
Mary Emma (Fairbrother)

836. EBSWORTH, Mary Emma
(Fairbrother), Mrs. Joseph Ebsworth
[Br. 1794-1881]
Payable at sight; or, The chaste
salute. A comedy in one act.
L: John Cumberland; S. French, 18--?
27p. NUC BL OCLC E
[Cumberland's Minor Theatre, XIV.
Adams also cites: "The sculptor of
Florence" and other dramatic pieces.]

837. -----The two brothers of Pisa.
A melodrama in three acts.
Edinburgh: Joseph Ebsworth, 1828.
36p. NUC
[Translated from French: "Le
delateur."]

EDDY, Jerome H., co-author see IVES,
Alice Emma

EDDY, MARION, pseud. see DELANOY,
Mary Frances (Hanford)

838. EDGAR, Miss [Br. 19c]
Tranquility. A poem. To which are
added other original poems and
translations from the Italian and
Spanish.
Edinburgh & Dundee: n.p., 1810. 2d.
ed. L: n.p., 1824. BL Inglis
[1824 ed. incl. "Bethulia delivered,
a drama."]

EDGARTON, S.C. see MAYO, Sarah Carter
(Edgarton)

EDGARTON, Mrs. Warren <u>see</u> DALY, Julia

839. EDGEWORTH, Maria [Br. 1767-1849]
Comic dramas, in three acts.
L: R. Hunter & Baldwin, Cradock &
Joy, 1817. 381p. Boston: Wells &
Lilly, 1817. 286p. NUC BL OCLC E N
[Also pub. as: Cornish dramas, in
three acts.]

840. -----Dramas and dialogues,
amusing and instructive.
L: Burns & Lambert, 1860. BL

841. -----Alfred the Great.
In: Dramas ... .
[Sketch]

842. -----The broken window; Being
the trial of a complaint made against
sundry persons for breaking the
window of Dorothy Careful, widow, and
dealer in Gingerbread.
In: Dramas ... .
[Sketch, 2 pts.]

843. -----Canute's reproof.
In: Dramas ... .
[Sketch]

844. -----The chestnut horse; or, New
logic. In: Dramas ... .
[Sketch]

845. -----The colonists.
In: Dramas ... .
[Sketch]

846. -----Hasty judgment. A drama.
In: Dramas ... .
[1 act]

847. -----How to tell news.
In: Dramas ... .
[Duologue]

848. -----Love and law; a drama, in
three acts.
In: Comic dramas ... .
[Irish setting & dialect. Prod.
Lyceum, 1810.]

849. -----The miser.
In: Dramas ... .
[Duologue]

850. -----The native village.
In: Dramas ... .
[2 scenes]

851. -----Old Poz.
In: Dramas ... .
[4 scenes, sketch]

852. -----The organ grinder.
L: T.H. Lacy, 1870? 27p. NUC OCLC E

853. -----The rose, thistle and
shamrock; a drama in three acts.
In: Comic dramas ... .
[Irish setting]

854. -----The three talismans.
In: Dramas ... .
[1 act]

855. -----The two guardians; a drama,
in three acts.
In: Comic dramas ... .
[Society comedy]

856. -----The two robbers.
In: Dramas ... .
[Sketch]

857. EDMEAD, Miss [Br. 18c]
The events of a day.
1795. N
[Comedy. Prod. in Norwich, 1795.]

858. EDMONDSON, Maysie [Br. 19c]
Duke of Christmas daisies and other
fairy plays.
L: Wells, Gardner, Darton & co., n.d.
96p. NUC BL

EDMUNDS, GEORGE, pseud. <u>see</u>
MERIWETHER, Elizabeth (Avery)

859. EDOUIN, Winnie [Am. 19c]
A bunch of keys; or, The hotel.
Comedy in three acts. With Charles
Hale Hoyt.
n.p.: n.p., 1883. H NUC
[Prompt book in Ms. 172 l. Also in:
America's lost plays. Vol. 9.
Princeton, NJ: Princeton UP, 1940.
pp. 3-51.]

860. EDWARDS, Miss [Br. 18c]
Miscellanies, in prose and verse.
Edinburgh: Pr. for author, sold by C.
Elliot, 1776. 181p. NUC BL
[Incl.: Otho and Rutha. A true story.
In 2 parts, pp. 137-181, more a prose
romance than a drama. Inglis attr.
to Miss Christian Edwards and also
attr. to her: "The Buchananshire
tragedy of Sir James the Ross, an
historical ballad."]

861. -----Otho and Rutha: a dramatic
tale.
Edinburgh: n.p.; Dublin: Pr. H.
Colbert, 1780, 1787. 238p. BL OCLC N
[Prose dialogue; speakers: 24 men &
women. Revised version of the work
in her miscellanies.]

862. EDWARDS, Anna Maria [Br. 18c]
PSEUD: Lady, A
The enchantress, or The happy island.
A favorite musical entertainment;
performed at the Opera House Capel
Street.
2 pt. Dublin: Pr. H. Colbert, 1787.
2v. in 1. NUC BL OCLC B N
[2 acts, prose with many songs. 1
perf. 1783. BL lists as Pub. in her
Poems on various subjects.]

863. EDWARDS, Annie, Mrs. [Br. 19c]
Ought we to visit her? With W.S.
Gilbert.
1874. M
[Comedy, 3 acts. Prod. Royalty,
1874. Dramatized from her novel of
the same name.]

864. EGLETON, Mrs. [Br. 18c]
The maggot.
1732. N
[Ballad opera. Prod. Lincoln's Inn.]

865. EHRLICH, Elma C. [Am. 19c]
The star of Judah; a Purim play.
Cincinnati, OH: n.p., 188-? 9p. NUC

866. ELDREDGE, Ruth [Am. 19c]
Parisina; a tragic romance. Prologue
and four acts. With Adam Darling, Jr.
Denver, CO: Pr. C.F. Hoeckel, 1897.
65p. NUC

867. ELE, Rona [Am. 19c]
Woman's lefts. Three acts.
Philadelphia & Boston: Geo. Maclean,
18--? 16p. L & Coventry: n.p., 1871.
NUC BL H

ELIOT, Annie see TRUMBULL, Annie
Eliot

ELIOT, GEORGE, pseud. see EVANS,
Marian

ELIZABETH see GRIFFITH, Elizabeth
(Griffith)

868. ELIZABETH I, Queen of England
[Br. 1533-1603]
Hercules Oetaeus (fragment).
1561. BioD
[Trans. of Seneca. Chetwood: "Sir
Robert Naunton and others inform us,
that she translated for her own
Amusement, one of the Tragedies of
Euripedes; but have not given us the
particular name of it."]

ELLET, E.F. see ELLET, Elizabeth
Fries (Lummis)

869. ELLET, Elizabeth Fries (Lummis),
Mrs. William Henry Ellet [Am. 1818-
1877] ALT: E., E. F.; Ellet, E. F.;
Lummis, Elizabeth Fries PSEUD:
Turner, Cyril
Euphemia of Messina. A tragedy.
NY: Monson Bancroft, 1834. 62p. NUC
OCLC H R
[Trans. from Italian of Silvio
Pallico.]

870. -----Poems, translated and
original.
Philadelphia: Key & Biddle, 1835.
229p. NUC BL OCLC R
[Incl. 5-act tragedy: Teresa
Contarini. Based on Venetian history.
Most poetry is original]

871. -----White lies, a drama in
three acts. From Charles Reade's
novel, entitled White Lies. Adapted
by Cyril Turner.
NY: O.A. Roorbach, 1858. 36p. NUC
OCLC R

ELLET, Mrs. William Henry see ELLET,
Elizabeth Fries (Lummis)

872. ELLIOT, Silvia Fogg [Br. 19c]
Doubly sold.
In: Dialogues of the day. Ed. Oswald
Crawfurd.
L: Chapman & Hall, 1895. 9p. NUC BL
OCLC E

873. ELLIOTT, Charlotte [Br. 1789-
1871] ALT: E., C. PSEUD: Lady, A
One fault. With Ernest Warren.
1885. N
[Comedy. Prod. at Wigan, 1885.]

874. ELLIS, Kate Florence [Am.
19/20c]
The family album; as exhibited by
Mrs. Almira Pease of Hockanum.
Boston: W.H. Baker & co., c1893. 16p.
NUC [Baker's novelties. Monologue]

875. ELLIS, R., Mrs. [Br. 19c]
The last of the Latouches. With
Charles R. Rennell.
1877. N
[Comedy. Prod. at Croyden, 1877.]

876. ELWYN, Lizzie May [Am. 19/20c]
Dot, the miner's daughter; or, One
glass of wine. A drama, in four
acts.
Clyde, OH: Ames' pub. co., 1888. 36p.
NUC OCLC
[Ames' series of standard and minor
drama, no. 254]

877. -----Millie, the quadroon; or,
Out of bondage. A drama in five
acts.
Clyde, OH: Ames' pub. co., 1888. 36p.
NUC OCLC
[Ames' series of standard and minor
drama; no. 251]

878. -----Murder will out, a farce in
one act for six female characters.
NY: Fitzgerald; H. Roorbach, 1890.
14p. NUC OCLC
[Roorbach's American edition of
acting plays, no. 25]

879. -----Rachel, the fire waif.
Four acts.
Clyde, OH: Ames, 1900. 29p. NUC OCLC
H
[Ames' Standard & Minor Drama, no.
420]

880. -----Sweetbriar, or, The flower
girl of New York. A drama in six
acts.
Clyde, OH: Ames' pub. co., 1889 [1899
H]. 31p. NUC OCLC H
[Ames' series of standard and minor
drama, no. 413]

881. -----Switched off. A temperance
farce in one act.
Clyde, OH: Ames pub. co., 1899. 16p.
NUC OCLC
[Ames' series of standard and minor
drama, no. 413]

882. ENEBUSKE, Sarah Folsom [Am. 19c]
A detective in petticoats.
Boston: W.H. Baker, c1900. 32p. NUC
OCLC
[Baker's ed. of plays]

ENELEH, H.B., pseud. see HERZOG,
Helene

EPHELIA, pseud. see PHILIPS, Joan

ERSKINE, Hon. Mrs. Esme Stewart see
NORTON, Eliza Bland (Smith) Erskine,
Hon. Mrs.

ERSKINE, Wallace, co-author see
STUART, Adeline

883. EVANS, Marian [Br. 1819-1880]
ALT: Cross, Mrs. J. W.; Cross, Marian
Evans; Evans, Mary Ann PSEUD: Eliot,
George; Lewes, Marian
The Spanish gypsy. A poem.
L & Edinburgh: W. Blackwood, 1868.
358p. Boston: Ticknor & Fields, 1868.
287p. NUC BL OCLC E
[Also incl.: "Armgart." Dramatic
poems. NUC has a 4-act typewritten

libretto, adapted from "The Spanish
gypsy," by Garrita Nash & Lily A.
Long, n.d.]

EVANS, Mary Ann see EVANS, Marian

884. EVANS, Rose [Br. 1850?-1875]
Disinherited; or, Left to her fate.
1874. N
[Drama. Prod. at Yarmouth, 1874.]

885. -----Quite alone.
1874. N
[Drama. Prod. at Yarmouth, 1874.]

886. EVELYN, J., Miss [Br. 19c]
A crown for love.
1874. Adams N
[Historical drama, 5 acts. Prod. in
Edinburgh, 1874 & at Gaiety, London,
1875.]

887. -----A life [life's] race.
1872. M N
[Prod. Royal Alfred, 1872.]

F., A. see FIELD, Annie (Adams)

F., A. see FLETCHER, Eliza Dawson

F., A. see FRANCIS, Ann (Gittins)

FABER, Rev. G.S., ed. see WOODROFFE,
Sophia

888. FAIRBAIRN, May Holt, Mrs. R.
Fairbairn [Br. 19c] ALT: Holt, May
Dark deeds.
1881. M N
[Drama, 4 acts. Prod. Oldham, 1881
as: "Jabez North"; Philharmonic,
1882. Adapt. from Mary Elizabeth
(Braddon) Maxwell's novel, "The trail
of the Serpent."]

889. -----Every man for himself.
1885. N
[Drama. Prod. in Yarmouth &
Pavillion, London, 1885.]

890. -----False pride.
1883. N
[Play. Prod. in Norwich, 1883;
Vaudeville, 1884.]

891. -----Men and women.
1882. N
[Drama. Prod. Surrey, 1882.]

892. -----Sweetheart, good-bye.
1881. M N

[Comedietta. Prod. Scarborough,
1881; Strand, 1884; & Criterion,
1890.]

893. -----Waiting consent.
1881. M N
[Comedietta. Prod. Folly, 1881.]

FAIRBAIRN, Mrs. R. see FAIRBAIRN, May
(Holt)

894. FAIRFAX, Mrs. [Br. 19c]
The best people.
1890. N
[Comedy, 4 acts. Prod. Globe, 1890.]

895. FAIRGRAVE, Amita B. [Am. 19c]
Purple and fine linen. With Helena
Miller.
NY: S. French, 1899?
[Comedy, 3 acts. On Puritan
England.]

896. FALKLAND, Elizabeth Tanfield)
Carew, Viscountess [Br. 1585-1639]
ALT: C., E.; Carew, Elizabeth
Tanfield), Viscountess Falkland;
Cary, Elizabeth
History [of Edward II].
L: C. Harper, 1680. 160p. OCLC
[Written 1627. Generally attr.
Viscount Falkland. OCLC]

897. -----Tragedie of Mariam, the
faire queene of Jewry. By E.C. L:
Creede, 1612. 34p. NUC BL OCLC B
[Written 1604. Pub. as: "Mariam the
queene of Jewry, L: Richard Hawkins,
1613.]

FANE, VIOLET, pseud. see CURRIE, Mary
Montgomerie (Lamb) Singleton,
Baroness

898. FARJEON, Eleanor [Am. 1881-1965]
Floretta. Opera in two acts.
Founded on a story by Heinrich
Zschokke.
L: Henderson & Spalding, pr., 1899.
31p. BL N E
[Opera. Music by Herbert Farjeon.
Prod. St. George Hall, 1899.]

FARMER, Lydia (Hoyt) see PAINTER,
Lydia Ethel (Hoyt) Farmer

FARREN, Mrs. William see FAUCIT,
Harriett Elizabeth (Diddear)

899. FAUCIT, Harriett Elizabeth
(Diddear), Mrs. John Saville Faucit
[Br. 1789-1857] ALT: Diddear,
Harriett; Farren, Mrs. William
Alfred the Great.

1811. N
[Prod. in Norwich. Larpent Ms. #54.]

FAUCIT, Mrs. J.S. see FAUCIT,
Harriett Elizabeth (Diddear)

FAUCIT, Mrs. John Saville see FAUCIT,
Harriett Elizabeth (Diddear)

900. FAUGÈRES, Margaretta Van Wyck
(Bleecker), Mrs. Peter Faugères [Am.
1771-1801] ALT: Bleecker, Margaretta;
Bleecker, Peggy
Belisarius, a tragedy.
NY: Pr. by T. & J. Swords, 1795. 53p.
NUC BL B Hill Wells
[Five acts, verse. Prob. never
perf.]

FAUGERES, Mrs. Peter see FAUGERES,
Margaretta Van Wyck (Bleecker)

FAWCETT, Mrs. Henry see FAWCETT,
Millicent (Garrett)

901. FAWCETT, Millicent Garrett, Mrs.
Henry Fawcett [Br. 1847-1929]
At the ferry.
1897. N
[Prod. at Kilburn, 1897. OCLC has
anon. entry, 1900: "At the ferry: a
trialogue."]

FELTHEIMER, Lillian, co-author see
DIXEY, Kate

902. FENTON, Stella [Am. 19c]
A born bohemian. A four act play.
NY: n.p., 1892. NUC

903. FIDDES, Josephine [Br. 1848?-
1923] ALT: Murray, Mrs. Dominick
Deadly foes.
1868. N
[Prod. in Belfast, 1868.]

FIELD, Kate see FIELD, Mary Katherine
Keemle

904. FIELD, Mary Katherine Keemle
[Am. 1838-1896] ALT: Field, Kate
Extremes meet; a comedietta.
L & NY: S. French, 1878. 16p. NUC
OCLC M N R
[Comedietta. Prod. St. James', 1877.
French's acting edition]

905. -----Mad on purpose. Translated
by Miss Kate Field.
NY: John A. Gray & Green, pr., 1868.
48p. NUC OCLC R
[Comedy, 4 acts. Trans. from Italian
of Baron Giovanni Carlo Cosenza.]
FIELD, MICHAEL, pseud. see BRADLEY,
Katherine Harris

FIELDING, Anna Maria see HALL, Anna
Maria (Fielding)

906. FIELDING, Mary [Br. 19c]
John Wharton; or, The wife of a
Liverpool mechanic.
1868. N
[Prod. in Manchester, 1868.]

907. FIELDS, Annie (Adams), Mrs.
James Thomas Fields [Am. 1834-1915]
ALT: Adams, Annie; F., A.
Under the olive.
Boston & NY: Houghton, Mifflin & co.,
1880. 317p. NUC OCLC H
[Title also given as: "Under the
olive tree."]

908. -----The return of Persephone.
A dramatic sketch. By A.F.
Cambridge, MA: Priv. pr. Welch,
Bigelow & co., 1877. 53p. NUC OCLC
[In verse, also in: "Under the
olive."]

909. -----Orpheus. A masque. In
three scenes.
Boston & NY: Houghton, Mifflin, 1900.
41p. NUC OCLC H R
[In verse.]

910. -----Pandora. A festival play.
In: Under the olive.
[Pp. 197-275.]

911. Sophocles.
In: Under the olive.
[Pp. 25-34]

FIELDS, Mrs. James Thomas see FIELDS,
Annie (Adams)

912. FIELDS, Louisa May [Am. 19c]
Twelve years a slave.
Indianapolis, IN: n.p., 1897. DLC
[Typescript]

913. FILIPPI, Rosina [Br. b. 1866]
ALT: Dowson, Mrs. H. M.; Dowson,
Rosina (Filippi)
Duologues and scenes from the novels
of Jane Austen, arranged and adapted
for drawing-room performance.
L: J.M. Dent, 1895. 139p. NUC BL OCLC

914. -----An idyll of New Year's Eve.
1890. M N
[Dramatic sketch. Prod. Chelsea,
1890. Also prod. at Prince of Wales,
1899, as: "An idyll of seven dials."
Music by Amy E. Horrocks.]

915. -----In the Italian quarter.
L: R.B. Johnson, 1899. 1900? 49p. NUC
BL N [Performed Vaudville Theatre.

Sketch of a street scene. Pub. in
series for amateur acting: Carpet
Plays.]

916. -----Little goody two shoes.
Music by A. Levey.
1888. N
[Pantomime. Prod. Court, 1888.]

FINCH, Anne (Kingsmill), Countess of
Winchelsea see WINCHELSEA, Anne
(Kingsmill) Finch, Countess of

FISH, George F., co-author see
FOREPAUGH, Luella

FISHER, Mrs. Bernhardt see BERNHARDT-
FISHER, Mrs.

FISKE, Mrs. Harrison Grey see FISKE,
Minnie Maddern (Davey)

FISKE, Marie Augusta (Davey) see
FISKE, Minnie Maddern (Davey)

917. FISKE, Minnie Maddern (Davey),
Mrs. Harrison Grey Fiske [Am. 1865-
1932] ALT: Fiske, Marie Augusta
(Davey); Maddern-Fiske, Minnie;
White, Mrs. LeGrand
The rose. Comedy in one act.
n.p.: n.p., 1893. OCLC H Hatch
[Typescript. 21 l. Perf. in Boston,
1892.]

918. FITCH, Anna Mariska, Mrs. [Am.
19c]
Items; a Washington society play, in
five acts.
NY: P.F. McBreen, pr., 1874. 52p. NUC

919. FITZ-SIMON, Ellen [Br. 19c]
Darrynane in Eighteen Hundred and
Thirty-two and other poems.
Dublin: W.B. Kelly, 1863. 250p. NUC
BL OCLC E
[Incl. a dramatic poem, "The boy of
Normandy," pp. 149-94.]

FLEMING, GEORGE, pseud. see FLETCHER,
Julia Constance

FLETCHER, Constance see FLETCHER,
Julia Constance

920. FLETCHER, Eliza Dawson [Br.
1770-1858] ALT: F., E.
Elidure and Edward. Two historical
dramatic sketches. By E.F.
L: Pr. Thomas Davison, 1825. 125p.
NUC BL OCLC
[5 acts each]

921. FLETCHER, Evelyn [Br. 19/20c]

Monologues a la mode and Ballads of
the comical couples. A book of
recitations.
L: S. French, 1895. 63p. BL
[7 ballads and 9 prose monologues for
female speakers.]

922. -----Seven duologues.
Manchester: Abel Heywood & son, 1899.
72p. NUC BL
[Heywood's winter amusements, 8.
Comedies, 1 act, prose]

923. FLETCHER, Julia Constance [Am.
1858-1936] ALT: Fletcher, Constance
PSEUD: Fleming, George
The canary: a sentimental farce in
three acts. By George Fleming.
NY: Z. & L. Rosenfield, 1899. 1900?
115p. NUC OCLC E M N
[Comedy. Prod. Prince of Wales,
1899.]

924. -----A man and his wife: a play
in three acts by George Fleming.
NY: Rosenfield stenography, 189-. 1v.
NUC

925. -----Mrs. Lessingham.
1894. M N
[Comic play, 4 acts. Prod. Garrick,
1894.]

926. FLEWELLYN, Julia Colliton [Am.
b. 1850]
It is the law; a drama in five acts.
Lockport? NY: n.p., 1896? 48p. NUC

927. FLINT, Mary MacHardy [Br. 19/20]
ALT: MacHardy, Mary; MacHardy Flint,
Mrs.; McHardy, Mary
"Pranks:" a farcical comedy in two
acts. By Mr. and Mrs. MacHardy
Flint.
L: George Phillip & son, 1894. 22p.
BL
[Irish drama]

928. FLORANCE, B. E., Mrs. [Br. 19c]
The Bohemian bandit.
1843. N
[Melodrama sometimes subtitled "The
shrine of St. Margaret's." Prod.
Olympic Theatre, 1843.]

FLOWER, Sarah Fuller see ADAMS, Sarah
Fuller (Flower)

929. FOGERTY, Elsie [Br. 1866-1945]
Love laughs at locksmiths.
1899. N
[Duologue. Prod. at Albert Hall,
1899. Also called "The Portrait."]

930. FORBES, Hon. Mrs. [Br. 19c]
All Hallow's Eve. With J.W.
Whitbread.
1891. N
[Prod. in Dublin, 1891.]

931. FORD, Emily S. [Br. 19c]
Rejected addresses. An episode in
one act.
L: E.S. Ford, 1882. 28p. BL
[Verse & prose]

932. FORD, Harriet [Am. 1863/68-1949]
ALT: Morgan, Mrs. Forde
The greatest thing in the world.
Four acts. With Beatrice M. DeMille.
L: Mrs. Marshall's typewriting
office, 1899. NUC H
[Prod. in NY, 1900. Typescript 18,
16, 16, 12 l.]

933. FOREPAUGH, Luella [Am. 19c]
Dr. Jekyll and Mr. Hyde; or, A mis-
spent life. Four acts. With George
F. Fish.
NY & L: S. French, c1879 OCLC, 1897.
40p. NUC OCLC H
[French's Intl. copyrighted ed. of
the works of the best authors, no.
15. Adapted from Robert Louis
Stevenson's novel]

934. FORREST, Amy [Br. 19c]
Out of evil.
1893. N
[Drama. Prod. at Battersea, 1893.]

935. -----Trick for trick.
1889. N
[Drama. Prod. at Stratford, 1889.]

936. FORRESTER, Elouise [Am. 19c]
A drama in six acts, entitled Hazel
Hampden.
Danbury, CT: n.p., 1897. 27p. NUC

937. FORRESTER, Stephanie [Br. 19c]
Black but comely.
1882. M N
[Adaptation of a story by George John
Whyte-Melville. Prod. Gaiety, 1882.]

938. -----My general.
1890. N
[Comedy. Prod. at Ryde, 1890.]

FORSYTH, Dorothy see JONSON, Dorothy
(Forsyth)

939. FORSYTH, Elizabeth [Br. 18c]
The siege of Quebec; or, The death of
General Wolfe. A tragedy.
Strabane: John Bellew, pr., 1789.
60p. NUC B

940. FOSTER, Carey [Am. 19c]
The moon menagerie.
Lebanon, OH: March bros., n.d. 5p.
NUC OCLC T
[Pub. 1903 as: "The moon menagerie: a
Mother Goose sketch." NY: Hinto pub.
co.]

FOX, Florence Lane- see LANE-FOX,
Florence

941. FRANCES, Miss [Br. 19c]
Charade dramas for home performance.
L: Thomas Hailes Lacy, 1863. 62p.
Lacy's Home Plays. NUC BL OCLC
[In English & French. Four dramatic
pieces.]

942. FRANCIS, Ann (Gittins), Mrs.
Robert Bransby Francis [Br. 1738-
1800] ALT: F., A. PSEUD: Lady, A
Sacred hymeneal drama.
1781. BioD [DNB: "A poetical
translation of the Song of Solomon
from the original Hebrew, with a
preliminary discourse and notes,
historical and explanatory." Pub.
1781.]

FRANCIS, Lydia Maria see CHILD, Lydia
Maria (Francis)

FRANCIS, Mrs. Robert Bransby see
FRANCIS, Ann (Gittins)

FRANKLIN, Eliza see LESLIE, Eliza
(Franklin)

943. FRANKLIN, Jenny [Br. 19c]
Cissy. With W.H. Dearlove.
1890. N
[Musical comedy. Prod. Harrowgate,
1890.]

944. FRASER, Julia Agnes [Br. 19c]
Barrington's busby; or, Weathering
the admiral. Comedietta in one act.
Plymouth: Trend & co., 1890. 26p. BL
E N
[Prod. at Devonport, 1890.]

945. -----Court lovers: or the
Sentinal of the King's guard. An
original musical comedy in four acts.
Plymouth: Trend & co., pr., 1891.
101p. BL E
[Words only]

946. -----Dermot O'Donoghue; or, The
stranger from Belfast.
1876. N
[Drama. Prod. at Strathaven, 1872;
Whitehaven, 1877; & Belfast, 1878.]

947. -----Hubert's pride. A comedy,
in one act.
Strathaven: Alexander Morton, pr.,
1871. BL E N
[Prod. at Strathaven, 1872. Extra
scene(s) of Hubert's pride, between
scenes first and second. 2 pt.
Strathaven: n.p., 1877. BL]

948. -----Idle words; or, death and
glory.
1896. N
[Drama. Prod. at Edinburgh, 1896,
amateur company.]

949. -----Pat of Mullingar; or, An
Irish lothario. An original Irish
comedy in three acts.
Greenock: Greenock Advertiser office,
pr., 1879. 66p. BL E
[Incl. songs]

950. -----Patrick's vow.
1873. N
[Drama. Prod. in Strathaven, 1873.]

951. -----A slight mistake. A farce
in one act.
L: Remington; Edinburgh, Strathaven:
John Menzies, 1872. 24p. BL E N
[Farce. Prod. in Strathaven, 1873.]

952. -----The star-spangled banner;
or, The far west. An ... Irish-
American military drama. In a
prologue and six acts.
Plymouth: Trend & co., pr., 1894.
163p. BL OCLC E

953. FRASER, Susan, Mrs. [Br. 19c]
PSEUD: Officer's wife, An
Camilla de Florian and other poems.
By an officer's wife.
L: Pr. for the author & sold by J.
Dick, 1809. 159p. NUC BL Inglis
[Incl. a dramatic poem, "Comala,"
adapted from Ossian.]

954. FREAKE, Mrs. [Br. 19c]
Deeds.
1879. N
[Comedy. Amateur prod. at Cromwell
House, S. Kensington, 1879.]

FREEMAN, Mrs. Charles Manning see
FREEMAN, Mary Eleanor (Wilkins)

FREEMAN, M.E. see FREEMAN, Mary
Eleanor (Wilkins)

FREEMAN, Mary E. see FREEMAN, Mary
Eleanor (Wilkins)

955. FREEMAN, Mary Eleanor (Wilkins),
Mrs. Charles Manning Freeman [Am.

1852-1930] ALT: Freeman, M. E.;
Freeman, Mary E. Wilkins; Wilkins,
Mary E.; Wilkins, Mary Eleanor
Giles Cory, yeoman.
NY: Harper & bros., 1893. 108p. NUC
BL OCLC R
[Tragedy, 6 acts. Dramatization of
Salem witch hunt. Harper's black &
white series.]

956. FREILIGRATH-KROEKER, Kathe, Frau
[Br. 1845-1904]
A domestic syndicate: original
drawing-room play in three acts.
L: Dean & sons, 1895. 51p. BL

957. FRENCH, Anne Warner [Am. 1869-
1913] ALT: Warner, Anne
The rejuvenation of Aunt Mary. By
Anne Warner.
NY: S. French, 1897? NUC BL DLC
[Comedy, 3 acts. Two later eds.,
1905 & 1916.]

FRENCH, L. Virginia (Smith) see
FRENCH, Lucy Virginia (Smith)

958. FRENCH, Lucy Virginia (Smith)
[Am. 1825-1881] ALT: French, L.
Virginia (Smith)
Istalilxo: the lady of Tula.
1856. Mainero
[Tragedy, 5 acts, verse. Set in
Mexico. Pub. after her first vol. of
poetry, "Wind whispers," 1856.]

959. FRERE, Mary Eliza Isabella [Br.
1845-1911]
Love's triumph.
1869. DNB N
[Play; published anon. DNB: a
pastoral, with sonnets.]

FREUND-LLOYD, Mabel see LLOYD, Mabel
Freund-

960. FREY, R. E., Mrs. [Am. 19c]
Eileen; a play in four acts.
St. Louis, MO: Mrs. R.E. Frey, 1898.
52p. NUC OCLC T

961. FRIEDLIEB, L. A., Mrs. [Am. 19c]
PSEUD: Horsford, F. Allen
"Gladys," or, a London beauty. A
comedy drama in five acts. By F.
Allen Horsford.
NY: H.A. Richardson, 1886. NUC

962. -----"Honor bright." Comedy
drama in three acts. By F. Allen
Horsford.
NY: H.A. Richardson, 1887. NUC

963. -----"My lady coquette." Comedy
drama in four acts. By F. Allen
Horsford.
NY: H.A. Richardson, 1886. NUC

964. FRIES, Adelaide Lisette [Am.
1871-1949]
Sigma Phi Alpha; an operetta for
ladies voices; the book of words.
Salem, NC: c1896. NUC

FROST, Annie see SHIELDS, Sarah Annie
(Frost)

FROST, S.A. see SHIELDS, Sarah Annie
(Frost)

FROST, S. Annie see SHIELDS, Sarah
Annie (Frost)

965. FROTHINGHAM, Ellen [Am. 1835-
1902]
Nathan the wise. A dramatic poem,
translated from Gotthold Ephraim
Lessing.
NY: H. Holt & co., 1867. NUC BL OCLC
H R

966. -----Sappho. A tragedy,
translated from German of Frans
Grillparzar.
Boston: 1876. NUC BL OCLC H R

967. FROTHINGHAM, Meredith S. [Am.
19c]
The Princess Tai, or a China tea set.
Two acts.
Saratoga Springs, NY: Saratogian book
& job print, 1887. 14p. NUC
[With orig. dances, ballet & marches,
by Jacob Mahler.]

968. FRY, Betsey [Am. 19c]
The area sylph; or, a Foot-boy's
dream, a bombastic, ... burlesque
burletta ... in one act.
L: J. Pattie, 18--? 16p. NUC E
[18-] [#12 in vol. lettered:
Burlesques, Vol. 5]

969. FULLER, Alice Cook, Mrs. [Am.
19/20c]
Hatchet march and drill; spectacular
entertainment for Washington's
birthday.
Lebanon, OH: March bros., 1899. 8p.
NUC
[Fin de siecle series]

970. -----November's crown;
spectacular entertainment for
Thanksgiving.
Lebanon, OH: March bros., c1898. 7p.
NUC OCLC

[Fin de siecle series]

FULLER, Frances see VICTOR, Frances
Auretta (Fuller) Barritt

FULLER, Metta Victoria, co-author see
VICTOR, Frances Auretta (Fuller)
Barritt

FULLERTON, Mrs. Alexander George see
FULLERTON, Lady Georgiana Charlotte
(Leveson Gower)

971. FULLERTON, Lady Georgiana
Charlotte (Leveson Gower), Mrs.
Alexander George Fullerton [Br. 1812-
1885]
The changelings; or, which is which?
A play.
NY: H. Roorbach, 187-? 22p. NUC
[The acting drama. no. 92]

972. FULLERTON, Lady Georgiana
Charlotte (Leveson Gower)
The fire of London; or, which is
which? A play in three acts.
L: Burns, Oates & co., 1882. 31p. NY:
D. & J. Sadlier, 1873. 45p. NUC BL E
N
[Comic drama. Title reversed in NY
ed.]

973. FURNISS, Grace Livingston [Am.
1863?-1938]
A box of monkeys, a parlor farce in
two acts.
Boston: W.H. Baker & co., c1889. 31p.
NUC OCLC R
[Baker's edition of plays]

974. -----Captain of his soul; a
play.
L: n.p., n.d. NUC
[Drama]

975. -----Colonial girl. With Abby
Sage Richardson.
n.p.: n.p., 1898. NUC

976. -----The corner lot chorus, a
farce in one act.
Boston: W.H. Baker & co., 1891. 19p.
NUC OCLC R
[Baker's edition of plays]

977. -----The flying wedge. A
football farce in one act.
Boston: Baker & co., 1896. 15p. NUC
OCLC
[Baker's edition of plays]

978. -----The Jack trust.
NY: Harper, c1891. 63p. NUC OCLC R
[3 act play]

979. -----The Nyctalops or Nyctalopia
or a Nyctalops, or Myctalops. In
three acts.
NY: n.p., 1891. 83p. NUC

980. -----Robert of Sicily. Romantic
drama in four acts.
NY: n.p., 1900. NUC OCLC H
[Typescript. Suggested by Henry
Wadsworth Longfellow's ballad.]

981. -----Second floor, Spoopendyke,
a farce in two [one R] acts. Boston:
W.H. Baker & co., 1892. 27p. NUC R
[Baker's edition of plays]

982. -----Tulu [Tula].
NY & L: Harper & bros., 1891. 97p.
NUC OCLC R
[3-act comedy. Satire on Americans
being scorned in England.]

983. -----The veneered savage.
NY & L: Harper & bros., 1891. 33p.
NUC R
[1 act satire on Americans visiting
England & playing the "veneered
savages."]

G., C.F. see GORE, Catherine Grace
Frances (Moody)

G., C.H. see GILMAN, Caroline
(Howard)

G., H.A. see GLAZEBROOK, Harriet A.

984. GADDESS, Mary L., Mrs. [Am.
19/20c]
A dream of fair women and brave men.
Tableaux vivants for any number of
males and females.
NY: E.S. Werner, c1891. 16p. NUC

985. -----The Ivy Queen. A cantata
for any number of girls.
NY: Edgar S. Werner; Boston: W.H.
Baker, 1891. 14p. NUC OCLC
[Masque]

986. -----Revels of the queen of May
and her fairies; a cantata for forty-
five girls.
Boston: Walter H. Baker & co., 1891.
14p. NUC OCLC
[Baker's edition of plays. Masque, in
verse]

987. GAILEY, Florence Louise [Am.
19c]

Ez-Zahra; a tragedy of tenth century.
Detroit, MI: n.p., 1898. NUC
[4 pts. in 1 vol.]

988. GALE, Rachel E. (Baker) [Am.
19/20c] ALT: Baker, Rachel E.
After taps, a drama in three acts.
Completed from notes and unfinished
manuscript of the late George M.
Baker.
Boston: W.H. Baker & co., 1891. 45p.
NUC OCLC H
[Baker's edition of plays]

989. -----Bachelor hall; a comedy in
three acts. With Robert Melville
Baker.
Boston: W.H. Baker & co., 1898. 64p.
NUC OCLC H
[Baker's edition of plays]

990. -----The chaperon, a comedy in
three acts, for female characters
only.
Boston: W.H. Baker & co., 1891
[c1889]. 56p. NUC OCLC H
[Baker's edition of plays]

991. -----Her picture; a comedy in
one act.
Boston: W.H. Baker & co., 1894. 17p.
NUC H
[Baker's edition of plays]

992. -----A king's daughter; a comedy
in three acts, for female characters
only.
Boston: W.H. Baker & co., c1893. 59p.
NUC OCLC H
[Baker's edition of plays]

993. -----Mr. Bob, a comedy in 2
acts.
Boston: W.H. Baker & co., 1894, 1899.
39p. NUC OCLC H
[Baker's edition of plays]

994. GANTHONY, Nellie [Br. 19c]
In want of an engagement.
1891. N
[Musical sketch. Prod. Vaudeville,
1891. Also prod. as: In search of an
engagement, Terry's, 1892.]

995. -----Last on the programme.
1892. N
[Musical sketch. Prod. at Ealing,
1892.]

996. -----Outward bound.
1896. N
[Musical sketch. Prod. Terry's,
1896.]

997. GARDNER, (Cheney) [Br. 18c] ALT:
Cheney, Miss
The advertisement; or A bold stroke
for a husband.
1777. N
[Comedy. Prod. Haymarket, 1777.
Also prod. as: "The matrimonial
advertisement; or, A bold stroke for
a husband."]

998. -----The female dramatist.
1782. N
[Operatic farce. Prod. Haymarket.]

GARNETT, Catherine Grace see GODWIN,
Catherine Grace (Garnett)

999. GARNETT, Constance Clara (Black)
[Br. 1862-1948]
The convert.
1848. M N
[Trans. of R. Sergius Stepaniak.
Prod. Avenue, 1898.]

1000. GARRARD, Louise [Am. 19c]
An unexpected fare, a comedy in one
act. Dramatized from the story by
Maxwell Gray [Mary Gleed Tuttiett].
NY: H. Roorbach, c1894. 15p. NUC OCLC
[Roorbach's Am. ed. of acting plays,
no. 67]

1001. GARRAWAY, Agnes J. [Br. 19c]
The marble arch. With Edward Rose.
Chicago: Dramatic pub. co., n.d. 16p.
NUC BL OCLC E M
[Comedietta. Prod. Prince of Wales,
1882. Adapted from the German of
Gustav von Moser. Sergel's acting
drama, no. 482.]

GARRICK, David, co-author see COWLEY,
Hannah (Parkhouse)

1002. GARTHWAITE, Fanny [Br. 19c]
Leah; or, The Jewish wanderer.
1866. M
[Drama, 4 acts. Adapted from the
German of Salomon Mosenthal's
"Deborah." Prod. Sadler's Wells,
1866.]

1003. GASKELL, Mrs. Penn [Br. 19c]
Run in.
1899. N
[Comedietta. Prod. at Harlesden,
1899.]

1004. GATHERCOLE, Mrs. [Br. 19c]
Trick for trick.
1877. N
[Prod. at Dewsbury, 1877.]

1005. GAY, Mary M. [Am. 19c]

The letter H. A drama in a prologue and three acts. With Charles Felton Pidgin.
Boston: n.p., 1883. NUC

1006. GAYLORD, Orrie M. [Am. 19c]
Heavenly foundations.
In: Dramatic leaflets.
Philadelphia: Phineas Garrett, 1877.
1 vol. in 20 pts. NUC BL OCLC

1007. GAYNOR, Lucy [Am. 19c] PSEUD: Romyag, L.
"Mignon." A drama in five acts. By L. Romyag.
NY: H. Overmann, 1882. NUC

1008. GEISWEILER, Maria [Br. 19c]
Crime from ambition: a play ... translated from the German of Wilhelm Augustus Iffland.
1799. NUC BL B N
[Drama. L: G. Sidney for C. Geisweiler et. al., 1800 B.]

1009. -----Joanna of Montfaucon; a dramatic romance of the fourteenth century: as performed at the Theatre-Royal, Covent Garden. Formed upon the plan of the German drama of Kotzebue.
1799. NUC N
[Drama, 2d ed. L: Lackington, Allen & co., 1800. Adapted for stage by Richard Cumberland.]

1010. -----The noble lie; a drama ... being a continuation of Misanthropy and repentance, or The stranger.
L: C. Geisweiler, et al, 1799. 39p.
BL OCLC N
[Drama. Trans. of August Friedrich Ferdinand von Kotzebue.]

1011. -----Poverty and nobleness of mind: a play.
L: C. Geisweiler, et al, 1799. 126p.
BL OCLC B N
[Drama. Trans. of August Friedrich Ferdinand von Kotzebue.]

1012. GEORGIA, Nevella [Am. 19c]
Elissa. A tragedy, in five acts.
NY: J. Brown, 1877. 25p. NUC

GIBBON, Anne (Trelawney) see
TRELAWNEY, Anne

1013. GIBBS, Bertha V. [Am. 19c]
A planter's son.
1895. DLC
[Typescript]

GIBBS, Mrs. Alexander see GIBBS, P.
(Graddon)

1014. GIBBS, Julia De Witt [Am. 19c]
A false note. Comedy in one act.
Boston: W.H. Baker & co., 1888. 23p.
H
[Baker's ed. of plays]

1015. -----Under a spell. Comedy in one act, from the French.
Boston: Walter H. Baker & co., 1888. 24p. H OCLC
[From French of Eugene Marin Labiche & Antoine Francois Jolly]

1016. GIBBS, P. Graddon, Mrs. Alexander Gibbs [Br. 1804-1854]
Mrs. Alexander Gibbs' musical and pictorial entertainment of the Emerald Isle and the Lakes of Killarney.
NY: C.K. Christopher, 18--. 24p. NUC
[She performed in her entertainments in New York, in the 1850's.]

1017. GIBSON, C., Miss [Br. 19c]
The chamois hunter.
1852. N
[Ballet. Prod. Queens, 1852.]

GIFFARD, Areton, co-author see
HINGESTON-RANDOLPH, Mary

GIFFORD, Helen Selina (Sheridan)
Blackwood Hay, Countess of see
DUFFERIN and CLANDEBOYE, Helen Selina (Sheridan) Blackwood, Baroness

GILBERT, W.S., co-author see EDWARDS, Annie

1018. GILBERT-GILMER, Julia [Br. 19c]
Life's parting ways.
1893. J
[Drama. Prod. at Parkhurst, 1893; at Hackney, 1894.]

GILLETTE, William H., co-author see
BURNETT, Frances Eliza (Hodgson)

GILLINGTON, May Clarissa see BYRON, May Clarissa (Gillington)

1019. GILMAN, Caroline (Howard), Mrs. Samuel Gilman [Am. 1794-1888] ALT: G., C. H.
Tales and ballads.
Boston: Wm. Crosby; NY: n.p., 1834. 190p. Boston: J. Munroe & co., 1839. 190p. NUC BL OCLC H
[Incl. "Isadore," a dramatic poem, pp. 90-94]

GILMAN, Mrs. Samuel see GILMAN, Caroline (Howard)

1020. GIRAUD, Mrs. [Br. 19c]
Dear Jack.
1892. N
[Dramatic sketch. Amateur prod. at
Colchester, 1892.]

1021. GLAZEBROOK, Harriet A. [Br.
19c] ALT: G., H. A.
The Brooklet reciter for temperance
societies.
L: National Temperance pub. depot,
1883. 176p. BL
[In verse, original & selected.]

1022. -----Justice's justice: a
dramatic dialogue. Founded upon the
three act comedy of [Theodore]
Barrière and [Lambert] Thiboust.
L: John Kempster & co., 1873. 8p. BL
[For home acting. In verse.]

1023. -----Readings and recitations,
chiefly upon temperance. Written and
selected by H.A.G.
L: Kempster's home library, 1874. BL
[In verse, original & selected.]

1024. -----Readings in rhyme from the
drama of drink.
L: Marshall bros., 1876. BL

GLEIG, G.R., co-author see CAMPBELL,
Hariette

1025. GLEN, Ida [Br. 19c]
A woman's error; or, The stolen
diamonds.
1876. N
[Melodrama. Prod. at Snrewsbury,
1876.]

GLENN, GRACE, pseud. see BATEMAN,
L.M. Beal, Mrs.

1026. GODDARD, Mrs. Edward [Am. 19c]
By force of love; or, Wedded and
parted, a domestic drama, in five
acts.
Clyde, OH: Ames' pub. co., 1895. 25p.
NUC OCLC T
[Prod. in Utah, 1891. OCLC attr. to
her husband. Ames' Series of
Standard & Minor Drama.]

1027. GODDARD, Kate [Br. 19c]
Mistaken identity.
L & NY: Samuel French, n.d. [1915?
NUC] [19-? OCLC]. 8p. NUC OCLC E
[Lacy's Acting Ed., No. 387; French's
Minor Drama, v. 149, no. 3.]

1028. -----Who won? A curtain
raiser.

NY & L: S. French, 18-- [1903 BL].
11p. NUC BL [French's acting edition,
2228.]

1029. GODWIN, Catherine Grace
(Garnett) [Br. 1798-1845] ALT:
Garnett, Catherine Grace
The night before the bridal, a
Spanish tale. Sappho, a dramatic
sketch, and other poems.
L: Longman, Hurst, Rees, Orme, Brown
& Green, 1824. 220p. NUC BL
[Sappho, dramatic poem in 10 scenes.
A revised version in her: The
poetical works ... Ed. A. Cleveland
Wigan. L: Chapman & Hall, 1854. 576p.
NUC BL OCLC]

1030. GOLDSCHMIDT, Anna [Br. 19c]
On strike. Music by Julia
Goldschmidt.
1894. N
[Operetta. Amateur prod. at
Nottingham, 1894.]

1031. GOLDSMITH, Mary [Br. 19c]
Angelina.
1804. N
[Comic opera. Prod. in the
provinces, 1804.]

1032. -----She lives! or, The
generous brother.
1800. NUC B N
[Comedy. Prod. Haymarket, 1803.
Larpent Ms. #1284.]

1033. GOODFELLOW, E. J. H., Mrs. [Am.
19/20c]
Vice versa; a comedy in three acts.
Philadelphia: Penn pub. co., 1899.
103p. NUC OCLC
[Dramatic library; v. 1, no. 122.
Keystone ed. of popular plays.]

1034. -----Young Dr. Devine; a
comedietta in two scenes.
Philadelphia: Penn, c1896. 12p. NUC
[2 acts, for 9 young ladies]

1035. GOODLOE, Abbie Carter [Am. b.
1867]
Antinous: a tragedy.
Philadelphia: J.B. Lippincott, 1891.
139p. NUC OCLC

1036. GOODRICH, F. M., Mrs. [Am. 19c]
Father Time's reception. A new
entertainment for the holidays.
Paola, KS: Western spirit-print,
1889. 18p. NUC

GORDON, Medora see BYRON, Medora
Gordon

GORE, C.G.F. see GORE, Catherine Grace Frances (Moody)

1037. GORE, Catherine Grace Frances (Moody), Mrs. Charles Gore [Br. 1799-1861] ALT: G., C. F.; Gore, C. G. F.; Moody, Catherine Grace Frances
The bond, a dramatic poem in the form of a play. By Mrs. Charles Gore.
L: John Murray, 1824. 100p. NUC BL OCLC E N
[3 acts]

1038. -----Dacre of the South; or, the olden time.
L: Richard Bentley, 1840. 95p. NUC BL OCLC E N
[Melodrama, 5 acts, verse]

1039. -----Don John of Austria.
1836. N
[Drama. Prod. Covent Garden, 1836. An adaptation of Jean Francois Casimir Delavigne, "Don Juan d'Autriche."]

1040. -----A good night's rest; or, Two in the morning: a farce, in one act.
L: J. Duncombe & co., 1839. 17p. NY & L: Samuel French, 1839? 12p. NUC BL OCLC E M N
[Prod. Strand, 1839 & Olympic, 1839. Duncombe's Acting Ed. of British Theatre, no. 307]

1041. -----King O'Neil; or, the Irish brigade, a comedy in two acts.
L: Chapman & Hall, 1835. 37p. NUC BL OCLC E M N
[Comedy. Prod. Covent Garden, 1839; St. James, 1867. R. Webster, The Acting National drama, v. 7; Dick's Standard Plays.]

1042. -----The king's seal. With James Kenney.
L: John Miller, 1835. 36p. E N
[Comedy. Prod. Drury Lane, 1835.]

1043. -----Lords and Commons.
1831. N
[Comedy. Prod. Drury Lane, 1831.]

1044. -----The maid of Croissey; or, Theresa's vow. A drama in two acts.
L: Chapman & Hall, 1835. 28p. NUC BL OCLC E M N
[Drama. Prod. Haymarket, 1835, 1837. Also known as: "The maid of Croissey; or, The return from Russia." R. Webster, The Acting National drama, v. 6]

1045. -----Modern honour; or, The sharper of high life.
1834. N
[comedy]

1046. -----The Queen's Champion.
L: J. Dicks, 18--. 16p. BL OCLC M N
[Melodrama, 2 acts. Prod. Haymarket, 1834, 1837. Trans. from Augustin Scribe. Dick's standard plays, no. 744.]

1047. -----Quid pro quo; or, The day of dupes. By C.G.F.
L: National acting drama office, 1844. 82p. NUC BL E N
[Comedy. Prod. Haymaket, 1844.]

1048. -----The school for coquettes.
1831. N
[Comedy. Prod. Haymarket, 1831.]

1049. -----A tale of a tub.
1837. M N
[Drama, 2 acts. Prod. Haymarket, 1837.]

GORE, Mrs. Charles see GORE, Catherine Grace Frances (Moody)

1050. GORTON, M. J., Mrs. [Am. 19c]
The drama of the cycle and other poems.
Boston: Joseph George Cupples, 1891. 117p. NUC OCLC
[Dramatic poem meant for reading, not acting]

1051. GOULD, Elizabeth Lincoln [Am. d. 1914]
The "little men." Two acts.
Philadelphia: Curtis pub. co., 1900. 103p. NUC OCLC H
[Adapt. from Louisa May Alcott's novel]

1052. -----The "little women." Play. Two acts.
Philadelphia: Curtis pub. co.; Boston: Little, Brown, c1900. 101p. NUC BL OCLC
[Adapted from Louisa May Alcott.]

GOWING, Mrs. Aylmer see GOWING, Emilia Julia (Blake) Aylmer

1053. GOWING, Emilia Julia (Blake) Aylmer, Mrs. William Aylmer Gowing [Br. 19/20c] ALT: Blake, Emilia; Gowing, Mrs. Aylmer
Boadicea. A play in four acts. Poems for recitation. By Mrs. Aylmer Gowing.
L: Kegan Paul, Trench, Trubner, 1899. 118p. BL OCLC E

[Boadicea is an historical tragedy in verse; others are narrative poems & sonnets]

1054. -----A crown for love. A play in five acts. By Emilia Blake.
L: E. Faithfull, 1875. 63p. NUC

1055. -----Nelson. A play in four acts and a tableau.
L: Chapman & Hall, 1878. 94p. NUC BL
[In verse]

GOWING, Mrs. William Aylmer see GOWING, Emilia Julia (Blake) Aylmer

1056. GRAHAM, Mary [Am. 19c]
Mademoiselle's Christmas gifts.
In: A dream of the centuries and other entertainments for parlor and hall. Comp. George B. Bartlett.
Boston: W.H. Baker, 1889. 23 1. NUC OCLC H
[Baker's novelties.]

GRAND, SARAH, pseud. see MCFALL, Frances Elizabeth (Clarke)

1057. GRATIENNE, Mlle. [19c]
Only an actress. 1898. N
[Prod. at Bournemouth, 1898.]

1058. GRAVES, Adelia Cleopatra (Spencer) [Am. 1821-1895]
Jephtha's daughter. A drama in five acts.
Memphis, TN: South-western pub. house, 1867. 144p. NUC OCLC R

1059. GRAVES, Clotilda Inez Mary [Br. 1863-1932] PSEUD: Dehan, Richard
Death and Rachel; a dramatic duologue.
n.p.: n.p., 18--? 8p. NUC E

1060. -----Dr. and Mrs. Neill.
1894. M N
[Play, 3 acts. Prod. Grand, 1895. Also prod. as: "The physicians," Lyceum, 1893.]

1061. -----A Florentine wooing.
1878. M N
[Comedy, 4 acts. Prod. Avenue, 1898. Also entered with Lord Chamberlain as: "The wooing"]

1062. -----A matchmaker. With Gertrude Kingston [Gertrude Angela Mary Konstam].
1896. M N
[Comedy, 4 acts. Prod. Shaftsbury, 1896.]

1063. -----A mother of three. By Richard Dehan.
L: S. French, 1909. 68p. NUC BL OCLC M N
[Farce, 3 acts. Prod. Comedy, 1896. French's acting edition of plays. v. 157]

1064. -----Nitocris.
1887. N
[Poetic drama. Prod. Drury Lane, 1887.]

1065. -----Nurse.
1890. M
[Farce, 2 acts. Prod. Vaudeville, 1890.]

1066. -----Princess Tarakanoff; or, The northern night.
1877. M N
[Drama, 5 acts. Prod. Prince of Wales, 1897.]

1067. -----Rachel.
1890. N
[Dramatic sketch. Prod. Haymarket, 1890.]

1068. -----She. With Edward Rose and W. Sidney.
1888. N
[Drama. Prod. Gaiety, 1888.]

1069. -----The skeleton. With Yorke Stephens.
1887. N [Farce. Prod. Vaudeville, 1887.]

1070. GRAY, Louisa [Br. 19c]
Between two stools.
1886. N
[Comic operetta. Prod. in Kensington, 1886.]

1071. -----Tricks and honours.
1897. N
[Operetta. Prod. Albert Hall, 1897.]

1072. GRAY, Mary C. [Am. 19c]
A Browning courtship. By Octave Thanet [Alice French]. Dramatized by Mary C. Gray.
Watkins, NY: n.p., 1889. 20p. NUC

1073. GREELY, M. A. [Am. 19c]
The chronothanatoletron; or, Old times made new; an entertainment for female characters only, written for the class-day exercises at Dana Hall School, Wellesley, MA, by two members of the class of '87 [M.A. Greely and M.M. Taylor].
Boston: Walter H. Baker co., c1889. 23p. NUC OCLC

[Baker's edition of plays]

GREEN, Anna Katharine see ROHLFS,
Anna Katharine (Green)

GREEN, John, co-author see HOWARD,
Mrs.

1074. GREEN, Katherine [Br. 19c]
What's in a name?
1895. N
[Duologue. Prod. Queen's Hall,
1895.]

1075. GREENE, Louisa Lilias
(Plunket), Baroness [Br. b. 1833]
ALT: Greene, Hon. Mrs. Richard Jonas
Drawing room dramas. With William
Gorman Wills.
Edinburgh & L: Wm. Blackwood & sons,
1873. 39p. BL OCLC E

1076. -----Nettle Coats; or, The
silent princess.
In: Drawing room dramas.

1077. -----Prince Croesus in search
of a wife.
In: Drawing room dramas.

GREENE, Hon. Mrs. Richard Jonas see
GREENE, Louisa Lilias Plunket,
Baroness

1078. GREER, Maria, Mrs. S. Greer
[Br. 19c] PSEUD: Greye, Armar
Kimbolton Castle; or, The last days
of Catherine of Arragon, and Lady
Jane Grey. Two dramatic sketches.
By Armar Greye.
L: Stevens & Richardson, pr., 1871.
100p. NUC BL

1079. GREER, Mary Autry [Am. 19c]
Pictures from the old time South; a
drama. Beaumont, TX: Press of the
Greer print, n.d. 52p. NUC

1080. -----Reconstruction in the
South (a tragedy founded on fact).
n.p.: n.p., 1876? 53p. NUC
[At head of title: Origin of the Ku
Klux Klan.]

GREER, Mrs. S. see GREER, Maria

1081. GREET, Dora Victoire, Mrs.
William Greet [Br. 19c] ALT: Greet,
Mrs. W.
Elsie's rival. A sketch in one act.
L: S. French; Lacy, 1893. 11p. L &
NY: S. French, 1888? 11p. NUC BL OCLC
E M N
[Comedietta. Prod. Strand, 1888.
French's acting edition. no. 1970]

1082. -----A flying visit. By Mrs.
W. Greet.
1889. M N
[Comedietta. Prod. Criterion, 1889,
& Princess', 1894.]

1083. -----A folded page.
1891. N
[Monologue. Prod. Steinway Hall,
1891.]

1084. -----Jackson's boy.
1891. N
[Melodrama. Prod. at Carlisle,
1891.]

1085. -----The little squire. With
Horace Sedger.
1894. N
[Comedy. Prod. Lyric, 1894.]

1086. -----A real prince.
1894. N
[Comic drama. Prod. Bijou, 1894.]

1087. -----Thrown together. A
sketch.
L & NY: S. French; Lacy, 1893. 9p.
NUC BL OCLC E N
[Comedietta, 1 act. Lacy's, French's
acting edition. no. 1972]

1088. -----To the rescue.
1889. M N
[Comedietta. Prod. Prince of Wales,
1889.]

GREET, Mrs. W. see GREET, Dora
Victoire, Mrs.

GREET, Mrs. William see GREET, Dora
Victoire, Mrs.

1089. GREGORY, H. S., Miss [Br. 19c]
Fate.
1874. N
[Drama. Prod. at Middlesborough,
1874.]

1090. GREVILLE, Beatrice Violet
(Graham), Baroness Greville [Br.
1842-1932] ALT: Greville, Violet;
Greville, Lady Violet
An aristocratic alliance.
1894. M N
[Comedy, 3 acts. Prod. Criterion,
1894. Adapted from French of Emile
Augier & Jules Sandeau, "Le Gendre de
M. Poirier."]

1091. -----Baby; or, a warning to
mesmerists.
1890. N
[Comic drama. Prod. in Brighton,
1890; at Terry's 1891.]

1092. -----Nadia.
1892. M N
[Drama, 4 acts. Prod. Lyric, 1892.
From French of Henry Greville [Alice
(Fleury) Durand].]

1093. -----Old friends; an original
one act comedy.
L: Lacy, 1893; NY: S. French, 1890.
22p. NUC BL OCLC E N
[Comedy. Prod. St. James, 1890.
Lacy's Acting Ed., no. 1975.]

GREVILLE, Lady Violet see GREVILLE,
Beatrice Violet (Graham), Baroness
Greville

GREVILLE, Violet see GREVILLE,
Beatrice Violet (Graham), Baroness
Greville

GREYE, ARMAR, pseud. see GREER, Maria

GRIFFITH, Eliza see GRIFFITH,
Elizabeth (Griffith)

1094. GRIFFITH, Elizabeth (Griffith),
Mrs. Richard Griffith [Br. 1720?-
1793] ALT: Elizabeth; Griffith, Eliza
PSEUD: Lady, A
Amana. A dramatic poem. By a lady.
L: Pr. by T. Harrison for W.
Johnston, 1764. 54p. NUC BL OCLC B N
[Tragedy, 5 acts. Longe, v. 186, no.
3.]

1095. -----The barber of Seville; or,
The useless precaution; a comedy in
four acts.
L: Pr. for the author, 1776. 70p. NUC
BL OCLC B N
[Comedy; trans. & adapt. of Pierre
Augustin Caron de Beaumarchais.
Longe, v. 318, no. 7]

1096. -----The double mistake: a
comedy.
L: J. Almon, T. Lowndes, S. Bladen &
J. Williams, 1766. 78p. NUC BL OCLC B
N
[5 acts. Prod. Covent Garden, 1766.
Pub. anon. Longe, v. 12, no. 1]

1097. -----The platonic wife, a
comedy. By a lady.
Dublin: P. Wilson, 1765; 74p. L: W.
Johnston, 1765. 97p. NUC OCLC B N
[Prod. Drury Lane, 1765. Based on
"L'heureux divorce" by Jean Francois
Marmontel. Longe, v. 25, no. 1]

1098. -----The school for rakes: a
comedy. Based on [Pierre Augustin
Caron de] Beaumarchais' "Eugenie".

L: T. Becket & P.A. DeHondt, 1769.
92p. Dublin: W. & W. Smith, 1769.
76p. NUC BL OCLC B N
[Comedy. Prod. Drury Lane, 1769.
Longe, v. 45, no. 1]

1099. -----The times, a comedy.
L: Fielding & Walker, 1779. 80p. NUC
BL OCLC B N
[Adaptation of Carlo Goldoni's "Le
bourru bien faisant." Prod. Drury
Lane, 1779. Longe, v. 99, no. 1]

1100. -----A wife in the right.
L: Pr. for the author, sold by E. &
C. Dilly, etc., 1772. 89p. NUC BL
OCLC B N
[Comedy. Prod. Covent Garden, 1772.
Also known as: "Patience, the best
remedy; or, A wife in the right."
Larpent Ms. #332. Longe, v. 25, no.
3]

1101. GRIFFITH, Helen Sherman [Am. b.
1873]
Borrowed luncheon, a farce.
Chicago: Denison, 1899. 16p. NUC
[T.P. lists: "The lady from
Philadelphia." Denison's acting
plays, amateur series]

1102. -----The burglar alarm. A
comedietta, in one act.
Philadelphia: Penn pub. co., 1899.
17p. NUC
[Dramatic Library, v. 1, no. 180.]

1103. -----A fallen idol; farce in
one act.
Philadelphia: Penn pub. co., 1900.
16p. NUC OCLC T

GRIFFITH, Mrs. Richard see GRIFFITH,
Elizabeth (Griffith)

GRIFFITHS, Cherry see GRIFFITHS, J.
Cherry

1104. GRIFFITHS, J. Cherry [Br. 19c]
ALT: Griffiths, Cherry
All for gold.
1878. M
[Drama, 3 acts. Prod. Britannia,
1878.]

1105. GROENEVELT, Sara B. [Am. 19c]
Otille the octaroone. Tragedy in
five acts.
n.p.: n.p., 1893. 59, 15 l. NUC OCLC
[Typescript]

1106. GROVE, Florence Craufurd [Br.
d. 1902]
Forget-me-not. With Herman Charles
Merivale.

L & NY: S. French, 1879? 45p. NUC
OCLC E
[Prod. NY, 1880. French's acting ed.
v. 1755. Adams also cites: "As in a
Looking-glass," adaptation with E.
Hamilton, 1887; "La Tosca," 1889; and
"The Bigot," 1890.]

1107. GUERNSEY, Alice Margaret [Am.
b. 1850]
1492. 1776. Five centuries: a
centennial drama, in five acts.
Boston: The New-England pub. co.,
1876. 41p. NUC OCLC

GUGGENBERGER, Louisa Sarah
(Bevington) see BEVINGTON, Louisa
Sarah

1108. GUION, Nettie Cortelyon [Br.
19c]
A modern Judas.
1892. M N
[Drama, 4 acts. Prod. Vaudeville,
1892.]

GUNNING, Elizabeth see PLUNKETT,
Elizabeth (Gunning)

1109. GUTHRIE, Mrs. [Am. 19c]
If I were a king. A drama in four
acts.
Notre Dame, IN: Joseph A. Lyons, UP,
1882. NUC
[NUC attr. Augustus Lemonnier.
Intro. indicates she is the author.
In verse.]

H., Eleanor see H_____, Eleanor (see
1347)

H., F.L. see HENDERSON, Florence
Leslie, Miss

H., L. see HOOPER, Lucy, Mrs.

H., L.J. see HALL, Louisa Jane (Park)

H., M.X. see HAYES, Maria Ximena

H., S.J. see HALE, Sarah Josepha
(Buell)

1110. HALE, Mrs. Challow [Br. 19c]
For the king's sake.
1897. N
[Drama. Prod. at Kingston, 1897/98.]

HALE, Mrs. David see HALE, Sarah
Josepha (Buell)

1111. HALE, Sarah Josepha (Buell),
Mrs. David Hale [Am. 1788-1879] ALT:
Buell, Sarah Josepha; H., S. J.
Ormond Grosvenor. A tragedy.
Boston: 1838. NUC
[A detached copy from The lady's
book.]

HALFORD, J., co-author see BINNS,
Gertrude

HALL, Anna Maria (Fielding) see
HALLETT, Mrs.

1112. HALL, Anna Maria (Fielding),
Mrs. Samuel Carter Hall [Br. 1800-
1881] ALT: Fielding, Anna Maria
Chester fair.
1844. N
[Drama. Prod. Queen's, 1844.]

1113. -----The French refugee.
L: John Macrone, 1837. 27p. E M N
[Comedy, 2 acts. Prod. St. James,
1837. Also known as: "St. Pierre,
the refugee."]

1114. -----The groves of Blarney. A
drama in three acts.
L: Chapman & Hall, 1836? 44p. NUC BL
E M N
[Drama. Prod. Adelphi, 1838.
Webster's acting national drama, no.
42]

1115. -----Mabel's curse. A musical
drama in two acts.
L: Lacy; Duncombe, 1837. 24p. NUC BL
OCLC E M N
[Pord. St. James, 1837. Duncombe's
ed. of the British Theatre, v. 28 &
Dicks']

1116. HALL, Caroline, Mrs. [Br. 19c]
The will and the way.
1853. N
[Drama. Prod. City of London
Theatre, 1853.]

HALL, Mrs. Edward B. see HALL, Louisa
Jane (Park)

1117. HALL, Louisa Jane (Park), Mrs.
Edward B. Hall [Am. 1802-1892] ALT:
H., L. J.; P., L. J., Miss; Park,
Louisa Jane
Hannah, the mother of Samuel the
prophet and judge of Israel. A
sacred drama.
Boston: J. Munroe & co., 1839. NUC
OCLC
[Dramatic poem, 5 acts]

1118. -----Miriam, a dramatic poem.

Boston: Hilliard, Gray & co., 1837.
124p. NUC BL R
[3 scenes, tragedy about early
Christians in Rome.]

HALL, Mrs. Samuel Carter see HALL,
Anna Maria (Fielding)

1119. HALLETT, Mrs. [Br. 19c]
Juniper Jack; or, My aunt's hobby. A
farce.
L: n.p., 1847. NUC BL E N
[N lists as a burletta, prod. Queen's
Theatre, 1845, under Anna Maria
(Fielding) Hall, but also lists this
work in vol. IV, Supplement.]

1120. -----Nobodies' at home;
somebodies' abroad. A farce in two
acts.
L: W.S. Johnson, 1847. 27p. NUC BL

1121. -----Woman's whims, or Who's to
win her? A comedietta in two acts.
L: T. Richardson, 1838. 48p. NUC BL

1122. HAMILTON, Catherine Jane [Br.
b. 1841]
Short plays for drawing-room
performances.
L: Ward Lock & co., 1890. 308p. BL
[Plays by various authors: F.C.
Broughton; R. Andre; Sir G. Campbell,
Bart.; F.C. Burnand, J. Tillotson &
C.J. Hamilton.]

1123. -----The four-leaved shamrock,
a comedy in three acts.
Chicago: Dramatic pub. co., n.d. 26p.
NUC BL OCLC
[Drawing room comedy, 3 acts, may be
acted as charade, "stoppage."
Sergel's acting drama, v. 552. Also
in Short plays.]

1124. -----Mr. Bootle's predicament.
In: Short plays ... .
[Drawing room comedy, 3 acts; may be
acted as a charade, "baggage."]

1125. -----To be let furnished. A
drawing-room comedy in three acts.
In: Short plays ... .
[Drawing-room comedy, 3 acts; may be
acted as a charade, "billet."]

HAMILTON, Henry, co-author see
BERINGER, Aimèe Danielle

1126. HAMILTON, Sarah [Br. 19c]
Alfred the Great, a drama, in five
acts.
L: Longman, Rees, Orme..., 1829. 71p.
NUC OCLC

1127. -----The liberation of Joseph,
a sacred dramatic poem, in two parts;
The beauties of vegetation, with
digressive sketches of Norwich, etc.
in four cantos; and other poems.
L: Pr. for J. Mawman, 1827. 178p. BL
OCLC
[Joseph, pp. 1-146]

HAMMOND, S.T., comp. see MCCONAUGHY,
Julia E. (Loomis)

HANKIN, St. John E.C., co-author see
VYNNE, Nora

1128. HARDWICKE, Elizabeth (Lindsay)
Yorke, Countess of [Br. 1763-1858]
ALT: Lindsay, Lady Elizabeth; Yorke,
Elizabeth Lindsay
The court of Oberon, or, The three
wishes. A drama.
L: W. Nichol, pr., 1831. 55p. L: T.H.
Lacy, n.d. 30p. NUC BL E N
[3 acts, verse & prose. Earlier
priv. ed. 1800. Written for her
children, but acted by adults in
private theatre at Wimpole Hall.
Inglis. Lacy's Acting Ed.]

HARKNESS, Mrs. A. Lawson see
HARKNESS, M. Lawson

1129. HARKNESS, M. Lawson, Mrs. A.
Lawson Harkness [Br. 19c]
Breeze! An episode. Manchester: A.
Heywood & sons, n.d. 14p. NUC
[Heywood & sons' original dramas, no.
265]

1130. -----A disciple of Plato: a
duologue.
Manchester: Abel Haywood, 19--? 16p.
OCLC

1131. -----Larks for an hour; or,
Humour in a registry office. A
comedy in one act. By Mrs. A. Lawson
Harkness.
Manchester: A. Heywood & sons, n.d.
18p. NUC

HARLEY, ST. JOHN, pseud. see POLLOCK,
Ellen

1132. HARLOW, Elizabeth [Br. 18c]
The English tavern at Berlin. A
comedy in three acts.
L: Elizabeth Harlow, 1789. 48p. NUC
BL OCLC B
[About Frederick II, King of Prussia,
1712-86]

HARRIES, Margaret see WILSON,
Margaret (Harries) Baron

HARRISON, Mrs. Burton N. see
HARRISON, Constance (Cary)

1133. HARRISON, Constance (Cary),
Mrs. Burton N. Harrison [Am. 19c]
Short comedies for amateur players.
As given at the Madison Square and
Lyceum Theatres, New York by
amateurs. Adapted and arranged by
Mrs. Burton Harrison.
NY: DeWitt pub. house, 1889. 116p.
NUC BL OCLC R
[From French plays]

1134. -----Behind a curtain; a
monologue in one act. By Mrs. Burton
Harrison.
Chicago: Dramatic pub. co., 1892. 6p.
NY: DeWitt pub. house, 1892. 6p. NUC
BL OCLC
[Also in: Short comedies. Perf. by
Mrs. Charles Denison at Madison
Square Theater. DeWitt's acting
plays, no. 374]

1135. -----The mouse-trap. A
comedietta, in one act.
NY: DeWitt pub. house, 1892. 14p. NUC
OCLC
[DeWitt's acting plays, no. 372.
Also in: Short comedies.]

1136. -----A Russian honeymoon.
Comedy in three acts. Adapted by
Mrs. Burton Harrison from French of
[Augustin] Eugene Scribe.
NY: DeWitt pub. house, 1890. NUC OCLC
[NUC & OCLC list under Scribe.
Critic of its first presentation at
the Madison Square Theatre credited
it to her.]

1137. -----Tea at four o'clock. A
drawing room comedy, in one act.
Chicago: Dramatic pub. co.; NY:
DeWitt pub. house, 1892. 29p. NUC
OCLC
[Sergel's acting drama, no. 375;
DeWitt's acting plays. First pub.
in: Short comedies.]

1138. -----Two strings to her bow. A
comedy in two acts. NY: DeWitt pub.
house; Chicago: Dramatic pub. co.,
1892. 36p. NUC OCLC
[DeWitt's acting plays, no. 376.
Sergel's acting drama; no. 376. Also
in: Short comedies. From the
French.]

1139. -----Weeping wives. A
comedietta in one act. From the
French of Paul Siraudin and Lambert
Thiboust.

NY: DeWitt, 1892. 31p. NUC
[NUC lists under Siraudin. Also in:
Short comedies.]

1140. HARRISON, Elizabeth [Br. 18c]
Miscellanies on moral and religious
subjects, in prose and verse. L: Pr.
for the author, 1756. 380p. NUC BL
OCLC N
[Incl.: The death of Socrates.
Tragedy, 1 act. Adaptation of
Plato's Crito.]

1141. HARRISON, Eva [Br. 19c]
Chaperoned.
1887. N
[Comedietta. Prod. Cheltenham,
1887.]

1142. HARRISON, Mary St. Leger
(Kingsley) [Br. 1852-1931] ALT:
Kingsley, Mary St. Leger PSEUD:
Malet, Lucas
"Forget-me-not." A true story of a
hat.
n.p.: n.p., 1899. 8p. BL
[Monologue Series, No. 3]

1143. -----Joan of Arc's missing
mother.
n.p.: n.p., 1890. 8p. BL
[Monologue Series, No. 10]

HART, Mrs. E.A. see HART, Fanny
(Wheeler)

1144. HART, Fanny (Wheeler), Mrs.
E.A. Hart [Br. 1822-1890?] PSEUD:
Clergyman's Wife, A
Charade: Armhole. By A Clergyman's
Wife.
L: n.p., 1868. 24p. BL

1145. -----Three epochs in the life
of a woman: being the record of three
Christmas days. By a Clergyman's
wife. Dramatized.
Manchester; L: John Heywood, 1881.
16p. BL

1146. HARVEY, Abbie M. [Am. 19c]
The discovery of America.
Boston: New England pub. co., 1892.
28p. NUC
[Patriotic masque; incl. songs]

1147. HARVEY, Margaret [Br. 19c]
Raymond de Percy; or, The tenant of
the tomb. A romantic melodrama.
Bishopswearmouth: G. Garbutt, pr.,
1822. 47p. BL E N
[3 acts, chiefly in verse. Prod. in
Sunderland, 1822.]

1148. HARWOOD, Isabella [Br. 1840?-
1888] PSEUD: Neil, Ross Plays. The
Cid; The King and the Angel; Duke for
a day; or, The tailor of Brussels.
L: Ellis & White, 1874. 307p. NUC BL
OCLC N

1149. -----Andrea the painter;
Claudia's choice; Orestes; Pandora;
plays by Ross Neil.
L: Ellis & White, 1883. 322p. NUC BL
OCLC E N
[Andrea is a tragedy, 4 acts, verse]

1150. -----Arabella Stuart; The heir
of Lynne; Tasso; plays by Ross Neil.
L: Ellis & White, 1879. 307p. NUC BL
OCLC E N
[Arabella Stuart is an historical
tragedy, 5 acts, verse]

1151. -----The Cid.
In: Plays.
[5 acts, verse. Preface notes: "the
present writer has worked
independently of either French or
Spanish predecessors."]

1152. -----Claudia's choice.
In: Andrea the painter, etc.
[Comedy, set in 17th c. 3 acts,
verse]

1153. -----Duke for a day; or, The
tailor of Brussels.
In: Plays.
[Comedy, 3 acts, verse. Based on
Eastern legend perhaps also the
source for Taming of the Shrew.]

1154. -----Eglantine.
L: Ellis & White, pr., n.d. 97p. E

1155. -----Elfinella; or, Home from
fairyland. Lord and Lady Russell.
By Ross Neil.
L: Ellis & White, 1876. 260p. NUC BL
E M N
[Elfinella is a comedy, 4 acts,
verse. Prod. at Edinburgh, 1875;
Princess' Theatre, 1878]

1156. -----The heir of Lynne.
In: Arabella Stuart, etc.
[Historical romance, 5 acts, verse,
based on an ancient ballad.]

1157. -----Inez; or, The bride of
Portugal.
In: Lady Jane Grey, etc.
[Tragedy, 5 acts, verse. The stage
version, in 4 acts, "Loyalty Love,"
prod. Gaiety, 1887. M N]

1158. -----The King and the Angel.
L: Pr. for priv. circ. by Ellis &
White, 1874. BL OCLC E N
[Drama, 5 acts, verse. Based on
Leigh Hunt's version of legend of
angel who takes the place of a king
in order to reform him. Also in:
Plays.]

1159. -----Lady Jane Grey. Inez; or,
The bride of Portugal.
L: Ellis & Green, 1871. 137p. NUC BL
E N [Tragedy, 5 acts, verse]

1160. -----Lord and Lady Russell.
In: Elfinella, etc.
[Historical drama, 5 acts, verse]

1161. -----Orestes.
In: Andrea the painter, etc.
[2 acts, verse. Based on the
classical myth.]

1162. -----Pandora.
In: Andrea the painter, etc.
[3 acts, verse. Based on the
classical myth]

1163. -----Paul and Virginia.
1881. N
[Comic drama. Also prod. at
Edinburgh, 1881, as: "The lovers of
Palma." Prod. at Dublin, 1881.]

1164. -----Tasso.
In: Arabella Stuart, etc.
[Tragedy, 5 acts, verse. Based on
the poet's life.]

1165. HASTINGS, Lady Flora [Br. 1806-
1839]
Poems by Lady Flora Hastings. Ed. her
sister, [Lady Sophia Hastings, aft.
Marchioness of Bute].
Edinburgh & L: n.p., 1841. 282p. NUC
BL OCLC Inglis
[Incl. fragments of a tragedy,
"Fiesco," scenes from another
tragedy, "Joanna of Naples," begun
1832, and in appendix, scenes from a
tragedy, "Eurycide," written 1819-
20.]

HASTINGS, Lady Sophia, ed. see
HASTINGS, Lady Flora

HATCHETT, William, co-author see
HAYWOOD, Eliza (Fowler)

HATFIELD, Sibella Elizabeth see
MILES, Sibella Elizabeth (Hatfield)

1166. HATTON, Ann Julia (Kemble),
Mrs. Curtis Hatton [Br. 1764-1838]
ALT: Kemble, Ann Julia

The songs of Tammany; or, the Indian chief. A serious opera.
NY: Pr. John Harrison, 1794. 16p. NUC BL
[Written when author visited America. Reduced to 2 acts in 1795, & called "America Discovered; or, Tammany, the Indian chief." Perf. several times in NY, Boston & Philadelphia. WNB mentions another play, "Zaffine."]

1167. HATTON, Bessie [Br. 19c]
The village of youth and other fairy tales.
L: Hutchinson & co.; NY: Stokes, 1895. 163p. NUC BL OCLC N
[Title work is an adaptation of the tale produced by amateur players on the rectory grounds, Radstock.]

HATTON, Mrs. Curtis see HATTON, Ann Julia (Kemble)

1168. HAUGHWOUT, L. May [Am. 19c]
Gossip pantomime.
NY: E.S. Werner, 1890. 14p. NUC

1169. -----Japanese fantastics; illustrated pantomime and drill with musical accompaniment. With Stanley Schell.
NY: E.S. Werner, c1890. 10p. NUC OCLC

1170. -----The princess, by Alfred, Lord Tennyson. Dramatized by L. May Haughwout.
NY: E.S. Werner, 1891. 39p. NUC OCLC

1171. HAWKINS, P. L., Mrs. [Br. 19c]
Ciceley's secret.
1895. N
[Comic drama. Prod. Bijou, 1895.]

1172. HAWTHORN, May [Br. 19c]
Day dreams.
1888. N
[Dramatic sketch. Prod. in Camden Town, 1888.]

HAWTREY, George P., co-author see BERINGER, Aimee Danielle

HAY, Helen Selina (Sheridan) Blackwood, Countess of Gifford see DUFFERIN and CLANDEBOYE, Helen Selina (Sheridan) Blackwood, Baroness

1173. HAYES, Maria Ximena [Br. 19c]
ALT: H., M. X.
Jean Buscaille. Trans. from E. Valnay. By M.X.H.
L: J. McDowell, 1879. 84p. BL OCLC E

1174. -----Paul and Virginia. Music by Victor Masse.

Paris: Theodore Michaelis, n.d. E
[Vocal score]

1175. HAYES, Maude Blanche [Am. 19c]
The royal revenge. Romantic drama in five acts.
n.p.: n.p., 1898. NUC H
[Typescript. 18, 20, 15, 24, 26 l.]

1176. HAYWOOD, Eliza (Fowler), Mrs. Valentine Haywood [Br. 1693-1756]
ALT: Heywood, Eliza (Fowler)
The fair captive: a tragedy.
L: T. Jauncy & H. Cole, 1721. 64p. NUC BL OCLC B N
[5 acts, verse. Prod. Lincoln's Inn, 1720/1.]

1177. -----Frederick, Duke of Brunswick-Lunenburgh. A tragedy.
L: W. Mears, J. Brindley, 1729. 56p. NUC BL OCLC B N
[5 acts, verse. Prod. Lincoln's Inn, 1728/29.]

1178. -----The opera of operas; or, Tom Thumb the great. Alter'd from the life and death of Tom Thumb the Great. And set to musick after the Italian manner. With William Hatchett.
L: William Rayner, 1733. OCLC B N Chetwood
[Ballad opera, a burlesque adapted from Henry Fielding. Prod. Haymarket, 1833.]

1179. -----A wife to be let.
1725. N
[Comedy.]

1180. -----A wife to be lett: a comedy.
L: n.p., 1723. 24p. L: D. Browne, jr., 1724. 72p. NUC BL OCLC N
[5 acts, prose. Prod. Drury Lane with Haywood in lead part. Chetwood, BioD. Enlarged version.]

HAYWOOD, Mrs. Valentine see HAYWOOD, Eliza (Fowler)

1181. HAZARD, Eleanor [Am. 19c]
An old plantation night. With Elizabeth Robinson Gibson Hazard [Am. 1799-1882].
NY: H. Roorbach; Dick & Fitzgerald, 1890. 44p. NUC
[Life in slave quarters, musical & dramatic entertainment for church, schools & drawing rooms]

HAZARD, Elizabeth Robinson Gibson, co-author see HAZARD, Eleanor

1182. HAZLEWOOD, Miss [Br. 19c]
Kevin's choice: an operetta, in two
acts. Music by T.A. Wallworth.
L: J. Bale, pr., 1867. 16p. E N
[Melodrama, verse and prose. Prod.
St. George Hall, 1867; Adelphi, 1882.
Also prod. as: "The Maid of
Glendalough," Prince of Wales',
1899.]

1183. -----London by gaslight.
1868. M N
[Drama, 5 acts. Adpt. from [John]
Augustin Daly's Under the gaslight.
Prod. Sadler's Wells, 1868.]

HEALY, Marie see BIGOT, Marie (Healy)

1184. HELME, Elizabeth [Br. d.
1813/16]
Cortez; or, The conquest of Mexico.
Trans. from Joachim Heinrich Campe.
Dublin: P. Wogan, et al, 1800. New
ed. L: C. Cradock & W. Joy, 1811.
259p. BL OCLC E N

1185. -----Pizarro; or, The conquest
of Peru. Trans. from Joachim
Heinrich Campe.
Dublin: P. Wogan, et al, 1800. 128p.
OCLC E N

1186. HELMORE, Margaret C. [Br. 19c]
Bandit, (an original charade) and The
snow helped. Written respectively by
M. Helmore and J.R. Ware.
L: J. Dicks, 1883. 6p. NUC BL [Dicks'
standard charades & comedies, no.
487]

HEMANS, Mrs. Alfred see HEMANS,
Felicia Dorothea (Browne)

1187. HEMANS, Felicia Dorothea
(Browne), Mrs. Alfred Hemans [Br.
1793-1835] ALT: Browne, Felicia
Dorothea PSEUD: Balfour, Clara; Lady,
A
The works of Mrs. Hemans; with a
memoir of her life, by her sister
[Harriet Hughes].
Edinburgh: W. Blackwood & sons; L:
Thomas Cadell, 1839. 7v. NUC BL OCLC
[The first collection of her works.
All works below are included in
this.]

1188. -----Dramatic works.
L & Edinburgh: William Blackwood &
sons, 1850. 270p. NUC OCLC E

1189. -----De Chatillon, or The
Crusaders. Five act tragedy.
In: Dramatic works.

E
[Tragedy, 5 acts, verse.]

1190. -----The forest sanctury, and
other poems.
Edinburgh: W. Blackwood & sons, 1825.
262p. L: J. Murray, 1825. 205p. BL
OCLC H
[H cites: The American forest girl
and Bernard del Carpio as dramatic
poems.]

1191. -----Sebastian of Portugal, a
dramatic fragment of four scenes.
In: Dramatic works.

1192. -----The siege of Valencia; a
dramatic poem of nine scenes based on
epic of The Cid. The last
Constantine: with other poems.
L: John Murray, 1823. 319p. NUC BL
OCLC E N
[Also in: Dramatic works]

1193. -----Vespers of Palermo; a
tragedy in five acts.
L: J. Murray, 1823. 116p. NUC BL OCLC
E N
[Verse. Prod. Covent Garden, 1823.
Also in: Dramatic works.]

1194. HEMENWAY, Abby Maria [Am. 1828-
1890] PSEUD: Marie Josephine
Fanny Allen, the first American nun.
A drama in five acts. By Marie
Josephine.
Boston: Noonan & co., 188-? 60p. NUC

1195. HENDERSHOT, Dell, Miss [Am.
19c]
The immortal Charles Ross; or, Stolen
from home. A drama in four acts.
Jackson, MI: Weeks, 1876. 32p. NUC

1196. HENDERSON, Edith [Br. 19c]
The mischief maker. 1891. M N
[Farce, comedy, 3 acts. Prod. Globe,
Vaudeville, 1891.]

HENDERSON, Ettie see HENDERSON,
Henrietta (Lewis)

1197. HENDERSON, Florence Leslie,
Miss [Br. b. 1859] ALT: H., F. L.
Three plays for drawing-room acting.
L: W. Swan Sonnenschein & co., 1885.
79p. BL

1198. -----Cinderella.
In: Three plays ... .
[4 scenes, verse]

1199. -----The lady-help.
In: Three plays ... .

[Comedietta, 3 scenes.]

1200. -----A story of the stars.
In: Three plays ... .
[Comedietta, 3 scenes.]

1201. HENDERSON, Henrietta (Lewis),
Mrs. William Henderson [Br. 1835-
1909] ALT: Henderson, Ettie
Almost a life.
NY: n.p., 1879. 1 sheet. OCLC N
[Prod. in Liverpool, 1882. Theall &
Carton's Novelty Theatre, Brooklyn,
N.Y. Program for week of April 28,
1879.]

1202. HENDERSON, L. Maggie [Br. 19c]
The rose queen; or, The real heiress
of Adonvale. A pastoral comedy in
two acts. With Stella Henderson.
L: J. Henderson, 1896. 32p. BL
[Society comedy, country gentry]

HENDERSON, Stella, co-author see
HENDERSON, L. Maggie

HENDERSON, Mrs. William see
HENDERSON, Henrietta (Lewis)

1203. HENRIETTA MARIA, Queen of
England [Fr./Br. 1609-1669]
Florimene.
1635. Har
[Pastoral. Now lost.]

1204. -----Queen's pastoral.
1626. Har
[MS. lost. In French.]

1205. HENRY, Re, Mrs. [Br. 19c]
Fast friends; comedietta in one act.
L & NY: S. French, 1884. 8p. NUC OCLC
[First performed in 1878. French's
acting edition, no. 1786]

1206. -----Going on the stage. Music
by E. Crook. 1895. N
[Musical comedy. Prod. in Blandford,
1895.]

1207. -----A narrow escape;
comedietta in one act.
Chicago: T.S. Denison, 18-? 10p. NUC
[Star Series]

1208. -----Norah. A drama in one
act.
Chicago: Dramatic pub. co., 1897?
12p. NUC OCLC M
[Prod. Grand, 1897. Sergel's acting
drama, no. 492]

1209. HENRY, Sarepta Myrenda Irish
[Am. 1839-1900]

Victoria: with other poems.
Cincinnati, OH: Poe & Hitchcock,
1865. 186p. NUC BL OCLC H
[Dramatic poem: "Victoria; or, The
triumph of virtue."]

1210. HENTZ, Caroline Lee (Whiting),
Mrs. Nicholas Marcellus Hentz [Am.
1800-1856]
De Lara, or, The Moorish bride. A
tragedy in five acts.
Tuscaloosa, AL: Woodruff & Olcott,
1843. 79p. NUC BL OCLC R
[In verse]

HENTZ, Mrs. Nicholas Marcellus see
HENTZ, Caroline Lee (Whiting)

1211. HERBERT, Miss [Br. 19c]
Up the ladder.
1876. N
[Comedy. Prod. in Limerick, 1876.]

HERBERT, Mary (Sidney), Countess of
Pembroke see PEMBROKE, Mary (Sidney)
Herbert, Countess of

HERING, Jeanie see ADAMS-ACTON,
Marion Hamilton

1212. HERNAMAN, Claudia Frances
(Ibotson) [Br. b. 1838]
The conversion and martyrdom of S.
Alban: a sacred drama.
South Norwood: Pr. Coventry & son,
1891. 16p. BL
[Historical drama, 4 acts, with
songs. Acting ed.]

HERON, Matilda see STOEPEL, Matilda
Agnes (Heron)

1213. HERRING, Ella C. [Br. 19c]
Lady Flora's namesake. A duologue.
L: Lacy, 1850. [1911 NUC & BL] 16p.
NUC BL
[French's acting edition of plays. v.
159, no. 14]

1214. HERVEY, Eleanora Louisa
(Montagu), Mrs. Thomas Kibble Hervey
[Br. 1811-1903] ALT: Montagu,
Eleanora Louisa PSEUD: Russell,
Margaret
The Landgrave, a play in five acts;
with dramatic illustrations of female
characters.
L: Smith, Elder & co., 1839. 286p.
NUC BL
[Verse. Dramatic illustrations are
prose dialogues: (1) Marie of
Moravia, 6 scenes; (2) The Fairy
Princess, 9 scenes; (3) The last of
the Cathari, 5 scenes; (4) The Bride

of the Alpo, 6 scenes. First 3 based
on French history]

1215. HERVEY, Rosamond [Br. 19c]
Duke Ernest, a tragedy, and other
poems.
L: Macmillan & co., 1866. NUC BL
[5 acts]

HERVEY, Mrs. Thomas see HERVEY,
Eleanora Louisa (Montagu)

1216. HERZOG, Helene [Am. 19c] PSEUD:
Eneleh, H.B.
One year. A comedy-drama. By H.B.
Eneleh.
Chicago: Dramatic pub. co., 1884.
20p. NUC OCLC
[4 acts. Sergel's acting drama. no.
319]

1217. -----Tempest tossed; an
original drama in four acts. By H.B.
Eneleh.
Chicago: Dramatic pub. co., 1885.
26p. NUC OCLC
[Sergel's acting drama, no. 337]

1218. HEYNE, Mary [Br. 19c]
The rose and the ring. Music by
Elena Norton.
1878. N
[Comic opera. Prod. in Dublin,
1878.]

1219. HEYWOOD, Delia A. [Am. 19c]
PSEUD: Pritchard, Polly Ann
Pritchard's choice dialogues.
Chicago: A. Flanagan co., 1896. 104p.
NUC OCLC
[Another 2 v. edition pub. 1866-98]

1220. -----Adam's fall.
In: Pritchard's ... .
[Comedy, 1 scene]

1221. -----Aestheticism versus common
sense.
In: Pritchard's ... .
[Comedy, 2 scenes.]

1222. -----Be truthful, be courteous.
In: Pritchard's ... .
[Comedy, 1 scene.]

1223. -----A character play.
In: Pritchard's ... .
[Comedy, 1 scene, for 9 actors]

1224. -----A cruel hoax.
In: Pritchard's ... .
[Comedy, 1 act]

1225. -----Grammatical difficulties.
In: Pritchard's ... .
[1/2 p. dialogue]

1226. -----Hospitality on the
frontier.
In: Pritchard's ... .
[1 scene in dialect]

1227. -----How the fun resulted.
In: Pritchard's ... .
[1 scene comedy]

1228. -----How the grown folks
minded.
In: Pritchard's ... .
[1 scene comedy]

1229. -----Insect - a charade.
In: Pritchard's ... .
[1 scene comedy]

1230. -----Keeping up appearances.
In: Pritchard's ... .
[4 scene melodrama]

1231. -----Kindness softens even
Savage Hearts.
In: Pritchard's ... .
[3 scenes. Adapted from "The Good
Old Times" a true account of life in
a Maine settlement during French &
Indian war.]

1232. -----Labor is honorable.
In: Pritchard's ... .
[1 act moral dialogue]

1233. -----Little pitchers.
In: Pritchard's ... .
[1 scene comedy]

1234. -----Mrs. Peabody's boarder.
In: Pritchard's ... .
[1 act comedy.]

1235. -----An object lesson.
In: Pritchard's ... .
[1 scene comedy]

1236. -----Perils of moderate
drinking.
In: Pritchard's ... .
[3 scenes]

1237. -----The professor is
interrupted.
In: Pritchard's ... .
[1 scene comedy]

1238. -----Quizzing a quack.
In: Pritchard's ... .
[1 scene comedy]

1238. -----Pseudo. A charade in
three scenes. In: Pritchard's ... .

1240. -----A reunion.
In: Pritchard's ... .
[1 scene comedy. Incl. a poem on the Civil War.]

1241. -----A shrewd guess.
In: Pritchard's ... .
[1 scene comedy]

1242. -----Sickly sentimentalism.
In: Pritchard's ... .
[1 scene comedy]

1243. -----A tea party.
In: Pritchard's ... .
[1 scene comedy]

1244. -----Trials of a country editor.
In: Pritchard's ... .
[1 scene, comedy]

HEYWOOD, Eliza (Fowler) see HAYWOOD, Eliza (Fowler)

HIGGINS, David K., co-author see HIGGINS, Georgia Waldron

1245. HIGGINS, Georgia Waldron, Mrs. [Am. 19c]
Darius Green and his flyin' machine: a comedy-drama, in four acts. With David K. Higgins.
Chicago: n.p., 1899. NUC

HILL, Mrs. Frank see LUTZ, Grace (Livingston) Hill

1246. HILL, Grace Livingston [Am. 1865-1947]
A colonial girl. Comedy in three acts. With Abbey Sage Richardson.
n.p.: n.p., 1898. 49, 42, 57 1. NUC OCLC
[Typescript prompt-book]

1247. HILL, Isabel [Br. 1800-1842]
Brian, the probationer: or, The red hand. A tragedy in five acts.
L: W.R. Sams, 1842. 100p. NUC BL E N
[In verse]

1248. -----The first of May; or, A royal love-match, a petite comedy, in two acts.
L: William Kenneth, 1829. 53p. NUC E N
[Comedy. Prod. Covent Garden, 1829.]

1249. -----The poet's child; a tragedy, in five acts.
L: John Warren, 1820. 64p. NUC BL OCLC E N
[In verse. Prod. Covent Garden, 1829.]

1250. HILL, Philippina Burton [Br. 18c] ALT: Burton, Philippina
Fashion displayed.
1770. N
[Comedy. Prod. Haymarket, 1770. She acted at the Haymarket theatre for 1 or 2 seasons & prod. 1 play. BioD.]

HILL-LOWE, Thomas, ed. see LOWE, Helen

1251. HILLS, Hammond, Miss [Br. 19c]
A lost Eden.
1897. M N
[Drama, 1 act. Prod. Novelty, 1897.]

1252. HILTON, Hilda [Br. d. 1888]
Princess Carlo's plot.
1887. M N
[Comedy, 3 acts. Prod. Novelty, 1887.]

1253. HINGESTON-RANDOLPH, Mary [Br. 19c]
The Beverley bogey. With Areton Giffard.
1897. N
[Comic drama. Prod. Bijou, 1897.]

HINKSON, Mrs. Henry Albert see HINKSON, Katharine (Tynan)

1254. HINKSON, Katharine (Tynan), Mrs. Henry Albert Hinkson [Br. 1859/61-1931] ALT: Tynan, Katherine
Miracle plays: Our Lord's coming, and childhood.
L: J. Lane, 1892. [1895 t.p.]. 98p. NUC BL OCLC E
[More properly, mystery plays; on Christ's life.]

1255. -----The annunciation.
In: Miracle plays ... .

1256. -----The finding in the temple.
In: Miracle plays ... .

1257. -----The flight into Egypt.
In: Miracle plays ... .

1258. -----The nativity.
In: Miracle plays ... .

1259. -----The presentation in the temple.
In: Miracle plays ... .

1260. -----The visitation.
In: Miracle plays ... .

1261. HOARE, Florence [Br. 19c]
Snow White. Music by Mme. Mely.
1899. N

[Fairy opera. Prod. St. George Hall, 1899.]

HOBBES, JOHN OLIVER, pseud. see CRAIGIE, Pearl Mary Teresa (Richards)

1262. HODGSON, Agatha H. [Br. 19c]
The captain's daughter. With Archibald C. Hodgson.
1890. M N
[Comedy, 1 act. Prod. Vaudeville, & at Southampton, 1890.]

1263. -----The clerk of the weather. With Kate Osborne.
1892. N
[Comedietta. Prod. at Torquay, 1892.]

1264. -----Doomed. With Archibald C. Hodgson.
1890. N
[Comic drama. Prod. at Southampton, 1890.]

1265. -----The gamekeeper's wife. With Archibald C. Hodgson.
1890. N
[Comic drama. Prod. at Southampton, 1890.]

1266. -----In olden days. With Archibald C. Hodgson.
1890. N
[Comedietta. Prod. at Southampton, 1890; Vaudeville, 1890.]

1267. -----On Zephyr's wings. With Archibald C. Hodgson.
1891. N
[Comic drama. Prod. at Teddington, 1891.]

1268. -----Watching and waiting. With Archibald C. Hodgson.
1891. M N
[Comedy, 3 acts. Prod. at Southampton; Terry's, 1891.]

HODGSON, Archibald C., co-author see HODGSON, Agatha H.

1269. HODSON, Emily [Br. 19c]
Another.
L: 1885. M N
[Farce-comedy, 3 acts. Prod. Vaudeville, 1885.]

1270. HOLBROOK, Margaret Louise [Am. 19c]
His heroine. A farce in one act.
Philadelphia: Penn. pub. co., [1906 OCLC] 1911. 14p. NUC OCLC H
[Earlier copyright: 1894.]

1271. HOLCROFT, Fanny [Br. d. 1844]
The baron. Translated from Celenio.
In: Theatrical Recorder, ed. Thomas Holcroft.
L: C. Mercier, pr., 1806. 322p. NUC BL OCLC E

1272. -----Emilia Galotti.
Translated from [Gotthold Ephraim] Lessing.
Philadelphia: Bradford & Inskeep, 1810. 18p.
[Also in: Theatrical Recorder ... .]

1273. -----Fortune mends.
Translanted from [Pedro] Calderon [de la Barca].
In: Theatrical Recorder ... .
OCLC

1274. -----From bad to worse.
Translated from [Pedro] Calderon [de la Barca].
In: Theatrical Recorder ... .

1275. -----The goldsmith.
1827. N
[Prod. Haymarket.]

1276. -----Minna von Barnhelm.
Translated from [Gotthold Ephraim] Lessing.
In: Theatrical Recorder ... .

1277. -----Philip the second.
Translated from [Count Vittorio] Alfieri.
In: Theatrical Recorder ... .

1278. -----Rosamond. Tr. from [Christian Felix] Weisse.
In: Theatrical Recorder ... .

1279. HOLFORD, Margaret Wrench [Br. d. 1834] ALT: Wrench, Margaret
Neither's the man: a comedy in five acts.
L: G. Sael; Chester: W. Minshull, 1799. 82p. NUC BL OCLC B N
[Prod. Chester, c1798. Ms. Larpent coll. 1798.]

1280. HOLFORD, Margaret Wrench
The way to win her; a comedy, in five acts.
L: n.p., 1814. BL OCLC E N
[The New Brit. Theatre, v. 2]

1281. HOLFORD, Mary Anne, Mrs. [Br. 19c] ALT: H., M.
Marie de Courcelles; or, a Republican marriage.
L: Pr. by W. Clowes & sons, 1876. 90p. NUC M N

[Drama, 5 acts. Prod. Olympic, 1878.]

1282. HOLLEY, Marietta [Am. 1836-1926] PSEUD: Josiah Allen's wife
Betsey Bobbett. A drama. By Josiah Allen's wife.
Adams, NY: W.J. Allen, pr., 1880. 40p. NUC OCLC

1283. HOLMES, Augusta (Macgregor), Mrs. Dalkeith Holmes [Br. d. 1857]
The law of Rouen: a dramatic tale. By Mrs. Dalkeith Holmes.
Dublin: Priv. pr., 1837. 63p. NUC BL
[3 acts, verse. Based on the trial of the Marquis d'Alligre]

HOLMES, Mrs. Dalkeith see HOLMES, Augusta (Macgregor)

1284. HOLT, Jane (Wiseman) [Br. 18c]
ALT: Wiseman, Jane
Antiochus the Great: or, The fatal relapse. A tragedy. L: Wm. Turner & Richard Bassett, 1702. 38p. NUC OCLC B N
[Verse. Prod. Lincoln's Inn, 1706. Chetwood. Longe, v. 138, no. 4]

HOLT, May see FAIRBAIRN, May (Holt)

1285. HOLT, Sarah Barton [Am. 19c]
The radish king. A drama, in four acts.
New Orleans, LA: W. Dunstan, 1887. NUC

1286. HOLTON, Florence [Br. 19c]
From the vanished past.
1888. N
[Drama. Prod. at Upton Park, 1888.]

1287. -----His hidden revenge.
1887. N
[Drama. Prod. at Upton Park, 1887.]

1288. HOOK, Harriet Horncastle (Madden), Mrs. James Hook [Br. d. 1805]
The double disguise, a comic opera in two acts.
L: J. Bell, 1784. 28p. NUC BL OCLC B N
[Music by James Hook. Longe, v. 95, no. 6]

HOOK, Mrs. James see HOOK, Harriet Horncastle (Madden)

1289. HOOPER, Lucy, Mrs. [Am. 1816?-1841] ALT: H., L.
Inherited. An emotional drama in four acts.

NY: n.p., 1890. NUC

1290. HOPE, Kate [Am. 19c]
Our Utopia, its rise and fall; an aesthetic comedietta [a farce BL], in two acts.
NY: Roorbach & Co., 1882. 18p. L: Simpkin & co., 21p. NUC BL
[Roorbach acting drama, 174]

1291. HOPE, Naomi [Br. 19c]
The armourer.
1894. N
[Drama. Prod. at Whitehaven, 1894.]

1292. -----Forgive us our trespasses.
1896. N
[Melodrama. Prod. at Brighton, 1896.]

1293. HOPE, Vivian [Br. 19c]
His second wife.
1892. N
[Play, 3 acts. Prod. Avenue, 1892.]

1294. HOPER, (Harford) [Br. 18c]
Edward the Black Prince; or, The battle of Poitiers.
1747. N [Tragedy. Prod. Goodman's Fields, 1746/7, and in 1747 as: "The battle of Poitiers, or, The English prince."]

1295. -----Queen's tragedy restor'd: a dramatick entertainement.
L: W. Owen, 1749. 46p. NUC BL OCLC B N
[Burlesque, 2 acts, prose & verse. Prod. Haymarket, 1749.]

1296. HOPKINS, Louisa Parsons (Stone) [Am. 1834-1895]
From Nazareth to Bethelehem.
Boston: Lee & Shepard; NY: Charles T. Dillingham, 1884. 16p. NUC OCLC BL
[Christmas duologue between Mary & Joseph; blank verse.]

1297. HORNBY, Mary [Br. 19c]
The battle of Waterloo: a tragedy.
Stratford-upon-Avon: n.p., 1819. BL
[5 acts]

1298. -----The broken vow: a comedy.
Stratford-upon-Avon: n.p., 1820. BL
[5 acts]

HORNE, Mrs. M.B., co-author see SILSBEE, Alice M.

1299. HORNE, Mary Barnard [Am. b. 1845]
The book of drills. A series of entertainments. Arranged by Mary B. Horne.

Boston: W.H. Baker & co., 1889-90.
2v. NUC OCLC
[Pt. 1: A national flag drill; The
shepherds' drill; The tambourine
drill; The Mother Goose quadrille.
Pt. 2: The nursery maids' drill.]

1300. -----A carnival of days.
Boston: W.H. Baker & co., 1887. 28p.
NUC

1301. -----The darktown bicycle club
scandal. A colored sketch in one act
for lady minstrels.
Boston: Walter H. Baker, 1897. 16p.
NUC OCLC
[Issued with Silsbee, Alice M.: Jolly
Joe's lady minstrels.]

1302. -----Glueck-auf; or, the four-
leaved clover. An operetta in three
acts.
Cambridge, MA: J. Wilson & bro.,
1886. 29p. NUC

1303. -----The great moral dime show,
an entertainment in one scene.
Boston: W.H. Baker & co., 1892. 17p.
NUC OCLC H
[Baker's edition of plays. Also pub.
as: "The last of the Peak sisters;
or, The great moral dime show."
Baker's Novelties, 1892.]

1304. -----Gulliver and the
Lilliputians up to date. One act.
Boston: W.H. Baker, 1903. 13p. NUC
OCLC H
[Earlier copyright: 1896. Adapted
from Jonathan Swift.]

1305. -----The ladies of Cranford; a
sketch of English village life fifty
years ago; in three acts.
Boston: W.H. Baker & co., 1899. 28p.
NUC OCLC
[Dramatized from Elizabeth (Cleghorn)
Gaskell's "Cranford."]

1306. -----The Peak sisters; an
entertainment.
Boston: W.H. Baker & co., 1887. 20p.
NUC OCLC
[For 7 female characters. Baker's
novelties]

1307. -----Plantation bitters; a
colored fantasy in two acts, for male
characters only.
Boston: W.H. Baker & co., 1892. 29p.
NUC OCLC
[Baker's edition of plays]

1308. -----Prof. Baxter's great
invention; an unclassified
entertainment in one act.
Boston: W.H. Baker & co., 1891. 24p.
NUC OCLC

1309. -----A Sevres cup; or, A bit of
bric-a-brac. A comedietta, in three
acts.
n.p.: n.p., 1886. 32 l. NUC

1310. -----A singing school of ye
olden time, as set down by M.B.
Horne.
Boston: W. Baker & co., 1894. 22p.
NUC OCLC
[Baker's novelties]

HORSFORD, F. ALLEN, pseud. see
FRIEDLIEB, L.A., Mrs.

1311. HOSMER, Harriet Goodhue [Am.
1830-1908] PSEUD: Chi-lo-sa
1975, a prophetic drama. By Chi-lo-
sa [who knows].
Rome: n.p., 1875. NUC

1312. HOUSTON, Lady [Br. d. 1780]
The coquettes; or, The gallant in the
closet.
1780. N
[Comedy. Prod. in Scotland; widow of
Sir Thomas Houston. Not printed.
BioD.]

1313. HOWARD, Mrs. [Br. 19c]
The forty thieves. Partly re-written
by John Green.
Newcastle: M. Benson, 1883. 63p. NUC
[pantomime]

HOWARD, Caroline (Gilman) see JERVEY,
Caroline (Gilman) Howard

1314. HOWARTH, Ellen Clementine
(Doran) [Am. 1827-1899]
The guerilla chief. A drama in five
acts.
Trenton, NJ: Murphy & Bechtel, 1872.
32p. NUC

1315. HOWE, Julia (Ward), Mrs. Samuel
G. Howe [Am. 1819-1910]
Leonore; or, the world's own, a
tragedy in five acts.
NY: Baker & Godwin, 1857. 63p. NUC
OCLC R [Stuart's repertory of
original American plays. no. 1. Also
pub. as: "The world's own." Boston:
Ticknor & Fields, 1857. 141p. NUC BL
OCLC R]

HOWE, Mrs. Samuel G. see HOWE, Julia
(Ward)

1316. HOWELL, Agnes Rous [Br. 19c]
Euphrosyne; or, the sculptor's bride.
Being the story of Pygmalion, with a
sequel. A libretto in three acts.
Norwich: Fletcher & son, 1886. 65p.
BL
[Prose & verse]

1317. HOWELL, S. [Am. 19c] PSEUD:
Sparks, Peter, gentleman
Cupid and Psyche: a mythological
play, in five acts, with grand
tableau.
New Orleans, LA: Pr. at the office of
the Picayune, 1873. 24p. NUC BL

1318. -----A marriage for revenge: a
drama in five acts.
New Orleans, LA: Pr. at the office of
the Picayune, 1874. 34p. NUC BL OCLC

1319. -----Upside down, an original
philosophical and mythological comedy
in five acts, with appropriate
tableaux. By Peter Sparks,
gentleman.
New Orleans, LA: Pr. at the
Commercial Bulletin Office, 1871.
31p. NUC BL OCLC

1320. HOWIE, Hellen Morrison [Am.
19c]
After the matinee. A comedy in one
act.
Philadelphia: The Penn. pub. co.,
1899. 19p. NUC
[Dramatic library, vol. 1, no. 185]

1321. -----His father's son. Farce
in one act.
Philadelphia: Penn pub. co., 1900.
20p. NUC OCLC H T

1322. -----The reformer reformed. A
comedy sketch.
Philadelphia: The Penn. pub. co.,
1899. 11p. NUC OCLC
[Dramatic library, vol. 1, no. 187]

1323. HOWITT, Mary (Botham), Mrs.
William Howitt [Br. 1799-1888] ALT:
Botham, Mary
The seven temptations.
L: R. Bentley, 1834. 373p. NUC BL
OCLC N
[Dramatic poems: The poor scholar;
Thomas of Torres; The pirate; The old
man; Raymond; Philip of Maine; The
sorrow of Teresa. Connecting
narrative in prose explains the devil
Achzib's temptations of these
characters. He wins four souls and
loses three (the old man, the scholar
& Teresa), the people around the lost
souls turn to God for sustenance.]

HOWITT, Mrs. William <u>see</u> HOWITT, Mary
(Botham)

1324. HOWLETT, Shirley [19c] A false
friend.
1893. N
[Drama. Prod. at Liverpool, 1893.
No biographical information
available, possibly a male author.]

1325. -----The gay chaperon.
1894. N
[Comedy. Prod. at Bootle, 1894.]

1326. -----A glimpse of the world.
1895. N
[Drama. Prod. at Liverpool, 1895.]

1327. -----Safe and sound.
1891. N
[Farce. Prod. at Bootle, 1891; at
Liverpool, 1896.]

HOYT, Charles Hale, co-author <u>see</u>
EDOUIN, Winnie

1328. HUGHES, Anne, Mrs. [Br. 18/19c]
Moral dramas intended for private
representation.
L: Pr. for William Lane, 1790. NUC BL
B N
[Blank verse. Longe, v. 285, no. 1]

1329. -----Aspacia, a tragedy in
three acts.
In: Moral dramas ... .

1330. -----Constantia, a tragedy; in
three acts.
In: Moral dramas ... .
[Verse]

1331. -----Cordelia, a tragedy in
five acts.
In: Moral dramas ... .
[Verse. Based on Shakespeare's King
Lear. Follows 18c revisions of
story, Edgar & Cordelia live to
restore order.]

1332. HUGHES, Annie [Br. 19c]
A husband's humiliation.
1896. M N
[Comedietta. Prod. Criterion, 1896.]

1333. HUGHES, Louise Marie [Am. 19c]
Love's stratagem; a comedy in two
acts.
Philadelphia: Penn pub. co., 1896.
10p. NUC
[Dramatic library, vol. 1, no. 43.
Keystone ed. of popular plays.]

HUMBOLDT, Charlotte de see DE
HUMBOLDT, Charlotte

HUME, Mary C. see HUME-ROTHERY, Mary
Catherine

1334. HUME-ROTHERY, Mary Catherine
[Br. 1824-1885] ALT: Hume, Mary C.;
Rothery, Mary Catherine (Hume)
Normiton: a dramatic poem, in two
parts. With other miscellaneous
pieces.
L: John W. Parker & son, 1857. 312p.
NUC BL OCLC
[Drama, Pt. 1 in 2 acts, Pt. 2 in 3
acts; misc. poems.]

1335. HUMPHREYS, Mary Gay [Am. d.
1915] PSEUD: Somerville, Henry
Beauchamp [or] Warwick-castle. By
Henry Somerville.
n.p.: n.p., 189-?

HUNGERFORD, Mrs. [Margaret Wolfe
(Hamilton) Argles], co-author see
PHILLIPS, Mrs. Newton

HUNT, Mrs. Alfred William see HUNT,
Margaret

1336. HUNT, Arzalea [Am. 19c]
A wedding notice.
Lebanon, OH: March bros., 189-? 8p.
NUC OCLC

1337. -----The wood fairies. An
Arbor Day entertainment.
Darrowville, OH: n.p., 1895. 1p. NUC

1338. HUNT, Margaret (Raine), Mrs.
Alfred William Hunt [Br. 1831-1912]
The girls he left behind him.
In: Dialogues of the day. Ed. Oswald
Crawfurd.
L: Chapman & Hall, 1895. 8p. NUC BL
OCLC E

1339. HUNT, Violet [Am. 1866-1942]
The way to keep her.
In: Dialogues of the day. Ed. Oswald
Crawfurd.
L: Chapman & Hall, 1895. NUC BL OCLC
E
[H also cites: The maiden's progress.
A novel in dialogue. NY: Harper &
bros., 1894. 252p. No evidence of a
stage adaptation.]

1340. -----The end of the beginning.
In: Dialogues of the day.

1341. -----The hour and the man.
In: Dialogues of the day ... .

1342. HUNTER, Grace Lillian [Am. 19c]
Twenty-five new and unique
entertainments; especially for church
entertainments, the Ladies' Aid
Society, the Epworth League, the
Christian endeavor.
2d ed. Des Moines, IA: Ladies Aid
Soc. pub. co., 1899. 83p. NUC OCLC

1343. HUNTER, Mrs. Talbot [Br. 19c]
Aurelian, the scion of the sun. An
original historic-romantic tragedy in
prologue and five acts.
L: Author's priv. copy, 1890. 119p.
NUC OCLC
[In verse. About Lucius Domitius
Aurelianus, Emperor of Rome, d. 275]

1344. -----Lost to the world. 1892. M
N
[Drama, 4 acts. Prod. Marylebone,
1892.]

1345. HUSE, Carolyn Evans [Am. 19c]
Under the greenwood tree; a Christmas
operetta in one act.
NY: E.S. Werner, c1895. 16p. NUC

1346. HYDE, Elizabeth A. [Am. 19c]
An engaged girl. A comedy.
Chicago: T.S. Denison, 1899. 18p. NUC
OCLC
[Amateur series; II, 208]

1347. H____, Eleanor [Br. 19c]
Matilda.
1803. BioD N
[Trans. from Jacques Boutet de
Monvel. Dramatic poem.]

1348. I., P. [Br. 18c]
Dramatic pieces, calculated to
exemplify the mode of conduct which
will render young ladies both amiable
and happy, when their school
education is completed.
New Haven: Pr. by Abel Morse, 1791.
3v. L: n.p., 1788. 3v. NUC BL OCLC
Wells

1349. -----The contract.
In: Dramatic pieces ... v. 3.
[3 acts]

1350. -----The good daughter-in-law.
In: Dramatic pieces ... v. 1.
[3 acts]

1351. -----The good mother-in-law.
In: Dramatic pieces ... v. 1.
[3 acts]

1352. -----The maternal sister.
In: Dramatic pieces ... v. 2.
[3 acts]

1353. -----The Reformation.
In: Dramatic pieces ... v. 2.
[3 acts]

1354. -----The triumph of reason. In:
Dramatic pieces ... v. 3.
[3 acts]

INCHBALD, Mrs. see INCHBALD,
Elizabeth (Simpson)

1355. INCHBALD, Elizabeth (Simpson),
Mrs. Joseph Inchbald [Br. 1753-1821]
ALT: Inchbald, Mrs.
The modern theatre; a collection of
successful modern plays ... printed
from the prompt books ... selected by
Mrs. Inchbald.
L: Longmans, Hurst, Rees, Orme &
Brown, 1811. 10v. NUC BL OCLC
[3 plays by Inchbald incl.]

1356. -----All on a summer's day.
1787. N
[Comedy. Prod. Covent Garden, 1787.
Larpent MS 46.]

1357. -----Animal magnetism, a farce.
Dublin: P. Byron, 1788? 36p. NUC BL
OCLC B E N
[3 acts, prose. Prod. Covent Garden,
1788. Also pub. as: The farce on
Animal magnetism. Dublin: Pr. for
the booksellers, 1792. 41p. N says a
pirated ed.]

1358. -----Appearance is against
them; a farce.
L: G.G.J. & J. Robinson, 1785. 48p.
NUC BL OCLC B E N
[2 acts. Prod. Covent Garden, 1785.
Revived 1804 under title: "Mistake
upon mistake."]

1359. -----A case of conscience.
In: Memoirs of Mrs. Inchbald. Ed.
James Boaden.
L: R. Bentley, 1833. 2v. NUC BL OCLC

1360. -----The child of nature, a
dramatic piece ... .
1788. Dublin: Mssrs. Byrne et al,
1789. 57p. NUC BL OCLC B E N
[2 acts.   Prod. Covent Garden, 1788.
Adapted from "Zelie" by [Stephanie
Felicite Ducrest de St. Aubin,
Comtesse de Genlis] Mme. de Genlis.
4 acts, printed separately. The
London Stage, vol. 2.]

1361. -----Every one has his fault; a
comedy, in five acts.
L: G.G.J. & J. Robinson, 1792. 114p.
NUC BL OCLC B E N
[Comedy. Prod. Covent Garden, 1793.]

1362. -----The hue and cry.
1792. N NUC OCLC
[Farce. Prod. Drury Lane, 1791.
Larpent MS 54. Adapted from
[Stephanie Felicite Ducrest de St.
Aubin, Comtesse de Genlis] Mme. de
Genlis]

1363. -----I'll tell you what.   A
comedy in five acts.
L: G.G.J. & J. Robinson, 1786. 88p.
NUC BL OCLC B E N
[Prod. Haymarket, 1785. With a
prologue and epilogue by G. Coleman,
the Elder.]

1364. -----Lover's vows, a play
[altered] from the German of [August
Friedrich Ferdinand von] Kotzebue.
L: Longman, Hurst, Rees & Orme, 1798.
72p. NUC BL OCLC B E N
[Prod. Covent Garden, 1798.
Adaptation of "Das Kind der liebe." 5
acts]

1365. -----Lovers no conjurors.
Farce in two acts.
1792. NUC B N BioD
[First prod. Theatre Royal, Drury
Lane, as: "Young men and old women,"
and at Haymarket, 1792. Larpent Ms.
#952.]

1366. -----The married man ... from
"Le Philosphe Marie" of Mr.
[Philippe] Nericault Destouches.
L: G.G.J. & J. Robinson, 1789. 63p.
1792. NUC OCLC B N
[Comedy, 3 acts. Prod. Haymarket,
1789. Longe, v. 196, no. 2]

1367. -----The massacre: taken from
the French. A tragedy, of three
acts, in prose.
L: G.G.J. & J. Robinson, 1792. 31p.
NUC OCLC
[On the French Revolution]

1368. -----The midnight hour; a
petite comedy.
L: G.G.J. & J. Robinson, 1787. 43p.
1824. NUC BL OCLC B E N
[3 acts. Prod. Covent Garden, 1787.
An adaptation of "Guerre ouverte" by
Antoine Jean [Dumaniant] Bourlin. In
the London Stage. Vol. 1.]

1369. -----A mogul tale: or, the
descent of the balloon. A farce.

Dublin: Pr. for the booksellers,
1788. [1778 OCLC]. 20p. NUC BL OCLC B
E N
[2 acts, prose. Prod. Haymarket,
1784. NUC has ed's L & Dublin.
Longe, v. 223, no. 8]

1370. -----Next door neighbours; a
comedy; in three acts.
L: G.G.J. & J. Robinson, 1791. 70p.
NUC BL OCLC B E N
[Prod. Haymarket, 1791. From the
French drama: "L'Indigent" by Louis
Sebastien Mercier and "Le
Dissipateur" by Philippe Nericault
Destouches. Longe, v. 220, no. 7.]

1371. -----Such things are. A play,
in five acts.
L: G.G.J. & J. Robinson, 1788. 74p.
NUC BL OCLC B E T
[Drama. Longe, v.99, no. 10.
In: The British Theatre, no. 1.]

1372. -----Such things are: a play,
in five acts.
L: Longman, Hurst, Rees, Orme &
Brown, n.d. 77p. N T
[Drama. Prod. Covent Garden, 1787.
The British theatre. L: 1808. v. 23,
no. 1]

1373. -----To marry or not to marry;
a comedy in five acts.
L: Longman, Hurst Rees, & Orme, 1805.
85p. NUC BL OCLC B N
[Comedy. Prod. Covent Garden, 1805.]

1374. -----The wedding-day; a farce
in two acts. L: G.G. & J. Robinson,
1794. 44p. NUC BL OCLC B E N
[Prod. Drury Lane, 1794. Longe,
v.228, no. 6]

1375. -----The widow's vow. A farce.
L: G.G.J. & J. Robinson, 1786. 35p.
NUC BL OCLC B N
[2 acts. Prod. Haymarket, 1786.
Plot taken from "L'heureuse erreur"
of Joseph Patrat. Longe, v.98, no.2]

1376. -----The wise man of the East.
A play altered from the German of
[August Friedrich Ferdinand von]
Kotzebue.
2d ed. L: G.G. & J. Robinson, 1799.
80p. NUC BL OCLC B E N
[Drama, 5 acts. Prod. Covent Garden,
1799.]

1377. -----Wives as they were, and
maids as they are. A comedy in five
acts.
L: G.G. & J. Robinson, 1797. 96p. NUC
BL OCLC B E N

[Prod. Covent Garden, 1797, & also
under title: "The Primitive wife and
modern maid."]

INCHBALD, Mrs. Joseph see INCHBALD,
Elizabeth (Simpson)

1378. INGELOW, Jean [Br. 1820-1897]
Annie's holiday, a little comedy.
With The old man's prayer.
Manchester: Heywood, 1895. 16p. BL
[In verse. A. Heywood & Sons series
of original dramas for amateur
entertainments, No. 157]

1379. INGRAHAM, Jean [Am. 19c]
The raw recruits; or, A day in camp
with the State National Guard. A
military comedy drama in two acts.
Clyde, OH: Ames, 1893. 10p. NUC OCLC
H
[Ames' Standard & Minor Drama, no.
322]

1380. IRISH, Annie [Br. 1862/65-1947]
ALT: Dodson, Mrs. J. E.
Across her path.
1890. M N
[Play, 4 acts, adapted from a novel
by Annie Swan [Burnett-Smith]. Prod.
Globe, Terry's, 1890.]

1381. IRVINE, Mary Catharine [Br.
19c] PSEUD: Aura
The friendly disputants; or, Future
punishment reconsidered. By Aura.
Edinburgh & L: A. Hall, Virtue & co.,
1859. 490p. NUC OCLC
[Dialogue. Inglis.]

1382. -----Heart repose. A dramatic
poem in three acts. By Aura.
L: Simpkin, Marshall & co., 1867.
175p. BL N
[3 acts. Moral & religious themes, a
group of 8 odes in Act III, Scene
XII]

1383. IRVING, Ethel [Br. 19c]
Hedvige; and poems.
L: W. Macintosh, 1872. 155p. BL OCLC
[Drama, 3 acts, verse; set in 14th c.
Budapest & Crackow. Stage directions
incl., though intended for reading.]

ISA see KNOX, Isa (Craig)

1384. ISDELL, Sarah [Br. 19c]
The cavern.
1825. N
[Comic opera. Prod. Hawkins-Street,
Dublin.]

1385. -----The poor gentlewoman.

1811. N
[Comedy. Prod. Crow-Street, Dublin. BioD.]

1386. IVES, Alice Emma [Am. d. 1930]
The village postmaster. A domestic drama in four acts. With Jerome H. Eddy.
NY & L: S. French, 1894. 93p. NUC OCLC H T
[French's standard library ed.]

J., M.E.M. see JONES, Margaret Elizabeth Mary

1387. JACKSON, Barbara [Br. 19c]
Monsieur Garrard's title. An original comedietta in one act.
L: Kegan Paul & co., 1888. 38p. BL

1388. JAMES, Ada [Br. 19c]
Arts and crafts. With Dudley James.
1897. N
[Comic drama. Prod. Ladbrooke Hall, 1897.]

JAMES, Dudley, co-author see JAMES, Ada

1389. JAMES, Florence Alice (Price) [Br. 1857-1929] ALT: Price, Florence Alice PSEUD: Warden, Florence
The guinea pigs. By Florence Warden.
1899. N
[Drama. Prod. in W. Kensington, 1899.]

1390. -----The house on the marsh.
By Florence Warden.
1885. M N
[Prod. Standard, 1885, & at Nottingham. Adapted from her novel.]

1391. -----In the lion's mouth. By Florence Warden.
1885. N
[Drama. Prod. at Bath, 1885.]

1392. -----Uncle Mike. By Florence Warden.
1892. N
[Drama. Prod. Terry's, 1892.]

1393. JAMESON, Mrs. [Br. 19c]
The odds are even.
1893. N
[Comedy. Prod. at Northampton, 1893.]

1394. JAMESON, Anna Brownell Murphy, Mrs. Robert Sympson Jameson [Br. 1794-1860]

Social life in Germany, illustrated in the acted dramas of Her Royal Highness, the Princess Amalie of Saxony.
L: Saunders & Otley, 1840. 2v. L: George Routledge, 1847. NUC OCLC E
[2nd Edition]

1395. -----The country cousin.
In: Social life in Germany.

1396. -----Falsehood and truth.
In: Evergreen I, 1840. pp. 58-71. E

1397. -----The princely bride.
In: Social life in Germany.

1398. -----Social life in Germany: An introductory dialogue.
In: Social life in Germany, 2d ed.

1399. -----The uncle.
In: Evergreen I, 1840, pp. 137-151. E

1400. -----The young ward.
In: Social life in Germany.

JAMESON, Mrs. Robert Sympson see JAMESON, Anna Brownell Murphy

1401. JAMIESON, Frances (Thurtle) [Br. 19c] ALT: Thurtle, Frances
Cadijah; or, The black palace. A tragedy in five acts.
L: G.B. Whittaker, 1825. NUC BL OCLC

1402. JAQUITH, Mrs. M.H. [Am. 19c]
The "deestrick skule" of fifty years ago.
Chicago: Dramatic pub. co., 1888. 37p. NUC BL OCLC
[Collection of humorous speeches, arranged as a day in school.]

1403. -----"Exerbition" of the deestrick skule of fifty years ago.
Topeka, KS: M.H. Jaquith, 1890. 29p. NUC BL

1404. -----Ma Dusenberry and her great humorous entertainment.
Chicago: Dramatic pub. co., 1896. 12p. NUC BL OCLC
[In OCLC as: Ma Dusenberry and her gearls: humorous entertainment.]

1405. -----Parson Poor's donation party. Burlesque entertainment, in two scenes.
Chicago: Dramatic pub. co., 1896. NUC BL
[Sergel's acting drama, no. 441]

1406. JAY, Harriett [Br. 1857-1932]
ALT: Buchanan, Mrs. Robert Williams
PSEUD: Marlowe, Charles
Alone in London. With Robert Williams
Buchanan.
n.p.: n.p., 1885. NUC E N
[Drama. Prod. Olympic, 1885.]

1407. -----Fascination. With Robert
Buchanan.
1887. M N
[Comedy, 3 acts. Prod. Novelty,
1887, & Vaudeville, 1888.]

1408. -----The mariners of England.
With Robert Buchanan.
1897. M N
[Romantic drama, 4 acts. Prod.
Olympic, 1897.]

1409. -----The new Don Quixote. With
Robert Buchanan.
1896. M N
[Play, 4 acts. Prod. Royalty, 1896.]

1410. -----The queen of Connaught.
With Robert Williams Buchanan.
1877. M
[Comedy, 4 acts, adaptation of a
novel. Prod. Olympic, 1877.]

1411. -----The romance of the
shopwalker. With Robert Buchanan.
1896. M N
[Comedy, 3 acts. Prod. Vaudeville,
1896.]

1412. -----The strange adventures of
Miss Brown. By Robert Williams
Buchanan and Charles Marlowe.
L: R. Buchanan, 1897. 36, 48, 25 f.
[prompt book NUC]. NUC BL E M N
[Farce, 3 acts. Prod. Vaudeville,
1895, & Terry's, 1895. NY & L: S.
French, 1909. NUC]

1413. -----Two little maids from
school. With Robert Buchanan.
1898. N
[Comic drama. Prod. in Camberwell,
1898.]

1414. -----The wanderer from Venus.
With Robert Buchanan.
1896. N
[Comedy. Prod. in Croyden, 1896.]

1415. JENNER, Annabel [Br. 19c]
My lady fanciful.
1899. N [Musical pastoral. Prod. at
Margate, 1899.]

1416. JERVEY, Caroline (Gilman)
Howard, Mrs. Lewis Jervey [Am. 1823-
1877] ALT: Howard, Caroline Gilman

The lost children. A musical
entertainment in five acts.
Boston: Walter H. Baker & co., 1889?
NUC OCLC H
[8 male, 5 female characters. Pub.
earlier: Plays for children, No. 1.
Boston: C.H. Spencer; Geo. H. Baker,
1870. 30p. OCLC]

JERVEY, Mrs. Lewis see JERVEY,
Caroline (Gilman) Howard

JEWRY, Laura see VALENTINE, Laura
(Jewry)

JO, pseud. see ALCOTT, Louisa May

1417. JOHNSON, Annie L. [Am. 19c]
In ole Virginny. With Hilgarde
Tyndale.
1889. DLC
[Typescript]

1418. JOHNSON, Ellen [Br. 19c]
My Aunt Grumble.
1877. N
[Comedietta. Prod. at Brighton,
1877.]

1419. JOHNSON, Fannie M. [Am. 19c]
Dotage, a Dickens charade in three
scenes.
In: George B. Bartlett's A dream of
the centuries and other
entertainments for parlor and hall.
Boston: W.H. Baker, 1899. 23 1. NUC
OCLC
[Baker's novelties]

1420. JOHNSON, Margaret [Am. b. 1860]
The wheel of fate. An operetta in
three acts.
NY: n.p., 1896. 24p. NUC

1421. JOHNSON, S. A., Miss [Br. 19c]
Caleb; or, The curse.
1893. N
[Comic drama. Prod. Terry's, 1893.]

1422. JOHNSTONE, Annie Lewis [Br.
19c]
On the frontier.
1891. N
[Melodrama. Prod. in Liverpool &
Greenwich, 1891, Pavillion, 1891.]

1423. JONES, Clara Augusta [Am. 19c]
ALT: Augusta, Clara; Clara Augusta
The matrimonial advertisement.
In: Dramatic leaflets.
Philadelphia: Phineas Garrett, 1877.
1 v. in 20 pts. NUC OCLC H
[Comedy, 1 act.]

1424. JONES, Gertrude (Price), Mrs.
J. Wilton Jones [Br. 19c] ALT: Devot,
Gertrude Price) Jones; Price,
Gertrude PSEUD: Warden, Gertrude
A cruel city; or, London by night.
With J. Wilton Jones.
1896. M N
[Drama, 4 acts. Prod. Surrey, 1896,
& Novelty, 1897.]

1425. -----Woman's proper place: a
duologue. By Gertrude Warden. With
J. Wilton Jones.
L: Lacy; L & NY: S. French, 1898.
14p. BL E N
[Duologue. Prod. St. James, 1896.
Lacy's acting edition, v. 140]

JONES, J. Wilton, co-author see
JONES, Gertrude (Price)

JONES, Mrs. J. Wilton see JONES,
Gertrude (Price)

1426. JONES, Lavinia, Mrs. [Br. 19c]
The Cloud King with his cloud castle.
An opera.
Bradford-on-Avon?: n.p., 1864. 15p.
BL
[Verse]

1427. -----The eleven white swans of
Denmark. An opera.
Bradford-on-Avon: Daniel Jones, 1864.
23p. BL
[Based on story by Hans Christian
Andersen]

1428. JONES, Margaret Elizabeth Mary
[Br. 19c] ALT: J., M. E. M.
Gawyim honor: a tragedy in five acts.
L: J.C. West, 1844. 110p. NUC BL

1429. JONSON, Dorothy (Forsyth) [Br.
19c] ALT: Forsyth, Dorothy PSEUD:
Leighton, Dorothy
Thyrya Fleming. By Dorothy Leighton.
1895. M N
[Play, 4 acts. Prod. Terry's, 1895.]

JOPLING, Louisa Goode, co-author see
PRAED, Rosa Caroline (Murray-Prior)

JOPLING, Mrs. Joseph Middleton, co-
author see PRAED, Rosa Caroline
(Murray-Prior)

1430. JORDAN, Dorothy (Bland) [Br.
1761-1816] ALT: Bland, Dorothy
The spoiled child; a farce.
Dublin: George Folingsby, 1801. 23p.
L: Pub. for Proprietors by W. Simpkin
& R. Marshall, 1822. NUC BL OCLC

[Ascribed variously to Isaac
Bickerstaff, Sir Richard Ford,
Dorothy Jordan, Prince Hoare, &
Elizabeth Inchbald. Cumberland's
British Theatre. v. 14.]

JOSEPH, DELISSA, pseud. see SMITH,
Adele Crafton

1431. JOSEPHINE, Katie [Am. 19c]
Love's disappointment. n.p.: n.p.,
1886. 16p. NUC OCLC
[Dramatic poem]

JOSIAH ALLEN'S WIFE, pseud. see
HOLLEY, Marietta

K., H. St. A. see KITCHING, H. Saint
A., Miss

1432. KARADJA, Mary Louise (Smith),
Princess [Br. b. 1868] ALT: Karatzas,
Maria Princess
"A.B.C.--poste restante" a farcical
comedy in three acts.
L: Pr. J. Miles & co., 1897. 60p. NUC
[BL has ed. in Swedish, 1898.]

KARATZAS, Maria, Princess see
KARADJA, Mary Louise (Smith),
Princess

1433. KATHERINE OF SUTTON, Abbess of
Barking [Br. 14c]
Latin liturgical drama and
ceremonials.
1363-1370. Har
[Her adaptations have been preserved
in the Ordinarium of Barking. Mod.
eds. incl. Drama of the Medieval
Church, ed. Karl Young. Oxford:
Clarendon press, 1933.]

1434. KAVANAUGH, Mrs. Russell [Am.
19c]
Original dramas, dialogues,
declarations and tableaux vivants for
school exhibitions, May-day
celebrating and parlor amusement.
Louisville, KY: John P. Morton, 1884.
252p. NUC OCLC H
[5 sections: Original dramas (for the
whole family); Declarations
(children's recitations); May Queen
celebration (masque); American
oratory (excerpts of speeches for
recitation); tableaux vivants.]

1435. -----Araminta Jenkins.
In: Original dramas ... .
[Comedietta, for female characters.]

1436. -----The aunt's legacy.
In: Original dramas ... .
[Dramatic sketch for female
characters.]

1437. -----Beauty and the beast.
In: Original dramas ... .

1438. -----Cinderella, or, The glass
slipper.
In: Original dramas ... .

1439. -----The dancing Dutchman.
In: Original dramas ... .
[Dramatic sketch. In dialect.]

1440. -----The elopement.
In: Original dramas ... .
[Comedietta for female characters.]

1441. -----Health vs. riches.
In: Original dramas ... .
[Dramatic sketch. Female
characters.]

1442. -----Marrying a fortune.
In: Original dramas ... .
[Comedietta]

1443. -----May Queen celebration.
In: Original dramas ... .
[In verse. Masque.]

1444. -----The minister's guests.
In: Original dramas ... .
[Comedietta]

1445. -----Mrs. Vatican Smythe's
party.
In: Original dramas ... .
[Comedietta for female characters.]

1446. -----The old man's pocket book.
In: Original dramas ... .
[Comic sketch]

1447. -----The pea-green glazed
cambric.
In: Original dramas ... .
[Comedietta.]

1448. -----The perfection of beauty.
In: Original dramas ... .
[Opera for female characters, the 9
muses & virtues.]

1449. -----Preposition v.
proposition.
In: Original dramas ... .
[Comedietta]

1450. -----The relief aid sewing
society, or Mrs. Jones' vow.

1451. -----The spelling lesson.
In: Original dramas ... .

1452. -----The tattler.
In: Original dramas ... .
[Comedietta]

1453. -----The wreath of virtue.
In: Original dramas ... .
[In verse. Masque of Minerva &
virtues.]

KEATING, Eliza H. see LACY, Katherine

1454. KEATING, Eliza H., Miss [Br.
19/20c]
Charade plays for the parlour.
2 pts. L: T.H. Lacy, 1865. NUC BL
[Pt. 2 Incl.: Nightgale, Matchlock &
Rebellion, Lacy's home plays.]

1455. -----Dramas for the drawing
room; or, Charades for Christmas.
2 pts. L: T.H. Lacy, 1855. 79, 100p.
NUC BL
[Part II title: Charade dramas for
the drawing room. Incl.: Blue Beard;
Phaeton; Cateline; Guy Fawkes;
Counterplot; Blindfold; Outlaw;
Sleeping-draught. Lacy's Home
Plays.]

1456. -----Fairy plays for home
performance. 10 pt.
L: T.H. Lacy, 1864-66. BL
[Incl. adult roles, sophisticated
enough for the whole family. NUC &
OCLC list plays sep. BL has sep. &
in 1 vol. coll.]

1457. -----Home plays for ladies;
arranged for school or family
performance.
L: T.H. Lacy, 187-? 102p. NUC
[Pt. 3 - Contents: 1. A Christmas of
Ambol in one act. 2. The harvest
queen, in one act. (Running title:
The peasant queen.) 3. Gaffer Grey's
legacy, in two acts. 4. The mystery
of Middlewitz.]

1458. -----Home plays. Dramas for
boys: a series of original comedies
comprising male characters only.
4 pt. L & NY: Samuel French & T.H.
Lacy, 1862. 20, 30, 19, 19p. NUC BL
[Incl. adult roles; sophisticated
enough for whole family.]

1459. -----Plays for the parlour: a
collection of acting charades.
L: T.H. Lacy, 1855. 2 pts. in 1 v.
NUC OCLC

[Contents: Banditti; Aladdin;
Inspector; & Nightmare.]

1460. -----Aladdin; or, The very
wonderful lamp! A fairy extravaganza
in two acts.
L: French, 18--? 33p. NUC BL OCLC E
[In French's standard drama; The
acting ed., v. 40; & Fairy plays, no.
6.]

1461. -----Ali Baba, a new duo-
(decimal) edition of the forty
thieves!!! A fairy extravaganza in
two acts.
L: T.H. Lacy, n.d. 38p. NUC BL OCLC E
[In: Fairy plays, no. 10. L & NY: S.
French, 1910? 38p. OCLC]

1462. -----Beauty and the beast. A
fairy extravaganza.
L & NY: T.H. Lacy, 1864. 32p. NUC BL
E
[In: Fairy plays, no. 1]

1463. -----Blue Beard: or, Female
curiousity and male atrocity: an
extravaganza in two acts.
L & NY: S> French, 1865? 28p. NUC BL
OCLC E
[In: Fairy plays, no. 2]

1464. ------A Christmas of Ambol in
one act.
In: Home plays for ladies.

1465. -----Cinderella; a fairy drama.
In one act.
L: S. French, 18--? 22p. NUC BL E
[In: Fairy plays, no. 4.]

1466. -----Gaffer Grey's legacy, in
two acts.
In: Home plays for ladies.

1467. -----The harvest queen, in one
act.
In: Home plays for ladies.
[Running title: "The peasant queen."]

1468. -----Incog; or, "Fine feathers
make fine birds." An original farce
in one act.
In: Home plays ... .

1469. -----Little Bo Peep.
1860. N
[Pantomime. Prod. at Brighton,
1860.]

1470. -----Little red riding hood;
or, The wolf, the wooer, and the
wizard: A fairy burlesque, in one
act.
L: T.H. Lacy, n.d. 37p. NUC BL E
[In Fairy plays, no. 8.]

1471. -----The mystery of Middlewitz.
In: Home plays for ladies.

1472. -----The plot of Potzentausend.
A comic drama in one act.
In: Home plays ... .

1473. -----The poor relation; or,
"Love me -- love my dog!" A comic
drama in two parts.
In: Home plays ... .

1474. -----Prince Nysee Nosey. Fairy
extravanganza in one act.
L & NY: S. French, 1864. 18p. NUC BL
[Also in: Fairy plays for Home
Performance]

1475. -----Puss in boots; or, The
marquis, the miller and the mouser.
A fairy extravaganza.
L: T.H. Lacy, 1864? 35p. NUC BL E
[In: Fairy plays, no. 7. L & NY: S.
French, 19--? 35p. OCLC]

1476. -----La roserie; or, The queen
of the fete. A comedy in one act.
L: T.H. Lacy, 186-? 35p. NUC

1477. -----Shamed. A drama in one
act.
In: Home plays ... .

1478. -----The sleeping beauty, or, one hundred and eighteen years in as many minutes, (stoppages included); a fairy extravaganza, in two parts.
L: T.H. Lacy, 18--? 30p. NUC BL E
[Fairy plays, no. 9]

1479. -----A slight mistake, or, A prize in a German lottery; a comedy in one act adapted from the French of Emile Souvestre.
L: T.H. Lacy, 186-? 34p. NUC
[In: Home plays for ladies, pt. 2, no. 2.]

1480. -----The talisman; or, "Truth may be blamed, but it cannot be shamed." An original drama in one act.
In: Home plays ... .

1481. -----The white cat, an old fairy tale made into a modern extravanganza.
L & NY: S. French and T.H. Lacy, 186-? 16p. NUC E
[In: Fairy plays, no. 3. Comedy, 1 act, verse.]

1482. -----The yellow dwarf. A fairy extravanganza, in one act.
L: S. French, T.H. Lacy, 1865? 32p. NUC BL E
[Farce, 6 scenes.
In: Fairy plays, no. 5.]

1483. KEEBLE, Mrs. [Br. 19c]
The Baronet's wager.
1869. N
[Comedietta. Prod. at Peterborough, 1869.]

1484. KEENE, Laura [Am. 19c]
The seven sons.
1861. C
[Keene established her own theatre in NY, 1855, and mounted a number of melodramas & tableaux, notably "Blanche of Brandywine." No copies of works found.]

1485. KELLOGG, Clara Louise [Am. 1842-1916] ALT: Strakosch, Clara Louise (Kellogg)
The Bohemian girl. Opera in three acts. [Lyrics] by Alfred Bunn. Music by Michael William Balfe. Revised and adapted by Miss Kellogg.
Baltimore, MD: Sun pr. establishment, 1874. 39p. H
[Libretto]

1486. -----The crown diamonds; grand opera in three acts. By D.F.E. Auber. Libretto revised and adapted by Kellogg.
Baltimore, MD: Sun pr. est., 1874. 48p. OCLC

1487. -----Faust. Grand opera in prologue and four acts.
Baltimore, MD: Sun pr. estab., 1874. 33p. NUC H
[Based on Goethe's Faust}

1488. -----Fra Diavolo, or, The inn of Terracina: comic opera in three acts, by D.F.E. Auber. Libretto revised and adapted by Kellogg.
Baltimore. MD: Sun pr. est., c1874. 32p. OCLC

1489. -----The Huguenots. Grand opera in five acts by Giacomo Meyerbeer.
Baltimore, MD: Sun pr. estab., 1875. 35p. OCLC H
[Libretto]

1490. -----The lily of Killarney: grand romantic opera in three acts by J. Benedict. Libretto revised and adapted by Kellogg.
Baltimore, MD: Sun pr. est., c1874. 32p. OCLC

1491. -----Lucia di Lammermoor.
Grand opera in three acts, by
Donizetti. Libretto revised and
adapted by Kellogg.
Baltimore, MD: Sun pr. est., 1874.
20p. NUC OCLC

1492. -----The star of the north.
Opera in three acts by Giacomo
Meyerbeer.
Baltimore, MD: Sun. pr. estab.,
c1874, 1876. 48p. NUC OCLC H
[Libretto]

KELLY, Fanny see KELLY, Frances Maria

1493. KELLY, Frances Maria [Br. 1790-
1882] ALT: Kelly, Fanny
A genuine report. Miss Kelly's new
entertainment entitled Dramatic
recollections: with studies of
character.
L: J. Duncombe, 1833? 38p. NUC OCLC

KEMBLE, Ann Julia see HATTON, Ann
Julia (Kemble)

KEMBLE, Mrs. Charles see KEMBLE,
Marie-Thérèse (DeCamp)

KEMBLE, Fanny see KEMBLE, Frances
Anne

1494. KEMBLE, Frances Anne [Br.
1800/09-1893] ALT: Butler, Frances
Anne (Kemble); Butler, Mrs. Pierce;
Kemble, Fanny
Plays. By F.A. Kemble. An English
tragedy: a play in five acts. Mary
Stuart; translated from the German of
[Johann Christoph Friedrich von]
Schiller. Mademoiselle de Belle
Isle; translated from the French of
Alexandre Dumas [the elder].
L: Longman, Green, Longman, Roberts &
Green, 1863. 582p. NUC BL OCLC E N
[First play: 5 acts, verse.]

1495. -----Francis the first, an
historical drama. L: J. Murray, 1832.
142p. NY: Peabody & co., 1832. 63p.
NUC BL OCLC E N
[5 acts, verse. Prod. Covent Garden,
1832.]

1496. -----Mademoiselle de Belle
Isle.
In: Plays ... .
M N
[Drama, 5 acts, adapted from the
French of Alexandre Dumas, Pere.
Prod. Haymarket, 1864.]

1497. -----The star of Seville: a
drama in five acts. By Mrs. Butler
(late Fanny Kemble).
L & NY: Saunders & Otley, 1837.
[130p. E] 146p. NUC BL OCLC E N
[verse]

1498. KEMBLE, Marie-Thérèse (DeCamp),
Mrs. Charles Kemble [Br. 1774-1838]
ALT: DeCamp, Marie Thérése
The day after the wedding; or, A
wife's first lesson. An interlude.
L: Appleyards, 1808. 32p. L: Thomas
Hailes Lacy, 1808. 19p. NUC BL OCLC E
N
[Farce, 1 act. Prod. Covent Garden,
1808.]

1499. -----Fairly taken in. A comic
interlude, in one act and one scene.
NY: n.p., 1870/ NY: Dick &
Fitzgerald, 190-? 11p. NUC
[In: Hudson, Francis, ed. Hudson's
private theatricals, pp. 171-179.]

1500. -----First faults.
1799. N
[Comedy. Prod. Drury Lane, 1799.
Larpent MS 37]

1501. -----Matchmaking; or, 'Tis a
wise child that knows its own father.
1808. N
[Comedy. Prod. Covent Garden, 1808.
Attr. to her.]

1502. -----Nigel; or, The crown
jewels. Five acts.
L: R. Wilks, pr., 1823. 97p. NUC
[OCLC attr. Isaac Pocock, 1st prod.
Theatre Royal.]

1503. -----Personation, or, Fairly
taken in: a comic interlude in one
act.
L: Dicks, 1805. 6p. NUC BL OCLC E N
[First performed at the Theatre Royal
in 1803. Adapted from the French,
"Defiance et malice," by Joseph Marie
Armand Michel Dieulafoy.]

1504. -----Smiles and tears; or, the
widow's stratagem: a comedy in five
acts.
L: John Miller, 1815. 88p. NUC BL
OCLC E N
[Prod. Covent Garden, 1815. Based in
part on Amelia (Alderson) Opie's "The
father and daughter" & upon the
French: "La suite d'un bal masque."]

1505. KENDAL, Mrs. Mark [Br. 19c]
Half seas over.
1882. M

[Drama. Prod. St. George Hall, 1882.
N lists author as Mrs. Mark and play
as prod. at Kendal.]

1506. KENNEDY, Grace [Br. 1782-1824]
The decision; or, Religion must be
all, or is nothing.
Edinburgh: n.p., 1821. NUC BL OCLC
[4th ed. Edinburgh: W. Oliphant,
1822. 108p. OCLC. Religious novel in
dramatic form. Inglis.]

1507. -----Profession not principle;
or The name of Christian is not
Christianity.
2d ed. Edinburgh: W. Oliphant, 1823.
286p. NUC BL OCLC
[Religious novel in dramatic form.
Inglis.]

1508. KENNERLEY, Juba [Br. 19c]
An entirely new and original comic
opera, in three acts entitled Melita;
or, The Parsee's daughter. Written
by J.K. Composed by H. Pontet.
L: W. Cubitt & co., 1883. 44p. BL N
[Prose & verse. Prod. Novelty,
1882.]

KENNEY, James, co-author see GORE,
Catherine Grace Frances (Moody)

1509. KENNION, Mrs. [Br. 19c]
Nina; or, The story of a heart.
1885. N
[Drama. Prod. at Wigan, 1885;
Strand, 1887.]

1510. KENYON, Emily E. [Am. 19c]
Rose McCrea; or, Congress and camp of
the American revolution.
Boston: A. Mudge & son, 1876. 19p.
NUC OCLC
[Historical drama]

1511. KETELTAS, Caroline M. [Am. 19c]
The last of the Plantagenets. Tragic
drama in three acts.
NY: Pr. by R. Craighead, 1844. 56p.
NUC OCLC H R
[Based on novel of same title by
William Heseltine, 1830.]

1512. KIDDER, Kathryn [Am. d. 1939]
ALT: Anspacher, Mrs. Louis Kauffman
The heart of her husband. Domestic
drama in three acts and two scenes.
NY: n.p., 187-? NUC H
[Supposed author. Typescript prompt-
book. 40, 62, 21 l.]

1513. KILLIGREW, Anne [Br. 1660-1685]
Poems.
L: S. Lowndes, 1686. 100p. NUC BL
OCLC [Incl.: A pastoral dialogue.]

1514. KIMBALL, Hannah Parker [Am. b.
1861]
Victory and other verses.
Boston: Copeland & Day, 1897. 76p.
NUC OCLC H
[Incl. Victory, a dramatic poem, pp.
1-12.]

KINGSLEY, Mary St. Leger see
HARRISON, Mary St. Leger (Kingsley)

KINGSTON, GERTRUDE, pseud., co-author
see GRAVES, Clotilda Inez Mary

1515. KINGSTON, Gertrude [Br. 19c]
The bear and the lady.
In: Dialogues of the day. Ed. Oswald
Crawford.
L: Chapman & Hall, 1895. 8p. NUC BL
OCLC E
[Author may be Gertrude Kingston,
aft. Silver, an actress or, more
probably, Gertrude Angela Mary
Konstam, who used this pseud.]

KINNAMAN, C.F., co-author see
KINNAMAN, Mrs. C.F.

1516. KINNAMAN, Mrs. C.F. [Am. 19c]
In a spider's web. Musical farce in
three acts. With C.F. Kinnaman.
Clyde, OH: Ames, 1900. 33p. NUC OCLC
H
[Ames' Standard & Minor Drama, no.
421]

1517. KINNEY, Elizabeth Clementine
(Dodge) Stedman [Am. 1810-1889]
Bianca Cappello. A tragedy.
Cambridge, MA & NY: Hurd & Houghton,
1873. 146p. NUC BL OCLC R
[5 acts, verse]

1518. KITCHEL, Mrs. Francis W. [Am.
19c]
The wager, a comedy duologue.
NY: E.S. Werner, 1894. 8p. NUC OCLC

1519. KITCHING, H. Saint A., Miss
[Br. 19c] ALT: K., H. St A. PSEUD:
Lady, A
Moral plays ... .
L: Calkin & Budd, 1832. 276p. NUC BL
OCLC

1520. -----The fate of Ivan, an
historical tragedy.
In: Moral plays ... .
[5 acts]

1521. -----Keep your temper! or Know
whom you marry, a comedy.
In: Moral plays ... .
[5 acts]

1522. -----Miss Betsy Bull, or the Johnnies in Spain, a melodrama. By a lady.
In: Moral plays ... . [3 acts]

1523. KNAPP, Lizzie Margaret [Am. 19c]
An afternoon rehearsal. Comedy in one act for female characters.
Boston: W.H. Baker, 1892. 14p. NUC OCLC H
[Baker's ed. of plays. Hartford, CT: United Workers & Women's exchange, 1892. 14p.]

KNIPE, Eliza see COBBOLD, Elizabeth (Knipe)

1524. KNOX, Isa (Craig) [Br. 1831-1903] ALT: Craig, Isa; Isa Duchessa [Duchess NUC OCLC] Agnes and other poems.
L: Alexander Strahan, 1864. 228p. NUC BL OCLC
[Verse drama]

KONSTAM, Gertrude Angela Mary, co-author see GRAVES, Clotilda Inez Mary

1525. KUMMER, Clare Rodman (Beecher) [Am. c1873-1958]
Captain Kidd; or, the Buccaneers. 1898. N
[comic opera]

KYLE, George, co-author see DALLAS, Mary (Kyle)

L., pseud. see SWANWICK, Catherine

L., co-author see SHORE, Arabella

L., A.E. see LEIGH, Agnes

L., B. see LINDSAY, Caroline Blanche Elizabeth (Fitzroy), Lady

L., L.E. see LANDON, Letitia Elizabeth

LACY, Katherine, ed. see SEYMOUR, Mary (Seamer)

1526. LACY, Katherine [Br. 19c]
Home plays for ladies, arranged for school or family performance. 10 pt.
L: T.H. Lacy, 1867-93. NUC BL OCLC
[Incl.: 5 plays by Mary Seymour and a few plays by male authors: Charles L. Young, Bart., Charles Masham Rae & Rev. G.S. Hodges. All other plays

without specific attribution assumed to be Lacy's. Also incl.: "Little plays for little children in one act." See juv. lit. vol. of this bibliography.]

1527. -----As you make your bed so you must lie in it. In one act.
In: Home plays ... .

1528. -----Caroline and Henrietta; or, Industry triumphant. Two acts.
In: Home plays ... .

1529. -----Choosing a bride. A comedy in one act.
In: Home plays ... .

1530. -----A Christmas gambol. A comedy in one act.
In: Home plays ... .

1531. -----Cousin Letty. A petite comedy in one act.
In: Home plays ... .

1532. -----The fox and the grapes. A sketch in one act.
In: Home plays ... .

1533. -----Gaffer Grey's legacy. A comedy in two acts.
In: Home plays ... .

1534. -----The governess. A petite comedy in one act.
In: Home plays ... .

1535. -----Lina and Gertrude; or, the Swiss chalet. A drama in one act.
L & NY: S. French, 186-. 35p. NUC
[In: Home plays for ladies. pt. 4, no. 2.]

1536. -----A little girl who tells fibs. A comedy in one act.
In: Home plays ... .

1537. -----My aunt's heiress; a comedy in one act.
L & NY: S. French, 186-. 65-103p. E
[Also pub. NY: Fitzgerald, n.d. 30p. E. Attrib. to Lacy.
In: Home plays for ladies. Authorship ascribed to author by Halkett & Laing, to Eliza H. Keating by Eldredge.]

1538. -----My daughter's daughter. A comedy in one act.
In: Home plays ... .

1539. -----The mystery of Muddlewitz. A comedy in one act.

In: Home plays ... .

1540. -----The peasant queen [The harvest queen]. A comedy in one act. In: Home plays ... .

1541. -----Polly. In three acts. In: Home plays ... .

1542. -----Pride and vanity. A comedy in one act. In: Home plays ...

1543. -----The prying little girl. A comedy. One act. In: Home plays ... .

1544. -----A wonderful cure. A farce. In one act. Female characters only.
L & NY: S. French, 186-. pp. 37-64. Boston: Walter H. Baker & co., 1889. 21p. NUC OCLC
[Also pub. as: The mystic charm, or, A wonderful cure. Listed in Halkett & Laing II, p. 98 under "Home plays for ladies." Baker's edition of plays. Also in: Home plays, pt. 4, no. 2.]

LACY, Maria see LOVELL, Maria Anne (Lacy)

LADY, A, pseud. see BROWN, Catherine

LADY, A, pseud. see CELESIA, Dorothea (Mallet)

LADY, A, pseud. see COBBOLD, Elizabeth (Knipe)

LADY, A, pseud. see EDWARDS, Anna Maria

LADY, A, pseud. see ELLIOTT, Charlotte

LADY, A, pseud. see FRANCIS, Ann (Gittins)

LADY, A, pseud. see GRIFFITH, Elizabeth (Griffith)

LADY, A, pseud. see HEMANS, Felicia Dorothea (Browne)

LADY, A, pseud. see KITCHING, H. Saint A., Miss

LADY, A, pseud. see PINCKNEY, Mary Henrietta

LADY, A, pseud. see PLUMPTRE, Annabella

LADY, A, pseud. see PYE, Jael Henrietta (Mendez)

LADY, A, pseud. see SHERIDAN, Frances (Chamberlaine)

LADY, A, pseud. see SIDDONS, Sarah (Kemble)

LADY, A, pseud. see SMITH, Sarah (Pogson)

LADY, A, pseud. see THOMAS, Elizabeth, Mrs.

LADY, A, pseud. see WINCHELSEA, Anne (Kingsmill) Finch, Countess of

LADY, A, pseud. see YOUNG, Mary Julia

1545. LADY, A, pseud. [Br. 18c] The conquest of Corsica by the French. A tragedy. By a lady. L: The author, 1771. NUC BL
[3 acts, verse]

1546. LADY, A, pseud. [Br. 18c] The court lady; or, the coquet's surrender. A comedy. Written by a lady.
L: T. Grey, 1733. NUC BL OCLC
[Running title: The Coquet's surrender, or, the Humourous punster. 5 acts, prose. Longe, F. Coll. of plays, v. 152, no. 1.]

1547. LADY, A, pseud. [Br. 18c] Cross partners, a comedy. In five acts. As performed at the Theatre Royal in the Haymarket.
L: C. & G. Kearsley, 1792. 108p. NUC BL OCLC
[Based on Philippe Nericault Destouches' "L'amour usé" and a novel, "The Kentish maid."]

1548. LADY, A, pseud. [Br. 19c] A lesson for lovers; a farce, in three acts; and The conjurer; a farce in three acts. By a lady.
L: S. Gosnell, 1823. 60p. OCLC

1549. LADY, A, pseud. [Br. 19c] The maiden queen, a pageant of olden times. Also, The countess, a play in five acts. By a lady.
Exeter: Pr. Trewman & co., 1829. NUC

1550. LADY, A, pseud. [Br. 18c] The Peruvian; a comic opera, in three acts. As performed at the Theatre Royal Covent Garden. By a lady. The music chiefly composed by Mr. Hook.
L: J. Bell, 1786. 81p. NUC BL OCLC

[Partly founded on Jean Francois
Marmontel's tale, Coralie, or
"L'amitie a l'epreuve."]

1551. LADY, A, pseud. [Br. 18c]
The South Briton: a comedy of five
acts: as it is performed at the
theatre in Smock-alley with great
applause. Written by a lady.
L: J. Williams, 1774. 72p. Dublin: G.
Allen, 1774. 79p. NUC BL OCLC
[Verse]

1552. LADY IN CONNECTICUT, A, pseud.
[Am. 18c]
The search after happiness: a
pastoral drama from the poetry of
Miss Moore.
Catskill, CT?: Pr. by M. Croswell &
co., 1794. 30p. Wells
[3 scenes, adapted from Hannah More]

LADY OF ENGLAND, A, pseud. see
TUCKER, Charlotte Maria

1553. LADY OF QUALITY, A, pseud. [Br.
18c]
The fate of Corsica: or, the female
politician. A comedy. Written by a
lady of quality.
L: E. Rayner, 1732. NUC
[Not performed. BioD.]

1554. LAHEE, M. R., Miss [Br. 19c]
ALT: L., M. R.
Next of kin.
Manchester: A. Heywood & sons, c1899.
[5 males, 1 female]

1555. LAKE, Barbara [Br. 19c]
The betrayal of Ruben Holt. A play
in prologue and three acts.
L: Wyman & sons, 1886. 16p. BL
[Adapted from her novel of same name]

LAMB, Mary Montgomerie see CURRIE,
Mary Montgomerie (Lamb) Singleton,
Baroness

1556. LAMBERT, Mary H. P. [Am. d.
1921] PSEUD: Luigi
An apple of discord; or, a warning to
young men who would marry for money.
By Luigi.
Mentone: Bertrand & Querot, 1875.
10p. NUC

1557. -----Vamba. An historical
drama. By Luigi.
Geneva: Burkhardt, 189-. 59p. NUC

1558. LAMBLA, Hattie L. [Am. 19c]
The bewitched closet, a dramatic
sketch in one act.

Clyde, OH: A.D. Ames, 1872. 6p. NUC

1559. -----Domestic felicity, a
domestic sketch, in one act.
Clyde, OH: A.D. Ames, 1872. 6p. NUC
OCLC H
[Ames' series of standard and minor
drama, no. 42]

1560. -----Obedience; or, Too mindful
by far; a comedietta in one act.
Clyde, OH: A.D. Ames, 1872? 6p. NUC H
[Ames' Standard & Minor Drama, no.
44]

1561. -----That mysterious bundle; a
farce in one act.
Clyde, OH: A.D. Ames, 1872. 7p. NUC
OCLC
[Ames' Standard & Minor Drama, no.
40]

LANCASTER, FLORENCE, pseud. see
LANCASTER-WALLIS, Ellen

1562. LANCASTER-WALLIS, Ellen [Br.
1856-1940] ALT: Wallis, Ellen
Lancaster PSEUD: Lancaster, Florence
Miss Wallis' ... Curtain-raisers.
(Little Miss Muffet; Cupid in ermine;
The prior claim; A sudden squall;
Cissy's engagement; My son and I).
6 pt. L & NY: Samuel French, 1899. BL

1563. -----An amateur wife.
1897. M N
[Farce comedy, 3 acts. Prod.
Criterion, 1897.]

1564. -----"Cissy's engagement." A
duologue by Ellen Lancaster-Wallis.
L: Lacy, 1895. 9p. L & NY: S. French,
NUC BL OCLC E N
[Prod. Steinway Hall, 1895. French's
acting edition, v. 2166. Also in:
Miss Wallis' Curtain raisers.]

1565. -----Cupid in ermine. A
comedietta in one act. By Ellen
Lancaster-Wallis.
L & NY: Lacy; S.French, 1899. 11p.
NUC BL OCLC E N
[Duologue. Produced at Princess of
Wales' Theatre, Kennington, March 27,
1899. French's acting edition, v.
2166. Also in: Miss Wallis' Curtain
raisers]

1566. -----For wife and state. With
James Winsett Boulding.
1883. N
[Drama. Prod. Edinburgh, 1883. Also
prod. at Belfast as: "A bitter
love."]

1567. -----Little Miss Muffet.
Comedietta in one act. By Ellen
Lancaster-Wallis.
L & NY: Lacy; S. French, 1899. 8p.
NUC BL E
[Duologue for female characters.
Produced at Steinway Hall, May 3,
1898. Also in: Miss Wallis' Curtain
raisers. Lacy's Acting ed.]

1568. -----"My son and I." An
original trifle in one act. By Ellen
Lancaster-Wallis.
L & NY: Lacy, 1894. 11p. NUC BL N E
[Produced at Steinway Hall, May 25,
1894. Also in: Miss Wallis' Curtain
raisers]

1569. -----The Pharisee. With T.
Malcolm Watson.
1894. M N
[Play, 3 acts. Prod. Shaftesbury,
1890.]

1570. -----The prior claim.
Comedietta in one act. By Florence
Lancaster.
In: Miss Wallis' curtain raisers.
L & NY: S. French, n.d. 13p. BL OCLC
E
[Female characters. Produced at
Steinway Hall, May 3, 1898. Lacy's
Acting ed.]

1571. -----"A sudden squall."
Comedietta in one act. By Ellen
Lancaster-Wallis.
L: Lacy, 1899. 7p. NUC BL
[Duologue. Also in: Miss Wallis'
curtain raisers]

1572. -----Summer clouds.
1899. N
[Dramatic sketch. Prod. at
Wolverhampton, 1899; Grand, 1899.]

1573. -----The wand of wedlock. With
Herbert MacPherson.
1896. N [Drama. Prod. in Cardiff,
1896.]

LANDER, Charles, co-author see
CASSILIS, Ina Leon

LANDER, George, co-author see WELDON,
Mrs.

1574. LANDON, Letitia Elizabeth [Br.
1802-1838] ALT: L., L. E.; Maclean,
Mrs. George
Life and literary remains of L.E.L.,
by Laman Blanchard.
L: H. Colburn, 1841. 2v. NUC OCLC E

[Incl. "Castruccio Castrucani; or,
The triumph of Lucca. A tragedy." in
5 acts, verse.]

1575. LANE, S., Mrs. [Br. 19c]
Albert de Rosen.
1875. M N
[Drama, 4 acts. Prod. Britannia,
1875.]

1576. -----The cobbler's daughter.
1878. M N
[Drama, 4 acts. Prod. Britannia,
1878.]

1577. -----Devotion; or, the
priceless wife.
1881. M N
[Drama, 3 acts, adapted from the
French. Prod. Britannia, 1881.]

1578. -----Dolores.
1874. M N
[Drama. Prod. Britannia, 1874.]

1579. -----The faithless wife.
1876. M N
[Drama. 4 acts. Prod. Britannia,
1876.]

1580. -----Red Josephine; or, Woman's
vengeance.
1880. M N
[Drama. Prod. Britannia, 1880.]

1581. -----St. Bartholomew; or, a
Queen's love.
1877. M N
[Drama. Prod. Britannia, 1877.]

1582. -----Taken from memory.
1873. M N
[Drama. Prod. Britannia, 1874.]

1583. LANE-FOX, Florence [Br. 19c]
ALT: Fox, Florence Lane-
The Jew's eye.
1899. N
[Drama. Prod. at Bayswater, 1889.]

1584. LANNER, Katti [19c]
Red riding hood.
1891. N [Ballet. Prod. Crystal
Palace, 1891.]

1585. LATHAM, Grace [Br. 19c]
Beside a cradle.
1888. N
[Monologue. Prod. 1888.]

1586. -----Florian. Music by I.
Walter.
1886. N
[Opera. Prod. Novelty, 1886.]

1587. LATIMER, K. M., Miss [Br. 19c]
Cousin Charlie.
1889. N
[Comedietta. Prod. at Eastbourne,
1889.]

1588. LATTER, Mary, Mrs. [Br. 1725-
1777] PSEUD: Vespasian, Titus
The siege of Jerusalem, by Titus
Vespasian, a tragedy. To which is
prefixed, by way of introduction, "An
essay on the mystery and mischiefs of
stagecraft.".
L: C. Bathurst, 1763. 87p. NUC BL
OCLC B N
[5 acts, verse. Ode, for music &
voices, pp. 86-87, intended as finale
for the play. Not prod. BioD.
Longe, v. 103, no.1]

1589. LAURENT, Mme. [Br. 19c]
The Truand Chief; or The provost of
Paris: a melodrama. With William
Henry Oxberry.
L: J. Duncombe, 1825. NUC BL
[3 acts. Duncombe's ed. of the
British Theatre, v. 32.]

LAW, Arthur, co-author see PURVIS,
Mrs. Herbert

1590. LAWRENCE, Eweretta, Miss [Br.
19c]
Isofel.
1887. N
[Drama. Prod. at Ipswich, 1887.]

1591. -----Jess. With J.J. Bisgood.
1890. M N
[Drama, adapted from H. Rider
Haggard. Prod. Adelphi, 1890.]

1592. -----On 'change; or The
professor's venture.
L & NY: Lacy, 1885. 53p. NUC BL OCLC
E M N
[Farce comedy, 3 acts. Adaptation of
Gustav von Moser's "On 'change."
Prod. Strand, 1885 & 1886, at
Toole's, 1885. French's Acting ed.,
2055.]

1593. LAWRENCE, Sarah, Miss [Br. 19c]
PSEUD: C., A.B.
Lausus and Lydia with Madam Bonso's
Three strings to her bow; or, Three
bows to her string!!! A comedy. By
A.B.C.
L: W. Earle, 1806. 78p. BL

1594. LAZARUS, Emma [Am. 1849-1887]
Admetus and other poems. NY: Hurd &
Houghton, 1871. 229p. NUC BL OCLC H

[Incl. Orpheus, p. 25-29; Prologue
for the theatre, p. 201-209; Scene
from Faust, p. 210-229]

1595. -----Songs of a Semite: the
dance to death and other poems.
NY: Office of "The American Hebrew,"
1882. 80p. NUC BL OCLC R
[The dance to death; a historical
tragedy in five acts, pp. 5-48, on
Pogrom in Germany, 1349.]

1596. -----The Spagnoletto: A drama
in verse.
NY: n.p. 1876. 56p. NUC OCLC R
[Tragedy, 5 acts, set in 17c Italy.]

1597. LEADBEATER, Mary (Shakleton),
Mrs. William Leadbeater [Br. 1758-
1826]
Cottage dialogues among the Irish
peasantry.
Philadelphia: Samuel R. Fisher, jr.,
1811. 270p. L: J. Johnson co., 1811.
343p. NUC BL OCLC E

LEADBEATER, Mrs. William see
LEADBEATER, Mary (Shakleton)

1598. LEAN, Florence (Marryat)
Church, Mrs. Francis Lean [Br.
1837/8-1899] ALT: Church, Mrs. Ross;
Marryat, Florence
The gamekeeper. With Henry
MacPherson.
1898. N
[Drama. Prod. at Brighton, 1898.]

1599. -----Her own enemy.
1884. M
[Adapted from her novel. Prod.
Gaiety, 1884.]

1600. -----Her world against a lie.
With George F. Neville.
1881. N
[Drama. Prod. Adelphi, 1881.]

1601. -----Miss Chester. Drama in
three acts. With Sir Charles Lawrence
Young, bart.
L & NY: Lacy; S. French, 1872 [1875
NUC]. 38p. NUC BL OCLC E N
[Drama. Prod. Holborn, 1872. Also
pub. as: "Charmyon" and "Her world
against a lie." French's acting
edition. no. 1549]

1602. -----Woman against woman.
n.p.: n.p., n.d. 42p. E
[Typescript]

LEAN, Mrs. Francis see LEAN, Florence
(Marryat) Church

1603. LEAPOR, Mary, Mrs. [Br. 1722-
1746] ALT: Leapor, Molly
Poems upon several occasions. Ed.
Isaac Hawkins Browne.
L: Pr. by J. Roberts, 1748-51. 2v.
NUC BL OCLC B N
[Vol. 2 contains a tragedy in blank
verse: "The unhappy father."]

LEAPOR, Molly see LEAPOR, Mary, Mrs.
LE BLONDE, H.M., co-author see
TEMPLE, Grace

1604. LECKIE, Elizabeth (Horner),
Mrs. George Leckie [Br. d. 1856]
The guardian: a dramatic poem.
Edinburgh: Edinburgh pr. & pub. co.;
L: Smith, Elder & co., 1843. BL
Inglis
[2 acts]

1605. -----The Hebrew boy. A
dramatic poem.
Edinburgh: Edinburgh pr. & pub. co.;
L: Smith, Elder & co., 1842. BL
Inglis
[2 acts. Preface says pub. as a
moral lesson & to inspire others to
write "short lyrical pieces,
combining music with action in blank
verse, in the style of Metastasio"]

1606. -----The power of conscience.
A dramatic poem.
Edinburgh: Edinburgh pr. & pub. co.;
L: Smith, Elder & co., 1841. 27p. BL
Inglis
[2 acts, music & poetry]

1607. -----The stepmother. A
dramatic poem.
Edinburgh: Edinburgh pr. & pub. co.;
L: Smith, Elder & co., 1842. BL
Inglis
[2 acts, music & poetry]

LECKIE, Mrs. George see LECKIE,
Elizabeth (Horner)

LEE, Miss see LEE, Eliza Buckminster

1608. LEE, Eliza Buckminster [Br.
1788-1864] ALT: Lee, Miss
Correggio. Trans. from Adam
Ochlenschlager.
In: Correggio ... .
Boston: Phillips & Sampson, 1846.
174p. NUC BL OCLC E

1609. -----Sappho. Trans. from Franz
Grillparzer.
In: Correggio ... .
[Pp. 175-303]

LEE, Mrs. Frank see LEE, Mary
(Chappell)

1610. LEE, Harriet [Br. 1757-1851]
The mysterious marriage, or the
heirship of Roselva. A play in three
acts.
L: G.G. & J. Robinson, 1798. 88p. NUC
BL OCLC B N
[Verse & prose. Longe, v. 245, no.
6]

1611. -----The new peerage, or, Our
eyes may deceive us, a comedy.
L: G.G. & J. Robinson, 1787. 72p. NUC
BL OCLC B N
[5 acts, prose. Prod. Drury Lane,
1787. Longe, v.99, no. 9]

1612. -----The three strangers. A
play in five acts. L: Longman, Rees,
Orme, Brown & Green, 1826. 76p. NUC E
N
[Based on her novel "Kruitzner."
Perf. Covent Garden, 1825.]

1613. LEE, Mary (Chappell), Mrs.
Frank Lee [Am. b. 1849]
The losing side, a poem, and why he
didn't insure, a dialogue.
Columbus, OH: W.G. Hubbard & co.,
1888. 18p. NUC
[Temperance recitations.]

LEE, Richard, co-author see PRAED,
Rosa Caroline (Murray-Prior)

1614. LEE, Sophia [Br. 1750-1824]
Almeyda, queen of Granada. A tragedy
in five acts.
L: Cadell & Davies, 1796. 121p. NUC
BL OCLC B N
[Blank verse. Prod. Drury Lane,
1796. Longe, v. 235, no. 3]

1615. -----The assignation, a comedy.
1807. N
[Prod. Drury Lane, 1807.]

1616. -----The chapter of accidents.
A comedy in five acts.
L: T. Caddell, 1780. 98p. BL OCLC B E
N
[Prod. Haymarket, 1780. Dicks'
standard plays, no. 257; Longe, v.
88, no. 1]

LEEDS, A., co-author see READE,
Gertrude

1617. LEETE, Jesse [Br. 19c]
Cinderella: a play for home acting.
Burgess Hill: F. Burnett, 1886. 22p.
BL

[one act, prose]

1618. LEFANU, Alicia (Sheridan), Mrs.
Joseph Lefanu [Br. 1753-1817]
The sons of Erin; or, Modern
sentiment; a comedy in five acts.
L: J. Ridgway, 1812. 98p. NUC BL OCLC
E
[Called on first performance,
"Prejudice; or, Modern Sentiment."
Prod. Lyceum, 1812.]

LEFANU, Mrs. Joseph see LEFANU,
Alicia (Sheridan)

1619. LEIGH, Agnes [Br. 19c] ALT: L.,
A. E.
Short plays and interludes.
L: S. French, 1899. 44p. BL

1620. -----Contradictions.
L & NY: Lacy, 1899. 8p. NUC BL E N
[Comic duologue for 2 female
characters. Also in: Short plays.]

1621. -----A lady in search of an
heiress.
L & NY: Lacy; S. French, 1899. 12p.
NUC BL E N
[Comedietta for female characters.
French's acting edition, no. 2149.
Also in Short plays.]

1622. -----The lunatic. L: Lacy,
1899. 11p. BL
[Comedietta. Also in: Short plays.]

1623. -----Number seventeen.
L & NY: Lacy; S. French, 1899. 11p.
NUC BL E N
[Comic duologue for 2 female
characters. Also in: Short plays.]

1624. -----A rainy day.
L & NY: Lacy; S. French, 1899. 11p.
NUC BL E
[Comedietta. Also in: Short plays.]

LEIGH, ARRAN, pseud. see BRADLEY,
Katharine Harris

LEIGH, ISLA, pseud. see COOPER, Edith
Emma

1625. LEIGH, Norma [Br. 19c]
Auld Lang Syne.
1891. N
[Drama. Prod. Ladbrooke Hall, 1891.]

LEIGHTON, DOROTHY, pseud. see JONSON,
Dorothy (Forsyth)

LEMORE, Clara see ROBERTS, Clara
(Lemore)

1626. LENNOX, Charlotte (Ramsay)
[Am./Br. 1720-1804] ALT: Ramsay,
Charlotte
Angelica; or, Quixote in petticoats.
L: Pr. for the author, 1758. 40p. NUC
OCLC Hill Wells
[Comedy, 2 acts.]

1627. -----The heiress. As performed
at the Theatre Royal, Drury Lane.
2d ed. L: J. Debrett, 1786. 112p. NUC
OCLC Hill
[Comedy, 5 acts. Adaptation by John
Burgoyne from her novel, "The
sister."]

1628. -----Old city manners. A
comedy. Altered from the original
Eastward Hoe, written by Ben Jonson,
[George] Chapman and [John] Marston.
As it is performed at the Theatre
Royal in Drury Lane.
L: T. Becket, 1775. 66p. NUC BL OCLC
B Hill N
[5 acts, prose. Prod. Drury Lane,
1775.]

1629. -----Philander. A dramatic
pastoral.
Dublin: R. Smith, 1758. 36p. L: A.
Millar, 1758. 48p. NUC BL OCLC B Hill
N
[Inspired by "Il Pastor Fido" by
Battista Guarini. Three acts, verse;
2 songs are by another hand. Longe,
v. 52, no. 8]

1630. -----The sister, a comedy.
L: J. Dodsley; T. Davies; Dublin: P.
& W. Wilson, 1769. 69p. NUC BL OCLC B
N Vaughn
[5 acts. Prod. Covent Garden, 1769.
Adaptation of her novel, "Henrietta."
Trans. into German 1776; first play
by Amer. woman & first trans. into
foreign language. R]

LESDERNIER, Emily P. see
DELESDERNIER, Emily Pierpont, Mrs.

LESLIE, Mrs. Frank see LESLIE, Miriam
Florence (Folline) Squier

1631. LESLIE, Eliza (Franklin) [Am.
1787-1858] ALT: Franklin, Eliza
Birth day stories.
Philadelphia: H.F. Anners, 1840.
179p. NUC OCLC
[Incl. dramatic dialogue & a poem.]

1632. LESLIE, Mary Eliza [Br. 19c]
Ina, and other poems.
Calcutta: W. Newman & co., 1856.
290p. BL Inglis

[Incl. "Ina, a drama," and "The death of Moses, a sacred drama."]

1633. LESLIE, Miriam Florence (Folline) Squier, Mrs. Frank Leslie [Am. 1836-1914] ALT: Squier, Mrs. E. G.
The "demi-monde." A satire on society. By Mrs. E.G. Squier. Philadelphia: J.B. Lippincott, 1858. 164p. NUC OCLC H R
[Based on "Le demi-monde" by Alexandre Dumas, the younger.]

1634. LETERRIER, Jennie [Br. 19c]
My courier.
1886. N
[Farce. Prod. in Manchester.]

1635. L'EVERSON, Mrs. Ernest [Br. 19c]
All for the best.
In: Dialogues of the day. Ed. Oswald Crawfurd.
L: Chapman & Hall, 1895. pp. 214-225. NUC BL OCLC E

1636. -----Engaged.
In: Dialogues of the day.
[pp. 44-53]

LEWES, MARIAN, pseud. see EVANS, Marian

LEWIS, Mrs. A.G. see LEWIS, Abbie Goodwin (Davies)

1637. LEWIS, Abbie Goodwin (Davies) [Am. 19c] ALT: Lewis, Mrs. A. G.
Caught napping; a one-act operetta for Christmas Eve. Music by Leo Rich Lewis.
Boston: O. Ditson, 1886. 22p. NUC OCLC
[OCLC: Juvenile opera]

1638. -----Christmas at the Kerchiefs'. A musical dialogue for use at Christmas tree festivals in the Sunday school and home and other entertainments. With Leo Rich Lewis.
Brattleboro, VT: E.P. Carpenter co., 1888. 46p. NUC

1639. -----The dairymaid's supper. A cantata for church and charity festivals. With Leo Rich Lewis.
Brattleboro, VT: E.P. Carpenter co., 1888. 48p. NUC OCLC

1640. -----Easter, 1885. The invisible house. With music by L.T. Lewis.
Boston: Sunday school helper, 1885. 5 l. NUC

1641. -----Jingle bells. An original operetta, in two scenes, for Christmas eve, in the home or Sunday school. Music by Leo R. Lewis.
Boston: Oliver Ditson & co.; NY: C.H. Ditson & co., 1887. 20p. NUC OCLC

1642. -----Our Easter offering; an Easter poem or cantata by Mrs. A.G. Lewis. With music by Leo R. Lewis.
Boston: O. Ditson co., 1888. NUC

1643. -----Programme for school celebration of Washington's birthday.
Boston: NY: Chicago: Ginn & co., 1894. 16p. NUC

1644. -----R.E. Porter, or the interviewer and the fairies. An original operetta in three acts. Music by Leo R. Lewis.
Boston: White, Smith & co., 1883. 88p. NUC OCLC

1645. LEWIS, Catharine [Br. 1856-1942]
Cupid's odds and ends.
1895. N
[Comedy. Prod. at Parkhurst, 1895.]

1646. -----My missis. With Donald Robertson.
1886. M N
[Drama. Prod. Opera Comique, 1886.]

1647. LEWIS, Clara M. [Am. 19/20c]
Mother Earth and her vegetable daughters: or, Crowning the queen of vegetables. An evening entertainment in one scene. By E.A. and C.M. Lewis. To which is added a description of the costumes ... and the whole of the stage business.
Clyde, OH: Ames' pub. co., 1898. NUC OCLC

LEWIS, E.A., co-author see LEWIS, Clara M.

1648. LEWIS, Eliza Gabriella [Am. 19c]
Poems.
Brooklyn, NY: Pr. by Shannon & co., 1850. 148p. NUC BL OCLC H R
[Incl.: "The outlaw. A dramatic sketch." pp. 1-51.]

1649. LEWIS, Estelle Anna Blanche (Robinson) [Am. 1824-1880] PSEUD: LEWIS, S. Anna; Lewis, Sarah; Stella Helemah; or, The fall of Montezuma. A tragedy.
NY: 1864. R

1650. -----The king's stratagem; or,
The pearl of Poland; a tragedy in
five acts.
L: Trubner, 1873. 94p. NUC BL OCLC R
[verse]

1651. -----Sappho of Lesbos; or, love
that kills. A tragedy in five acts.
By Stella.
L: Trubner & co., 1868. 132p. NUC BL
OCLC R
[verse]

LEWIS, Leo Rich, co-author see LEWIS,
Abbie Goodwin (Davies)

LEWIS, M.G. see LEWIS, Mary G.

1652. LEWIS, Mary G., Miss [Br. 19c]
ALT: Lewis, M. G.
Zelinda, a poem, and Cardiff castle,
a dramatic-historical sketch ... By
M.G. Lewis.
L: Simpkin & Marshall, 1823. 144p.
NUC

LEWIS, S. ANNA, pseud. see LEWIS,
Estelle Anna Blanche (Robinson)

LEWIS, SARAH, pseud. see LEWIS,
Estelle Anna Blanche (Robinson)

1653. LIBBY, Laura Jean [Br. 1862-
1924]
Parted on the bridal hour.
1888. N
[Drama. Prod. Sadler's Wells, 1888.
She also pub. novel, Parted at the
altar, 1893. NUC OCLC]

LIDDIARD, I.S. Anna (Wilkinson) see
LIDDIARD, J.S. Anna (Wilkinson)

1654. LIDDIARD, J. [I. BL]S. Anna
(Wilkinson) [Br. 19c]
Kenilworth: a mask. [With] The
phantom knight; or, Farley Castle. A
chivalric tale.
Dublin: A. at Hibernia press off,
1813. 133p.; Dublin: John Cumming; L:
Longman, Hurst, Rees, Orme, & Browne,
1815. 112p. NUC BL
[Based on the entertainment presented
for Elizabeth I; 3 days' pageants]

1655. LILJENCRANTZ, Ottilie Adelina
F. [Am. 1876-1910]
"A prince who would a wooing go." A
fairy drama in three acts.
n.p., 1895.

1656. LINDLEY, Henrietta [Br. 19c]
For England's sake.
1889. M N

[Drama, 4 acts. Dramatized from the
novel by Robert Cromie. Prod.
Haymarket, 1889.]

1657. -----Her dearest foe.
1894. M N
[Comic drama, 4 acts. Adapted from a
novel by Mrs. Alexander, pseud.
[Annie (French) Hector, Mrs.
Alexander Hector]. Prod. Criterion,
1894.]

1658. -----The power of love.
1888. M N
[Drama, 4 acts, adapted from a novel
by Michael Connelly. Prod. Prince of
Wales, 1885.]

1659. -----A tangled chain.
1888. M
[Adapted from a novel by Mrs. Jane
Ellen Panton. Prod. Prince of Wales,
1888.]

LINDSAY, Lady see CAMPBELL, Anna
(Mackenzie) Lindsay, Countess of
Argyll

LINDSAY, Anna (Mackenzie), Countess
of Balcarres see CAMPBELL, Anna
(Mackenzie) Lindsay, Countess of
Argyll

1660. LINDSAY, Caroline Blanche
Elizabeth (Fitzroy), Lady [Br. 1844-
1912] ALT: L., B.
Original plays. By B.L.
L: Pr. Bradbury, Agnew & co., 1875?
20, 14, 18, 24p. NUC

1661. -----Forget-me-not. A play in
two short acts.
In: Original plays.

1662. -----Runa. A sketch.
In: Original plays.

1663. -----Three girls. A comedietta
in one act.
In: Original plays.

1664. -----A weak plot. A comedietta
in one act.
In: Original plays.

LINDSAY, Lady Elizabeth see
HARDWICKE, Elizabeth (Lindsay) Yorke,
Countess of

1665. -----Martha by-the-day.
NY: S. French, 1899? DLC
[Comedy, 3 acts. Adapt. of her novel
by same name.]

1666. LIPPMANN, Julie Mathilde [Am. 1864-1952]
Cousin faithful.   Comedy in one act.
Philadelphia: Penn pub. co., 1908.
18p. NUC OCLC H
[Earlier copyright: 1897.]

1667. -----The facts in the case; a farce in one act.
Philadelphia: Penn pub. co., 1897.
18p. NUC OCLC
[Keystone edition of popular plays; Dramatic library, v. 1, no. 88]

1668. -----A fool and his money. Comedy in two acts.
Philadelphia: Penn pub. co., 1901.
28p. NUC OCLC H [Earlier copyright: 1897.]

1669. LIPTHWAITE, Olive [Br. 19c]
Brothers; or, A plunge in the dark.
1885. M
[Drama, 4 acts.   Prod. Marylebone, 1885.]

LITTLE, Sarah see LITTLE, Sophia Louisa (Robbins)

1670. LITTLE, Sophia Louisa (Robbins), Mrs. William Little, Jr. [Am. b. 1799] ALT: Little, Sarah
The branded hand: a dramatic sketch, commemorative of the tragedies at the South in the winter of 1844-45.
Pawtucket, RI: R.W. Potter, 1845.
46p. NUC OCLC C R
[Verse dramatization of Jonathan Walker episode treated in John Greenleaf Whittier's poem.]

LITTLE, Mrs. William, Jr. see LITTLE, Sophia Louisa (Robbins)

1671. LITTLETON, Mary L., Mrs. [Am. 19c]
Christopher Columbus, an historical spectacle, presenting the most magnificent scenes and dramatic events in connection with the discovery of America, arranged for presentation during the World's fair at Chicago.
Nashville, TN: n.p., 1891. 10p. NUC

1672. -----DeSoto; or, The fall of the Incas.   In four acts. With Frank C. Drake.
n.p.: n.p., 1895.   23 1. NUC

LIVINGSTON, Grace see LUTZ, Grace (Livingston) Hill

1673. LIVINGSTON, Margaret Vere (Farrington) [Am. b. 1863]

Sauce for the goose; a farce in one act.
Boston: W.H. Baker & co., 1899. 11p. NUC
[Baker's edition of plays]

LIVONDAIS, A, pseud. see CHANDOS, Alice

LIVONDAIS, A.V., pseud. see CHANDOS, Alice

1674. LLOYD, Mabel Freund- [Br. 19c]
ALT: Freund-Lloyd, Mabel
A breach of promise.
L: 1891. M N
[Comedietta.   Prod. Opera Comique, 1891.]

1675. -----For Claudia's sake.
1891. M N
[Comedy, 3 acts.   Prod. Vaudeville, 1891.]

1676. -----Sacrificed.
1891. M N
[Drama, 1 act.   Prod. Vaudeville, 1891.]

1677. LOCHLAN, Helen Beatrice [Am. 19c]
The spirit of Christmas. A prelude to the distribution of presents on Christmas Eve at the Independent Liberal Church, Greenwich Mass., Dec. 25, 1893.
Greenwich, MA: n.p., 1893.   7 1. NUC OCLC
[A short Christmas play, probably printed as a souvenir.]

1678. LOCKE, Belle Marshall [Am. 19/20c] ALT: Locke, Nellie M.
Breezy Point; a comedy in three acts for female characters only.
Boston: W.H. Baker, c1898. 50p. NUC OCLC
[Baker's edition of plays]

1679. -----The great catastrophe: a comedy in two acts. By Nellie M. Locke.
Philadelphia: Penn pub. co., c1895.
30p. NUC OCLC

1680. -----A heartrending affair.   A monologue. By Nellie M. Locke.
Philadelphia: Penn pub. co., 1911.
NUC OCLC H
[Earlier copyright: 1895.]

1681. -----The Hiartville Shakespeare Club; a farce in one act.
Philadelphia: Penn pub. co., c1896.
149-159p. NUC OCLC

[In: One hundred choice selections. No. 35]

1682. -----Marie's secret, a duologue in one scene.
Boston: W.H. Baker & co., c1894. 8p. NUC OCLC
[Baker's edition of plays]

1683. -----A victim of woman's rights. A monologue. By Nellie M. Locke.
Clyde, OH: Ames' pub. co., 1896. 4p. NUC OCLC T

1684. LOCKE, Helen M. [Am. 19c] ALT: Locke, Nellie M.
All due to the management; monologue for a gentleman.
Chicago: Dramatic pub. co., c1897. 6p. NUC OCLC

1685. -----A victim of woman's rights. A monologue.
Clyde, OH: Ames' pub. co., 1896. 4p. T
[Also attr. Belle Locke.]

LOCKE, Nellie M. see LOCKE, Belle Marshall

LOCKE, Nellie M. see LOCKE, Helen M.

1686. LOGAN, Olive [Am. 1839-1909] ALT: Sikes, Olive Logan; Sikes, Mrs. Wirt; Sikes, Mrs. William Wirt; O'Neil, Mrs. James; DeLille, Mrs. Henry A.; Sykes, Olive
Armadale.
c1870. Mainero
[Adaptation of Wilkie Collins' story. Prod., not printed.]

1687. -----Newport.
1879. Mainero [Satire of high society. Prod., but not printed.]

1688. -----The stroller.
1877. N
[Comedy. Prod. Princess, 1887. Also prod. in NY as: "La Cigaille," 1878.]

1689. -----Surf.
1870. Mainero
[Satire of high society. Prod., but not printed.]

1690. LONERGAN, Mrs. E. Argent [Br. 19c] ALT: Argent-Lonergau, Mrs. E.
Betwixt the cup and the lip.
1896. N
[Comedietta. Prod. at Hackney, 1896.]

1691. -----A love letter.
1894. M
[Drama, 1 act. Prod. Strand, 1894.]

1692. -----Love versus science.
1896. N
[Dramatic sketch. Prod. London Polytechnic, 1896.]

1693. -----To be or not to be.
1894. N
[Duologue. Prod. at Hornsey, 1894.]

1694. -----A woman's secret.
1894. N
[Drama. Prod. Watford, 1894. Prod. as: "A love letter," Strand, 1894.]

1695. LONG, Lily Augusta [Am. d. 1927]
The masque of the year.
Chicago: Charles H. Kerr & co., 1886 [1887 OCLC]. 20p. NUC OCLC
[With music by Sarah D. Chapin]

1696. LORD, Alice Emma (Sauerwein) [Am. 1848-1930]
A vision's quest. A drama in five acts, representing the hopes and ambitions, the love, marriage, pleadings, discouragements, and achievements of Christopher Columbus, discoverer of America.
Baltimore, MD: Cushing & co., 1899. 123p. NUC OCLC

1697. LORD, Henrietta Frances [Br. 19c]
Ghosts. Translated from Ibsen.
New ed. Chicago: Lily pub. house; L: Griffith, Farran, Okeden & Walsh, 1890. NUC BL OCLC

1698. -----Nora; or, The doll's house. Translated from Henrik Ibsen.
L: Griffith, Farran, Okeden & Welsh, 1885, 1890. 116p. NUC OCLC E N
[Drama. Prod. School of Dramatic Art, 1885. Pub. as: The doll's house. NY: D. Appleton, 1907. 148p.]

LOUISA, pseud. see BOYD, Elizabeth

LOVELL, Mrs. George William see LOVELL, Maria Anne (Lacy)

1699. LOVELL, Maria Anne (Lacy), Mrs. George William Lovell [Br. 1803-1877]
ALT: Lacy, Maria
The beginning and the end: a domestic drama, in four acts.
L: Cumberland; G.H. Davidson, 1840? 1855. 44p. NY: S. French, 186-? NUC BL OCLC E N

[Prod. Haymarket, 1855. Cumberland's
British theatre, V. 47, no. 393]

1700. -----Ingomar, the barbarian: a
play in five acts. Translation of
Friedrich Halm's "Der Sohn der
Wildniss." Altered and adapted to
the English stage by Maria Lovell.
NY: S. French, 1855? 65p. Boston:
W.H. Baker, 1851? 64p. L: G.H.
Davidson, 18--? 61p. NUC BL OCLC E M
N
[Drama, 5 acts. In verse. Prod.
Drury Lane, 1851 & 1857. Cumberland's
British Theatre, v. 47, no. 386]

1701. LOWE, Helen [Br. 19c]
Poems, chiefly dramatic, edited by
Thomas Hill-Lowe, Dean of Exeter.
L: W. Pickering, 1840. 140p. NUC OCLC
[Attr. to Helen Lowe, Thomas's
daughter.]

1702. -----Cephalus and Procris. A
lyrical drama.
In: Poems ... .

1703. -----Joan of Arc in prison. A
dramatic poem.
In: Poems ... .

1704. LOWE, Helen Tracy (Porter) [Br.
b. 1876] ALT: Porter, Helen Tracy
The three heron feathers. Translated
from Hermann Sudermann.
In: Poet-Lore, New Series, 1900, p.
161-234.
NUC OCLC E

1705. LOWTHER, Aimee [Br. 19c]
The dream flower.
1898. N
[Extravaganza. Prod. Comedy, 1898.]

1706. LUCE, Grace A. [Am. 19c]
Brass buttons. Comedy in three acts.
Boston: W.H. Baker, 1900. 37p. NUC
OCLC H
[Baker's ed. of plays. Orig.
produced under title: "S. Sutherland
Breyfogle."]

1707. LUDLOW, Anna D. [Am. 19c]
Shall I marry a moderate drinker?
Rockland, ME: Z.P. Vose, 1875. 15p.
NUC
[Temperance recitation]

LUIGI, pseud. see LAMBERT, Mary H.P.

1708. LUMLEY, Lady Jane (Fitzalan),
Baroness [Br. 1537?-1576/77] ALT:
Lumley, Lady Joanna
Iphegenia in Aulis.

1558. NUC BL Har
[Closet trans. of Euripedes in prose.
Ed. Harold H. Child for Malone
Society. L: Chiswick Prss, 1909.]

LUMLEY, Lady Joanna see LUMLEY, Lady
Jane (Fitzalan), Baroness

LUMMIS, Elizabeth Fries see ELLET,
Elizabeth Fries (Lummis)

1709. LUTKENHAUS, Anna May Irwin [Am.
b. 1874]
Master Skylark.
NY: Century, 1896. 31p. NUC H
[Dramatization of John Bennett's
"Master Skylark. A story of
Shakespeare's time."]

1710. LUTZ, Grace (Livingston) Hill,
Mrs. Frank Hill [Am. 1865-1947] ALT:
Hill, Grace Livingston; Livingston,
Grace
A colonial girl; comedy in three
acts. With Abbey Sage Richardson.
n.p.: n.p., 189-? NUC H
[Produced at Lyceum theatre, NY, Oct.
31, 1898. Typescript prompt book.
49, 42, 57 l.]

1711. LYNCH, Hannah [Br. d. 1904]
The great Galeoto. Trans. from Jose
Echegaray.
In: Great Galeoto ... .
L: John Lane; Boston: Lamson Wolffe,
1895. [195p. OCLC] 97p. NUC BL OCLC E

1712. -----Folly or saintliness.
Trans. from Jose Echegaray.
In: Great Galeoto ... .

M., C.M.E. see MCFIE, Mrs.

1713. MABERLEY, Mrs. [Br. 19c]
A day near Turin.
1841. N
[Operetta. Prod. English Opera
House, 1841.]
 MCCARTHY, Justin, co-author see
PRAED, Rosa Caroline (Murray-Prior)

1714. MACAULAY, Elizabeth (Wright)
[Br. 1786?-1837]
Marmion, a melo-drama, founded on
Walter Scott's celebrated poem of
Marmion; or, the battle of
Floddenfield.
2d ed. Cork: John Connor, pr., 1811.
45p. E

1715. MACCARTHY, Charlotte [Br. 18c]

The author and bookseller. A dramatic piece. With proposals for printing by subscription, justice and reason, faithful guides to truth.
L: Pr. for the author, 1765. 12p. NUC
[Satirical play]

1716. MCCOLLUM, Elsie Malone [Am. 19c]
In grandma's chest; a monologue for a lady.
NY: E.S. Werner, 1897. 7p. NUC
[verse]

1717. MCCONAUGHY, Julia E. (Loomis) [Can. b. 1834]
Debates of conscience with a distiller, a wholesale dealer and a retailer.
In: A collection of temperance dialogues. Comp. S.T. Hammond.
Ottawa: S.T. Hammond, 1869. 112p. H

1718. -----The drunkard's daughter.
In: A collection of temperance dialogues. Comp. S.T. Hammond.
Ottawa: S.T. Hammond, 1869. 112p. H

MCCORD, Mrs. David James see MCCORD, Louisa Susannah (Cheves)

1719. MCCORD, Louisa Susannah (Cheves), Mrs. David James McCord [Am. 1810-1880]
Caius Gracchus, a tragedy in five acts.
NY: H. Kernot, 1851. 128p. NUC BL OCLC R
[Verse]

MACCRAY, Florine Thayer see MCCRAY, Florine Thayer

1720. MCCRAY, Florine Thayer [Am. 19c] ALT: MacCray, Florine Thayer
Columbus, a historical drama.
Hartford, CT: Plimpton mfg. co., 1892. 14p. NUC

MACDONNELL, Mrs. A.J. see MACDONNELL, Cicely

1721. MACDONNELL, Cicely, Mrs. A.J. MacDonnell [Br. 19c]
For good and evil.
1894. M N
[Play, 3 acts. Prod. Royalty, 1894.]

1722. -----Life's sarcasm.
1898. N [Duologue. Prod. Matinee Theatre, 1898.]

MACDOWELL, Mrs. William Melbourne see DAVENPORT, Fanny Lily Gypsy

MCFALL, [Chambers] Haldane, co-author see MCFALL, Frances Elizabeth (Clarke)

1723. MCFALL, Frances Elizabeth (Clarke) [Am. 1862-1943/5] PSEUD: Grand, Sarah
The fear of Robert Clive. By Sarah Grand [Chambers]. With Haldane McFall.
1896. M N
[Play, 1 act. Prod. Lyceum, 1896.]

MCFALL, Haldane, co-author see MCFALL, Frances Elizabeth (Clarke)

1724. MACFARREN, Natalia [Br. 19/20c]
The barber of Seville. Music by Rossini.
NY: G. Schirmer, n.d. 328p. OCLC E
[Trans. Vocal score. This and the following 5 works are cited in E. She translated numerous opera libretti & other works by well known composers. OCLC]

1725. -----Bride of Lammermoor. Music by Donizetti.
NY: G. Schirmer, 1898. 240p. OCLC E
[Trans. Vocal score.]

1726. -----The dumb girl of Portici. Music by Auber.
L: Novello, Ewer; Simpkin, Marshall, n.d. 333p. OCLC E
[Trans. Vocal score.]

1727. -----Lohengrin. Music by Wagner.
L: Novello, Ewer, 1875. 267p. OCLC E
[Trans. Vocal score.]

1728. -----Tannhauser and the tournament of song at Wartburg. Music by Wagner.
L: Novello, Ewer; Simpkin, Marshall, 187-? 273p. NUC OCLC E
[Trans. Vocal score.]

1729. -----William Tell. Music by Rossini.
L: Novello, Ewer, 1873? 421p. NUC OCLC E
[Trans. Vocal score.]

1730. MCFIE, Mrs. [Br. 19c] ALT: M., C. M. E.
Stolen hours by C.M.E.M.
Glasgow: n.p., 1836. BL
[Miscellany. Incl.: "The bridal, a mask." Inglis.]

1731. MCGRATH, E.R., Mrs. [Br. 19c]
The maid of Cashmere. A drama. In two acts.

Calcutta: W. Newman & co., 1885. 30p.
BL

MACHARDY, Mary <u>see</u> FLINT, Mary
MacHardy
MACHARDY FLINT, Mr., co-author <u>see</u>
FLINT, Mary MacHardy

MACHARDY FLINT, Mrs. <u>see</u> FLINT, Mary
MacHardy

1732. MCINTYRE, Anna E., Mrs. [Am.
19c] PSEUD: Allen, Mrs. Fairchild
... A morning in court ... Pleading
the cause of those dumb mouths which
have not our speech. Together with
mercy songs and recitations. By Mrs.
Anna E. McIntyre, Mrs. Fairchild
Allen.
Aurora, IL: Anti-Vivisection press,
1894. 84p. NUC OCLC
[A 45p. play in which people are
judged for cruelty to animals. Pp.
46-84 poems and sketches on
preventing cruelty to animals.]

MACKARNESS, Mrs. Henry D. <u>see</u>
MACKARNESS, Matilda Anne (Planché)

1733. MACKARNESS, Matilda Anne
(Planché), Mrs. Henry D. Mackarness
[Br. 1826-1881] ALT: Planché, Matilda
Anne
New charades for the drawing room.
L: George Routledge & sons, 1866.
150p. BL
[12 charades, all 3-part plays]

1734. MCKAY, Sarah Lucy, Mrs. [Am.
19c]
Lucy, the sold orphan.
Bay City, MI: n.p., 1882. 61p. NUC
[Play in 12 acts]

MACKAYE, Percy Wallace, co-author <u>see</u>
SUTHERLAND, Evelyn Greenleaf

1735. MCKEAN, May Field [Am. 19c]
Red-letter days. Anniversary,
concert and entertainment exercises.
NY: Phillips & Hunt; Cincinnati, OH:
Cranston & Stowe, 1886. 91p. NUC

1736. -----Anniversary welcome. Poem
in: Red letter days.

1737. -----Christmas tree.
In: Red letter days.
[21 children and a teacher.]

1738. -----Christmas welcome.
In: Red letter days.
[Poem spoken by one character. In
imitation of Henry Wadsworth
Longfellow's Hiawatha.]

1739. -----Clinging-resting.
In: Red letter days.
[Poems, lines & songs for 3 young
ladies & 8 little girls.]

1740. -----Flowers' lesson.
In: Red letter days.
[10 children represent different
trees & flowers.]

1741. -----Gold, frankincense and
myrrh, a Christmas exercise.
In: Red letter days.
[Nativity exercise for 1 adult and 2
children, chorus of 24 children.]

1742. -----Rock of ages.
In: Red letter days.
[Poems for 4 young ladies.]

1743. -----Ruth, the Moabitess.
In: Red letter days.
[Story told by several characters in
turn.]

1744. -----The temple we build.
In: Red letter days.
[Short devotional poems for 11
children & 2 young adults.]

1745. MACKENZIE, Fanny (Locke) [Am.
19c]
The Willoughsby Browns' dinner, a
comedy in two acts.
Chicago: Blakely pr. co., 1897. 22p.
NUC

MACLEAN, Mrs. George <u>see</u> LANDON,
Letitia Elizabeth

1746. MACNAMARA, Annie [Br. 19c]
Our garden. Music by C. Shafer.
1894. N
[Operetta. Prod. at Parkhurst,
1894.]

MACPHERSON, Henry, co-author <u>see</u>
LEAN, Florence (Marryat) Church

MACPHERSON, Herbert, co-author <u>see</u>
LANCASTER-WALLIS, Ellen

MACRAE, F., co-author <u>see</u> PHILLIPS,
Mrs. Newton

1747. M'TAGGART, Ann (Hamilton) [Br.
1753?-1834]
Constantia, a tragedy, in five acts;
and Valville; or The prejudices of
past times; a drama, in five acts.
L: M.A. Nattali, 1824. 201p. NUC BL
[In verse. Constantia is based on
story by Stephanie Felicite Ducrest
de St. Aubin, Comtesse de Genlis.
Also in: Plays.]

1748. -----Plays: Valville; or, The prejudices of past times; Theodora; Hortensia; Villario; A search after perfection; and Constantia.
2nd ed. L: Pr. A.J. Valpy, 1832. 2v. NUC BL

1749. -----Hortensia; a tragedy, in five acts.
In: Plays ... .
[Verse]

1750. -----A search after perfection. A comedy, in five acts.
In: Plays ... .
[She says in preface that the character, Mrs. Rational, is intended to be a self portrait. Orig. title: "The school for mothers; or, A search after perfection."]

1751. -----Theodora: a tragedy.
In: Plays ... .
[5 acts, verse. Taken from Francois Thomas Marie Baculard d'Arnaud.]

1752. -----Villario; a play, in five acts.
In: Plays ... .
[Verse]

1753. -----Valville.
In: Constantia ... .
[In verse. Written 1790. Also in: Plays.]

MADDERN-FISKE, Minnie see FISKE, Minnie Maddern (Davey)

1754. MADDISON, Katherine Dorothy [Br. 19c]
All in one day. A farce.
L: Digby & Long, 1891. BL
[One act]

1755. MAGIN, Mary, Miss [Am. 19c]
On 'change.
Chicago: n.p., 1892. NUC
[4 acts]

1756. MAGUIRE, Mrs. John Francis [Br. d. 1905]
Beauty and the beast: a play, with a new version of old fables.
Dublin: M.H. Gill & son, 1878. 95p. BL
[Drawing room play, 3 acts, verse. 12 prose fables, proverb stories & an allegory]

1757. -----Two plays: Blue Beard and Cinderella.
Cork: J. Mahony & son, 1879. 54p. NUC

MALET, LUCAS, pseud. see HARRISON, Mary St. Leger (Kingsley)

MALLOY, Louise see MALLOY, Marie Louise

1758. MALLOY, Marie Louise [Am. 19/20c] ALT: Malloy, Louise
The prince's wooing. A dramatic poem. By Louise Malloy.
Baltimore, MD: American job pr. off., 1894. 31p. NUC H

MANCHESTER, Miss H.E., co-author see DOREMUS, Elizabeth Johnson (Ward)

MANLEY, Mrs. John see MANLEY, Mary de la Rivière (Manley)

1759. MANLEY, Mary de la Rivière (Manley), Mrs. John Manley [Br. 1663-1724] ALT: Manley, de la Rivière
Almyna; or, The Arabian vow.
1706. L: William Turner & Egbert Sanger, 1707. 68p. NUC BL OCLC B N S
[Tragedy, 5 acts, verse. Prod. Haymarket, 1706.]

1760. -----The court legacy. A new ballad opera by the author of the New Atlantis.
L: J. Dormer, 1733. 55p. NUC OCLC B N S

1761. -----The lost lover; or, the jealous husband: a comedy.
L: R. Bently; J. Knapton & R. Wellington; F. Saunders, 1696. 39p. NUC BL OCLC B N S WM
[5 acts, verse. Perf. Drury Lane, 1695/6.]

1762. -----Lucius, the first Christian king of Britain. A tragedy.
L: J. Barber, 1717. 54p. NUC BL OCLC B N S
[5 acts, verse. Prod. Drury Lane, 1717.]

1763. -----The royal mischief. A tragedy.
L: R. Bentley, F. Saunders & J. Knapton, 1696. 47p. NUC BL OCLC B N S WM
[5 acts, verse. Perf. Lincoln's Inn Fields, 1696.]

MANLY, De La Rivière see MANLEY, Mary de la Rivière (Manley)

1764. MANNING, Kathryn [Am. 19c]
Francesco Carrara; a drama in three acts. "From the French."

Chicago: Dramatic pub. co., 1899.
32p.
[Sergel's acting drama, no. 550]

1765. MAREAN, Beatrice [Am. 19/20c]
An original drama. In six acts,
entitled Cherry, or Labor vs.
Capital. Written in compliment to
the Greensboro Fire Department.
Greensboro, NC: Reece & Elam, 1897.
81p. NUC

MARIE see SKIDMORE, Harriet Marie

MARIE JOSEPHINE, pseud. see HEMENWAY,
Abby Maria

1766. MARISHALL, Jean [Br. 18c] ALT:
Marshall, Jane
Sir Harry Gaylove; or, Comedy in
embryo. In five acts.
Edinburgh: A. Kincaid & W. Creech,
1772. 66p. NUC BL OCLC B

MARKS, Josephine Preston (Peabody)
see PEABODY, Josephine Preston

MARKS, Mrs. Lionel S. see PEABODY,
Josephine Preston

MARLOWE, CHARLES, pseud. see JAY,
Harriett

1767. MARRIOTT, Mrs. [Am. 18c]
The chimera; or, Effusions of fancy:
a farce in two acts.
NY: T. & J. Swords, pr., 1795. 24p.
NUC OCLC B Hills Wells
[Played in Philadelphia, 1794.]

1768. MARRIOTT, Fanny [Br. 19]
Capers. With A. Kenward Matthews.
1899. N
[Farce. Amateur prod. at Hampstead,
1899.]

MARRYAT, Florence see LEAN, Florence
(Marryat) Church

MARSHALL, Jane see MARISHALL, Jean

1769. MARTIN, Mrs. [Br. 18/19c]
Reparation; or, The Savoyards. A
play in three acts.
L: Pr. J. Nichols & son, 1823. 115p.
NUC E

MARTYN, Mrs. Job H. see MARTYN, Sarah
Towne (Smith)

MARTYN, Mrs. S.T. see MARTYN, Sarah
Towne (Smith)

1770. MARTYN, Sarah Towne (Smith),
Mrs. Job H. Martyn [Am. 1805-1879]
ALT: Martyn, Mrs. S. T.
Ione: a dramatic sketch.
NY: n.p., 1848. 35p. NUC OCLC
[From The Ladies' Wreath, May, 1848]

1771. MARX, Eleanor [Br. 1855-1898]
ALT: Aveling, Mrs. Edward; Aveling,
Eleanor; Marx-Aveling, Eleanor
An enemy of the people. Trans. from
Henrik Ibsen.
In: Ibsen's Prose Dramas. Ed. William
Archer.
NY: Scribner & Welford, 1890; L:
Walter Scott, 1904. 5v. NUC BL OCLC E

1772. -----The lady from the sea.
Trans. from Henrik Ibsen.
L: T. Fisher Unwin, 1890. 184p. NUC
BL OCLC E M N
[Prod. Terry's, 1891.]

MARX-AVELING, Eleanor see MARX,
Eleanor

MASON, Alfred Edward Woodley, co-
author see BATEMAN, Isabel

MASSEY, Charles, comp. see COOK,
Eliza

MASSEY, Charles, comp. see NORTON,
Mrs.

1773. MASTERS, Julia M. [Br. 19c]
The scarlet dye; drama in three acts.
Brighton: A.M. Robinson & son, 18--.
NUC M N
[Drama. Prod. St. George hall,
1888.]

1774. -----Les Scelles.
1888. N
[Comedy. Prod. St. George Hall,
1888.]

1775. MATHER, Mary H. [Am. 19c]
Ye hatchet partie and other
entertainments.
Chicago: Woman's temperance pub.
assoc., 1889. 52p. NUC OCLC
[Temperance recitations]

MATHEWS, Fannie Aymar see MATHEWS,
Frances Aymar

1776. MATHEWS, Frances Aymar [Am.
1855-1925] ALT: Mathews, Fannie Aymar
Tonight at eight; comedies and
comediettas. By Fannie Aymar
Mathews.
Chicago: Belford, Clarke & co., 1889.
260p. NUC OCLC

[All 1-act comedies. She also wrote: "Bigamy, a society play in 5 acts" staged 1881; "Joan," 1898, written for Fanny Davenport who wanted to play Joan of Arc. Not printed.]

1777. -----All for sweet charity. Comedy.
NY: Edgar S. Werner, 1907. 17p. NUC OCLC H
[Werner ed. T.P. c1889. Also in: Tonight at eight.]

1778. -----American hearts. Comedy.
NY: E.S. Werner, 1907. 13p. NUC OCLC H
[Werner ed. T.P. c1889. Also in: Tonight at eight.]

1779. -----The apartment. Comedy.
NY: E.S. Werner, 1907. 14p. NUC OCLC H
[Werner ed. T.P. c1889.]

1780. -----At the Grand Central.
In: Tonight at eight.

1781. -----Both sides of the counter. Almost a tragedy.
In: Tonight at eight.

1782. -----A charming conversationalist.
In: Tonight at eight.

1783. -----The chatterbox. A monologue.
In: Tonight at eight.

1784. -----The courier.
In: Tonight at eight.

1785. -----Cousin Frank, a farce in one act, for female characters only.
Boston: W.H. Baker & co., 1896. 9p. NUC OCLC
[Baker's edition of plays]

1786. -----En Voyage. A farce.
In: Tonight at eight.

1787. -----A finished coquette, a comedietta in one act.
Boston: W.H. Baker & co., 1895. 16p. NUC
[Also in: Tonight at eight.]

1788. -----The honeymoon-Fourth quarter. One act.
In: Tonight at eight.

1789. -----A knight of the quill. A farce.
In: Tonight at eight.

1790. -----On the staircase.
In: Tonight at eight.

1791. -----Paying the piper.
In: Tonight at eight.

1792. -----The proposal. A duologue, one act.
In: Tonight at eight.

1793. -----Six to one; or, The scapegrace. A comedietta in one act.
Boston: Baker & co., 1889. 14p. NUC OCLC
[T.P. c1887. Also pub. as: "The scapegrace." Baker's edition of plays]

1794. -----Snow-bound.
In: Tonight at eight.

1795. -----Teacups.
In: Tonight at eight.

1796. -----The title and the money. One act.
In: Tonight at eight.

1797. -----War to the knife.
In: Tonight at eight.

1798. -----The wedding tour. One act.
In: Tonight at eight.

1799. -----A woman's forever.
In: Tonight at eight.

1800. -----Wooing a widow, a comedietta in one act.
Boston: W.H. Baker & co., 1895. 12p. NUC
[Baker's edition of plays]

MATTHEWS, A. Kenward, co-author see MARRIOTT, Fanny

1801. MATTHEWS, Edith Virginia Brander [Am. 19c]
Six cups of chocolate. A piece of gossip in one act.
NY & L: Harper & bros., 1897. 32p. NUC OCLC H
[T.P. "Freely Englished from a 'Kaffeeklatsch' of E. Schmithof."]

MAXWELL, Mrs. John see MAXWELL, Mary Elizabeth (Braddon)

1802. MAXWELL, Mary Elizabeth (Braddon), Mrs. John Maxwell [Br. 1837-1915] ALT: Braddon, Mary Elizabeth
Dross; or, the root of evil. A comedy [domestic drama NUC] in four

acts. L: J. & R. Maxwell, 1882. [56p.
E] 23p. NUC BL E N
[Sergel's acting drama, no. 344]

1803. -----For better, for worse.
1890. N
[Melodrama. Prod. Whitby, 1890;
Brighton, 1891.]

1804. -----Genevieve.
1874. N
[Drama. Prod. Liverpool, 1874.]

1805. -----Griselda; or, The patient
wife.
1873. M N
[Drama, 4 acts. Perf. Princess's,
1873.]

1806. -----The loves of Arcadia.
1860. N
[Comedietta. Prod. Strand, 1860.]

1807. -----Marjorie Daw. A household
idyl in two acts.
L: J. & R. Maxwell, 1882. 23p. NUC BL
OCLC E H
[DeWitt's acting plays. No. 338.
Prepared for the Am. stage by Henry
Llewellyn Williams.]

1808. -----Married beneath him. A
comedy in four acts.
L: J. & R. Maxwell, 1882. 55p. BL E N

1809. -----The missing witness. An
original drama in four acts.
L: J. & R. Maxwell, 1880. 53p. BL E N

1810. -----The model husband.
1868. M
[Comedy. Perf. Surrey, 1868.]

MAYO, Mrs. Amory Dwight see MAYO,
Sarah Carter (Edgarton)

1811. MAYO, Sarah Carter (Edgarton),
Mrs. Amory Dwight Mayo [Am. 1819-
1849] ALT: Edgarton, S. C.
The beauty of piety. By S.C.
Edgarton.
In: Dramatic leaflets.
Philadelphia: Phineas Garrett, 1877.
1 v. in 20 pts. NUC OCLC H
[Masque in verse & prose.]

1812. MEADOWS, Alice Maud [Br. d.
1913]
A run down to Brighton.
1893. N
[Musical sketch. Prod. St. Martin's,
1893.]

1813. MEDD, Mabel S. [Br. 19c]

Broken idylls. A comedietta in one
act.
L & NY: Lacy, 1899. 12p. NUC BL E
[French's acting edition, no. 2144]

1814. -----Imogen's new cook.
Duologue for two ladies in one act.
L: Lacy, 1898. 12p. NUC BL E N
[Duologue. Amateur prod. at
Ladbrooke Hall, 1898. French's
acting edition, v. 142, no. 1]

1815. MEDINA, Louisa H. [Am. 19c]
ALT: Medina, Louise H.
Ernest Maltravers. A drama, in three
acts.
NY: French, [1857 R] 1860. 37p. NUC
BL OCLC M N R
[Adaptation of Edward Bulwer Lytton,
Baron Lytton's novel. Prod.
Britannia, 1874. N & M attr. Miss
Rose Medina. French's standard
drama. no. 143; Dicks' standard
plays, no. 379]

1816. -----The last days of Pompeii:
a dramatic spectacle, taken from
[Edward Bulwer Lytton, Baron Lytton]
Bulwer's celebrated novel of the same
title.
NY & L: Samuel French, 1844. 31p. NUC
BL OCLC R
[French's standard drama, no. 146]

1817. -----Nick of the woods. A
drama, in three acts.
NY & L: French, 1843. 30p. NUC BL
OCLC R
[Adaptation of Robert Montgomery
Bird's novel, "Nick of the woods; A
story of Kentucky;" Dicks' standard
plays, no. 547; French's standard
drama. no. 269]

MEDINA, Louise H. see MEDINA, Louisa
H.

MEDINA, Miss Rose see MEDINA, Louisa
H.

MEG, pseud., co-author see ALCOTT,
Louisa May

MELFORD, Mark, co-author see
BRADSHAW, Annie M. (Tree)

1818. MELLER, Rose [Br. 19c]
The light of other days.
1889. N
[Dramatic sketch. Prod. at Middlesex
County Asylum, 1889.]

1819. -----A summer's dream.
1891. M N

[Dramatic sketch. Prod. Avenue, 1891.]

1820. MERCEDES, Sister [Am. b. 1846]
Wild flowers from "The mountainside."
Poems and dramas.
Philadelphia: J.B. Lippincott & co.,
1885. 260p. NUC

1821. -----The child heroine Marie.
In: Wild flowers ... .
[One act, verse.]

1822. -----Dolores: or, Through the
fires of sorrow.
In: Wild flowers ... .
[Three acts, verse.]

1823. -----Dottie's dream. In: Wild
flowers ... .
[One act, verse, for little girls]

1824. -----A legend of the rainbow.
In: Wild flowers ... .
[One act, verse.]

1825. -----The reproof of the flower-
angel.
In: Wild flowers ... .
[One, act, verse.]

1826. MEREDITH, Katherine Mary
Cheever [Am. 19/20c] PSEUD: Staats,
Johanna
Ambition; a one act play. By Johanna
Staats.
NUC
[Manuscript, not pub.]

1827. MERINGTON, Marguerite [Am. d.
1951]
Captain Lettarblair; a comedy in
three acts written for [the American
actor] E.H. Sothern.
NY: n.p., 1891. Boston: C.E. French,
1899. 19p. NUC BL OCLC
[First prod. NY Lyceum, 1891.]

1828. -----Daphne; or, The pipes of
Arcadia. Three acts of singing
nonsense.
NY: Century co., 1896. 166p. NUC BL
OCLC

1829. -----Good-bye. A comedy.
Boston: Lincoln, 1893. 8p. NUC OCLC

MERIVALE, Herman Charles, co-author
see GROVE, Florence Craufurd

MERIVALE, Herman Charles, co-author
see MERIVALE, Mrs. Herman Charles

1830. MERIVALE, Mrs. Herman Charles
[Br. 1847?-1932]

The butler. With Herman Charles
Merivale.
1886. M N
[Comedy, 3 acts. Prod. Toole's, & at
Manchester, 1886.]

1831. -----The don. With Herman
Charles Merivale.
1888. M N
[Comedy, 3 acts, adapted from the
German. Prod. Toole's, 1888.]

1832. -----Our Joan. With Herman
Charles Merivale.
n.p.: n.p., 1885. NUC E M N
[3 act drama; based on William
Black's novel "A Princess of Thule."
Prod. Grand & in Birmingham, 1887.
NUC attr. to her husband alone. Act
3 incomplete. Typewritten prompt
book.]

MERIWETHER, E.A. see MERIWETHER,
Elizabeth (Avery)

1833. MERIWETHER, Elizabeth (Avery),
Mrs. Minor Meriwether [Am. 1824-1917]
ALT: Meriwether, E. A. PSEUD:
Edmunds, George The devil's dance. A
play for the times. By E.A.
Meriwether.
St. Louis, MO: Hailman Bros., 1886.
67p. NUC
[Temperance]

1834. -----Ku Klux Klan; or, The
carpet bagger in New Orleans.
Memphis, TN: South Bapt. pub. co.,
1877. 51p. NUC OCLC

MERIWETHER, Mrs. Minor see
MERIWETHER, Elizabeth (Avery)

1835. MERRIMAN, Effie Woodward [Am.
b. 1857]
Diamonds and hearts; comedy-drama in
three acts.
Chicago: Dramatic pub. co., 1897.
40p. NUC

1836. -----Maud Muller; a burlesque
entertainment in three acts.
Chicago: Dramatic pub. co., 1891. 63-
88p. NUC OCLC
[On cover: American amateur drama.]

1837. -----A pair of artists; a
comedy.
Chicago: Dramatic pub. co., 1892.
48p. NUC OCLC
[Sergel's acting drama, no. 436]

1838. -----Socials.
Chicago: C.H. Sergel & co., 1891.
88p. NUC OCLC

[Suggestions for money-raising
activities. Incl.: Maud Muller's
Social, a comedy, 3 acts.]

1839. -----Their first meeting; a
comedietta in one act.
Chicago: Dramatic pub. co., 1899.
10p. NUC OCLC
[American acting drama]

1840. -----Through a matrimonial
bureau; a comedietta in one act.
Chicago: Dramatic pub. co., 1898. 9p.
NUC OCLC
[Sergel's acting drama, no. 495]

1841. -----Tompkins' hired man. A
drama in three acts.
Chicago: Dramatic pub. co., 35p. NUC
OCLC
[Sergel's acting drama]

1842. MERRITT, Catharine Nina [Can.
1859-1926]
"When George the Third was king." An
historical drama in three acts.
Toronto: Rowsell & Hutchinson, 1897.
30p. NUC BL OCLC

1843. MERRON, Eleanor [Am. 19c]
The dairy farm, a romance of Sleepy
Hollow.
n.p.: n.p., 1899. NUC
[4 acts. Produced in NY in 1903 &
pub. NY: G.W. Kauser, 1903.]

1844. METCALFE, Catharine [Br. 18c]
Julia de Rouligne.
1790. N
[Tragedy. Also prod. as: "Julia."
She died before it was performed.
BioD.]

MILES, Mrs. Alfred see MILES, Sibella
Elizabeth (Hatfield)

1845. MILES, Sibella Elizabeth
(Hatfield), Mrs. Alfred Miles [Br.
1800-1882] ALT: Hatfield, Sibella
Elizabeth
Leisure evenings; or, Records of the
past. A collection of prose and
poetical miscellanies. By Mrs.
Alfred Miles.
L: Geo. Phipps, 1860. 166p. BL
[Incl. dramatic monologue in verse &
"Two dramatic scenes from British
History," in verse, based on death of
Edward VI.]

MILLER, Alice Maud (Duer), co-author
see DUER, Caroline

1846. MILLER, Annie Jenness [Am. b.
1859]

The master passion; a drama in five
acts.
n.p.: n.p., n.d. NUC

MILLER, Helena, co-author see
FAIRGRAVE, Amita B.

1847. MILLER, Mrs. Thomas [Am. 19c]
Nella Duglas, or 100 pound reward; a
play of powerful interest, in 5 acts.
NY: John Polhemus, 1880. 96p. OCLC

1848. MILLIGAN, Alice Letitia [Br. b.
1880]
The last feast of the Fianna.
L: David Nutt, 1900. 29p. NUC BL E

1849. MILNER, Frances S. [Br. 19c]
Brothers in name. Drama in 5 [6 NUC]
acts.
n.p.: n.p., 1899. NUC H
[Typescript prompt-book 19, 19, 15,
17, 24, 31 l.]

1850. MINTON, Ann [Br. 19c]
The comedy of a wife to be lett, or,
The miser cured ... compressed into
two acts.
L: A. Seale, pr., 1802. NUC BL E N
[Adaptation of Eliza (Fowler)
Haywood's comedy]

MITFORD, M.R. see MITFORD, Mary
Russell

1851. MITFORD, Mary Russell [Br.
1787-1855] ALT: Mitford, M. R.
Dramatic scenes, sonnets, and other
poems.
L: Geo. B. Whittaker, 1827. 392p. NUC
BL OCLC E N
[All in verse]

1852. -----The dramatic works of Mary
Russell Mitford.
L: Hurst & Blackett, 1854. 2v. NUC BL
OCLC T

1853. -----Alice.
In: Dramatic scenes ... .
[1 scene.]

1854. -----The bridal eve.
In: Dramatic scenes ... . [1 scene.]

1855. -----The captive.
In: Dramatic scenes ... .

1856. -----Charles the First. An
historical tragedy, in five acts.
L: J. Dicks, 1834. 22p.; John
Duncombe, 1834. 80p. NUC BL OCLC E N
[Verse. Also in Dramatic Works.
Refused a license in 1825. First

prod. Victoria Theatre, 1834. Dicks'
standard plays, no. 667]

1857. -----Cunigunda's vow.
In: Dramatic scenes ... .
[Adaptation of Voltaire's "Candide."]

1858. -----Emily.
In: Dramatic scenes ... .
[1 scene.]

1859. -----Fair Rosamond.
In: Dramatic scenes ... .
[Historical, 1 scene.]

1860. -----The fawn.
In: Dramatic scenes ... .
[1 scene.]

1861. -----The Foscari. A tragedy in
five acts.
L: G.B. Whittaker, 1826. 78p. NUC BL
OCLC E N
[Verse. Prod. Covent Garden, 1826.
Also in Dramatic Works.]

1862. -----Gaston de Blondeville.
In: Dramatic works ... .
[Historical]

1863. -----Henry Talbot.
In: Dramatic scenes ... .
[1 scene.]

1864. -----Inez de Castro; a tragedy
in five acts.
L: G.B. Whittaker, 1842. 20p. NUC BL
OCLC E N
[First performed 1841. Also in
Dramatic Works. Dicks' standard
plays, no. 672]

1865. -----Julian, a tragedy in five
acts.
L: John Cumberland, 1823. 58p. 3d ed.
L: G. & W.B. Whittaker, 1823. 83p.
NUC BL OCLC E N
[Verse. Prod. Covent Garden, 1823.
Also in Dramatic Works.]

1866. -----The masque of the seasons.
In: Dramatic scenes ... .
[1 scene.]

1867. -----Otto of Wittelsbach.
In: Dramatic works ... .

1868. -----The painter's daughter.
In: Dramatic scenes ... .
[1 scene.]

1869. -----Rienzi. A tragedy in five
acts.
L: John Cumberland, 1828. 66p. NUC BL
OCLC E M N

[Verse. Prod. Drury Lane, 1828;
Sadler's Wells, 1839. Also in:
Dramatic Works.]

1870. -----Sadak and Kalasrade; or,
The waters of oblivion. A romantic
opera in two acts.
L: Pr. by S.G. Fairbrother, 1835.
31p. NUC BL OCLC E N
[Perf. English Opera House, 1835.
Also in Dramatic Works.]

1871. -----The siege.
In: Dramatic scenes ... .
[1 scene.]

1872. -----The wedding ring.
In: Dramatic scenes ... .
[1 scene, romance.]

1873. MOLINI, Miss [19c]
William Tell.
1846. N
[Trans. of drama by Johann Christoph
Friedrich von Schiller.]

1874. MONCKTON, Lady [Br. d. 1920]
The countess.
1882. N
[Drama. Amateur prod. at Sir Percy
Shelley's theatre, 1882.]

1875. -----Tobacco jars. Music by H.
Young.
1889. N
[Operetta. Prod. St. George Hall,
1889.]

1876. MONROE, Harriet [Am. 1860-1936]
Valeria and other poems.
Chicago: Pr. for the author at the
DeVinne press, 1891; A.C. McClurg,
1892. 287p. NUC OCLC H
[Valeria, pp. 1-194, tragedy in
prologue and five acts.]

MONTAGU, Eleanora Louisa see HERVEY,
Eleanora Louisa (Montagu)

1877. MONTAGU, Lady Mary (Pierrepont)
Wortley [Br. 1689-1762] ALT:
Montague, Lady Mary (Pierrepont)
Wortley
Simplicity.
c1735. BioD
[Never performed or published.]

1878. MONTGOMERY, Eleanor Elizabeth
[Br. 19/20c]
Madame Beranger, an original drama,
one act.
Wanganui, N.Z.: Wanganui Herald
Newspaper co., 1887. 15p. BL

1879. -----The snow vision! An
original comedy drama in a prologue
and three acts.
Wanganui, N.Z.: Wanganui Herald
Newspaper co., 1891. 45p. BL

1880. MONTGOMERY, Margaret [Am. 19c]
Per telephone. Farce in one act.
Boston: W.H. Baker, 1893. 17p. NUC
OCLC H
[Baker's ed. of plays]

MOODY, Catherine Grace Frances <u>see</u>
GORE, Catherine Grace Frances (<u>M</u>oody)

1881. MOORE, Ada [Br. 19c]
A sneaking regard.
1870. N
[Farce. Prod. Surrey, 1870.]

MOORE, George, co-author <u>see</u> CRAIGIE,
Pearl Mary Teresa (Richar<u>ds</u>)

MOORE, Mary Evelyn <u>see</u> DAVIS, Mary
Evelyn (Moore)

MOORE, Mollie E. <u>see</u> DAVIS, Mary
Evelyn (Moore)

1882. MORE, Hannah [Br. 1745-1833]
PSEUD: Young lady, A
Sacred dramas.
L: T. Cadell, 1782. NUC BL OCLC B N
[She says in the preface that these
are for the improvement of young
ladies.]

1883. -----The works of Hannah More.
L: T. Cadell & W. Davies, 1801. 8v.
NUC BL OCLC

1884. -----Belshazzar.
In: Sacred dramas.

1885. -----Daniel.
In: Sacred dramas.

1886. -----David and Goliath.
In: Sacred dramas.

1887. -----
Earl Percy: a tragedy.
Dublin: Pr. R. Marchbank, 1778. NUC
BL OCLC B E N
[5 acts, verse. Prod. Covent Garden,
1777. Pub. as: Percy: a tragedy. L:
T. Cadell, 1778. 87p.]

1888. -----The fatal falsehood, a
tragedy.
L: T. Cadell, 1779. 83p. NUC BL OCLC
B N [5 acts, verse. Prod. Covent
Garden, 1779.]

1889. -----The inflexible captive: a
tragedy.
Bristol: S. Farley, 1774. 83p. BL
OCLC B N
[5 acts, verse]

1890. -----Moses in the bulrushes.
In: Sacred dramas.

1891. -----Reflections of King
Hezekiah in his sickness.
In: Works ... .

1892. -----Three dialogues. By a
young lady.
Bristol: S. Farley, 1766? 37p. NUC BL
B N
[Incl.: "The search after happiness:
a pastoral." 1 act, verse. Two verse
prologues to "Hamlet" and "King
Lear." Longe, v. 204, no. 5]

1893. -----Village politics.
In: Works ... .
[Dialogue written to counteract
influence of Tom Paine and the French
Revolution.]

1894. MORGAN, Carrie A., Mrs. [Am.
19c]
Five thousand pounds sterling. A
play in five acts.
NY: n.p., 1885. 67 1. NUC

MORGAN, Mrs. Ford <u>see</u> FORD, Harriet

1895. MORGAN, Geraldine (Woods), Mrs.
John P. Morgan [Am. 19c]
Tannhauser and the minstrels
tournament on the Wartburg. Grand
romantic opera in three acts.
New ed. Berlin: Adolph Furstner,
1891. 96p. H OCLC
[Libretto]

MORGAN, Mrs. John P. <u>see</u> MORGAN,
Geraldine (Woods)

1896. MORGAN, Sydney (Owenson), Lady
[Br. 1783?-1859] ALT: Morgan, Mrs.
Thomas Charles; Owenson, Sydney
Dramatic scenes from real life. By
Lady Morgan.
L: Saunders & Otley, 1833. 329p. 2v.
NUC BL OCLC E
[Contents: v. 1. Manor Sackville. v.
2. Manor Sackville (cont.) The Easter
recess; or, The tapestry workers.
Temper.]

1897. -----The first attempt. BioD
1807.
[Comic opera which ran only a few
nights]

MORGAN, Mrs. Thomas Charles see
MORGAN, Sydney (Owenson), Lady

1898. MORISON, Christina W. [Br. 19c]
The Uhlans: comic opera in three
acts.
L?: n.p., 1884. 36p. BL

MORISON, Jeanie see CAMPBELL, Jean
(Morison)

1899. MORISON, Mary [Br. 19c]
Lonely lives. Tr. from Gerhart
Hauptmann.
L: Wm. Heinemann, 1898. 179p. NUC BL
OCLC E

1900. -----The Weavers. Tr. from
Gerhart Hauptmann.
L: Wm. Heinemann, 1899. 148p. NUC BL
OCLC E

1901. MORLAND, Charlotte E. [Br. 19c]
The matrimonial agency; an original
farce in one act.
L: Capper & Newton, 1893. 20p. NUC BL
OCLC E N
[Prod. at Bayswater, 1888. N attr.
to Emily Beauchamps. Lynn's acting
edition; no. 15]

1902. -----Quicksands.
1890. M N
[Comic drama. Adapted from: "The
devout lover," a novel by Caroline
Emily Cameron, Mrs. Lovatt Cameron.
Prod. Comedy, 1890.]

1903. -----A shower of kisses.
1893. N
[Comic drama. Prod. at Hammersmith,
1893.]

MORLAND, Frank H., co-author see
CASSILIS, Ina Leon

1904. MORSE, Evelyn L. (Blake) [Am.
19c]
The drunkard's journey.
Boston: Congregational pub. soc.,
1876. 10p. NUC
[Temperance recitation]

1905. MORSE, Mabel [Am. 19c]
A foolish investment. A comedietta,
in one act. Adapted from the German.
NY: DeWitt, 1888. 15p. NUC OCLC
[DeWitt's acting plays, no. 350]

1906. -----A warm reception. A
comedietta, in one act. Tr. from the
German "Im schneegestober" of Rudolf
Jarosy, adapted for the American
stage.

NY: DeWitt pub. house, 1890. NUC OCLC
H
[Sergel's acting drama, no. 345]

1907. MORTON, Marguerite W. [Am. 19c]
Poison. Farce in one scene for four
females.
NY: E.S. Werner, 1895. 8p. NUC OCLC H

1908. -----Scenes from the last days
of Pompeii.
Philadelphia: Penn pub. co., 1894.
NUC
[Adapted from George Bulwer Lytton,
Baron Lytton. Keystone ed. of
plays.]

1909. -----The two roses. Farce in
two acts. NY: E.S. Werner, 1894. 11p.
NUC OCLC H

1910. MORTON, Martha [Am. 1865/70-
1925] ALT: Conheim, Mrs. Herman
A bachelor's romance; an original
play in four acts.
NY: n.p., 1896. Detroit, MI: R.J.
Laughlin, 1898. 16p. NUC OCLC M
[Comedy. Prod. Gaiety, 1886, 1897 &
1898. She also wrote and prod. at
own expense, "Helene," 1898. Her
play, "The merchant," won the NY
World drama contest. Mainero.]

1911. -----Brother John.
n.p.: n.p., n.d. 30, 32, 30f. NUC
[Typescript]

1912. -----A fool of fortune.
Boston: E.O. Skelton, 1897. 14p. NUC
OCLC

1913. -----His wife's father. Based
on a central idea in German by A.
L'Aronge.
NY: n.p., 1895. NY: Frank V. Strauss,
1896. 12p. NUC
[Produced at the Fifth Ave. Theatre,
NY, 25 Feb., 1895. Typescript.]

1914. -----The sleeping partner.
1897. M N
[Comedy, 3 acts. Further adapted
from "His wife's father." Prod.
London at Criterion, 1897.]

1915. MOSES, Annie Jonas, Mrs. [Am.
19/20c]
Esther. A drama in five acts.
Cincinnati, OH: Bloch, 1887. 27p. NUC

1916. MOUBREY, Lilian [Br. 1875?-
1970] ALT: Mowbrey, Lilian
King and artist, a romantic play in
five acts. With Walter Herries
Pollock.

NY; L: W. Heinemann, 1897. 88p. NUC
BL E
[Prod. Strand, 1897.]

1917. -----The werewolf, a romantic
play in one act. With Walter Herries
Pollock.
NY: Mershon co., 1898. 43p. L: W.
Heinemann, 1898. 44p. NUC BL E M
[Prod. Avenue, 1898.]

MOUILLOT, Frederick, co-author see
STEER, Janet

MOWATT, Anna Cora (Ogden) see
RITCHIE, Anna Cora (Ogden) Mowatt

MOWATT, Mrs. James see RITCHIE, Anna
Cora (Ogden) Mowatt

MOWBREY, Lilian see MOUBREY, Lilian

1918. MUNDAY, Lurania A. H. [Am. b.
1828]
Lasalvarietta; or, The female
patriot. A tragedy in five acts.
Cincinnati, OH: Elm St. pr. co.,
1876. 32p. NUC

1919. MUNSON, Kate C. [Am. 19c]
Zilla; an operetta.
Rochester, NY: n.p., 1870. 19p. NUC

MURRAY, Mrs. Dominick see FIDDES,
Josephine

1920. MURRAY, Ellen [Am. 19c]
Cain: ancient and modern.
In: Dramatic leaflets.
Philadelphia: Phineas Garrett, 1877.
1 v. in 20 pts. NUC OCLC H
[Temperance play.]

1921. -----The crusaders.
In: Dramatic leaflets.

1922. -----Esau and Jacob.
In: Dramatic leaflets.
[Sabbath school entertainment.
Dialogue.]

1923. -----Licensed snakes:
temperance dialogue.
In: Dramatic leaflets.

1924. MURRAY, Ellen [Am. 19c]
The women of Lowenburg. Historical
comedy in five scenes.
Chicago: T.S. Denison, 1886. 12p. H
[The amateur series]

MURRAY, Mrs. John see MURRAY, Judith
(Sargent) Stevens

1925. MURRAY, Judith (Sargent)
Stevens, Mrs. John Murray [Am. 1751-
1820] ALT: Sargent, Judith; Stevens,
Mrs. John; Stevens, Judith PSEUD:
Constantia
The gleaner. A miscellaneous
production. By Constantia.
Boston: Pr. by I. Thomas & E.T.
Andrews, 1798. 3v. NUC BL OCLC B Hill
Wells
[Collection, mostly original. Incl.
2 5-act plays, & poems, but primarily
prose letters to a periodical, The
Gleaner.]

1926. -----The traveller returned.
Boston: I. Thomas & E.T. Andrews,
1798. OCLC
[Comedy, 5 acts. Perf. in Boston,
1796. Also in: The gleaner.]

1927. -----Virtue triumphant.
In: The gleaner.
[Comedy, 5 acts. Perf. 1795 at
Federal St. Theater, Boston as: "The
medium; or, Happy tea party." Her
husband publicly denied her
authorship. Prod. anon. to avoid
criticism.]

1928. MURRAY, Kate [Am. 19c]
A Christmas play, including the
mystery of the three wise men.
Garden City Press, Letchworth, Herts,
n.d. 52p. NUC

1929. MUSGRAVE, H., Mrs. [Br. 19c]
Cerise and co.
1890. M N
[Farce comedy, 3 acts. Prod. Prince
of Wales, 1890.]

1930. -----Dick Wilder.
1891. M N
[Play, 4 acts. Prod. Vaudeville,
1891. Entered with Lord Chamberlain
as: "The Weeping Cross."]

1931. -----Our flat.
1889. M N
[Farce comedy. Prod. Prince of Wales
& Opera Comique, 1889; Strand, 1894.]

1932. N., M. [Br. 18c] PSEUD: Young
lady, A
The faithful general. A tragedy as
it is acted at the Queen's Theatre in
Haymarket by her Majesty's sworn
servants. By a young lady.
L: Pr. for R. Wellington, 1706. NUC
BL OCLC N
[Dedication signed: M.N. Adapted in
part from Francis Beaumont & John
Fletcher, "The loyal subject."]

1933. NAUCAZE, Anna de [Br. 19c]
The Peruvian.
1891. M N
[Play, 1 act, adaptation. Prod.
Opera Comique, 1891.]

1934. NEAL, May [Am. 19c]
The dairy-maid's festival.
Boston: W.H. Baker & co., 1887. 19p.
NUC

NEIL, ROSS, pseud. see HARWOOD,
Isabella

NETTIE see CLARK, Jeanette R.

NEVILLE, George F., co-author see
LEAN, Florence (Marryat) Church

1935. NEWCASTLE, Margaret (Lucas)
Cavendish, Duchess of [Br. 1624-1673]
ALT: Cavendish, Margaret (Lucas),
Duchess of Newcastle
Playes written by the thrice noble,
illustrious and excellent princess,
the lady Marchioness of Newcastle.
L: J. Martyn, J. Allestry, & T.
Dicas, 1662. 675p. NUC BL OCLC N
[None have been acted.]

1936. -----Plays, never before
printed.
A. Warren for J. Martyn, J. Allestry
& T. Dicas, 1662. 675 p.; 5pt. L:
Pr. A. Maxwell, 1668. 95, 155, 80,
53, 20p. NUC BL OCLC N Wm
[Contains: 1. The sociable
companions; or, The female wits; 2.
The presence; 3. The bridals; 4. The
convent of pleasure; 5. "A piece of a
play." Plays composed between 1662
and 1668. Incl. Blazing World;
Bridals; Convent of Pleasure,
Presence; Sociable Companions, &
fragments.]

1937. -----The apocriphal ladies.
In: Playes ... .
[Comedy. Chetwood.]

1938. -----Bell in Campo.
In: Playes ... .
[2 pts. Tragedy. Chetwood.]

1939. -----The blazing world.
In: Plays, never ... .
[2 pt. comedy. Chetwood.]

1940. -----The bridals.
In: Plays, never ... .
[Comedy, 5 acts. Chetwood.]

1941. -----The comical hash.
In: Playes ... .

[Comedy. Chetwood.]

1942. -----The convent of pleasure.
In: Plays, never ... .
[Comedy, 5 acts, not acted.
Chetwood.]

1943. -----The female academy.
In: Playes ... .
[Comedy, c1662. Chetwood.]

1944. -----The lady contemplation.
In: Playes ... .
[2 pt. comedy. Chetwood.]

1945. -----Loves adventures.
In: Playes ... .
[2 pts. Comedy. Chetwood.]

1946. -----The matrimonial trouble.
In: Playes ... .
[2 pts. Pt. 1 comedy. Pt. 2
tragedy. Chetwood.]

1947. -----Nature's three daughters:
beauty, love and wit.
In: Playes ... .
[2 pts. Comedy. Chetwood.]

1948. -----"A piece of play." In:
Plays, never ... .
[Comedy, 5 acts, not acted.]

1949. -----The presence.
In: Plays, never ... .
[Comedy, 5 acts. Chetwood.]

1950. -----The publick wooing.
In: Playes ... .
[Comedy. Chetwood.]

1951. -----The religious.
In: Playes ... .
[Comedy. Chetwood.]

1952. -----Several wits: the wise
wit, the wild wit, the cholerick wit,
the humble wit.
In: Playes ... .
[Comedy. Chetwood.]

1953. -----The sociable companions;
or, The female wits.
In: Plays, never ... .
[Comedy, 5 acts. Chetwood.]

1954. -----The unnatural tragedie.
In: Playes ... .

1955. -----Wits cabal.
In: Playes ... .
[2 pts. Comedy. Chetwood.]

1956. -----Youth's glory and death's
banquet.

In: Playes ... .
[2 pts. Tragedy. Chetwood.]

1957. NICHOLSON, Mrs. Alfred [Br. 19c]
The sleeping beauty and the wide-awake prince. A burlesque.
Manchester: J. Heywood, 1890. 48p. BL
[4 acts, verse]

1958. NIGHTINGALE, Lady Clarence [Br. 19c]
The three graces, faith, hope, and charity. Their arrival. Their reception ... and speeches to the people.
L: Passmore & Alabaster, 1881. 58p. BL
[Masque]

1959. NILES, Mrs. Clifford [Am. 19c]
Deoine. Pastoral drama for young ladies.
Griffin, GA: Daily News book & job office print, 1876. 32p. NUC OCLC

NOMAD, pseud. see SMITH, Adele Crafton

1960. NOOTH, Charlotte [Br. 19c]
Original poems, and a play.
L: Pr. for Longman, Hurst, Rees, Orme, & Brown, 1815. 156p. NUC BL OCLC
["Clara; or, The nuns of charity"; 5 acts, verse]

1961. NORDON, Julia B. [Br. 19c]
Misunderstood.
1899. N
[Duologue. Prod. Steinway Hall, 1899.]

1962. NORTON, Mrs. [Am. 19c]
The soldier from Bingen.
In: Massey's exhibition reciter, and drawing room entertainments. Comp. Charles Massey. NY: S. French, 1856. 98p. NUC OCLC H

1963. NORTON, Eliza Bland (Smith) Erskine, Hon. Mrs. [Br. 19c] ALT: Erskine, Hon Mrs. Esme Stewart
The martyr: a tragedy.
L: Saunders & Otley, 1848. 80p. NUC BL
[5 acts, verse]

1964. NORTON, Jessie [Am. 19c]
Sappho. Classical historical play for girls.
NY: E.S. Werner, 1894. 28p. NUC OCLC H

1965. NORTON, Morilla Maria [Am. b. 1865]
Gloria Victis.
Warner, NH: E.C. Cole, 1900. 50p. NUC OCLC H
[Drama on Esther, Queen of Persia.]

1966. NOVELLO, Mary Sabilla (Hehl), Mrs. Vincent Novello [Br. 1789-1854]
Turandot: the Chinese sphinx.
L: Samuel French, 1872. 35p. E

NOVELLO, Mrs. Vincent see NOVELLO, Mary Sabilla (Hehl)

1967. O'BRIEN, Charlotte Grace [Br. 1845-1909]
A tale of Venice: a drama. And lyrics.
Dublin: M.H. Gill & Sons, 1880. 138p. BL
[4 acts, verse. Misc. poems, pp. 93-138]

1968. O'BRIEN, Constance [Am. 19c]
Possible plays for private players.
4 pt. L: Griffith Farran, Okeden & Welsh, 1891. 36, 27, 30, 35p. NUC BL OCLC

1969. -----Cross purposes. A comedy in one act.
NY: DeWitt, 189-? 38p. NUC BL OCLC
[DeWitt's acting plays, no. 382. Also in: Possible plays.]

1970. -----Love in a flue; or, The sweep and the magistrate; a comedy in two acts.
NY: DeWitt, n.d. 35p. NUC BL OCLC
[DeWitt's acting plays, no. 385. Also in: Possible plays as "The sweep and the magistrate; or, Love in a flue."]

1971. -----A lover and a half. A comedy in two acts.
NY: DeWitt, n.d. 30p. NUC BL OCLC
[DeWitt's acting plays, no. 384. Also in: Possible plays.]

1972. -----The wager. Comedy in one act.
NY: DeWitt, 189-? 27p. NUC BL OCLC H
[Also in: Possible plays. DeWitt's acting plays, no. 383.]

1973. O'BRIEN, Mary, Mrs. [Br. 18c]
The fallen patriot. A comedy, in five acts. Dublin: Pr. William Gilbert, 1790. 58p. NUC BL

1974. O'CONNELL, Alice [Br. 19c]
All Jackon's fault.

1889. N
[Farce.   Prod. Tottenham Ct. Rd.,
1889.]

OFFICER'S WIFE, AN, pseud. <u>see</u>
FRASER, Susan, Mrs.

OGILVIE, Mrs. David <u>see</u> OGILVIE,
Eliza Ann Harris (Dick)

1975. OGILVIE, Eliza Ann Harris
(Dick), Mrs. David Ogilvie [Br. 19c]
Traditions of Tuscany.
L: n.p., 1851. Inglis
[Incl. a drama on Bianca Capello.
She also pub. a charade in Mrs.
Valentine's Girls' Home Book, 1867,
and "Lars Porsena," a dramatic
extravaganza, in Warne's Christmas
Annual, 1867-8.]

OLIPHANT, E.H.C., co-author <u>see</u>
CHAPIN, Alice

OLIVER, Isabella <u>see</u> SHARP, Isabella
(Oliver)

OLWINE, Mrs. Wayne <u>see</u> DALY, Julia

O'NEIL, Mrs. James <u>see</u> LOGAN, Olive

1976. OPENSHAW, Mary [Br. 19c] ALT:
Binstead, Mary Openshaw
My first client: duologue.
L & NY: Samuel French, 1903. 8p. BL
OCLC E
[Lacy's Acting ed.]

1977. OPIE, Amelia (Alderson), Mrs.
John Opie [Br. 1769-1853?] ALT:
Alderson, Miss; Alderson, Amelia
Adelaide.   By Miss Alderson.
1791. N
[Tragedy.   Prod. Plumptre's private
theatre, Norwich, 1791.]

OPIE, Mrs. John <u>see</u> OPIE, Amelia
(Alderson)

ORINDA, pseud. <u>see</u> PHILIPS, Katherine
(Fowler)

1978. ORNE, Martha Russell [Am. 19c]
A black diamond.   A comic drama in
two acts.
Boston: W.H. Baker & co., 1890. 24p.
NUC OCLC
[Baker's edition of plays]

1979. -----The country school.   An
entertainment in two scenes.
Boston: W.H. Baker & co., 1890. 20p.
NUC OCLC
[Baker's "Novelty" list]

1980. -----The donation party; or,
Thanksgiving eve at the parsonage.   A
comedy in three acts.
Boston: W.H. Baker, 1894. 43p. NUC
OCLC [Baker's edition of plays]

1981. -----A limb o'the law.   A
comedy in two acts.
Boston: W.H. Baker & co., 1892. 18p.
NUC OCLC
[Baker's edition of plays]

1982. -----An old maid's wooing; a
drama in two acts.
Boston: W.H. Baker & co., 1899. 22p.
NUC OCLC
[Baker's edition of plays]

1983. -----Timothy Delano's
courtship; a comedy in two acts.
NY: H. Roorbach; Dick & Fitzgerald,
1892. 27p. NUC BL OCLC
[Prose; Roorbach's American ed. of
acting plays, no. 50]

OSBORNE, Kate, co-author <u>see</u> HODGSON,
Agatha H.

1984. OSGOOD, Frances Sargent
(Locke), Mrs. Samuel Stillman Osgood
[Am. 1811-1850]
Osgood's poetical works, containing a
choice collection of sacred and
miscellaneous poems, and songs,
ballads and floral fancies.
Philadelphia: J.E. Potter & co.,
1880. 466p. NUC OCLC

1985. -----A wreath of wild flowers
from New England.
L: Edward Churton, 1838. 364p. NUC BL
OCLC
[Incl.: "Elfrida," a dramatic poem in
5 acts.   Also in Poetical Works.]

OSGOOD, Mrs. Samuel Stillman <u>see</u>
OSGOOD, Frances Sargent (Locke)

1986. OVERBECK, E. Miss [Br. 19c]
Round the links.
1895. N
[Dramatic sketch.   Prod. Albert Hall,
1895.   Also prod. as: "The Tipster."]

1987. -----Sonia.
1895. N
[Dramatic sketch.   Prod. Albert Hall,
1895.]

OWENSON, Sydney <u>see</u> MORGAN, Sydney
(Owenson), Lady

OXBERRY, William Henry, co-author <u>see</u>
LAURENT, Mme.

P*****, MISS, pseud. see PLUMPTRE,
Anne

P., A. see PENNY, Anne (Hughes)
Christian
P., A.M. see PORTER, Anna Maria

P., L.J., Miss see HALL, Louisa Jane
(Park)

P., Mrs. K. see PHILIPS, Katherine
(Fowler)

1988. PACHECO, Mrs. Romauldo [Am.
19/20c]
Ireland; or, The voice of the people;
a drama of real life in four acts.
NY: Trow's pr. & bookbinding co.,
1890. 48p. NUC OCLC

1989. -----"Tom, Dick and Harry." A
farcical comedy in three acts.
L & NY: French, 1899. 57p. NUC BL M N
[Prod. Trafalgar, 1893. Prod. in
U.S. as: "Incog."]

1990. PACKARD, Hannah James [Am.
1815-1831]
The choice: a tragedy; with
miscellaneous poems.
Boston: L.C. Bowles, 1832. 142p. NUC
OCLC R
[3-acts, verse]

PAINE, Jennie E., co-author see COBB,
Josephine H.

1991. PAINTER, Lydia Ethel (Hoyt)
Farmer [Am. 1842-1903] ALT: Farmer,
Lydia (Hoyt) PSEUD: X., G.E.
The rosary, by G.E.X.
Cleveland, Oh: Pr. by Fenton & Stair,
1899. NUC OCLC
[62p. poems, chiefly love poetry;
Incl. allegorical play, "The rose
tree," 29p.]

1992. PALMER, Mrs. Bandmann [Br. 19c]
Catherine Howard; or, The tomb, the
throne and the scaffold.
1892. N
[Drama. Prod. at Weymouth, 1892.]

1993. PALMER, Bell Elliot [Am. b.
1873]
Dodging an heiress; or, His uncle's
choice. Two act comedy.
Franklin, OH: Eldridge entertainment
house, 18--? [1918? NUC] 41p. NUC
OCLC T

1994. -----A social crisis; or,
Almost a tragedy of tongues. Comedy
in one act.

Franklin, OH: Eldridge entertainment
house, 18--? [1918? NUC] 11p. NUC
OCLC T

1995. PARDOE, Julia S. H. [Br. 1806-
1862]
Agnes St. Aubin, the wife of two
husbands.
1841. M N
[Drama, 3 acts. Prod. Adelphi,
1841.]

1996. -----Louise de Lignerolles; or,
A lesson for husbands.
L: T.H. Lacy, 1838. 33p. E M
[Drama, 3 acts. Prod. Adelphi, 1838.
Lacy's Acting ed.]

1997. PARK, Elisabeth [Am. 19c]
Miriam; a dramatic poem.
2d ed. Boston: H.P. Nichols & co.,
1838. 122p. TXU
[1st ed. 1837. 2d ed. incl.
corrections. 3 long scenes on early
Christians in Rome.]

PARK, Louisa Jane see HALL, Louisa
Jane (Park)

1998. PARKER, Charlotte (Blair), Mrs.
Harry Doel Parker [Am. 1858-1937]
ALT: Parker, Lottie Blair
Way down East; a pastoral drama in
four acts.
NY: priv. pr., 1898. NUC OCLC
[Quinn: prod. at Manhattan Theatre,
Jan. 19, 1898]

PARKER, Mrs. Harry Doel see PARKER,
Charlotte (Blair)

PARKER, Lottie (Blair) see PARKER,
Charlotte (Blair)

1999. PARKER, Mary Saltonstall, Mrs.
W.P. Parker [Am. 19/20c]
Charades. A baker's dozen of
charades.
Salem, MA: I.K. Annable?, 1897. 13p.
NUC

2000. PARKER, Nella [Br. 19c]
Home acting for amateurs. [Two
series] By N. Parker [and others].
13 pts.
L: F. Warne & co., 1892. NUC BL

2001. -----After long years.
In: Home acting, Series 2.
[Musical comedy; incl. 6 songs]

2002. -----Cynthia's captive.
In: Home acting, Series 1.
[Duologue, set in 1814]

2003. -----Fairly caught.
In: Home acting, Series 1.
[Romantic comedietta]

2004. -----For Cyril's sake.
In: Home acting, Series 2.
[Romantic comedietta]

2005. -----For the honour of the
house.
In: Home acting, Series 1.
[Set in Restoration, romantic
comedietta]

2006. -----In danger's hour.
In: Home acting, Series 1.
[Set mid 18th c., romantic
comedietta]

2007. -----"Kitty." In: Home acting,
Series 2.
[Duologue]

2008. -----A midsumer jest.
In: Home acting, Series 1.
[Romantic comedietta]

2009. -----My lady of Levenmore.
In: Home acting, Series 2.
[Set in 18th c., romantic comedietta]

2010. -----Theo.
In: Home acting, series 1.
[Domestic comedietta]

PARKER, Nella, comp. see VALENTINE,
Laura Jewry

2011. PARKER, Nella [Br. 19c]
Tom's wife.
1896. N
[Comedietta. Prod. at Worthing,
1896.]

2012. -----Uncle Malot's return.
In: Home acting, Series 2.
[Duologue]

PARKER, Mrs. W.P. see PARKER, Mary
Saltonstall

2013. PARSONS, Eliza Phelp [Br. d.
1811]
The intrigues of a morning. In two
acts.
L: W. Lane, 1792. 31p. NUC BL B N
[A farce, from Moliere's "M. de
Pourceaugnac." Prod. Covent Garden,
1792. Longe, v. 234, no. 7]

2014. PARSONS, Laura Matilda
(Stephenson) [Am. b. 1855]
The district school at Blueberry
Corners. A farce in three scenes.

NY: Bunnell & O. Berdorf, 1889. NUC
OCLC

2015. -----Jerusha Dow's Album #2,
her friends and neighbors.
Boston: Walter H. Baker co., 1892.
25p. NUC OCLC
[Both bound in Aunt Jerusha's
Quilting Party, 1901. Monologues in
rhyme. Also incl. 6 short plays for
use by jr. high students.]

2016. -----Jerusha Dow's family
album.
Boston: Walter H. Baker co., 1892.
25p. NUC OCLC
[Baker's specialties. Dramatic
monologues in rhyme. Jerusha, an
old-fashioned lady, describes her
family, with homely wisdom.]

2017. -----Living pictures of the
Civil War.
Boston: W.H. Baker & co., 1894. 28p.
NUC OCLC
[Tableaux. Baker's Novelties.]

2018. -----The old maid's convention;
an entertainment in one scene.
Boston: Walter S. Baker, 1899. 18p.
NUC

2019. -----Scenes and songs of ye
olden time; an old folks'
entertainment.
Boston: W.H. Baker & co., 1894. 20p.
NUC
[Baker's novelties]

2020. PATRY, Rose Isabel [Br. 19/20c]
Mrs. Jacobson's account of the
Jubilee. Dialogue 1898.
L: S. French, 1898. 6p. NUC BL
[Recital piece in Westmorland
dialect]

2021. PAYN, Dorothea [Br. 19c]
A midnight shriek.
1896. N
[Burlesque. Prod. in Dublin, 1896.]

2022. PAYSON, Frances M. [Am. 19c]
Elma, the fairy child. An operetta.
Chicago: T.S. Denison, 1889. 43p. NUC

2023. PEABODY, Josephine Preston [Am.
1874-1922] ALT: Marks, Josephine
Preston (Peabody); Marks, Mrs. Lionel
S.
Fortune and men's eyes. New poems
with a play.
Boston: Houghton, Mifflin; Small,
Maynard & co., 1900. pp. 1-49. NUC
OCLC H

[Incl.: "Fortune and men's eyes." 1 act.]

2024. PEARD, Frances Mary [Br. 1835-1923]
Pins and needles. Comedietta.
Torquay: Standard pr., pub. & newspaper co., 18--? 12p. OCLC E

PEATTIE, Mrs. E.W. see PEATTIE, Elia (Wilkinson)

2025. PEATTIE, Elia (Wilkinson), Mrs. Robert Burns Peattie [Am. 1862-1935]
ALT: Peattie, Mrs. E. W.
The love of a Caliban, a romantic opera in one act.
Wausau, WI: Van Vechten & Ellis, 1898. NUC

PEATTIE, Mrs. Robert Burns see PEATTIE, Elia (Wilkinson)

PECK, E.W. see PECK, Elizabeth Weller

2026. PECK, Elizabeth Weller [Am. 19c] ALT: PECK, E. W.
Nathaniel Hawthorne's Scarlet Letter dramatized. A play in five acts by E.W. Peck.
Boston: Franklin Press; Rand, Avery & co., 1876. 72p. NUC BL OCLC R

2027. PEEL, Lady Georgiana Adelaide (Russell) [Br. b. 1836] ALT: Russell, Lady Georgina Adelaide
Dewdrop and Glorio; or, The sleeping beauty in the wood. Written and dedicated to Lord John Russell, by [Lady G.A. Russell and Lady Victoria Russell]. Acted at Pembroke Lodge, December 23 and 28, 1858.
L: Charles Westerton, priv. pr., (1858 NUC) c1860. 32p. NUC BL E
[Masque in verse]

2028. PELHAM, Nettie H. [Am. 19/20c]
The belles of Blackville, a Negro minstrel entertainment for young ladies, concluding with a specialty farce entitled "Patchwork.".
NY: Fitzgerald; H. Roorbach, 1897. 20p. NUC OCLC

2029. -----The Christmas ship, a Christmas entertainment.
Chicago: T.S. Denison, 1888. 10p. NUC OCLC
[Amateur series]

2030. -----The old fashioned husking bee; an old folks' entertainment in one scene.
Boston: W.H. Baker, 1891. 17p. NUC OCLC

[Baker's novelties]

2031. -----The realm of time, a pageant for young people and children.
Chicago: T.S. Denison, 1890. 20p. NUC OCLC H T
[Amateur series]

2032. -----The white caps.
Chicago: T.S. Denison, 1891. 12p. NUC OCLC H
[Amateur series. Play for children.]

PEMBERTON, Harriet Louisa Childe see CHILDE-PEMBERTON, Harriet Louisa

2033. PEMBROKE, Mary (Sidney) Herbert, Countess of [Br. 1561-1621]
ALT: Herbert, Mary (Sidney,) Countess of Pembroke; Sidney, Mary
A discourse of life and death.
Written in French by Ph[ilippe de] Mornay. Antoinius, a tragedie written also in French by Ro[bert] Garnier. Both done in English by the Countess of Pembroke.
L: Pr. for William. Ponsonby, 1592. NUC BL B G
[The tragedie of Antoine. Translated into English by the Countess of Pembroke. L: P.S. For Wm. Ponsonby, 1595.]

2034. PENDLETON, Charlotte [Am. 19c]
The admiral, a dramatic triad.
Philadelphia: Allen, Lane & Scott, 1889. 22p. NUC
[Play about Christopher Columbus]

2035. -----Blue Beard. Kermesse, for the benefit of the village improvement society, Bar Harbour, Maine, 1890.
Philadelphia: n.p., 1890. 8p. NUC
[A humorous version of Bluebeard in verse]

PENN, RACHEL, pseud. see WILLARD, Catherine McCoy (White)

2036. PENNY, Anne (Hughes) Christian, Mrs. Peter Penny [Br. 1731-1784] ALT: Christian, Mrs. Thomas; P., A.
Poems.
L: Pr. for the author & sold by J. Dodsley, 1780. 242p. NUC BL OCLC B N
[Incl.: "The Birth-day, an entertainment in 3 acts."]

PENNY, Mrs. Peter see PENNY, Anne (Hughes) Christian

2037. PERKINS, Mary R. [Am. 19c]

Annette. A melodrama in five acts.
NY: n.p., 1890. NUC

2038. -----His mother and I, in four
acts.
NY: n.p., 1890. NUC

2039. -----Uncle Dollie, or
notwithstanding; a one act comedie.
NY: n.p., 1890. NUC

2040. -----Who is the man? A comedy
in four acts.
NY: n.p., 1892. NUC

2041. PERRY, Mrs. [Br. 19c]
Our last rehearsal. Music by A.
Oake.
1893. N
[Musical comedy. Prod. at Folkstone,
1893.]

PFEIFFER, Emily Jane (Daub) see
PFEIFFER, Emily Jane (Davis)

2042. PFEIFFER, Emily Jane (Davis
[Daub E]) [Br. 1827-1890]
The Wynnes of Wynhavod: A drama of
modern life.
L: n.p., 1881. 79p. NUC BL E
[Five acts, verse. Also pub. in:
Under the aspens: lyrical and
dramatic. L: K. Paul, Trench & co.,
1881, 1882. NUC BL OCLC E]

2043. PHELAN, Agnes Vivien [Am. 19c]
Margaret of Anjou; a drama.
Chicago: Donahue & Henneberry, 1888.
48p. NUC OCLC

2044. PHELPS, Jessie Adeline (Cole)
[Am. b. 1864]
Robert Emmet; or, true Irish hearts.
In six acts.
Denver, CO: Colorado pr. co., 1884.
76p. NUC

2045. PHELPS, Pauline [Am. 19/20c]
Aunt Elnora's hero. Humorous
monologue for a woman.
NY: n.p., c1900. 4p. NUC
[Pauline Phelps' pieces.]

2046. PHELPS, Pauline [Am. 19/20c]
Aunt Sarah on bicycles. Humorous
monologue for a woman.
NY: n.p., 1899. 4p. NUC
[Pauline Phelps' pieces]

2047. -----A cyclone for a cent, a
farce in one act. Boston: W.H. Baker
& co., 1894. 17p. NUC OCLC H
[Baker's edition of plays]

2048. -----Dialect. Compiled and
arranged by Pauline Phelps.
NY: E.S. Werner & co., c1899. 192p.
NUC
[Werner's readings and recitations,
no. 21.]

2049. -----Minister's Black Nance.
The story of a country horse race, as
described by an eye witness.
NY: n.p., 1899. 5p. NUC
[Pauline Phelps' pieces]

2050. -----A Shakespearian
conference.
NY: E.S. Werner, 1899. 15p. H

2051. -----The sweet girl graduate.
Humorous monologue for a lady.
NY: E.S. Werner, 1900. 7p. NUC

2052. -----A telephone romance.
Humorous monologue for a lady.
NY: E.S. Werner, 1899. 8p. T

2053. -----A telephone romance.
Humorous monologue for a lady.
NY: E.S. Werner, 1900. 8p. NUC

2054. PHELPS, Sydney, Miss [Br. 19c]
The lady volunteers.
1894. N
[Comedietta. Prod. Parkhurst, 1894.]

2055. PHIBBS, Mary [Br. 19c]
Alice Western; or, The dangers of
coquetry. A drama in four acts.
L: C. Westerton, 1855. 35p. NUC

PHILANTHEA, pseud. see DEVERELL,
Mary, Mrs.

PHILIPS, Mrs. James see PHILIPS,
Katherine (Fowler)

2056. PHILIPS, Joan [Br. 17c] ALT:
Wogan, Joan (Philips) PSEUD: Ephelia
Female poems on several occasions.
By Ephelia.
L: Pr. William Downing for James
Courtney, 1679. 112p. NUC BL OCLC
[Incl. prologue, epilogue and songs
from her play, "The pair royal of
Coxcombs," now lost. It was acted at
a dancing school.]

2057. PHILIPS, Katherine Fowler, Mrs.
James Philips [Br. 1631-1664] ALT:
P., Mrs. K. PSEUD: Orinda
Poems by the most deservedly admired
Mrs. Katherine Philips, the matchless
Orinda. To which is added M.
Corneille's Pompey and house
tragedies. With several other
translations out of French.

L: Pr. by J.M. for H. Herringman,
1667. 112p. NUC BL OCLC B N WM
[Perf. by amateurs at court, Feb.
1667/8, Theatre Royal in Bridges St.,
1668/9. Philips' work was finished
by Sir John Denham. Incl. "Horace."
Translated from Philippe Corneille.]

2058. -----Pompey. A tragedy.
L: J. Crooke; Dublin: Jerre Crooke
for S. Dancer, 1663. NUC BL OCLC B N
WM
[Tragedy, trans. from Philippe
Corneille. Perf. Smock Alley,
Dublin, 1662/3. Also in: Poems,
1667, 1669 & 1678.]

PHILLIPS, Mrs. Alfred P. see
PHILLIPS, Elizabeth

2059. PHILLIPS, Elizabeth, Mrs.
Alfred P. Phillips [Br. 1822?-1876]
Caught in his own trap. An original
comedietta, in one act.
L & NY: S. French, 1851. 18p. BL E M
[Prod. Olympia, 1851. Lacy's acting
ed.]

2060. -----Cupid in Brighton; or, a
visit from the celestials.
1848. N
[Interlude]

2061. -----Katty from Connaught.
1849. N
[Comedietta. Prod. Strand, 1849.]

2062. -----The king's choice.
1848. N
[Interlude. Prod. Strand, 1848.]

2063. -----Life in Australia, from
our own correspondent.
1853. N
[Drama. Prod. Olympia, 1853.]

2064. -----The master passion, a
comedy in two acts.
L: T.H. Lacy, 1852. 30p. BL OCLC E M
N
[Comedy. Prod. Olympia, 1852.]

2065. -----My husband's will.
1853. N
[Comedietta. Prod. Olympia, 1853.]

2066. -----An organic affection, a
farce in one act.
L: T.H. Lacy, 1852. 20p. BL OCLC E M
N
[Prod. Olympia, 1852. Also known as:
"An affection of the heart."]

2067. -----Prejudice; or, a
bachelor's vow.

1848. M N
[Farce, 1 act. Prod. Strand, 1848.
Prod. as: "The batchelor's vow,"
Olympia, 1852.]

2068. -----Uncle Crotchet, a farce in
one act.
L: Lacy, 1853. 22p. BL E N
[Farce. Prod. Olympia, 1853.]

2069. PHILLIPS, Mrs. Newton [Br. 19c]
All a mistake.
1890. N
[Comedietta. Prod. Ladbrooke Hall,
1890. Also known as: "Polly
Plumtree."]

2070. -----Alpine tourists.
1888. N
[Comedietta. Prod. Ladbrooke Hall,
1888.]

2071. -----Broken off.
1892. N
[Comedietta. Prod. Ladbrooke Hall,
1892.]

2072. -----Charlotte Maria. With F.
Macrae.
1892. N
[Farce. Prod. Ladbrooke Hall, 1892.]

2073. -----Donna. With Mrs. [Margaret
Wolfe (Hamilton) Argles] Hungerford.
1892. N
[Drama. Prod. Ladbrooke Hall, 1892.]

2074. -----Some day. With John
Tresahar.
1889. M N
[Play, 3 acts. Prod. St. George
Hall, 1889.]

2075. PICKERING, Ellen [Br. d. 1843]
Charades for acting.
L: Lacy, 1843. 104p. NUC BL
[Contents: Homely; Backbiting;
Candidate; Mistake; Final. Each
charade has 3 parts.]

2076. -----Proverbs for acting.
L: T.C. Newby, 1844. 121p. NUC BL
OCLC

PIDGIN, Charles Felton, co-author see
GAY, Mary M.

2077. PIERCE, Sarah Emily, Mrs. [Am.
19c]
Old Moneybag's will. A farce comedy
in three acts.
n.p.: n.p., 1890. NUC

2078. -----The poor girl, a romantic
drama in four acts and one tableaux.

Adapted from the works of Pierce Egan
[the younger].
NY: n.p., 1883. NUC

2079. PILKINGTON, Laetitia (Van
Lewen), Mrs. Matthew Pilkington [Br.
1712-1750]
Memoirs of Mrs. Laetitia Pilkington,
wife to the Rev. Mr. Matthew
Pilkington. Written by herself.
Dublin: Pr. for author, 1748. 2v. NUC
BL OCLC
[2d v. incl. a 1 act tragedy, "The
Roman father." A burlesque satiric
piece, "The Turkish Court, or, The
land on prentice," perf. at theatre
in Capel St., 1748, but never
printed. Chetwood.]

PILKINGTON, Mrs. Matthew see
PILKINGTON, Laetitia (Van Lewen)

2080. PINCKNEY, Maria Henrietta [Am.
d. 1836] PSEUD: Lady, A
Essays, religious, moral, dramatic
and poetical: addressed to youth and
published for a benevolent purpose.
Charleston, SC: A.E. Miller, 1818.
[148p. Wells] 242p. NUC OCLC B Hill
Wells
[The article on Sarah (Pogson) Smith
in Mainero attr. this work to her.]

2081. -----The orphans.
In: Essays ... .
[Melodrama, 5 acts.]

2082. -----A tyrant's victims.
In: Essays ... .
B Hill Wells
[Tragedy of Greek tyrant.]

2083. -----The young Carolinians; or,
Americans in Algiers.
Charleston, SC: Pr. E. Miller, 1898.
NUC B Hill Wells
[5 acts. 1st pub. in: Essays ... .]

2084. PINEO, Mabel [Br. 19c] PSEUD:
Pireau, Max
The double deception. By Max Pireau.
With Lois Royd.
1897. N
[Comedy. Prod. Bijou, 1897 & in 1899
as: "Phyllis."]

PIREAU, MAX, pseud. see PINEO, Mabel

2085. PITTMAN, Hannah Daviess [Am. b.
1840]
Manette, a comic opera in three acts.
St. Louis, MO: Nixon-Jones pr. co.,
1883. 58p. NUC
[libretto by Pittman; music by A.G.
Robyn]

PIX, Mrs. George see PIX, Mary
(Griffith)

2086. PIX, Mary (Griffith), Mrs.
George Pix [Br. 1666-1709]
The adventures in Madrid. Comedy.
L: W. Turner, 1706? 1709. 70p. NUC BL
OCLC B N S
[Prod. Haymarket, 1706. Longe, v.
179, no. 10]

2087. -----The beau defeated: or, The
lucky younger brother. A comedy.
L: W. Turner; R. Basset, 1700? 47p.
NUC BL OCLC B N S WM
[Prod. Lincoln's Inn, 1699/1700.
Ascribed also to a Mr. Barker.
Sometimes called "The beau
demolished." Longe, v. 208, no. 1]

2088. -----The conquest of Spain, a
tragedy.
L: R. Wellington, 1705. 76p. NUC BL
OCLC B N S
[Tragedy. Prod. Haymarket, 1705. No
records of perf. Partly taken from
William Rowley's "All's lost by
lust."]

2089. -----The Czar of Muscovy. A
tragedy.
L: B. Bernard Lintott, 1701. 57p. NUC
BL OCLC N S
[Tragedy. Prod. Lincoln's Inn,
1700/01. No records of perf. On
Pseudo Demetrius I, Czar of Russia]

2090. -----The deceiver deceived. A
comedy.
L: R. Bassett, 1698. 47p. NUC BL OCLC
B N S WM
[Comedy, 5 acts, prose. Perf.
Lincoln's Inn Fields, 1697. Prod.
1699 as: "The French beau." Longe,
v. 127, no. 7]

2091. -----The different widows; or,
Intrigue all-a-mode. A comedy. Pub.
anon.
L: Henry Playford & Bernard Lintott,
1703. 62p. NUC BL OCLC B N S
[Comedy, 5 acts, prose. Prod.
Lincoln's Inn, 1703, no records of
performance. Longe, v. 160. no. 2]

2092. -----The double distress. A
tragedy.
L: R. Wellington, 1701. 56p. NUC BL
OCLC B N S
[Tragedy, 5 acts, verse. Prod.
Lincoln's Inn, 1700/01.]

2093. -----The false friend; or, The
fate of disobedience. A tragedy.

L: Richard Bassett, 1699. 60p. NUC BL OCLC B N S WM
[Tragedy, 5 acts, verse. Perf. Lincoln's Inn Fields, 1699. Longe, v. 171, no. 7]

2094. -----Ibrahim, the thirteenth, Emperour of the Turks: a tragedy.
L: John Harding & Richard Wilkin, 1696. 41p. NUC BL OCLC B N S WM
[Tragedy, 5 acts, verse. Pef. Drury Lane, 1696.]

2095. -----The innocent mistress. A comedy.
L: J. Orme for R. Bassett & F. Cogan, 1697. 52p. NUC BL OCLC B N S WM
[Comedy, 5 acts. Perf. Lincoln's Inn Fields, 1697. Taken in part from Sir George Etherege's "The man of mode." Longe, v. 108, no. 4.]

2096. -----Queen Catherine: or, The ruines of love.
L: William Turner & Richard Bassett, 1698. 52p. NUC BL OCLC B N S WM
[Tragedy, 5 acts, verse. Perf. Lincoln's Inn Fields, 1698. Longe, v. 1, no. 3.]

2097. -----The Spanish wives. A farce.
L: R. Wellington, 1696. 48p. NUC BL OCLC B N S WM
[Farce, 3 acts. Perf. Drury Lane, 1696. Plot borrowed from Sebastien Bremond's novel: "The pilgrim."]

2098. -----Violenta, or The rewards of virtue: turn'd from Boccace into verse.
L: John Nutt, 1704. 128p. NUC BL OCLC
[Based on 8th tale, 2nd day of Decameron by Giovanni Boccaccio.]

2099. -----Zelmane: or, The Corinthian queen.
1704. N
[Tragedy begun by William Mountfort. Perf. Lincoln's Inn Fields. Completion of work attr. to Pix in Avery, London Stage.]

PLANCHE, Eliza see PLANCHE, Elizabeth (St. George)

2100. PLANCHÉ, Elizabeth (St. George), Mrs. James Robinson Planché [Br. 1796-1846] ALT: Planché, Eliza
A handsome husband: a farce.
L: J. Miller, 1836; L & NY: Samuel French, 1836. 28p. NUC BL OCLC E M N
[Farce, 1 act. Prod. Olympic, 1836 & in 1839, 42, 46, 50 & 95. Modern

acting drama New Series. no. 14. Lacy's Acting edition, no. 157]

2101. -----A hasty conclusion. A burletta, in one act.
L: Chapman & Hall, 1838. 22p. NUC BL OCLC E M N
[A version in 2 acts, "Hasty conclusions," prod. Olympic, 1838, & Lyceum, 1844. BL has ed. with "A handsome husband." L: Dick's Standard plays, 1887. 21p. Webster, R., Acting national drama, no. 43.]

2102. -----Ivan Daniloff; or, The Russian mandate.
1835. M N
[Drama. Prod. Surrey, 1835; Sadler's Wells, 1844.]

2103. -----A pleasant neighbour. A farce.
L: John Miller, 1836. 22p. NY: S. French, 186-? 16p. NUC BL OCLC E M
[Farce, 1 act. Prod. Olympic, 1836; Sadler's Wells, 1837; & Globe in 1871. French's American drama. Acting ed.; no. 8.]

2104. -----The ransom: an anecdote of Montesquieu. A drama in two acts.
L: J. Miller, 1836. 36p. Philadelphia: Turner & Fisher, 183-? 40p. NUC BL OCLC E M N
[Prod. Haymarket, 1836, 37. Turner's dramatic library. Miller's Modern Acting Drama.]

2105. -----The sledge-driver: a drama in two acts.
L: John Miller, 1834. 40p. NUC BL E N
[Prod. Haymarket, 1834. Miller's Modern Acting Drama, v. 5]

2106. -----The Welsh girl; a vaudeville in one act. By Mrs. J.R. Planché.
L: John Miller, 1834. 37p. NUC BL E M N
[Farce. OCLC attr. James Robinson Planche. First prod. at Olympic Theatre, 1833. Revived in 1842 & 1846. BL has ed. with "A pleasant neighbor." L: Dicks' Standard Plays, 1887. 21p. Miller's Modern Acting Drama, v. 5]

PLANCHÉ, Mrs. James Robinson see PLANCHÉ, Elizabeth (St. George)

PLANCHÉ, Matilda Anne see MACKARNESS, Matilda Anne (Planché)

2107. PLOWDEN, Dorothea (Phillips), Mrs. Francis Plowden [Br. d. 1827]

Virginia: a comic opera in three acts.   By Mrs. Francis Plowden.   L: J. Barker, 1800.   63p.   NUC BL OCLC E [Prod. Drury Lane, 1800.]

PLOWDEN, Mrs. Francis <u>see</u> PLOWDEN, Dorothea (Phillips)

2108.   PLUMB, Harriet Pixley [Br. 19c] Charlotte Temple; a historical drama. Three acts with prologue. Chicago: Publishers' pr. co.; L: T.F. Unwin, 1899.   47p.   NUC BL [Based on Susanna Rowson's novel, "Charlotte Temple."]

2109.   PLUMPTRE, Annabella [Br. b. 1755?] ALT: Plumptre, Bell PSEUD: Lady, A The foresters.   By Bell Plumptre. L: Vernor & Hood, 1799.   119p.   NUC OCLC B N [Drama.   Trans. from German of "Die Jager" by August Wilhelm Iffland.]

2110.   PLUMPTRE, Anne [Br. 1759/60- 1818] PSEUD: P*****, Miss Count of Burgundy. L: R. Phillips, 1798.   77p.   NUC BL OCLC N B [4 acts.   Tr. from German]

2111.   -----The force of calumny. L: R. Phillips, 1799.   108p.   NUC BL OCLC B N [5 acts.   From German of August Friedrich Ferdinand Von Kotzebue.]

2112.   -----The natural son. Dublin: H. Fitzpatrick, 1798.   83p. NUC BL OCLC B N [5 acts.   From German of August Friedrich Ferdinand Von Kotzebue.]

2113.   -----La peyrouse. L: R. Phillips, 1799.   34p.   BL OCLC B N [From German of August Friedrich Ferdinand Von Kotzebue.]

2114.   -----Pizarro. L: R. Phillips, 1799.   93p.   NUC BL OCLC B N [Tragedy, 5 acts.   From German of August Friedrich Ferdinand Von Kotzebue.   Title also given as: "The Spaniards in Peru; or, The death of Rolla."]

2115.   -----Virgin of the sun. L: R. Phillips, 1799.   96p.   NUC BL OCLC B N [From German of August Friedrich Ferdinand Von Kotzebue.]

2116.   -----The widow and the riding horse.   A dramatic trifle in one act. L: R. Phillips, 1799.   NUC BL OCLC B N [5 acts.   From the German of August Friedrich Ferdinand Von Kotzebue. Title also given as: The horse and the widow.   NUC has adaptation by Thomas Dibden from Plumptre.]

PLUMPTRE, Bell <u>see</u> PLUMPTRE, Annabella

2117.   PLUNKETT, Elizabeth (Gunning), Mrs. James Plunkett [Br. 1769-1823] ALT: Gunning, Elizabeth The wife with two husbands.   Tragi- comedy in three acts. L: H.D. Symonds, 1803.   104p.   BL OCLC E N [Melodrama, trans. of René Charles Guilbert de Pixérécourt, "La femme á deux maris."   Pub. 1803, not produced.]

PLUNKETT, Mrs. James <u>see</u> PLUNKETT, Elizabeth (Gunning)

POGSON, Sarah <u>see</u> SMITH, Sarah (Pogson)

2118.   POLACK, Elizabeth [Br. 19c] Esther, the royal Jewess: or, The death of Haman!   An historical drama, in three acts. L: J. Duncombe & co., 1825.   30p.   L: J. Duncombe, 1835?   30p.   NUC BL OCLC E N [Prod. in 1835.   Duncombe's acting edition of the British theatre, no. 128]

2119.   -----St. Clair of the isles; or, The outlaw of Barra.   A Scottish historical melodrama; in three acts. L: J. Dicks, 1838.   18p.; James Pattie, 1838.   50p.   NUC BL OCLC E M [Prod. Victoria, 1838.   Dicks' standard plays, no. 794]

2120.   POLLARD, Josephine [Am. 1834- 1892] Artistic tableaux with picturesque diagrams and description of costumes. With Walter Satterlee. NY: White, Stokes & Allen, 1884.   56p. NUC OCLC

2121.   POLLOCK, Ellen, Mrs. Julius Pollock [Br. 19c] PSEUD: Harley, St. John Eunice.   A drama in five acts. L: n.p., 1877.   BL [Adapted from her novel of the same name.]

2122. -----Judael.
L: Vinton, pr., 1881, 1885. 60p. E M
N
[Drama, 5 acts. Prod. Olympic,
1885.]

2123. -----A violent passion.
L: Vinton, pr., 1880. 44p. E

POLLOCK, Mrs. Julius see POLLOCK,
Ellen

POLLOCK, Walter H., co-author see
CLIFFORD, Lucy (Lane)

POLLOCK, Walter Herries, co-author
see MOUBREY, Lilian

2124. POLSON, Minnie [Am. 19c]
Our Kittie. A comedy drama in three
acts.
Clyde, OH: Ames pub. co., 1894. 20p.
NUC OCLC
[Ames' Standard & Minor Drama; no.
333]

2125. -----Wild Mab, a border drama,
in four acts.
Clyde, OH: Ames' pub. co., 1891. 19p.
NUC OCLC H
[Ames' Standard & Minor Drama. no.
290]

2126. POLWHELE, Elizabeth [Br. c1651-
1691]
The frolicks; or, the lawyer cheated.
1671. Har N
[Not performed. Rediscovered & ed.,
Judith Milhous & Robert D. Hume.
Ithaca, NY: Cornell UP, 1977. She
also wrote "Elysium," now lost, and a
verse tragedy, "The faithful
virgins."]

2127. POPE, Miss [Br. 18c]
The young couple.
1767. N
[Farce, altered from Frances
(Chamberlaine) Sheridan's "The
discovery." Prod. Drury Lane, 1761,
where she was a comic actress for 40
yrs. Bio.D..]

PORTER, A.M. see PORTER, Anna Maria

2128. PORTER, Anna Maria [Br. 1780-
1832/5] ALT: P., A. M.; Porter, A. M.
The fair fugitives, a musical
entertainment. Music by Thomas
Busby.
L: T.N Longman & O. Rees, 1803. 17p.
OCLC N
[Melodrama. Prod. Covent Garden,
1803.]

2129. -----Switzerland.
1819. N
[Tragedy. Prod. Drury Lane, 1819.
DNB attr. to Jane Porter & indicates
it had to be withdrawn.]

2130. PORTER, Charlotte Endymion [Am.
1859-1942]
Alladine and Palomides. With Helen
Archibald Clarke.
Boston: Poet-Lore, 1895. H
[V. 7, nos. 6 & &, p. 281-301. From
Count Maurice Maeterlinck.]

2131. -----Monna Vanna. Translated
from French of [Count Maurice]
Maeterlinck.
n.p.: n.p., n.d. NUC

2132. -----The seven princesses.
Boston: Poet-Lore, 1895. NUC H
[Vol. 4, nos. 1-3, based on Count
Maurice Maeterlinck.]

2133. -----The sightless.
Boston: Poet-Lore, 1893. NUC [Vol. 5,
nos. 3, 4, 5, 6-9. Based on Count
Maurice Maeterlinck.]

PORTER, Helen Tracy see LOWE, Helen
Tracy (Porter)

PORTER, Jane see PORTER, Anna Maria

2134. PORTER, Jane [Br. 1776-1850]
Owen, Prince of Powys; or, Welsh
feuds.
1822. DNB N
[Prod. Drury Lane, 1822. N lists
with unknown authors. DNB attr. to
her, "Egmont; or, The eve of St.
Alyne." Never prod. or printed.]

2135. POTTER, Mary [Br. 19c]
A bag of tricks.
1896. N
[Duologue. Prod. at Brighton, 1896.]

2136. POYAS, Catharine Gendron [Am.
1813-1882]
The Huguenot daughters and other
poems.
Charleston, SC: John Russell, 1849.
167p. NUC OCLC H
[Title poem, pp. 5-21 & The Convert,
pp. 145-8, dramatic poems.]

PRAED, Mrs. Campbell see PRAED, Rosa
Caroline (Murray-Prior)

2137. PRAED, Rosa Caroline (Murray-
Prior), Mrs. Campbell Praed [Br.
1851-1933]
Affinities. A drama in three acts.
Adapted from Mrs. Campbell Praed's

novel "Affinities" by Mrs. Campbell
Praed and Mrs. Jopling [Louisa Goode
Jopling, Mrs. Joseph Middleton
Jopling, later Mrs. Rowe].
NY: L: Bentley & son, 1885. 17p. BL E
N

2138. -----Ariane. With Richard Lee.
NY & L: G. Routledge, 1888. 278p. BL
N
[Comedy. Adapted from her novel.
Also pub. as: "The bond of wedlock."]

2139. -----The Binbian mine. With
Justin McCarthy.
1888. N
[Romantic drama. Also pub. as: "Two
friends."]

2140. PRAEGER, Nita [Br. 19c]
Outwitted.
1890. N
[Comedietta. Prod. at
Meistersingers' club, 1890.]

PRATT, Anna Bronson (Alcott), co-
author see ALCOTT, Louisa May

2141. PRATT, Sarah H. [Am. 19c]
Penelope's symposium; a dialogue
illustrating life in ancient Greece.
Containing full directions for
presentations.
Chicago: T.S. Denison, 1891. 16p. NUC
OCLC
[For 9 female characters. Written
for a Chautauqua women's meeting.]

2142. PRENTISS, Elizabeth (Payson),
Mrs. George Lewis Prentiss [Am. 1818-
1878] ALT: Prentiss, Mrs. G. L.
Griselda. Dramatic poem in five
acts.
NY: YWCA, 1876. 152p. NUC OCLC H
[Trans. from German of [Fredrich
Halm], Eligius Franz Joseph, Baron
Munch-Bellinghausen.]

PRENTISS, Mrs. G.L. see PRENTISS,
Elizabeth (Payson)

PRENTISS, Mrs. George Lewis see
PRENTISS, Elizabeth (Payson)

2143. PREVOST, Constance M., Miss
[Br. 19c] PSEUD: Terra Cotta
Meadowsweet; a play in one act.
L & NY: Samuel French, 1890? 22p.
OCLC E M N
[Comedietta. Prod. Vaudeville, 1890.
Lacy's Acting ed.]

2144. -----The silence of a
chatterbox.

1899. M N
[Play, 1 act, adapted from story by
Miss [Florence] Wilford. Prod.
Terry's, 1899.]

PRICE, Mrs. Edwin H. see DAVENPORT,
Fanny Lily Gypsy

PRICE, Florence Alice see JAMES,
Florence Alice (Price)

PRICE, Gertrude see JONES, Gertrude
(Price)

PRIDEAUX, Fanny Ann (Bell) see
PRIDEAUX, Fanny Ash (Bell)

2145. PRIDEAUX, Fanny Ash (Bell),
Mrs. Frederick Prideaux [Br. d. 1894]
ALT: Prideaux, Fanny Ann (Bell)
Basil the iconoclast. A drama of
modern Russia. By Mrs. Frederick
Prideaux.
L: D. Nutt, 1892. 236p. BL OCLC
[3 acts; verse]

2146. -----The nine days' queen. A
dramatic poem. By Mrs. Frederick
Prideaux.
L: Bell & Daldy, 1869. 244p. BL OCLC
[Four acts, verse, tragedy of Lady
Jane Grey]

PRIDEAUX, Mrs. Frederick see
PRIDEAUX, Fanny Ash (Bell)

2147. PRITCHARD, Johanna [Br. 19c]
Auromania; or, the diamond's
daughter.
1871. M N
[Drama, 4 acts. Prod. Alfred, 1871.]

PRITCHARD, POLLY ANN, pseud. see
HEYWOOD, Delia A.

2148. PULLEN, Elisabeth (Jones)
Cavazza [Am. d. 1926] ALT: Cavazza,
Elisabeth (Jones) Algernon in London,
a tragedy. By Elisabeth Cavazza.
Portland, ME: Pr. Wm. Marks, 1880.
16p. NUC
[Satire on Algernon Charles
Swinburne. In verse. Written for
the Portland Press.]

2149. PURVIS, Mrs. Herbert [Br. 19c]
After long years. With Arthur Law.
1886. N
[Comic drama. Prod. at Torquay,
1886; Criterion, 1887.]

2150. PUTNAM, Mary Traill Spence
(Lowell), Mrs. Samuel R. Putnam [Am.
1810-1898] PSEUD: Colvil, Edward

Tragedy of errors.
Boston: Ticknor & Fields, 1861. 249p.
NUC OCLC
[Verse drama, on slavery in the U.S.]

2151. -----Tragedy of success.
Boston: Ticknor and Fields, 1862.
191p. NUC OCLC
[Verse drama, sequel to: Tragedy of
Errors]

PUTNAM, Mrs. Samuel R. see PUTNAM,
Mary Traill Spence (Lowell)

PYE, Hon. Mrs. Hampden see PYE, Jael
Henrietta (Mendez)

PYE, Mrs. Henry James see PYE, Jael
Henrieta (Mendez)

PYE, J. Henrietta see PYE, Jael
Henrietta (Mendez)

2152. PYE, Jael Henrietta (Mendez),
Hon. Mrs. Hampden Pye [Br. d. 1782]
ALT: Pye, J. Henrietta PSEUD: Lady, A
The capricious lady.
1771. NUC B N
[Farce. Prod. Drury Lane, 1771.
BioD. & Wearing attr. to Mrs. Henry
James Pye, nee Hook. Larpent Ms.
#323.]

2153. PYER, Kate [Br. 19c]
Dialogues for recitation. Three pt.
L: W. Tweedie, 1858. NUC BL
[Temperance; verse and prose. In
vol. lettered: VTZ, v. 39, no. 6]

R., S. see ROWSON, Susanna (Haswell)

2154. RAE, Josephine [Br. 19c]
Bars of gold. With Thomas Sidney.
1892. N [Dramatic sketch. Prod. St.
Leonard's, 1892.]

2155. -----Interviewed. With Thomas
Sidney.
1896. N
[Dramatic sketch. Prod. at Brighton,
1896.]

2156. -----Love, the magician. With
Thomas Sidney.
1892. M N
[Play, 3 acts. Prod. Shaftesbury,
1892.]

2157. -----My little red riding hood.
With Thomas Sidney.
1895. N

[Comic drama. Prod. St. Leonard's,
1892.]

2158. -----Pretty Mollie Barrington.
With Thomas Sidney.
1892. N
[Comic drama. Prod. St. Leonard's,
1892.]

2159. -----The ruby heart. With
Thomas Sidney.
1892. N
[Dramatic sketch. Prod. St.
Leonard's, 1892.]

2160. RAMSAY, Alicia [Br. 19c]
As a man sows. With Rudolph de
Cordova.
1898. M N
[Drama, 4 acts. Prod. Grand, 1898.]

2161. -----The executioner's
daughter. With Rudolph de Cordova.
1896. M N
[Drama, 1 act, also prod. as:
"Monsieur de Paris," Royalty, 1896.]

2162. -----Gaffer Jarge.
1896. M N
[Comedietta. Prod. Comedy, 1896.]

RAMSAY, Charlotte see LENNOX,
Charlotte (Ramsay)

2163. RAND, Katharine Ellen [Am. 19c]
New Hampshire gold; a comedy drama in
three acts.
Boston: W.H. Baker, 1897. 40p. NUC
OCLC
[Baker's edition of plays. Earlier
copyright 1872? Intended for
amateurs, a "homely and domestic"
melodrama.]

RANDALL-DIEHL, Anna T. see DIEHL,
Anna T. (Randall)

2164. RANDFORD, Maud [Br. 19c]
A harvest of crime.
1897. N
[Drama. Prod. at Brierly Hill,
1897.]

2165. -----Streaks of gold.
1878. N
[Comedy. Prod. at Sunderland, 1876.]
RAVENSWOOD, pseud. see WALKER, Agnes
M.A., Mrs.

2166. RAY, Eileen [Br. 19c]
Caroona.
1899. M N
[Drama, 4 acts. Prod. St. George
Hall, 1899.]

RAYMOND, Fanny Malone see RITTER,
Catherine Frances Malone (Raymond)

2167. RAYMOND, Kate [Br. 19c]
The waifs of New York.
1875. N
[Drama. Prod. in Liverpool, 1875.]

RAYMOND-RITTER, Frances see RITTER,
Catherine Frances Malone (Raymond)

2168. RAYNOR, Verna M. [Am. 19c]
The Bird family and their friends. A
comedy in three acts.
Clyde, OH: Ames' pub. co., 1898. 38p.
NUC OCLC
[Ames' Standard & Minor Drama, no.
394]

2169. -----Noel Corson's oath; or,
Leonia's repentance. A drama in four
acts.
Clyde, OH: Ames, 1899. 16 l. NUC
OCLC
[Ames' Standard & Minor Drama, no.
408]

2170. READ, Harriette Fanning, Miss
[Am. 19c]
Dramatic poems; Medea, Erminia, and
the New world.
Boston: W. Crosby & H.P. Nichols,
1847, 1848. 297p. NUC BL OCLC R
[All three are 5-act tragedies]

2171. READE, Gertrude [Br. 19c]
The Minkalay. With A. Leeds.
1896. N
[Comic opera. Prod. in Devonport,
1896.]

2172. REID, Bessie [Br. 19c]
The colonel's wife. With Lita Smith.
1888. N
[Drama. Prod. at Coventry, 1888.]

2173. -----Desperation. With George
Roy.
1887. N
[Drama. Prod. at W. Bromwick, 1887.]

RENNELL, Charles R., co-author see
ELLIS, Mrs. R.

REVEL, Mollie, co-author see DORAN,
Marie

2174. REYNARTZ, Dorothy [Am. 19/20c]
Carnival; or, Mardigras in New
Orleans. Comedy in one act. Adapted
from the French.
NY: Roxbury pub. co., 1899. 16p. NUC
OCLC
[The wizard series. Sergel's Acting
Drama. No. 558]

2175. -----A cup of coffee; comedy in
one act for young ladies.
Chicago: Dramatic pub. co., 1899.
22p. NUC OCLC
[Sergel's Acting Drama. No. 526]

2176. -----It is never too late to
mend; comedy in one act. For young
ladies.
NY: Roxbury pub. co., 1899. 8p. NUC
[Wizard series]

2177. -----Two mothers. Drama in
four acts, for young ladies.
NY: J.F. Wagner, 189-? [191-? NUC].
30p. NUC OCLC

RICHARDSON, Abbey Sage, co-author see
HILL, Grace Livingston

2178. RICHARDSON, Abbey Sage [Am.
1837-1900]
Americans abroad. Comedy in three
acts.
NY: Z. & L. Rosenfield, 1892. NUC
OCLC H
[Typescript, prompt-book 58, 61, 51
l. Based on Victorien Sardou.]

2179. RICHARDSON, Anna Steese
(Sausser) [Am. 1865-1949]
Miss Mosher of Colorado; or, A
mountain psyche. Comedy-drama in
four acts.
NY: Dick & Fitzgerald, 1899. 48p. NUC
H

2180. RICHARDSON, Elizabeth [Br. d.
1799]
The double deception.
1779. N
[Comedy. Prod. Drury Lane, 1779, and
also under title: "The double
deception, or, The lovers perplexed."
Larpent MS 21.]

RICHARDSON, Mrs. Joseph see
RICHARDSON, Sarah (Watts)

2181. RICHARDSON, Sarah Watts, Mrs.
Joseph Richardson [Br. d. 1823?]
Ethelred, a legendary tragic drama,
by Mrs. Richardson, one of the
patentees of the late Theatre Royal,
Drury Lane, and widow of the late
Joseph Richardson, esq.
L: Pr. Lowndes & Hobbs, 1809. 92p.
NUC BL OCLC E
[5 acts; verse]

2182. -----Gertrude; a tragic drama
in five acts.
L: C. Lowndes, 1810. 66p. BL OCLC E
[prose & verse]

2183. RICHEY, Octavia [Am. 19c]
The earl's daughter, a drama in five
acts. Re-arranged and dramatized
from Mrs. Elizabeth Vanlyon's
celebrated novel "A heart twice won".
Clyde, OH: Ames, 1882. 26p. NUC
[Ames' Standard & Minor Drama, 145]

2184. RICORD, Elizabeth Stryker [Am.
1788-1865]
Zampa, or the insurrection. A
dramatic poem, in five acts.
Cambridge, MA: J. Owen, 1842. 139p.
NUC BL OCLC C R
[History of Martinique]

2185. RIGHTON, Mary [Br. 19c]
Cupid and Psyche.
1895. N
[Musical sketch. Amateur prod. at
Bijou, 1895.]

2186. -----Little nobody.
1890. M N
[Comedietta. Prod. Vaudeville,
1890.]

2187. -----Our [Dear M] friends.
1890. M N
[Comedietta. Prod. Ladbrooke Hall,
1888; Vaudeville, 1890.]

2188. RILEY, Catherine [Am. 19c]
On and off.
NY: Frank V. Strauss, 1898. 24p. OCLC
M
[Comedy, 3 acts, adapted from the
French of Alexandre Bisson. Prod.
Madison Square Garden, NY, and
Vaudeville, London, 1898.]

RINGWALT, Mrs. J.L. see RINGWALT,
Jessie (Elder)

2189. RINGWALT, Jessie (Elder), Mrs.
J.L. Ringwalt [Am. 19c]
Paul and Virginia; or, The runaway
slave. Three acts.
Philadelphia: Ringwalt & Brown, 1864.
35p. NUC OCLC H
[Dramatized from novel by Bernardin
de Saint-Pierre]

2190. RITCHIE, Anna Cora (Ogden)
Mowatt, Mrs. William Fouchée Ritchie
[Am. 1819(1822 R)-1870] ALT: Mowatt,
Anna Cora (Ogden); Mowatt, Mrs. James
Armand; or, the peer and the peasant.
A romantic drama in five acts.
NY & L: W. Newberry; French, 1849.
60p. NUC BL OCLC M R Vaughn
[Verse & prose. Premiered in 1847 in
NY & Boston with subtitle: "The child
of the people." Prod. Marylebone,

1849 & Drury Lane, 1853. Revived at
Sadler's Wells, 1864, as: "The peer
and the peasant." French's standard
drama, no. 214. Also in: Plays.]

2191. -----Fashion; or, life in New
York. A comedy in five acts.
NY: S. French, [1845 Vaughn] 1849.
62p. NUC BL OCLC M N R Vaughn
[Comedy. Premiered in NY, 1845.
Prod. Olympic, London, 1850. French's
standard drama, no. 215. Also in:
Plays.]

2192. -----Gulzara; or, The Persian
slave.
NY: R. Vaughn, 1841.
[Written for her father's birthday in
1840, perf. for NY society. Pub. 1840
in "The new world."]

2193. -----Plays.
New & rev. ed. Boston: Ticknor &
Fields, 1855. 60p. NUC BL
[Cont.: "Armand" & "Fashion."]

2194. RITCHIE, Fannie [Am. 19c]
Pleasant wedding guests; comedy in
one act.
Chicago: Dramatic pub. co., 1899.
22p. OCLC
[Sergel's acting drama; no. 566]

2195. RITCHIE, Maria Kate [Br. 19c]
Poems.
Edinburgh: Priv. pr., 1865. BL Inglis
[Incl.: "Love and hatred; or, Which
shall conquer." Drama in 13 scenes.]

RITCHIE, Mrs. William Fouchée see
RITCHIE, Anna Cora (Ogden) Mowatt

2196. RITTENHOUSE, Laura J. [Am. 19c]
The interstate milkmaids' convention.
Chicago: Women's temperance pub.
assoc., 1889. 29p. NUC OCLC
[Burlesque]

2197. RITTER, Catherine Frances
Malone (Raymond) [Br. 1830-1890] ALT:
Raymond, Fanny Malone; Raymond-
Ritter, Frances; Ritter, Frances
Malone (Raymond)
The devil's share.
1843. N
[drama]

2198. -----Mariette; or, the Reward.
1843. N
[vaudeville]

2199. -----Orpheus. Opera in four
acts.
NY: Academy of music, 1863. H

[Libretto]

2200. -----The two sisters; or, The godfather's legacy.
1843. N
[vaudeville]

RITTER, Frances Malone (Raymond) see RITTER, Catherine Frances Malone (Raymond)

RIVES, Amelie see TROUBETZKOY, Amelie (Rives)

2201. RIVERS, Florence [Br. 19c]
A quiet half-hour. A farce, in one act.
L: Kennett, Towerzey & co., 1884. 20p. BL

2202. ROBBINS, Caroline A. [Am. 19c]
Poems and an anti-slavery drama in prose and verse. Providence, RI: J.A. & R.A. Reid, pr., 1876. 82p. NUC OCLC
[Poetry honors John Brown & other abolitionists. Drama on escaping slavery.]

ROBE, J., Miss see ROBE, J., Mrs.

2203. ROBE, J., Mrs. [Br. 18c] ALT: Robe, J. Miss
The fatal legacy.
L: E. Symon, et al, 1723. 79p. OCLC B
[Tragedy. Prod. Theatre Royal.]

2204. ROBERTS, Clara (Lemore) [Br. d. 1898] ALT: Lemore, Clara
A crooked mile.
L: 1885. M N
[Play, 3 acts. Prod. at Manchester, 1885; Vaudeville, 1888.]

2205. ROBERTS, Emma [Br. 1794?-1840]
Oriental scenes, dramatic sketches and tales, with other poems.
Calcutta: N. Grant, 1830. 263p. NUC BL OCLC
[T.P. mentions: "Conrad, a tragedy," & "The Kinsman of Naples."]

2206. -----Constantine the great.
In: Oriental scenes ... .
[Sketch]

2207. -----The Florentines.
In: Oriental scenes ... .
[Sketch]

2208. -----Geraldi Sforza.
In: Oriental scenes ... .
[Sketch]

2209. -----The incantation.

In: Oriental scenes ... .
[Sketch]

2210. -----The witch's ordeal.
In: Oriental scenes ... .
[Sketch]

2211. ROBERTS, R., Miss [Br. d. 1788]
Malcolm, a tragedy.
L: the author, 1779. 76p. NUC BL OCLC B N
[5 acts, blank verse. On Malcolm III, King of Scotland. Longe, v. 126, no. 2]

2212. ROBERTS, Sara (Lacy), Mrs. Valentine Roberts [Br. 1822?-1881]
Mark the blacksmith. An original operetta, in one act.
L: Pr. for priv. circ., 1862. NUC BL
[Verse]

2213. -----The young recruit, an original operetta, in two acts. L: n.p., 1860. NUC BL
[prose & verse]

ROBERTS, Mrs. Valentine see ROBERTS, Sara (Lacy)

2214. ROBERTSON, Mrs. [Br. 19c]
Ellinda; or, The Abbey of St. Aubert. A dramatic romance.
1800. N
[Melodrama. Prod. Newark, 1800. She was a member of the Newark acting company. BioD.]

ROBERTSON, Donald, co-author see LEWIS, Catherine

2215. ROBERTSON, Jessie [Br. 19c]
Dan the outlaw.
1888. N
[Drama. Prod. at Kilburn, 1888; Novelty, 1892.]

2216. -----Venus.
1896. N
[Farce. Prod. Novelty, 1896.]

2217. ROBERTSON, T., Mrs. [Br. 18c]
The enchanted island.
1796. Bio.D.
[Musical entertainment.]

ROBINS, Elizabeth, co-author see BELL, Florence Eveleen Eleanore (Olliffe)

2218. ROBINS, Mary Ellis [Am. 19c]
The forerunners.
Woodstock, NY: Maverick press, 18--? 82p. NUC H

[Dramatic poem in 3 acts.]

ROBINSON, A. Mary F. see DUCLAUX,
Agnes Mary Frances (Robinson)

ROBINSON, Mrs. C. see ZECH, Marie

2219. ROBINSON, Emma [Br. 1814-1890]
The revolt of Flanders: an historical
tragedy in five acts.
L: H. Colburn, 1848. 196p. NUC

2220. -----Richelieu in love; or, The
youth of Charles I.
NY: Benjamin & Young, 1844. 54p. L:
Henry Colburn, 1844. 80p. NUC BL OCLC
E
[Historical comedy in 5 acts. Perf.
prohibited by Lord Chamberlain.]

2221. ROBINSON, Harriet Jane
(Hanson), Mrs. William Stevens
Robinson [Am. 1825-1911]
Captain Mary Miller. A drama.
Boston: Walter H. Baker & co., 1887.
47p. NUC OCLC E
[5 acts, on women's rights.]

2222. -----The new Pandora, a drama.
NY: The Knickerbocker press; NY & L:
G.P. Putnam's sons, 1889. 151p. NUC
OCLC
[In verse]

ROBINSON, Lucy Catlin (Bull) see
BULL, Lucy Catlin

2223. ROBINSON, Mary Darby [Br. 1758-
1800]
The lucky escape; songs, choruses,
etc.
L: For the author, 1778. NUC OCLC B N
[Comic opera. Prod. Drury Lane,
1778. Larpent MS. 15.]

2224. -----Nobody.
1794. N
[Comedy. Prod. Drury Lane, 1794.
Larpent MS 62.]

2225. -----The Sicilian lover; a
tragedy in five acts.
L: Pr. for author by Hookham &
Carpenter, 1796. 80p. NUC BL OCLC B N
[Verse. Longe, v. 238, no. 6]

ROBINSON, Mrs. William Stevens see
ROBINSON, Harriet Jane (Hanson)

2226. ROGERS, Maud M. [Br. 19c]
Held in trust, and other plays for
amateurs.
L: Marshall, Russell & co., 1898.
113p. BL OCLC

[Title play is a 1-act comedy.]

2227. -----Edelweiss.
In: Held in trust ... .
[Comedietta]

2228. -----Fate.
In: Held in trust ... .
[Comedietta in two scenes]

2229. -----The sixth woman.
In: Held in trust ... .
[Duologue]

2230. -----When the wheels run down.
A play in one act.
NY & L: Lacy, 1899. 15p. NUC BL OCLC
E N
[Amateur prod. at St. George Hall,
1899. French's edition of the works
of the best authors, no. 27. 19th
century English & American drama, no.
674.]

ROGERSON, Mrs. Whit see SANDFORD,
Edith

2231. ROHLFS, Anna Katharine (Green),
Mrs. Charles Rohlfs [Am. 1846-1935]
ALT: Green, Anna Katharine
Risifi's daughter. A drama.
NY: G.P. Putnam's sons, 1887. 109p.
NUC OCLC H R
RHOLFS, Mrs. Charles see ROHLFS, Anna
Katharine (Green)

ROLLS, Mrs. Alexander see BARRY,
Helen

ROMYAG, L., pseud. see GAYNOR, Lucy

2232. ROSE, Ada M. [Br. 19/20c]
At cross purposes. Comedietta, in
one act.
NY & L: Lacy; S. French, 1899. 12p.
NUC BL
[French's minor drama. The acting
edition. no. 393]

ROSE, Edward, co-author see GARRAWAY,
Agnes J.

ROSE, Edward, co-author see GRAVES,
Clotilda Inez Mary

ROSE, Heloise (Durant) see DURANT,
Heloise

ROSS, Anna see BRUNTON, Anna (Ross)

ROSS, R.S. see ROSS, Rebecca Sophia,
Lady

2233. ROSS, Rebecca Sophia, Lady [Br. 19c] ALT: Ross, R. S.; Ross of Balnagown, Lady
Antiope: a tragedy.
L: Kegan Paul & Co., 1880. 151p. BL
[verse]

2234. -----Ariadne in Naxos. By Lady Ross of Balnagown.
L: Trubner & co., 1882. 199p. BL OCLC
[verse]

2235. -----The monk of St. Gall. A dramatic adaptation of [Joseph Victor Von] Scheffel's "Ekkehard." By R.S. Ross.
L: n.p., 1879. BL
[5 acts, verse]

ROSS OF BALNAGOWN, Lady see ROSS, Rebecca Sophia, Lady

2236. ROSSE, Jeanie Quinton [Am. 19c]
The Egyptian princess. Romantic operetta in two acts.
Boston: Boston Music co., 1899. 106p. NUC OCLC H
[Music by Charles John Vincent]

2237. -----The Japanese girl (O Hame San). Operetta in two acts.
Boston: Boston Music co., 1899. 74p. NUC OCLC H
[Music by Charles John Vincent]

ROTHERY, Mary Catherine (Hume) see HUME-ROTHERY, Mary Catherine

2238. ROUSE, E., Miss [Br. 19c]
Buy-em-dears, alias bay-a-deres.
1838. N [Burlesque. Prod. Strand, 1838.]

2239. ROUSE, T., Miss [Br. 19c]
Naomi; a dramatic poem, and other pieces.
L: Hamilton, Adams; Norwich: Jarrold & sons, 1845? [1850? BL] 90p. NUC BL OCLC E

2240. ROVER, Winnie [Am. 19c]
The children of to-day. A farce in five acts.
NY: Catholic pub. soc., 1877. 32p. NUC

2241. -----The house on the avenue; or, The little mischief-makers. A drama in six scenes.
NY: Catholic pub. soc., 1877. 62p. NUC OCLC

2242. -----Wealth and wisdom. A drama in six scenes.

NY: Catholic pub. soc., 1877. 63p. NUC

ROWE, Louisa Goode Jopling, co-author see PRAED, Rosa Caroline (Murray-Prior)

2243. ROWLEY, Mary S. [Am. 19c]
Froth and foam.
Rochester, NY: Union & Advertiser co., pr., 1888. 85p. NUC OCLC
[Incl. dramatic poem, rhymed comedy about modern love.]

2244. ROWSELL, Mary Catherine [Br. 19/20c]
The friend of the people. With H.A. Saintsbury.
1893. M N
[Drama, 5 acts. Perf. Haymarket, 1898.]

2245. -----Plays for home performance. Thornrose and Sparkeldor. Riquet with the Tuft.
New & rev. ed. L: S. French, 1890? 63p. BL

2246. -----Prince Riquet with the tuft; or, the deformed transformed; a happie conceit, wherein is endeavoured to be set forth ye mighty power of love. A musical fairy extravaganza.
L: Lacy, 1855? 1874? 28p. NUC BL
[Also in: Plays. Based on "Riquet a la Houpe." Verse, with songs.]

2247. -----Richard's play. A comedietta. With Joseph J. Dilley.
L: S. French; Lacy, 1893. 16p. NUC BL OCLC M N
[Perf. Terry's, 1891. French's acting ed. no. 2020]

2248. -----Thornrose and Sparkledor, or the Sleeping beauty in the wood; a musical extravaganza.
New ed. L: Lacy, 1873. 1885? 23p. NUC BL
[Based on the sleeping beauty story. Verse with songs. Also in: Plays.]

2249. -----Whips of steel. With Joseph J. Dilley.
1889. M N [Comedy, 4 acts. Perf. St. George Hall, 1889.]

2250. ROWSON, Susanna (Haswell), Mrs. William Rowson [Br/Am. c1762-1824]
ALT: R., S.
Americans in England.
1797. DNB Meserve Hill
[Farce emphasizing English eccentricities and sturdy American

qualities. Prod. as: "The Columbian
Daughter," Boston, 1800. Play now
lost.]

2251. -----The female patriot, a
farce.
1795. Meserve
[Now lost.]

2252. -----Slaves in Algiers; or, A
struggle for freedom.
Philadelphia: pr. for author by
Wrigley and Berriman, 1794. 72p. NUC
OCLC B C Hill Wells
[Opera, 3 acts]

2253. -----The volunteers.
Philadelphia: Pr. for the author,
1795. NUC Meserve
[Comic opera performed twice. About
Whiskey Rebellion in PA in 1794. Now
lost.]

2254. -----Hearts of Oak.
1810. Meserve
[Written for 1810-11 season in
Boston. Now lost.]

ROWSON, Mrs. William see ROWSON,
Susanna (Haswell)

ROY, George, co-author see REID,
Bessie

ROYD, Lois, co-author see PINEO,
Mabel

RUMSEY, Mrs. B.C. see RUMSEY, Eveline
(Hall)

2255. RUMSEY, Eveline (Hall), Mrs.
B.C. Rumsey [Am. 1822-1900]
St. Augustine episode.
Buffalo, NY: Press of Peter Paul &
bro., [c1884? OCLC] 1890? 39p. NUC
OCLC H

2256. RUNCIE, Constance Owen (Faunt
Le Roy) [Am. 1836-1911]
Poems, dramatic and lyric.
NY & L: G.P. Putnam's sons, 1888.
98p. NUC OCLC
[Dramatic poems, not intended for
production.]

RUSSELL, Lady Georgiana Adelaide see
PEEL, Lady Georgiana Adelaide
(Russell)

RUSSELL, Lady Victoria, co-author see
PEEL, Lady Georgiana Adelaide
(Russell)

RUSSELL, MARGARET, pseud. see HERVEY,
Eleanora Louisa (Montagu)

RYES, Elizabeth see RYVES, Elizabeth

RYLEY, Mrs. J.H. see RYLEY, Madeleine
Lucette

2257. RYLEY, Madeleine Lucette, Mrs.
J.H. Ryley [Am. 1868-1934]
An American citizen; an original
comedy in four acts.
NY: Samuel French, 1895. 63p. NUC BL
OCLC M N
[Prod. Duke of York's, 1899.
French's standard library edition.
Novel of the same title pub. 1899.]

2258. -----Christopher Junior; comedy
in four acts.
NY: Samuel French, 1889. 65p. NUC
OCLC

2259. -----Jedbury Junior.
L & NY: S. French, 1900. 65p. BL OCLC
E M N
[Terry's, 1896; Prod. Empire, NY,
1895.]

2260. -----The mysterious Mr. Bugle.
1897. N
[In N as: "The vanishing husband."
Prod. at Stockton-on-Tees, 1897; &
Strand, 1900, under title above.]

2261. RYLEY, Maude [Br. 19c]
A coat of many colours.
1897. M N
[Comedy, 4 acts. Prod. West London,
1897.]

2262. RYVES, Elizabeth [Br. 1750-
1797] ALT: Ryes, Elizabeth
Poems on several occasions.
L: Pr. for the author & sold by J.
Dodsley, 1777. 176p. NUC BL OCLC N
[Incl.: The prude and The triumph of
Hymen, a dramatic poem.]

2263. -----The debt of honour.
n.d. N
[DNB: comedy, never acted. Bio.D..]

2264. -----Dialogue in the Elysian
Fields between Caesar and Cato.
L: n.p., 1784. BL
[In verse, Ms.]

2265. -----The prude: a comic opera.
In: Poems ... .
[3 acts, meant for production.]

S., A. see SWANWICK, Anna

S., C. see SYMMONS, Caroline

S., E.C. see SMALE, Edith C.

S., F. see SHERIDAN, Frances
(Chamberlaine)

S., L.F.M., pseud. see SWAN, Myra

S., M. see SMEDLEY, Menella Bute

S., M. see STUART, M., Mrs.

S., M.F. see SEYMOUR, Mary (Seamer)

S., Olivia W. see SERRES, Olivia
(Wilmot)

SADLIER, Mrs. James see SADLIER, Mary
Anne (Madden)

2266. SADLIER, Mary Anne (Madden),
Mrs. James Sadlier [Am. 1820-1903]
The invisible hand. A drama in two
acts. By Mrs. James Sadlier.
NY: D. & J. Sadlier & co., 1873. 36p.
NUC OCLC

2267. -----The secret.
NY: D. & J. Sadlier, 1865. 32p. NUC
BL H

2268. -----The talisman. One act.
NY: D. & J. Sadlier, 1863. 33p. NUC
BL H

2269. ST. AUBYN, Daisy, Mrs. [Br.
19c]
The dark hour.
L: n.p., 1885. BL M N
[Melodrama, 4 acts. Prod. St. George
Hall, 1885.]

2270. ST. RUTH, Abbey, Miss [Br. 19c]
The key to King Solomon's riches,
limited.
1896. N
[Burlesque. Prod. Opera Comique,
1896.]

SAINTSBURY, H.A., co-author see
ROWSELL, Mary Catherine

SAKER, Mrs. Edward see SAKER, Marie
(O'Brien)

2271. SAKER, Marie O'Brien, Mrs.
Edward Saker [Br. 19c]
Duplicity.
1883. N
[Comedy. Prod. at Birkenhead, 1883.]

2272. -----A sinless sinner.
1896. N

[Drama. Prod. at Ealing, 1896.]

2273. -----Till we meet again.
1898. N
[Drama. Prod. at Kingston, 1898.]

SAMUEL, S.M., co-author see COWEN,
Henrietta

SANDBACH, Mrs. Henry Roscoe see
SANDBACH, Margaret Roscoe

2274. SANDBACH, Margaret Roscoe, Mrs.
Henry Roscoe Sandbach [Br. 1812-1852]
The Amidei. A tragedy in five acts.
L: William Pickering, 1845. 151p. NUC
BL OCLC
[Verse]

2275. -----Giuliano de' Medici. A
drama in five acts; with other poems.
L: W. Pickering, 1842. 213p. NUC BL
OCLC E

2276. SANDERSON, Mary [Am. 19c]
The mistake on both sides; a petite
comedy, in one act.
NY: Baker, Godwin & co., prs., 1852.
12p. NUC H R
[Written when author was 10 yrs.
old.]

2277. SANDFORD, Edith [Br. 1847-1923]
ALT: Rogerson, Mrs. Whit
The firefly [Firefly M].
1869. M N
[Drama, 3 acts. From a story by
Ouida [Louise de la Ramée], "Under
two flags." Prod. Surrey, 1869; &
Britannia, 1870.]

2278. SANFORD, Amelia [Am. 19/20c]
The advertising girls. Two scenes.
Boston: W.H. Baker, 1900 [1909 OCLC].
18p. NUC OCLC H
[Baker's ed. of plays]

2279. -----A commanding position.
Philadelphia: Penn pub. co., 18--?
[1909. 23p. NUC]. NUC
[Farcical entertainment]

2280. -----The ghost of an idea; a
comedietta in one act and three
scenes.
Philadelphia: Penn pub. co., 1898.
13p. NUC

2281. -----Maids, modes and manners;
or, Madame Grundy's dilemma.
Philadelphia: Penn pub. co., [1903
NUC] 1911. 14p. NUC H
[Earlier copyright: 1896.]

2282. SANFORD, Mary Williams [Am. 19c]
Pompair. A chemical union of fusion and confusion. A comic opera in three acts.
Albany, NY: Weed, Parsons & co., 1883. 29p. NUC

2283. SANTLEY, Kate [Br. d. 1923]
Vetah.
1886. N
[Comic opera. Prod. at Portsmouth, 1886.]

2284. SARGANT, Jane Alice [Br. b. 1832]
Joan of Arc: a play in five acts.
L: Joseph Rickerby, 1840. 99p. NUC BL
[Verse]

SARGENT, Judith see MURRAY, Judith (Sargent) Stevens

SATTERLEE, Walter, co-author see POLLARD, Josephine

SAULL, J.A., Miss see SAULL, Julie A.

2285. SAULL, Julie A. [Br. 19c] ALT: Saull, J. A., Miss
Book of words of the new burlesque operetta ... entitled: Mokanna, the veiled Prophet; or, the Feast of roses.
Nottingham: The authoress, 1895. 24p. BL
[Libretto, one act]

2286. -----Prince Pedrillo; or, who's the heir?
1893. N
[Musical extravaganza. Prod. in Nottingham, 1893.]

2287. SAVORGNAN, Cora Ann (Slocomb) Brazza-, Contesa di [Am. b. 1862] ALT: Brazza-Savorgnan, Cora Ann (Slocomb), Countess of; Slocomb, Cora A.
A literary farce.
Boston: Arena pub. co., 1896. 36p. NUC BL OCLC H

SCHELL, Stanley, co-author see HAUGHWOUT, L. May

2288. SCHIFF, Emma [Br. 19c]
The countess; or, A sister's love.
1870. N
[Drama. Prod. Alfred, 1870.]

2289. -----On the brink.
1875. N
[Comic drama. Prod. in Liverpool, 1875.]

2290. -----The rights of women.
1871. M N
[Comedietta. Prod. Globe, 1870.]

2291. -----The twin sisters.
1870. N
[Comedy. Prod. Charing Cross, 1870.]

2292. SCHMALL, Alice F. [Am. 19c]
Zanetto [and] At sunset.
NY?: n.p., 18--? 23p. H
[Libretti for 2 1-act operas.]

2293. SCOTT, Jane M. [Br. 19c]
Asgard, the Demon hunter; or, Le diable a la chasse.
1812. N
[Spectacle; prod. Sans Pareil, 1812.]

2294. -----The old oak chest; or, The smuggler's son and the robber's daughter. A melodrama in two acts.
L: J. Duncombe, 1816. 36p. NUC OCLC E N
[Prod. Sans Pareil, 1816. Duncombe's acting ed. of the British Theatre, 3.]

2295. SCOTT, Mary Affleck [Br. 19c]
The tarantula.
1897. M N
[Comedy, 4 acts. Prod. Criterion, 1884.]

SCOTTI, Mme. C. see SCOTTI, Sophie

2296. SCOTTI, Sophie, Mme. C. Scotti [Br. 19c]
Happier days.
1886. N
[Comic drama. Prod. Ladbrooke Hall, 1886.]

2297. -----Peaceful war. With Leopold Wagner.
1887. M N
[Farce, adapted from the German of Gustav von Moser. Prod. Prince of Wales, 1887.]

2298. -----Resemblance.
1885. M N
[Drama, 4 acts. Prod. Vaudeville, 1885.]

SCRIBNER, Lizzie B., co-author see BREWSTER, Emma E.

2299. SCUDDER, Vida Dutton [Am. 1861-1954]
Mitsu-yu-nissi; or, The Japanese wedding. With F.M. Brooks.
Chicago: T.S. Denison, 1887. 20p. NUC OCLC H

[Denison's specialties. Young's standard series of plays]

SEAMER, Mary see SEYMOUR, Mary (Seamer)

2300. SEATON, Rose [Br. 19/20c]
Andromeda. The promised gift. A dramatic poem in two parts.
In: Romances and poems.
L: Simpkin, Marshall, Hamilton, Kent & co., 1891. 119p. NUC BL OCLC M N
[Tragedy, 1 act. Perf. Vaudeville, 1890.]

2301. -----Mr. Donnithorpe's rent.
1890. N
[Comedietta. Prod. at Chatham, 1890.]

2302. -----Music at home. 1890. N
[Comedy. Prod. at Chatham, 1890; Opera Comique, 1892.]

SEAWELL, Miss Elliot see SEAWELL, Molly Elliot, Miss

2303. SEAWELL, Molly Elliot, Miss
[Am. 1860-1916] ALT: Seawell, Miss Elliot
The sprightly romance of Marsac.
1898. N
[Dramatic sketch. Based on her novel, pub. 1896. Prod. Ladbrooke Hall, 1898.]

SEDGER, Horace, co-author see GREET, Dora Victoire, Mrs.

2304. SELDEN, Almira [Am. 19c]
Effusions of the heart.
Bennington, VT: Pr. by Darius Clark, 1820. 152p. NUC BL OCLC B Hill Wells
[Incl.: "Lady Jane Grey and Lord Guilford Dudley," a dramatic poem.]

2305. -----The Irish exiles in America.
In: Effusions ... .
[5 scenes, prose.]

2306. -----Naomi.
In: Effusions ... .
[5 scenes, verse.]

2307. SELOUS, Millie [Br. 19c]
The stage in the drawing-room: short one-act sketches for two and three players.
L: Leadenhall press, 1893. 169p. BL

2308. -----Almost! A dramatic sketch.
In: The stage ... .

[Duologue for female characters]

2309. -----Buying one's experience.
A duologue.
In: The stage ... .
[duologue/home performance

2310. -----A conjugal duologue.
In: The stage ... .

2311. -----A happy expedient. A dramatic sketch in one scene.
In: The stage ... .

2312. -----In the garden. Dramatic scene.
In: The stage ... .
[Duologue]

2313. -----A little breeze-snow-afterwards fair weather. A dramatic sketch in one scene. In: The stage ... .

2314. -----Ten minutes' serious conversation. A dialogue.
In: The stage ... .
[Duologue for female characters]

2315. -----Tomorrow! A dramatic sketch.
In: The stage ... .
[Duologue]

2316. SERGEL, Annie Myers [Am. 19c]
The Midway: a burlesque entertainment, based on the famous Midway plaisance of the World's Columbian expositions.
Chicago: The Dramatic pub. co., c1894. 26p. NUC

2317. SERLE, Mrs. Walter [Br. 19c]
Outwitted.
1884. N
[Comedietta. Prod. at Scarborough, 1884.]

SERRES, Mrs. J.T. see SERRES, Olivia (Wilmot)

2318. SERRES, Olivia (Wilmot), Mrs. J.T. Serres [Br. 1772-1834] ALT: S., Olivia W.; Wilmot, Olivia
Flights of fancy; consisting of miscellaneous poems. With the Castle of Avola; an opera in three acts. By Mrs. J.T. Serres.
L: Pr. by D.N. Shury for J. Ridgway, 1805. 190p. NUC BL OCLC
[The opera is in prose.]

SEWARD, Anna, co-author see SHORT, C.

SEYMOUR, Mrs. F. see SEYMOUR, Mary (Seamer)

2319. SEYMOUR, Mary (Seamer), Mrs. F. Seymour [Br. 19c] ALT: S., M. F.; Seamer, Mary
Bonds, a drama in two acts.
n.p.: n.p., 1880? 28p. NUC

2320. -----A daughter-in-law: a comedy in one act.
Boston: W.H. Baker and Co., 1893. 7p. NUC E
[Also pub. in Home Plays for Ladies and pub. anon. in S. French's Home plays for ladies, pt. 9.]

2321. -----Friends. A comedy in two acts by Mary Seymour.
In: Home plays for ladies. Ed. Katherine Lacy.
10 pt. L: T.H. Lacy, 1867-93. NUC BL OCLC E
[Seymour is named in Lacy's ed.; plays incl. anon. in the French ed.]

2322. -----The heiress.
In: Home plays for ladies ... .
[Pub. anon. NY: S. French, n.d. pt. 7. 18p. E]

2323. -----Only a jest. In: Home plays for ladies.
[Pub. anon. in French's ed.]

2324. -----Ten years hence; a comedy in one act.
Chicago: Dramatic pub. co., 18--? 14p. NUC E
[Also in Lacy's Home plays & pub. anon. in S. French's ed. The world acting drama]

SHAEL, Vernon, co-author see WYCOMBE, Magdeline

SHANNON, Charles M., co-author see SHANNON, Mrs. F.S.

2325. SHANNON, Mrs. F. S. [Br. 19c]
Jealousy, a petite comedy, in two acts. With Charles M. Shannon.
L: Duncombe; Samuel French; NY: Henry French, 1838? 25p. NUC BL OCLC E M
[Prod. Covent Garden, 1838. Lacy's Acting ed. Dick's, no. 928]

2326. -----The mountain sylph, a romantic grand opera in two acts.
2d ed. L: Miller, 1834. 19p. BL OCLC
[Shannon wrote the songs, duets, choruses. First perf. Royal Lyceum, 1884. Also pub. L: Duncombe; T. Lacy, 1852. 34p. Lacy's Acting ed.]

2327. SHARP, Evelyn [Br. 1869-1955]
The green enchantress.
1898. N
[Fairy drama. Prod. at home of E.J. Griffiths, Regent's Park, 1898.]

2328. SHARP, Isabella (Oliver) [Am. 19c] ALT: Oliver, Isabella
Poems on various subjects.
Carlisle, PA: A. Loudon, 1805. NUC OCLC B Wells

2329. -----Frances and Mila, a dialogue.
In: Poems ... .
[Dialogue between a pretty, vain girl & an ugly, sensible girl, pp. 150-155.]

2330. -----Philander and Lucinda.
In: Poems ... .
[pp. 156-160.]

SHARP, Janet (Achurch) see ACHURCH, Janet

2331. SHATTUCK, Harriette Robinson [Am. 1850-1937]
Our mutual friend. A comedy in four acts. Dramatized from Charles Dickens.
Boston: Walter H. Baker & co., c1879. 42p. NUC OCLC

2332. SHEARS, L. D., Mrs. [Am. 19c]
The captain of "the Plover." An original libretto for comic opera.
Peekskill, NY: n.p., 1886. 75 l. NUC

2333. -----The emperor and the peasant.
Peekskill, NY: n.p., 1887. 56 l. NUC
[Drama, 5 acts]

2334. -----Golden locks, the little tramp. Comedy.
Huntington, L.I.: n.p., 1889. 84 l. NUC

2335. -----The wife's appeal: a temperance drama in six acts.
NY: n.p., 1878. 48p. NUC

2336. SHEDLOCK, Marie L. [Br. 1854-1935]
A happy medium in all things. A comedy in two acts.
L: n.p., 189-? 31p. NUC

2337. SHERIDAN, Miss [Br. 18c]
The ambiguous lover.
1781. N
[Farce. Prod. Crow-Street, Dublin. BioD says by a sister of Richard Brinsley Sheridan.]

2338. SHERIDAN, Frances
(Chamberlaine), Mrs. Thomas Sheridan
[Br. 1724-1766] ALT: S., F. PSEUD:
Lady, A
The discovery. A comedy.
L: T. Davies, 1763. 139p. NUC BL OCLC
N
[5 acts. Drury Lane, 1763.]

2339. -----The dupe, a comedy.
L: A. Millar, 1764. 68p. NUC BL OCLC
N
[5 acts. Prod. Drury Lane, 1763.]

2340. -----A journey to Bath, a
comedy.
L: n.p., 1890. 70p. NUC BL
[BL has as in R.B.B. Sheridan's wks.
1902 ed.]

SHERIDAN, Mrs. Thomas see SHERIDAN,
Frances (Chamberlaine)

SHERIDAN-FRY, Emma, co-author see
SUTHERLAND, Evelyn Greenleaf

2341. SHERMAN, Helen Hoyt [Am. 19c]
The lady from Philadelphia. Farce in
one act.
Philadelphia: Penn pub. co., [1901
OCLC] 1912. 16p. NUC OCLC H
[Earlier copyright: 1896.]

2342. SHERWOOD, Clara Harriet [Br.
19c]
The alumni play. A farce in one act.
NY: T.H. French; L: Lacy & Samuel
French, 1891. 13p. NUC BL OCLC

2343. -----The cable car. A
Howellian burlesque. In two acts.
L & NY: Lacy; French, 1891. 13p. NUC
BL OCLC
[Satire on William Dean Howells.
French's acting ed., v. 133]

2344. -----The early bird. A farce
in two acts. NY: T.H. French; L:
Samuel French, 1891. 17p. L: Lacy,
1893. 17p. BL OCLC

2345. -----For half a million. A
play in one act.
NY: S. French, 1891. 12p. L: Lacy,
1893. 12p. NUC BL OCLC
[French's minor drama. The acting
edition; no. 338]

2346. SHIELDS, Lottie [Am. 19c]
Kate's infatuation. A comedy in one
act, for young ladies.
NY & Chicago: The dramatic pub. co.,
1899. 16p. NUC OCLC
[Sergel's acting drama; no. 545; The
wizard series]

2347. -----When the cat's away; a
comedy in one act for young ladies.
Chicago: Dramatic pub. co., c1890.
14p. NUC
[Sergel's acting drama. no. 454]

2348. SHIELDS, Sarah Annie (Frost)
[Am. 19/20c] ALT: Frost, Annie;
Frost, S. A.; Frost, S. Annie
Amateur theatricals and fairy-tale
dramas. A collection of original
plays, expressly designed for
drawing-room performance.
NY: Dick & Fitzgerald, 1868. 180p.
NUC OCLC

2349. -----Dramatic proverbs and
charades, containing a collection of
original proverbs and charades, some
of which are for dramatic
performances, and others arranged for
tableaux-vivants.
NY: Dick & Fitzgerald, 1866. 176p.
NUC OCLC

2350. -----Evening amusements: or,
Merry hours for merry people,
comprising fireside games, tricks of
conjuring, tricks in cards, riddles,
enigmas, fortune-telling, charades,
tableaux, home occupations, etc. By
Henry T. Williams and S. Annie Frost.
NY: H.T. Williams, 1878. 352p. NUC
OCLC
[Williams' Household Series, v. 5.
Incl. 2 charade comedies, other
charades with suggested characters &
plots, but no script, & tableaux.]

2351. -----New book of dialogues ...
designed for performance at school
anniversaries and exhibitions.
NY: Dick & Fitzgerald, 1872. 180p.
NUC OCLC

2352. -----Parlor acting charades ...
for performance in the drawing room
... .
NY: Dick & Fitzgerald, 1876. 182p.
NUC OCLC
[Same as 1859 ed. with some added
scenes, 2 additional plays & added
tableaux.]

2353. -----Parlor charades and
proverbs, intended for the parlor or
saloon ... .
Philadelphia: J.B. Lippincott & co.,
1859. 262p. NUC OCLC
[Incl. 7 charades & 7 proverbs to be
presented in tableaux.]

2354. -----The parlor stage, a
collection of charades and proverbs,

intended for the drawing room or saloon ... .
NY: Dick & Fitzgerald, 1866. 368p.
NUC OCLC

2355. -----All that glitters is not gold.
In: Dramatic proverbs ... .
[1 scene.]

2356. -----All's well that ends well; a petite comedy in one act.
NY: Dick & Fitzgerald, 189-? 17p. NUC OCLC
[Dick's American edition. Also in: Amateur theatricals.]

2357. -----Antecedents.
In: Evening amusements.
[Comedy, 4 scenes.]

2358. -----Antidote.
In: Dramatic proverbs ... .
[Comedy, 3 scenes.]

2359. -----Beauty and the beast.
In: Amateur theatricals ... .
[6 scenes.]

2360. -----Blue beard, a melodramatic travesty.
In: Amateur theatricals ... .
NUC
[2 scenes. Dick's American edition]

2361. -----Bolts and bars. Comedy in one act.
NY: Dick & Fitzgerald, n.d. 28p. NUC OCLC H
[Dicks' American ed. Also in: Amateur theatricals.]

2362. -----Bridegroom.
In: Parlor acting ... .
[3 scene comedy]

2363. -----Cinderella.
In: Amateur theatricals ... .
[4 scenes.]

2364. -----Domestic.
In: Parlor acting ... .
[Comedy, 4 scenes.]

2365. -----Dramatic.
In: Dramatic proverbs ... .
[Comedy, 3 scenes.]

2366. -----Faint heart never won fair lady.
In: Dramatic proverbs ... .
[Comedy, 1 scene.]

2367. -----Inconstant. In: Parlor acting ... .

[3 scene comedy]

2368. -----Love-sick.
In: Dramatic proverbs ... .
[Romantic comedy, 3 scenes.]

2369. -----Mad-cap.
In: Parlor acting ... .
[3 scene comedy]

2370. -----Manager.
In: Dramatic proverbs ... .
[Comedy, 4 scenes. Also in: Parlor acting charades.]

2371. -----Marplot.
In: Parlor acting ... .
[3 scene comedy]

2372. -----Masquerade.
In: Parlor acting ... .
[Comedy, 3 scenes.]

2373. -----Matrimony.
In: Parlor acting ... .
[Comedy, 4 scenes.]

2374. -----Misfortune.
In: Parlor acting ... .
[3 scene comedy]

2375. -----Mistake.
In: Parlor acting ... .
[3 scene comedy]

2376. -----Mr. John Smith.
In: Amateur theatricals ... .
[Comedy, 2 scenes.]

2377. -----Purse-proud.
In: Parlor acting ... .
[3 scene comedy]

2378. -----Refinement.
In: Dramatic proverbs ... .
[Comedy, 3 scenes.]

2379. -----Stage struck.
In: Parlor acting ... .
[3 scene comedy]

2380. -----Stratagem.
In: Dramatic proverbs ... .
[Romantic comedy, 3 scenes.]

2381. -----There's many a a slip 'twixt the cup and the lip.
In: Dramatic proverbs ... .
[Romantic comedy, 1 scene.]

2382. -----The train to Mauro. An original interlude in one act. By S.A. Frost.
NY: Dick & Fitzgerald, 1870. 9p. OCLC H

2383. -----Wayward.
In: Dramatic proverbs ... .
[3 scenes; comedy.]

2384. -----When poverty comes in at
the door, loves flies out at the
window.
In: Dramatic proverbs ... .
[1 scene.]

2385. -----Wind-fall.
In: Evening amusements.
[Romantic comedy, 3 scenes.]

2386. -----Wooing under difficulties.
In: Amateur theatricals ... .
[Romantic comedy, 4 scenes. Set in
War of 1812.]

2387. -----The young amazon, a farce
comedy in one act.
NY: Dick & Fitzgerald, 187? 19p. NUC
OCLC
[Dicks' American edition. Also in:
Amateur theatricals.]

2388. SHOEMAKER, Dora Adele [Am. 19c]
A fighting chance; or, For the blue
or the gray. Three acts for female
characters.
Boston: W.H. Baker, 1900. 46p. NUC
OCLC H
[Baker's ed. of plays]

2389. SHORE, Arabella [Br. b. 1826?]
ALT: A.
Gemma of the isles, a lyrical drama,
and other poems. By A. & L.
[Arabella & Louisa Catherine Shore].
L: Saunders & Otley, 1859. 194p. NUC
BL

SHORE, Louisa Catherine, co-author
see SHORE, Arabella

2390. SHORE, Louisa Catherine [Br.
1824-1895] ALT: L.
Hannibal: a drama in two parts.
L: n.p. 1861. L: G. Richards, 1898.
225p. NUC BL E N
[Verse, each part 5 acts]

2391. SHORT, C., Mrs. [Br. 18c]
Dramas for the use of young ladies.
Birmingham: G.G.J. & J. Robinson, J.
Balfour & C. Elliott, 1792. 178p. NUC
BL
[Written for a group of young ladies,
to promote "the habit of speaking
with grace & propriety."]

2392. -----Domestic woe.
In: Dramas ... .
[Drama, 3 acts, for female
characters]

2393. -----The fortunate
disappointment.
In: Dramas ... .
[Drama, 3 acts, for female
characters. Poetic prologue and
epilogue by Anna Seward]

2394. SHORT, Marion [Am. 19c]
Miss somebody else.
NY: S. French, 1899? [1918?]. NUC DLC
[Comedy, 4 acts.]

2395. -----The touchdown. Comedy in
four acts.
NY & L: S. French, 1913. 83p. NUC DLC

SIDDONS, Mrs. see SIDDONS, Sarah
(Kemble)

2396. SIDDONS, Sarah (Kemble) [Br.
1755-1831] ALT: Siddons, Mrs. PSEUD:
Lady, A
The siege of Mansoul, a drama, in
five acts. The diction of which
consists altogether in an
accommodation of words from
Shakespeare and other poets. By a
lady.
L: n.p.; Bristol: W. Bulgin, 1801.
NUC BL
[Based on the "Holy War" by John
Bunyan. NUC attr. Mrs. Siddons; in
BL only under pseud.]

SIDNEY, Mary see PEMBROKE, Mary
(Sidney) Herbert, Countess of

SIDNEY, Thomas, co-author see RAE,
Josephine

SIDNEY, W., co-author see GRAVES,
Clotilde Inez Mary

SIKES, Olive (Logan) see LOGAN, Olive

SIKES, Mrs. William Wirt see LOGAN,
Olive

SIKES, Mrs. Wirt see LOGAN, Olive

2397. SILSBEE, Alice M., Mrs. H.M.
Silsbee [Am. 19c]
Jolly Joe's lady minstrels;
selections for the "sisters". With
Mrs. M.B. Horne.
Boston: W.H. Baker & co., 1893. 33p.
NUC OCLC

SILSBEE, Mrs. H.M. see SILSBEE, Alice
M.

SIMPSON, Ella G. see SIMPSON, Ella
Graham

2398. SIMPSON, Ella Graham [Br. 19c]
ALT: Simpson, Ella G.
The demon spider; or, The catcher
caught. Music by W.E. Lawson.
L & Newcastle-on-Tyne: Andrew Reid,
1895. 20p. BL E N
[Operetta. Prod. at Newcastle,
1895.]

2399. SIMPSON, Kate [Br. 19c]
Elfiana; or, the witch of the
woodlands. Music by W.M. Wood.
1895. N
[Operetta. Prod. Newcastle, 1895.]

2400. -----Nanette. Music by E.
Lorence.
1895. N
[Operetta. Prod. at Newcastle,
1895.]

2401. SINCLAIR, Kate [Br. 19c]
A broken sixpence. With Mrs. G.
Thompson.
1889. M N
[Comedietta. Prod. Ladbrooke Hall,
1889; Toole's, 1890.]

2402. -----Duskie. With Mrs. G.
Thompson.
1890. M N
[Play, 1 act. Prod. Ladbrooke Hall,
1890; St. George Hall, 1893.]

2403. -----Mademoiselle de Lira. With
Mrs. G. Thompson.
1890. M N
[Comedietta. Prod. Comedy, 1890.]

2404. -----Plucky Nancy. With Mrs. G.
Thompson.
1889. N
[Comic drama. Prod. at Kilburn,
1889.]

2405. -----Pounds, shillings and
pence. With Mrs. G. Thompson.
1892. N
[Dramatic sketch. Prod. at Kilburn,
1892.]

2406. -----Saint Angela. With Mrs. G.
Thompson.
1892. N
[Drama. Prod. at Kilburn, 1892.]

SINGLETON, Mary Montgomery (Lamb) see
CURRIE, Mary Montgomerie (Lamb)
Singleton, Baroness

2407. SKELTON, Sophia [Br. 19c]
Arnold of Brescia, a dramatic poem.
L: Simpkin, Marshall & co., 1866.
123p. BL

[Historical tragedy, 5 acts.]

2408. -----Saul; a dramatic poem.
L: Simpkin & Marshall, 1864. 86p. BL
[5 acts]

2409. SKIDMORE, Harriet Marie [Am.
1837-1904] ALT: Marie
Beside the western sea: a collection
of poems.
NY: P. O'Shea, 1877. 536p. NUC OCLC
[Cover title: Poems of Marie. Incl.
4 plays in verse, religious poetry.]

2410. -----The cross and the
crescent: a drama of the first
crusade.
In: Beside the western sea.
[6 scenes, verse.]

2411. -----The nativity.
In: Beside the western sea.
[4 scenes, verse.]

2412. -----The ransomed captive; or,
The regeneration of earth: an
allegorical drama.
In: Beside the western sea.
[1 act, 5 scenes, characters: Earth,
Paganism, Violence, Truth, Peace,
Mercy, Faith, Hope, Charity, Europe,
Asia, Africa, America, Science,
Music, Poetry, Painting, etc.]

2413. -----The siege of Granada.
In: Beside the western sea.
[2 act dramatic poem.]

SLOCOMB, Cora A. see SAVORGNAN, Cora
Ann (Slocomb) Brazza-, Contesa di

2414. SMALE, Edith C., Mrs. T.E.
Smale [Br. 19/20c] ALT: S., E. C.
The baffled spinster.
L & NY: S. French, 1901. 9p. NUC BL
OCLC E
[Lacy's Acting Ed.]

2415. -----Bravado.
1889. M N
[Farce, adapted from the French.
Prod. Strand, 1889.]

2416. -----A compromising case. A
little comedy, in one act.
L & NY: S. French, 1888. 22p. OCLC E
M N
[Adapted from the French. Prod.
Haymarket, 1888. French's Acting
ed.]

2417. -----Forty winks: an operatic
absurdity, in one act. Written by
E.C.S. Composed by G.H. Stone.

L: Lacy, 1896. 13p. BL

2418. -----Old spoons.
1899. N
[Comedietta. Prod. at Turnham Green, 1899.]

SMALE, Mrs. T.E. see SMALE, Edith C.

2419. SMART, Mrs. Alec [Br. 19c] ALT:
De Smart, Mrs. Alec
"Purely platonic".
L & NY: Lacy; S. French, 1898. 12p.
NUC BL OCLC E N
[French's & Lacy's Acting ed. no. 2115.]

2420. SMEDLEY, Menella Bute [Br. 1820-1877] ALT: S., M. Two dramatic poems.
L: Macmillan & co., 1874. 346p. NUC BL
[Blind love, tragedy, 5 acts, pp. 3-195; 4 scenes from a life: Choice, Trial, Love, Thirty years afterwards, pp. 199-386. T.P. mentions another wk.: "Lady Grace."]

2421. SMITH, A., Miss [Br. 19c]
A rainy day. Music by Virginia Gabriel.
1868. N
[Operetta. Amateur prod. at Gallery of Music, 1868.]

2422. SMITH, Adele Crafton [Br. 19/20c] PSEUD: Joseph, Delissa; Nomad
The blue stocking. A comedietta in one act.
NY: DeWitt, 1884. BL
[DeWitt's Acting Plays, no. 333. Sergel's Acting Drama, no. 532.]

2423. SMITH, Amanda M. [Am. 19c]
The other Tom, a comedy, in four acts.
NY: n.p., 1875. 28p. NUC

SMITH, Mrs. Benjamin see SMITH, Charlotte (Turner)

2424. SMITH, Bessie Blair [Am. 19c]
A considerable courtship. Farce in one act.
Philadelphia: Penn pub. co., 1900, 1914. 11p. NUC OCLC H

2425. SMITH, Charlotte (Turner), Mrs. Benjamin Smith [Br. 1749-1806]
What is she? A comedy in five acts.
As performed by the Theatre Royal Convent Garden.
L: T.N. Longman & O. Rees; Dublin: A. George Folingsby, 1799. 88p. NUC BL OCLC B N

[Prod. Covent Garden, 1799.]

SMITH, E. Oakes see SMITH, Elizabeth Oakes (Prince)

2426. SMITH, Elizabeth Oakes (Prince), Mrs. Seba Smith [Am. 1806-1893] ALT: Smith, E. Oakes
Old New York: or, Democracy in 1689.
A tragedy, in five acts.
NY: Stringer & Townsend, 1853. 65p.
NUC BL OCLC R

2427. -----The Roman tribute.
NY: n.p., 1850. R
[Tragedy.]

2428. SMITH, Julia Holmes [Am. 19c]
The butterflies' ball; a spectacular drama in two parts.
Chicago: Hazlitt & Reed, pr., c1877, 1878. 11p. NUC OCLC
[Tableaux, incl. some verse.]

2429. SMITH, Lilli Huger [Am. 19/20c]
A rank deception; a farce. Boston: Walter H. Baker & co., c1899. 28p.
NUC OCLC H
[Baker's ed. of plays]

SMITH, Lita, co-author see REID, Bessie

2430. SMITH, Lita [Br. 19c]
Bridget's blunders. A farce in one act.
L: Capper & Newton, 1893. 26p. NUC BL OCLC E N
[Lynn's acting edition, 7; "One at a time series." Prod. at Eastbourne, 1892. French's acting ed. no. 2275]

2431. -----Domestic medicine.
1887. N
[Comedietta. Prod. at Grantham, 1887.]

2432. -----Mistress Peg.
1892. N
[Dramatic sketch. Prod. Vaudeville, 1892.]

2433. -----Mr. and Mrs. Muffet; or, a domestic experiment.
L: Lacy; L & NY: S. French, 1893.
12p. NUC BL OCLC E N
[Farce, one act. Prod. at Hastings, 1892. French's acting edition, no. 2021]

2434. -----My friend Gomez. Music by E. Stanley.
1896. N
[Operetta. Prod. at Preston, 1896.]

2435. SMITH, Lydia Annie (Jocelyn)
[Am. b. 1836]
Aunt Sally's prediction.
Worcester, MA: n.p., 1889.   31 l. NUC
[Drama in 3 acts]

SMITH, Margaret Cameron Kilvert,
comp. see BRADBURY, Louise A.

SMITH, Margaret Cameron Kilvert,
comp. see CASTLE, H.D., Miss

SMITH, Margaret Cameron Kilvert,
comp. see GOODFELLOW, Mrs. E.J.H.

SMITH, Margaret Cameron Kilvert,
comp. see SMITH, S. Jennie

2436. SMITH, Margaret Cameron Kilvert
[Am. 1867-1947]
Captain Hearne.
1893. Hatch
[Source: Black Images on the American
Stage.]

2437. -----A loyal renegade, comedy
in one act.
Oakland, CA: Enquirer pub. co., 1900.
7p. NUC T

2438. -----A pipe of peace; comedy in
one act.
Oakland, CA: Enquirer pub. co., 1900.
10p. NUC OCLC T

SMITH, Mrs. Peter see SMITH, Sarah
(Pogson)

2439. SMITH, S. Jennie [Am. d. 1904]
Doctor Cureall, a comedy in two acts.
In: Easy entertainments for young
people. Comp. Margaret Cameron
Kilvert Smith.
Philadelphia: Penn pub. co., 1892.
NUC OCLC

2440. -----A free knowledge-ist; or,
Too much for one head. Comedy in two
acts.
Chicago: T.S. Denison, 1893. 12p. NUC
OCLC H
[Amateur series]

2441. -----Not a man in the house.
Comedy in two acts.
Chicago: T.S. Denison, 1897. 21p. NUC
OCLC H
[Amateur series]

2442. -----A perplexing situation.
Comedy in two parts.
Philadelphia: Penn pub. co., 1916.
19p. NUC OCLC H
[Earlier copyright: 1895.]

SMITH, Sarah (Pogson) see PINCKNEY,
Maria

2443. SMITH, Sarah (Pogson), Mrs.
Peter Smith [Am. 19c] ALT: Pogson,
Sarah PSEUD: Lady, A
The female enthusiast. A tragedy in
five acts. By a lady.
Charleston, SC: pr. for the author by
J. Hoff, 1807. 51p. NUC OCLC BM Hill
Wells
[In verse, tragedy of Charlotte
Corday. Smith supposed author. NUC]

SMITH, Mrs. Seba see SMITH, Elizabeth
Oakes (Prince)

2444. SMITH, Sophia Mary [Br. 19c]
The Eastern princess, and other
poems: together with Walberg; or,
Temptation: a drama.
L: Simpkin, Marshall & co., 1844.
338p. BL
[Walberg is historical drama of the
Reformation, 3 acts]

SOMERVILLE, HENRY, pseud. see
HUMPHREYS, Mary Gay

SOUTHAM, Gertrude, co-author see
ARMITAGE, Ethel

SPARKS, PETER, GENTLEMAN, pseud. see
HOWELL, S.

SPEED, Belle Lewis see SPEED, Belle
Tevis

2445. SPEED, Belle Tevis [Lewis
OCLC], Mrs. [Am. 19c]
Columbia; drama in one act, for
thirty-one females.
NY: E.S. Werner, 1894. 15p. NUC OCLC

2446. SPENCER, Bella Zilfa, Mrs. [Am.
1840-1867]
The two wives of Lynn, an original
play.
San Francisco: Alta California pr.
house, 1866. 42p. NUC

2447. SPRAGUE, Mary Aplin [Am. b.
1849]
Mr. Hudson's tiger hunt; a drama in
two acts.
Clyde, OH: A.D. Ames, c1885. 7p.
[Ames' Standard & Minor Drama, no.
158]

SQUIER, Mrs. E.G. see LESLIE, Miriam
Florence (Folline)

STAATS, JOHANNA, pseud. see MEREDITH,
Katherine Mary Cheever

2448. STANNARD, Henrietta Eliza
Vaughan (Palmer) [Br. 1856-1911]
PSEUD: Winter, John Strange
A ring fence.
1893. N
[Comedietta.   Prod. at Portsmouth,
1893.]

2449. -----Rumour.
1889. N
[Drama.   Prod. Vaudeville, 1889.]

2450. STAPLES, Edith Blair [Br. 19c]
Was it a dream?
1896. N
[Comedietta.   Prod. Stockport, 1896.]

2451. STARKE, Mariana [Br. 1762?-
1838]
The British orphan.
1790. N
[Tragedy.   Prod. at Mrs. Crespigny's
private theatre at Camberwell.]

2452. -----The poor soldier; An
American tale.
2d ed. L: J. Walter, 1789. 43p. NUC
OCLC
[In verse.   Attr. to her.   Account of
misfortunes of Charles Short, South
Carolina loyalist.]

2453. -----The sword of peace; or, A
voyage of love, a comedy, in five
acts.
L: J. Debrett, 1789. 66p. OCLC B N
[Comedy.   Prod. Haymarket, 1788.]

2454. -----The tournament, a tragedy;
imitated from the celebrated German
drama entitled Agnes Bernaver ...
written by a nobleman of high rank
[Joseph August Torring-Gutenzell].
NY: David Longworth, 1803. 60p. L: R.
Phillips, 1800. 64p. NUC BL OCLC B
[5 acts, verse.]

2455. -----The widow of Malabar, a
tragedy in three acts.
L: Wm. Lane, 1791. NUC BL OCLC B N
[In verse, imitated from Antoine
Marin Le Mierre's "La Veuve de
Malabar."   Prod. at Mrs. Crespigny's
private theatre at Camberwell.
Longe, v. 214, no. 3]

2456. STEELE, Anna Caroline (Wood)
[Br. d. 1914] A red republican: an
original drama, in three acts.
Privately printed, dedicated to Lady
Barrett Lennard Witham.
Essex: W.R. King, pr., 1874. 67p. NUC
E

2457. -----Under false colours.
1869. N
[Drama.   Prod. St. George Hall,
1869.]

2458. STEER, Janet [Br. 19c] ALT:
Steer, Jannette
The cloven foot. With Frederick
Mouillot.
1890. M N
[Drama from a novel of Mary Elizabeth
(Braddon) Maxwell.   Prod. Pavillion,
1890 & Grand, 1891.]

2459. -----Idols of the heart.
1890. M N
[Play, 1 act.   Prod. in Liverpool,
1890; Grand, 1891, & Criterion,
1892.]

STEER, Jannette see STEER, Janet

STEINBERG, Amy see DOUGLASS, Amy
(Steinberg)

STELLA, pseud. see LEWIS, Estelle
Anna Blanche (Robinson)

2460. STERLING, Sara Hawks [Am.
19/20c]
Hamlet's brides: a Shakespearean
burlesque in one act.
Boston: W.H. Baker & co., 1900. 19p.
NUC OCLC T
[Baker's ed. of plays]

STERNE, S., pseud. see BLOEDE,
Gertrude

STERNE, STUART, pseud. see BLOEDE,
Gertrude

STEVENS, Mrs. John see MURRAY, Judith
(Sargent) Stevens

STEVENS, Judith see MURRAY, Judith
(Sargent) Stevens

2461. STEVENSON, Kate Claxton Cone
[Am. 19c]
Two orphans.   Six acts.
NY: n.p., 187-? 70p. NUC H
[Based on "Les deux orphelines" by
Adolph Philippe Dennery & Pierre
Etienne Piestre]

STEWART, Mrs. Colonel see STEWART,
Harriet (Wainewright)

2462. STEWART, Harriet (Wainwright),
Mrs. Colonel Stewart [Br. 19c] ALT:
Wainewright, Harriet
Don Quixote; or, the knight de la
Mancha, a comic opera. By Mrs.
Colonel Stewart.

L: E. & J. Thomas, 1834. 57p. BL OCLC
[3 acts. Adaptation from Miguel de
Cervantes.]

2463. STEWART, Katherine [Br. 19c] An
episode.
1895. N
[Comedietta. Prod. in Folkestone,
1895.]

2464. STOCKTON, Ella [Br. 19c]
Madcap Violet.
1882. M N
[Comedy, 4 acts from a novel by
William Black. Prod. Sadler's Wells,
1882.]

2465. STOEPEL, Matilda Agnes (Heron),
Mrs. Robert Stoepel [Br. 19c] ALT:
Heron, Matilda
Camille; or, The fate of a coquette.
NY: Samuel French, 185-? 42p. NUC BL
OCLC E R
[Tragedy, 5 acts. French's standard
drama, 129. From the French of
Alexandre Dumas, the younger, "La
dame au Camelias."]

2466. -----Medea. Translated from
[Gabriel] Ernest Legouvé.
NY: S. French, 1857; L: T.H. Lacy,
1861. 27p. NUC BL OCLC E N R
[Tragedy, 3 acts. Prod. Drury Lane,
1861.]

2467. -----Phaedra. Adapted to the
English stage.
NY: S. French, 1867. 32p.
Cincinnati, OH: Wrightson, 1858. 32p.
NUC OCLC R E

STOEPEL, Mrs. Robert see STOEPEL,
Matilda Agnes (Heron)

2468. STONE, Abbie Anna [Am. 19c]
A.D. 1813; or, America's triumph, a
historical spectacular naval
melodrama in five acts.
Milwaukee, WI: n.p., 1893. 42p. NUC T

STOWE, Mrs. Calvin see STOWE, Harriet
Elizabeth (Beecher)

2469. STOWE, Harriet Elizabeth
(Beecher), Mrs. Calvin Stowe [Am.
1811-1896]
The Christian slave, a drama.
Founded on a portion of Uncle Tom's
cabin.
Boston: Phillips, Sampson, & co.,
1855. 67p. NUC OCLC R
[U.S. debut at National, 1852.
Innumerable adaptations & productions
thereafter. M lists 9 separate

adaptations of "Uncle Tom's Cabin"
prod. in London 1852-1896.]

STRAKOSCH, Clara Louise (Kellogg) see
KELLOGG, Clara Louise

2470. STRATHMORE, Mary Eleanor
(Bowes) Lyon, Countess of [Br. 1749-
1800] ALT: Bowes, Mary Eleanor Lyon,
Countess of Strathmore
The siege of Jerusalem.
L: n.p., 1774. 63p. NUC BL OCLC N
[Tragedy]

2471. STRETTLE, Miss [Br. 19c]
The Dorias; a historical drama.
Edinburgh: W. Blackwood, 1835. 95p.
NUC BL [5 acts, verse]

2472. STUART, Adeline [Br. 19c]
In search of a father. With Wallace
Erskine.
1898. N
[Musical comedy. Prod. at Derby,
1898.]

2473. STUART, M., Mrs. [Br. 19c] ALT:
S., M.
Romance of a rose: a drama. By M.S.
L: Digby, Long & co., 1847. 256p. BL

2474. STUART, Mary [Br. 19c]
Out of the shadow-land.
1899. N
[Drama. Prod. at Bijou, 1899.]

2475. STUART, Ruth McEnery [Am.
1849/56-1917]
The snow-cap sisters. A burlesque.
NY & L: Harper & bros., 1901. 32p.
NUC OCLC H
[Earlier copyright: 1897]

STUART-WORTLEY, Mrs. Charles see
STUART-WORTLEY, Lady Emmeline
Charlotte Elizabeth (Manners)

2476. STUART-WORTLEY, Lady Emmeline
Charlotte Elizabeth (Manners), Mrs.
Charles Stuart-Wortley [Br. 1806-
1855] ALT: Wortley, Lady Emmeline
Charlotte Elizabeth (Manners) Stuart-
Alphonzo Algarves. A play in five
acts.
L: Joseph Rickerby, 1841. 167p. NUC
BL E
[verse]

2477. -----Angiolina del' Albano; or,
Truth and treachery.
L: How & Parsons, 1841. 112p. NUC BL
[Drama in verse, 5 acts]

2478. -----Ernest Mountjoy, a
comedietta.

L: n.p., 1844. NUC BL
[3 acts]

2479. -----Eva, or The error. A play
in five acts.
L: J. Rickerby, 1840. 154p. NUC BL E
[Verse]

2480. -----Jairah, a dramatic
mystery; and other poems.
L: J. Rickerby, 1840. 380p. NUC BL
[2 acts]

2481. -----Moonshine: a comedy in
five acts.
L: W.S. Johnson, 1843. 91p. NUC BL E
[Dicks' standard plays, no. 668]

2482. STURM, Olga Louise, Mrs. [Am.
19c]
Under the red flag, a tragedy in five
acts.
n.p.: n.p., 1891. 36 l. NUC

2483. STURROCK, Mrs. [Br. 19c]
Bromley's wife.
1863. Inglis
[Farce. Prod. Theatre Royal,
Glasgow, 1863.]

2484. -----The triple dilemma.
1864. Inglis
[Comedietta. Prod. Theatre Royal,
Glasgow, 1864.]

2485. SUTHERLAND, Evelyn Greenleaf
(Baker) [Am. 1855-1908]
In office hours and other sketches
for vaudeville or private acting.
Boston: W.H. Baker, 1900. 61p. NUC
OCLC H
[Incl: In office hours, a sketch.]

2486. -----Po' white trash and other
one act dramas ... certain of the
plays being written in collaboration
with Emma Sheridan-Fry and Percy
Wallace Mackaye.
Chicago: Herbert J. Stone & co.,
1900. 232p. NUC BL OCLC H
[Most of these plays produced before
1900. Title play, 1 act, in dialect
prod. at Bijou Theater, Boston,
1897.]

2487. -----At the barricade, an
episode of the commune of '71.
In: Po' white trash ... .
[Drama, 1 act]

2488. -----A bit of instruction, a
little comedy.
In: Po' white trash ... .
[Duologue produced at Brattle Hall,
Cambridge, 1898 & Lyceum, NY, 1898.]

2489. -----A comedie royall, being a
forgotten episode of Elizabeth's day.
In: Po' white trash ... .
[Elizabeth I appears as a character.
Romantic comedy, 1 act. Produced at a
benefit, Hollis St. Theatre, 1898 &
Am. Academy of Dramatic Arts.]

2490. -----The end of the way.
In: Po' white trash ... .
[Romantic duologue between Will
Scarlett of Sherwood Forest & Lady
Werewood. Produced at Bijou Theatre,
Boston, 1897 & Lyceum, NY, 1898.]

2491. -----Galatea of the toy-shop.
A fantasy in one act.
In: Po' white trash.
[Duologue based on the legend.]

2492. -----In Aunt Chloe's cabin.
In: In office hours ... .

2493. -----In far Bohemia.
In: Po' white trash ... . With Emma
Sheridan-Fry. [1 act, in dialect.
Produced Bijou Theatre, Boston,
1898.]

2494. -----A quilting party in the
thirties.
In: In office hours ... .

2495. -----Rohan the silent. A
romantic drama in one act.
In: Po' white trash ... . With Emma
Sheridan-Fry.
[Produced by Alexander Salvini,
Tremont Theatre, Boston, 1896. Set
13c English castle.]

2496. -----A song at the castle, a
romantic comedy in one act. With
Percy Wallace Mackaye.
In: Po' white trash ... .
[Set in 1798 in Dublin Castle]

2497. -----The story of a famous
wedding.
In: In office hours ... .

2498. SWAN, Myra [Br. 19/20c] PSEUD:
S., L.F.M.
Her first engagement.
1894. N
[Comedietta. Prod. at Middleborough,
1894.]

2499. SWANWICK, Anna [Br. 1813-1899]
ALT: S., A.
Dramas of Aeschylus. Translated by
A.S.
1865. 1873. 3d ed. L: G. Bell, 1881.
NUC BL OCLC

2500. -----Dramatic works of [Johann Wolfgang von] Goethe ... comprising Faust, Iphigenia in Taurus, Torquato Tasso, Egmont. Translated by A.S.
L: H.G. Bohn, 1846. BL OCLC E

2501. -----Iphegenia in Taurus. Translated from [Johann Wolfgang von] Goethe.
NY: A. Hinds & co., 1884? 64p. NUC

2502. -----The maid of Orleans. Translated from [Johann Christoph Frederick von] Schiller.
In: The works of Frederick Schiller.
L: G. Bell & sons, 1881. E
[Also in: Historical dramas. L: Bell & Daldy, 1870. NUC]

2503. SWANWICK, Catherine [Br. 19c] PSEUD: L.
Plays and poems of L.
NY: Delisser & Procter, 1859. 98p. OCLC H
[OCLC & H enter these plays under Miss L.B. Adams]

2504. -----Eva [and] A tragic poem. In one scene.
In: Plays and poems ... .
[1 scene, 3 acts]

2505. -----Hofer. A drama.
L: Griffith & Farran, 1879. 83p. BL
[Tragedy in 5 acts & in verse]

2506. -----Poems: narrative and dramatic.
L: E.T. Whitfield, 1872. 208p. NUC

2507. -----Richard Coeur de Lion, a legendary drama.
L: Griffith & Farran, 1880. 160p. BL E
[5 acts & verse]

2508. -----The talisman, a drama. A tale of the eleventh century.
L: n.p., 1864. 2d ed. L: H.K. Lewis, 1882. 150p. BL
[5 acts, verse]

SWAYZE, Mrs. J.C. see SWAYZE, Kate Lucy (Edwards)

2509. SWAYZE, Kate Lucy (Edwards), Mrs. J.C. Swayze [Am. b. 1833]
Nigger sweethearts.
Kansas State Historical Society [Manuscript.]

2510. -----Ossawattomie Brown; or, The insurrection at Harper's Ferry. A drama, in three acts.

NY: French, 1859. 27p. NUC BL OCLC R
[Melodrama presented a few days after Brown's execution. French's standard drama. The acting ed. no. 226]

SYKES, Olive see LOGAN, Olive (Logan)

2511. SYLVESTER, Clara A. [Am. 19c]
Trusty and true.
In: Dramatic leaflets.
Philadelphia: Phineas Garrett & co., 1877. 1v. in 20 pts. NUC OCLC H
[Proverb play]

2512. SYMMONS, Caroline [Br. 1789-1803] ALT: S., C.
The Sicilian captive, a tragedy.
L: n.p., 1800. BL N

TADEMA, Laurence Alma- see ALMA-TADEMA, Laurence, Miss

2513. TALLADAY, Jennie [Am. 19c]
The little country store. One act.
Auburn, NY: Wm. J. Moses, 1894. 36p. NUC OCLC H

2514. TALLANT, Anne [Br. 19c] Octavia Elphinstone, a Manx story: and Lois, a drama founded on a legend in the noble family of ... .
J. Hatchard, 1834. 2v. NUC BL OCLC
[5 acts & in verse]

2515. TAMMIE, Carrie [Am. 19c]
The birthday cake. Comedy in two acts.
Chicago: Dramatic pub. co., 1899. 19p. NUC OCLC H
[For female characters. Sergel's acting drama, no. 551]

2516. TANNER, Minnie H. [Am. 19c]
Cinderella; a drama.
NY: Hastings & Habberton, c1872. 12p. NUC T
[verse]

2517. TAWNEY, Mabel E. [Br. 19c]
The matrimonial market, and other duologues for female characters.
Oxford: B.H. Blackwell, 1899. 69p. NUC BL

2518. TAYLOR, A. H., Mrs. [Am. 19c]
The new recruits. A temperance dialogue.
Boston: 1885. H

TAYLOR, M.N., co-author see GREELY, M.A.

2519. TEMPLE, Grace [Br. 19c]
The ocean waif. With H.M. LeBlonde.
1893. N
[Drama. Prod. at Wrexham, 1893.]

TERRA COTTA, pseud. see PREVOST,
Constance M., Miss

2520. TERROT, Anna J. [Br. 19c]
Scenes from the life of the first
Benedictines.
n.p.: n.p., 1877. BL
[A drama, in verse]

2521. THAYER, Ella Cheever [Am. 19c]
Lords of creation. Woman suffrage
drama.
Boston: W.H. Baker, c1883. 39p. NUC
OCLC
[Baker's ed. of plays]

2522. THAYER, Julia M. [Am. 19c]
Fighting the rum-fiend.
In: Dramatic leaflets.
Philadelphia: Phineas Garrett, 1877.
1 v. in 2 pts. OCLC H
[1 scene.]

THOMAS, Arthur, co-author see BARRY,
Helen

2523. THOMAS, Edith Matilda [Am.
1854-1925]
A New Year's masque, and other poems.
Boston & NY: Houghton, Mifflin & co.,
1885. 138p. NUC BL OCLC R

2524. -----A winter swallow, with
other verse.
NY: C. Scribner's sons, 1896. 120p.
NUC OCLC

THOMAS, Mrs. Edward see THOMAS, Jane
(Hamilton) Penhorn

2525. THOMAS, Elizabeth, Mrs. [Br.
18c] PSEUD: Lady, A
A dramatick pastoral, occasioned by
the collection at Gloucester on the
Coronation day, for portioning young
women of virtuous character. By a
Lady.
Gloucester: Pr. R. Raikes, 1762. 16p.
BL N
[In verse. Bio.D. calls her a sister
of Sir Jeffrey Amherst.]

2526. THOMAS, Jane (Hamilton) Penhorn
[Pinhorn NUC], Mrs. Edward Thomas
[Br. 19c]
The merchant's daughter of Toulon. A
play in five acts.
L: T.H. Lacy, 1856? 75p. NUC BL E N

[Verse, set in 17c France. Performed
Marylebone Theatre, 1855; Strand,
1856.]

2527. -----The wife's tragedy. By
Mrs. Edward Thomas.
1870. M N
[Drama, 5 acts. Prod. Standard,
1870.]

THOMAS, Jane (Hamilton) Pinhorn see
THOMAS, Jane (Hamilton) Penhorn

2528. THOMPSON, A., Miss [Br. 19c]
A woman's freak.
1882. N
[Comic drama. Prod. at Chester,
1882.]

2529. THOMPSON, Almira Carpenter [Am.
19c]
The lyre of Tioga.
Geneva, NY: Pr. for the author by J.
Rogers, 1829. 180p. BV Hill T Wells
[Contains: A sacred drama on the Book
of Esther and a pastoral play in one
act, designed for the 4th of July.]

2530. THOMPSON, Caroline Eunice [Am.
19c]
Blind Margaret, a dramatic sketch,
adapted from [Henry Wadsworth]
Longfellow's "Blind girl of Castle-
Cuille".
Chicago: T.S. Denison, c1890. 12p.
NUC H
[Denison's specialties. Libretto.
Music by G.T. Page.]

THOMPSON, Eliza see THOMPSON,
Elizabeth Jane (Sweetland)

2531. THOMPSON, Elizabeth Jane
(Sweetland) [Can. b. 1858] ALT:
Thompson, Eliza
A double life. A drama in five acts.
By Eliza Thompson.
Toronto, Canada: Hill & Weir, pr.,
1884. 34p. NUC OCLC

THOMPSON, Mrs. G., co-author see
SINCLAIR, Kate

2532. THOMPSON, Helen, Mrs. Noel
Thompson [Br. 19c]
My Maggie.
1884. N
[Drama. Also prod. as: "Darkest
London." Prod. Liverpool, 1884.]

2533. -----Myra; or, Will the
fisherman.
Maidstone: Burgiss-Brown, pr., 1888.
39p. E N

[Drama.   Prod. in Richmond, 1880.]

2534. -----Rex Cann, the whipper-in.
1884. N
[Drama.   Prod. in Liverpool, 1884.]

2535. -----The shades.
1884. N
[Drama.   Prod. in Liverpool, 1884.]

2536. THOMPSON, Mary Anne [Br. 19c]
O'Shaughan; or, the fatal secret.
1850. N
[Drama.   Prod. in Birmingham, 1850.]

THOMPSON, Mrs. Noel see THOMPSON,
Helen

THOMSON, Mrs. A.T. see THOMSON,
Katherine (Byerley)

2537. THOMSON, Augusta [Br. d. 1877]
Sunshine and shadow.
1867. Inglis N
[Melodrama.   Inglis calls it a
musical drama.   Prod. Marylebone,
1867.]

2538. -----True until death, a drama.
1868. Inglis
[Prod. Theatre Royal Glasgow, 1868.]

2539. -----Violet's playthings.
1867. N
[Musical farce.   Prod. Marylebone,
1867.   Inglis.]

2540. THOMSON, Katherine (Byerley),
Mrs. A.T. Thomson [Br. 1797-1862]
PSEUD: Wharton, Grace
Allaooddeen, a tragedy, and other
poems.
L: Smith, Elder, Thomson? 1880. 230p.
NUC
[Tragedy, 3 acts, verse, based on
historical Indian king.]

2541. THORNE, Eliza [Br. 19c]
Bleak house; or, Poor Jo the crossing
sweeper.
1876. N
[Drama, based on Charles Dickens'
character.   Prod. at Sheffield,
1876.]

THURTLE, Frances see JAMIESON,
Frances (Thurtle)

2542. TIBBETTS, Martie E. [Am. 19c]
Two Aunt Emilys; or, Quits. A farce
for eight female characters.
Clyde, OH: Ames, c1890. 8p. NUC OCLC
[Ames' Standard & Minor Drama. no.
281]

2543. TIFFANY, Esther Brown [Am. b.
1858]
The angel at the sepulchre.
Boston: L. Prang & co., c1889. 9p.
NUC OCLC
[Dramatic poem in 2 scenes.]

2544. -----Anita's trial; or, Our
girls in camp, a comedy in three acts
for female characters.
Boston: W.H. Baker & co., 1889. 42p.
NUC OCLC
[Walter H. Baker & co.'s Boston list]

2545. -----Apollo's oracle, an
entertainment in three acts.
Boston: W.H. Baker, 1897. 8p. NUC
OCLC T
[T cites a version in 1 act.   Baker's
novelties.]

2546. -----An autograph letter, a
comedy in three acts.
Boston: W.H. Baker & co., 1889. 42p.
NUC OCLC
[Baker's edition of plays]

2547. -----Bachelor maids; a comedy
in one act for female characters.
Boston: W.H. Baker, c1897. 12p. NUC
OCLC
[Baker's edition of plays]

2548. -----A blind attachment; a
comedy in one act.
Boston: W.H. Baker & co., 1895. 17p.
NUC OCLC
[Baker's edition of plays]

2549. -----A borrowed umbrella, a
comedietta in one act.
Boston: W.H. Baker & co., 1893. 7p.
NUC OCLC
[Baker's edition of plays]

2550. -----A model lover, a comedy in
two acts.
Boston: W.H. Baker & co., 1893. 22p.
NUC OCLC
[Baker's edition of plays]

2551. -----A rice pudding, a comedy
in two acts.
Boston: W.H. Baker & co., 1889. 30p.
NUC OCLC
[Baker's edition of plays.   Boston
list]

2552. -----The spirit of the pine.
Boston: L. Prang & co., 1890. 12p.
NUC OCLC
[Christmas play]

2553. -----A tell-tale eyebrow, a
comedy in two acts.

Boston: W.H. Baker, c1897. 23p. NUC
OCLC
[Baker's edition of plays. Earlier
copyrt. 1872?]

2554. -----That Patrick! A comedy in
one act.
Boston: W.H. Baker & co., 1886. 13p.
NUC OCLC
[Walter H. Baker & co.'s list]

2555. -----The way to his pocket: a
comedy in one act.
Boston: W.H. Baker & co., 1889. 24p.
NUC OCLC
[Baker's edition of plays]

2556. -----Young Mr. Pritchard. A
comedy in two scenes.
Boston: W.H. Baker & co., 1886. 17p.
NUC OCLC
[W.H. Baker & co.'s Boston list]

2557. TINSLEY, Lily [Br. 19c]
Cinders.
NY: S. French; L: Lacy, 1899. 20p.
NUC BL OCLC E
[Drama in one act. French's
international edition of the works of
the best authors, no. 24. Lacy's
Acting Ed.]

2558. -----The Devil's luck; or, The
man she loved. With George Conquest.
1885. M N
[Drama, 5 acts. Prod. Surrey, 1885.]

2559. TOLER, H. M., Mrs. [Am. 19c]
Eh? What did you say? A farce.
Clyde, OH: A.D. Ames, c1885. 10p. NUC
OCLC
[Ames's eries of standard & minor
drama. no. 148]

2560. -----Thekla, a fairy drama, in
three acts.
Clyde, OH: A.D. Ames, c1884. 14p. NUC
OCLC
[Ames' Standard & Minor Drama; no.
144]

2561. -----Waking him up. A farce,
in one act.
Clyde, OH: A.D. Ames, 1885. 9p. NUC
[Ames' Standard & Minor Drama, no.
147]

2562. TOLER, Sallie F., Mrs. [Am.
19c]
Bird's Island; a drama in four acts.
Chicago: Dramatic pub. co., c1897.
42p. NUC OCLC
[Sergel's acting drama.]

2563. -----Handicapped; or, a racing
romance. An original comedy, in two
acts.
NY: DeWitt pub. house; Chicago:
Dramatic pub. co., 1894. 13p. NUC
OCLC
[Sergel's acting drama, no. 399]

2564. TOLLEMACHE, Beatrix Lucia
Catherine (Egerton), Hon. Mrs. Lionel
Tollemache [Br. d. 1926]
The early bird and other drawing-room
plays.
L: Remington & co., 1894. 123p. NUC
BL
[Title play, romantic comedy, 1 act]

2565. -----The art critic. In: The
early bird ... .
[Comedy, 3 scenes.]

2566. -----The bandbox. A monologue.
In: The early bird ... .
[For a young woman]

2567. -----Exchange is no robbery.
In: The early bird ... .
[Comic duologue]

2568. -----Explanations.
In: The early bird ... .
[Romantic comedy, 3 scenes]

2569. -----The gooseberries.
In: The early bird ... .
[Comedy, 1 scene. Adapted & trans.
from the Spanish of Lope de Rueda.]

2570. -----The pretty duckling.
In: The early bird ... .
[Comedy, 3 scenes]

2571. -----The Solomon Islands.
In: The early bird ... .
[Comedy, 1 act]

2572. -----The two counts.
In: The early bird ... .
[Comedy, 1 act, adapted & trans. from
German of [Karl] Theodore Korner.]

TOLLET, Elizabeth <u>see</u> TOLLETT,
Elizabeth

2573. TOLLETT, Elizabeth [Br. 1694-
1754] ALT: Tollet, Elizabeth
Poems on several occasions. With
Anne Boleyn to King Henry VIII, an
epistle.
Enl. ed. L: John Clarke, 1755. NUC BL
OCLC B N
[Incl.: "Susanna; or, Innocence
preserved," according to Bio.D., a
musical drama.]

2574. TOWNSEND, Eliza [Am. 1789-1854]
Poems and miscellanies, selected from
the writings of Miss Eliza Townsend.
Printed, but not published.
Boston: Press of G.C. Rand & Avery,
1856. 355p. NUC OCLC R
[Misc. poetry, and "The Wife of
Seaton; or, the Siege of Berwick,"
historical tragedy, 5 acts.]

2575. TOWNSEND, G. M., Miss [Am. 19c]
The ugliest of seven.
In: Dramatic leaflets.
Philadelphia: P. Garrett, 1877. 1
vol. in 2 pts. NUC OCLC H
[Romantic comedy, 3 acts. Adapt.
from the German]
TOWNSEND, Stephen, co-author see
BURNETT, Frances Eliza (Hodgson)

TREE, Ann Marie see BRADSHAW, Annie
M. (Tree)

TREE, Annie M. see BRADSHAW, Annie M.
(Tree)

2576. TRELAWNEY, Anne [Br. 19c] ALT:
Gibbon, Anne Trelawney
Mary Stuart. A tragedy. Translated
from [Johann Christoph Friedrich von]
Schiller.
Devonport: n.p., 1838. BL N
[Drama]

TRESAHAR, John, co-author see
PHILLIPS, Mrs. Newton

TRETBAR, H.D. see TRETBAR, Helen D.

2577. TRETBAR, Helen D. [Am. 19c]
ALT: Tretbar, H. D.
Mataswintha. Opera ... libretto
after Fredrich Dahn's "A battle for
Rome," by Dr. E. Koppel. English
version by H.D. Tretbar.
n.p.: n.p., 1893. BL

2578. -----Rustic chivalry (Caveleria
rusticana). Melodrama in one act.
NY: Richard A. Soalfield, 189-? 146p.
NY: Charles F. Tretbar, 1891. 20p.
OCLC H
[Vocal score, music by Mascagni]

TRIMMER, Mrs. James see TRIMMER,
Sarah (Kirby)

2579. TRIMMER, Sarah Kirby, Mrs.
James Trimmer [Br. 1741-1810]
The little hermit.
1788. N BioD
[Drama. Pub in: The juvenile
magazine. No record of performance
in N or Bio.D.]

TROTTER, Catherine see COCKBURN,
Catherine (Trotter)

2580. TROTTER, Elizabeth Hill [Br.
19c]
Cindabright; or, The fatal flowers.
A fairy tale, with minor poems.
Kensington: Pr. & sold by John Wild,
1838. 145p. BL
[Allegorical dramatic poem, title
character an Irish patriot]

2581. TROUBETZKOY, Amelie (Rives)
Chanler, Princess [Am. 1863-1945]
ALT: Chanler, Amelie (Rives); Rives,
Amelie
Athelwold.
NY: Harper & bros., 1893. 118p. NUC
BL OCLC R
[Tragedy; 4 acts; verse & prose]

2582. -----Herod and Marianne (a
drama in verse). Tragedy.
Philadelphia: J.B. Lippincott Co.,
c1888, 1889. NUC OCLC R
[Extracted from Lippincott's Monthly
Magazine. V. 42, pp. 305-89.]

2583. TRUMBULL, Annie (Eliot) [Am.
1857-1949] ALT: E., A.; Eliot, Annie
From four to six, a comedietta.
In: Stories of New York.
NY: C. Scribner's sons, 1894. NUC
OCLC

2584. -----The green-room rivals; a
comedietta in one act.
Boston: W.H. Baker & co., 1894. NY:
Werner, 1894. 16p. NUC OCLC T
[Baker's edition of plays]

2585. -----A masque of culture.
Hartford, CT?: Case, Lockwood &
Brainard co., 1893. 54p. NUC OCLC

2586. -----Matchmakers, a comedy in
one act.
Boston: W.H. Baker & Co., c1884. 30p.
NUC OCLC
[Baker's edition of plays]

2587. -----Mind cure; or, When
doctors agree. A farce.
Hartford, CT?: Press of Case,
Lockwood & Brainard Co., 1896. 29p.
NUC OCLC

2588. -----St. Valentine's Day; a
comedy in one act, for female
characters only.
Boston: W.H. Baker & co., 1892. 17p.
NUC OCLC
[Baker's edition of plays]

2589. -----A Virginia reel. A
comedietta in two parts.
Hartford, CT?: n.p., c1888. 24p. NUC
OCLC

2590. -----The wheel of progress.
Hartford, CT?: Press of Case,
Lockwood & Brainard co., 1898. 50p.
NUC OCLC

2591. TUCKER, Charlotte Maria [Br.
1821-1893] PSEUD: E., A.L.O. [A Lady
of England]
A lady of England; the life and
letters of Charlotte Maria Tucker.
NY: A.C. Armstrong & son, 1895. 514p.
NUC BL OCLC

2592. -----The fatal vow, a tragedy
in 3 acts.
In: A lady of England ... .
[Written in 1840.]

2593. -----The iron mask.
In: A lady of England ... .
[Historical drama, written in 1839.]

2594. -----The pretender, a farce in
two acts.
NY: A.C. Armstrong & son, 1895. 514p.
NUC BL OCLC
[In: A lady of England; the life and
letters of Charlotte Maria Tucker.
Written in 1842. Printed as Chapter
IV of her biography.]

2595. TUDOR, Catherine [Br. 19/20c]
Aunt Minerva. A comedietta in one
act.
L & NY: Lacy; Samuel French, 1899.
20p. NUC BL OCLC E

2596. TULLOCK, Augusta [Br. 19c]
The web of fate.
1899. N
[Drama. Prod. at Braintree, 1899.]

TURNBULL, Anne Charlotte see
BARTHOLOMEW, Anne Charlotte
(Fayermann) Turnbull

TURNBULL, Mrs. Walter see
BARTHOLOMEW, Anne Charlotte
(Fayermann) Turnbull

TURNER, CYRIL, pseud. see ELLET,
Elizabeth Fries (Lummis)

2597. TURNER, Margaret, Mrs. [Br.
18c]
The gentle shepherd ... by Allan
Ramsay. Attempted in English.
L: Pr. for author by T. Bensley,
1790. 103p. BL OCLC N

[Based on "The gentle shepherd, a
pastoral comedy." From the Scots.]

TYNAN, Katharine see HINKSON,
Katharine (Tynan)

TYNDALE, Hilgarde, co-author see
JOHNSON, Annie L.

2598. ULMER, Lizzie May [Am. 19c]
"Dad's girl." Play.
n.p.: n.p., n.d. NUC

2599. -----The new "mulberry bend."
A dramatic comedy in four acts and
six scenes.
NY: n.p., 1896. NUC

UNSWORTH, Evelyn see ASHLEY, Evelyn
(Unsworth)

V., L. see VALENTINE, Laura Jewry

2600. V., Mary V. [Am. 19c]
A dialogue, between a southern
delegate and his spouse, on his
return from the Grand Continental
Congress.
NY: Pr. James Rivington, 1774. 14p.
BL OCLC B Wells
[In verse.]

VALENTINE, Mrs. L. see VALENTINE,
Laura Jewry

2601. VALENTINE, Laura Jewry [Br.
19/20c] ALT: V., L.; Jewry, Laura;
Valentine, Mrs. L.
Bluebeard.
In: Home acting for amateurs. By
Nella Parker. 2d series.
13 pts. L: F. Warne & co., 1892. NUC
BL
[Folk tale romance in verse]

VAN ALSTYNE, Mrs. Alexander see
CROSBY, Frances Jane

VAN ALSTYNE, Frances Jane (Crosby)
see CROSBY, Frances Jane

2602. VAN DE VELDE, Mme. [19c]
A bijou residence to let.
1889. N
[Comedietta. Prod. in Nottingham,
1889.]

2603. -----Lena.

1889. N
[Drama. Prod. Lyceum, 1889.]

2604. VANDENHOFF, Charlotte Elizabeth
[Br. 1818-1860]
Woman's heart.
1852. M N
[Play, 5 acts. Prod. Haymarket,
1852.]

2605. VARRIE, Vida [Am. 19c]
The coming man; or, Fifty years
hence.
Philadelphia: E.C. Markley & sons,
1872. 37p. NUC H

2606. VAUGHAN, Mrs. [Br. 19c]
The Grecians. A tragedy. In five
acts.
L: The author, 1824. 56p. NUC BL E
[verse & prose]

2607. VAUGHAN, Virginia [Br. d. 1913]
Heaven and earth.
L: Chiswick press, 1877? 57p. NUC
OCLC
[Prelude to unpub. lyric drama: Adam
and Eve, a new Paradise Lost]

2608. -----The new era; a dramatic
poem.
L: Chapman & Hall, 1880. 238p. NUC BL
OCLC E
[Allegorical poem in 4 scenes]

2609. -----Orpheus and the sirens. A
drama in lyrics. L: Chapman & Hall,
1882. 241p. NUC OCLC
[Divided into sections, too long for
presentation]

2610. VAUGHN, Mrs. [Br. 19c]
Mated.
1879. M N
[Comedy, 3 acts. Prod. Criterion,
1879.]

2611. -----Monsieur Alphonse.
1875. N
[Comic drama. Prod. in Liverpool,
1875.]

2612. -----Outwitted.
1871. M N
[Comedy, 3 acts. Prod. St. George
Hall, 1871.]

2613. VERNIER, Isabella [Br. 19c]
The barber and the bravo; or, The
princess with the raven locks. A ...
farcical drama, in one act.
L: J. Duncombe, 1825. NUC BL E M N
[Prod. Surrey, 1846. Duncombe's
British Theatre, v. 57]

VESPASIAN, TITUS, pseud. see LATTER,
Mary, Mrs.

2614. VICTOR, Frances Auretta
(Fuller) Barritt, Mrs. Henry Clay
Victor [Am. 1826-1902] ALT: Fuller,
Frances; Barritt, Frances; Barritt,
Mrs. Jackson; Victor, Frances
(Fuller)
Poems of sentiment and imagination:
with dramatic and descriptive pieces.
With Metta Victoria Fuller [Victor,
1831-1886].
NY: A.S. Barnes & co., 1851. 264p.
NUC OCLC
[Incl.: "Azlea" by Frances Fuller.
Tragedy, 4 acts, verse.]

VICTOR, Frances (Fuller) see VICTOR,
Frances Auretta (Fuller) Barritt

VICTOR, Mrs. Henry Clay see VICTOR,
Frances Auretta (Fuller) Barritt

VICTOR, Metta Victoria (Fuller), co-
author see VICTOR, Frances Auretta
(Fuller) Barritt

VILLARS, GEORGE, pseud. see CLAY,
Mrs. Randolph

2615. VINCENT, LaBelle Brooks [Am.
19c]
The witch of the woods; or, The land
of way off. A spectacular operatic
extravaganza.
Chicago: Vincent & co., 1897. 30p. BL

2616. VOKES, Victoria [Br. 1853-1894]
In camp.
1883. N
[Drama. Prod. in Liverpool, 1883.]

VOTEER, Adeline see VOTIERI, Adeline

2617. VOTIERI, Adeline [Br. 19c] ALT:
Voteer, Adeline
A fool's trick.
1891. M N
[Farce. Prod. St. George Hall,
1891.]

2618. -----Prudes and pros.
1891. M N
[Farce, 2 acts. Prod. St. George
Hall, 1891.]

2619. -----The syndicate.
1897. M N
[Farce, 2 acts. Prod. St. George
Hall, Matinee Theatre, 1897.]

2620. -----That charming Mrs.
Spencer.

1899. N
[Comedy. Prod. in Ipswich, 1899.]

2621. -----An unknown quantity.
Music by D. Harrison.
1897. N
[Duologue. Prod. Bijou, 1897.]

2622. VOX, CLARA, pseud. [Br. 19c]
San(n)itation: an epic and dramatic
poem in two parts: by Clara Vox.
L: Vickers; Wandsworth: Cooke &
Cooke, 1876. 116p. BL
[Pt. 1: Epic, heroic couplets. Pt.
2: Play, also heroic couplets, 2
acts, satire on women's health
organizations.]

2623. VYNNE, Nora [Br. d. 1914]
Aftermath.
1893. N
[Drama. Prod. Bijou, 1893.]

2624. -----Andrew Paterson. With St.
John E.C. Hankin.
1893. N
[Drama. Prod. Bijou, 1893.]

W., Lady see WALLACE, Eglantine
(Maxwell), Lady

W., A. see WEBSTER, Julia Augusta
(Davies)

W., A. see WILSON, Ann, Mrs.

W., E. see WALLACE, Eglantine
(Maxwell), Lady

W., E.C. see WILSON, Ella Calista
(Hardy)

W., H.G. see WHEELER, H.G., Mrs.

W., M. see WINTER, Mary

W., M.J. see WILLIAMS, Marie
Josephine

W_____. see WEDDELL, Mrs.

2625. WADE, Florence [Br. d. 1896]
Madge. With H. Austin.
1890. N
[Comic sketch. Prod. at Southend,
1890; St. George, 1891, Royalty,
1892.]

WAGNER, Leopold, co-author see
SCOTTI, Sophie

WAINEWRIGHT, Harriet see STEWART,
Harriet (Wainewright)

2626. WALCOT, Maria Grace [Br. 19c]
The cup and the lip. Translated and
adapted from Adolphe Belot Charles
Edmond Villetard de Prunieres and
Edmond Villetard.
NY: Samuel French, [1861. NUC] 1886.
48p. NUC BL OCLC N
[Comedy, 5 acts. Prod. Olympia,
1886.]

WALFORD, Miss H.L. see CORDER,
Henrietta Louisa (Walford)

WALFORD, Henrietta Louisa see CORDER,
Henrietta Louisa (Walford)

2627. WALKER, Agnes M. A., Mrs. [Br.
19c] PSEUD: Ravenswood
A Venetian festival. A spectacular
cantata. Words by Ravenswood.
Birmingham: Hulston & son, 1892. 14p.
BL

2628. WALKER, Ann [Br. 19c]
"Dr. Trueman's visit to Edinburgh in
1840.".
Edinburgh: W. Innes, 1840/41. BL
Inglis
[Satire in dramatic form.]

WALKER, J.E. see WALKER, Janet
Edmondson

2629. WALKER, Janet Edmondson [Am.
19c] ALT: Walker, J. E.
Fortune by land and sea. By Thomas
Heywood and William Rowley. Acting
version arranged by J.E. Walker for
annual theatricals of Harvard chapter
of Delta Upsilon.
Boston: W.B. Clarke co., 1899. NUC BL
OCLC

2630. -----The new governess; a
comedy in one act. Adapted from the
German.
Chicago: Dramatic pub. co.; NY:
Roxbury pub. co., c1899. 16p. NUC
OCLC
[The Wizard series. Sergel's acting
drama. no. 537]

2631. WALL, Annie Russell [Am. 19c]
The lying easy? A comedy.
St. Louis, MO: G.I. Jones, 1877. 72p.
NUC OCLC H
[From the German of Julius Roderich
Benedix]

2632. WALLACE, Belle [Am. 19c]
The battle of Chichamauga.

1864. C
[Pro-Confederate.]

2633. WALLACE, Eglantine (Maxwell),
Lady [Br. d. 1803] ALT: W., E.; W.,
Lady
Cortes, a tragedy.
N
[Bio.D. indicates it was never
printed.]

2634. -----Diamond cut diamond, a
comedy in two acts.
L: J. Debrett, 1787. 58p. NUC OCLC B
N
[Trans. & adapted from the French of
Antoine Jean Bourlin (Dumaniant).]

2635. -----The ton; or, Follies in
fashion: a comedy.
Dublin: H. Chamberlaine, 1788. 70p.
L: T. Hookham, 1788. 99p. NUC BL OCLC
B N
[5 acts. Prod. Covent Garden, 1788.
Longe, v. 110, no. 4]

2636. -----The whim; a comedy in
three acts.
Margate: Pr. W. Epps; L: S. & J.
Reed, 1795. 79p. NUC BL OCLC B N
[Longe, v. 232, no. 1]

2637. WALLACE, Margaret [Br. 19c]
Tiger Lily.
1892. N
[Drama. Prod. St. George Hall,
1892.]

2638. WALLBERG, Anna Cronhjelm [Am.
19c]
Fridthjof and Ingeborg; opera in
three acts. Translated from Swedish.
Worcester, MA: C.F. Hanson & sons,
1898. 138p. NUC OCLC
[Libretto.]

WALLIS, Ellen Lancaster see
LANCASTER-WALLIS, Ellen

2639. WALTON, Kate A. [Br. 19c]
Drop by drop; or, Old England's
curse.
1884. N
[Drama. Prod. in Liverpool, 1884.]

2640. WALWORTH, Reubena Hyde [Am. d.
1898]
Where was Elsie; or, The Saratoga
fairies. Comedietta in one act.
NY: Edgar S. Werner, 1900. 15p. NUC
OCLC H

2641. WARD, Miss [Br. 19c] The buried
bride, &c.

L: Simpkin, Marshall & co.;
Southampton: W. Sharland, 1840? 173p.
BL OCLC
[A drama in verse, founded on
Domenico Maria Manni's novel "La
Sepotta viva." With other poems]

WARDEN, FLORENCE, pseud. see JAMES,
Florence Alice (Price)

WARDEN, GERTRUDE, pseud. see JONES,
Gertrude (Price)

WARE, J.R., co-author see HELMORE,
Margaret C.

WARNER, Anne see FRENCH, Anne
(Warner)

WARREN, Ernest, co-author see
ELLIOTT, Charlotte

WARREN, Mrs. James see WARREN, Mercy
(Otis)

2642. WARREN, Mercy Otis, Mrs. James
Warren [Am. 1728-1814]
Poems, dramatic and miscellaneous.
Boston: Pr. I. Thomas & E. J.
Andrews, 1790. 252p. NUC BL OCLC Hill

2643. -----The adulateur. A tragedy
as it is now acted in Upper Servia.
Boston: Pr. & sold @ New printing
off. near Concert hall, 1773. 30p.
NUC OCLC B Hill Wells
[5 acts, but author claimed the last
2 by an unknown hand. Satire on
Thomas Hutchinson, Gov. of Mass.]

2644. -----The blockheads; or, The
affrighted officers.
1776. Hill Vaughn
[Lampoon of Gen. Burgoyne. Sometimes
attr. to Warren.]

2645. -----The defeat.
1773. Vaughn
[Satiric pamphlet play which
ridicules Hutchinson. Sometimes
attr. to Warren.]

2646. -----The group. Satire, in
verse, play. Two parts as lately
acted, and to be re-acted to the
wonder of all superior intelligences:
nigh headquarters at Amboyne,
Jamaica.
Boston: Pr. & sold by Edes & Gill,
1775. 22p. NUC B Hill Wells Vaughn
[Satire on the Mass. Council
appointed by George III.]

2647. -----Ladies of Castile.

In: Poems, dramatic and
miscellaneous.
Boston: Pr. I Thomas & E.T. Andrews,
1790. 252p. NUC BL OCLC B

2648. -----The ladies of Castille.
In: Poems, dramatic ... .
[Tragedy, 5 acts.]

2649. -----The motley assembly, a
farce.
Boston: Printed and sold by Nathaniel
Coverly, 1779. 15p. NUC OCLC B Hill
Wells

2650. -----The sack of Rome.
In: Poems, dramatic ... .
B Hill Wells
[Tragedy, 5 acts.]

2651. -----Sans souci, alias free and
easy; or, An evening's peep into a
polite circle.
Boston: Pr. by Warden & Russell,
1785. 24p. B Hill Wells
[Hill says attr. to Mrs. Warren is
doubtful.]

2652. WASHINGTON, Lucy Hall (Walker)
[Am. 19c]
Echoes of song.
Springfield, IL: E.S. Walker, 1878.
200p. NUC OCLC
[Incl. a 20p. masque: The Court of
the muses.]

2653. WATSON, A., Miss [Br. 19c]
PSEUD: DeYonge, Annemina
Joy; or, new dramatical charades for
home performance. By Annemina
DeYonge.
L: J. Blackwood, c1860. 190p. NUC

WATSON, T. Malcolm, co-author see
LANCASTER-WALLIS, Ellen

2654. WEBB, Marion Grace [Br. 19c]
Puck; or, The lass o' moorside.
1883. M N
[Drama, 3 acts, adapted from a novel
by Ouida [Louise de la Ramee]. Prod.
in Bournemouth, 1883. At Olympic,
1885, as: "Heartless."]

WEBSTER, Augusta see WEBSTER, Julia
Augusta (Davies)

2655. WEBSTER, Julia Augusta
(Davies), Mrs. Thomas Webster [Br.
1837-1894] ALT: W., A.; Webster,
Augusta
Dramatic studies.
L & Cambridge: Macmillan & co., 1866.
165p. NUC BL OCLC

2656. -----The auspicious day.
L: Macmillan & co., 1872. 220p. NUC
BL OCLC
[5 acts, verse]

2657. -----By the looking glass.
In: Dramatic studies.
[Dramatic sketch in verse.]

2658. -----Disguises; a drama.
L: C. Kegan Paul & co., 1879. 202p.
NUC BL OCLC
[In verse; 5 acts]

2659. -----In a day: a drama.
L: Kegan Paul, Trench, & co., 1882.
93p. NUC BL OCLC E M N [3 acts, in
verse. Prod. Terry's, 1890.]

2660. -----Jeanne d' Arc.
In: Dramatic studies.
[Dramatic sketch in verse.]

2661. -----Medea. Translated from
Euripedes.
L & Cambridge: Macmillan, 1868. 90p.
E

2662. -----A painter.
In: Dramatic studies.
[Dramatic sketch in verse.]

2663. -----A preacher.
In: Dramatic studies.
[Dramatic sketch in verse.]

2664. -----Prometheus bound.
Translated from Aeschylus.
L & Cambridge: Macmillan, 1866. 77p.
E

2665. -----The sentence: a drama.
L: T. Fisher Unwin, 1887. 138p. NUC
BL OCLC E N
[verse]

2666. -----Sister Annunciata: I. An
anniversary. II. Abbess Urania's
lecture.
In: Dramatic studies.
[Dramatic sketches in verse.]

2667. -----The snowwaste.
In: Dramatic studies.
[Dramatic sketch in verse.]

2668. -----Too late.
In: Dramatic studies.
[Dramatic sketch in verse.]

2669. -----With the dead.
In: Dramatic studies.
[Dramatic sketch in verse.]

2670. WEBSTER, Miss R. Davies [Br. 19c]
Mine hostess.
1899. N
[Comedy. Prod. Bijou, 1899.]

WEBSTER, Mrs. Thomas see WEBSTER, Julia Augusta (Davies)

2671. WEDDELL, Mrs. [Br. 18c] ALT: W____.
The city farce. By W____.
L: for G. Hawkins; J. Roberts, 1737. 46p. NUC BL OCLC B N
[Longe, v. 54, no. 13.]

2672. -----Incle and Yarico. L: T. Cooper, 1742. 69p. NUC OCLC B N
[Tragedy, 3 acts, verse. Longe, v. 60, no. 4.]

2673. WEED, Emma Herrick [Am. 19c]
A professional gardner, or, Hard of hearing, a farce in one act.
Clyde, OH: Ames pub. co., 1891. 9p. NUC
[Ames' Standard & Minor Drama, no. 286]

2674. WELDON, Mrs. [Br. 19c]
Not alone. With George Lander.
1885. M N
[Drama, 5 acts. Prod. Grand, 1885.]

2675. WELLS, Anna Maria (Foster) [Am. 1795?-1868]
Poems and juvenile sketches.
Boston: Carter, Hendee & Babcock, 1830. 104p. NUC BL Wells
[Incl.: "The owl and the swallow," pp. 93-96. Dialogue in verse.]

2676. WEST, A. Laurie [Am. 19c]
Shades of Shakespeare's women. Entertainment in 10 scenes.
NY: E.S. Werner, 1894-6. 32p. NUC OCLC H
[Werner's plays]

2677. WEST, Emma Elise [Am. b. 1870]
Their graduating essays. Comedietta in one scene for two young ladies.
NY: E.S. Werner, 1900. 11p. H

2678. WEST, Jane (Iliffe), Mrs. Thomas West [Br. 1758-1852]
Poems and plays.
L: Pr. by C. Whittingham for T.N. Longman & Rees, 1799-1805. 4v. NUC BL OCLC B N
[3 tragedies, 1 comedy. None were prod. Bio.D..]

2679. -----Adela, or, The barons of old, tragedy, 5 acts, verse.

In: Poems and plays.

2680. -----Edmund, surnamed Ironside.
In: Miscellaneous poems ... .
York: Pr. W. Blanchard, sold by R. Faulder, 1791. 127p. NUC BL N
[Verse, 5 acts. Also in: Poems and Plays.]

2681. -----"How will it end?" A comedy.
In: Poems and plays.

2682. -----The minstrel; or, the heirs of Arundell.
In: Poems and plays.
1805. N
[Tragedy, 5 acts.]

WEST, Mrs. Thomas see WEST, Jane (Iliffe)

2683. WESTON, Effie Ellsler [Am. 1858-1942] As who shall say? A play.
n.p.: n.p., n.d. 1v. NUC
[Prompt-book]

2684. -----The columbine trail. A romantic drama ... .
n.p.: n.p., n.d. 51f. NUC
[Prompt-book]

2685. -----Good ground; an original play.
n.p.: n.p., n.d. 28, 31, 30 f. NUC
[Prompt-book]

2686. -----Hawks and doves; an original play.
n.p.: n.p., n.d. 29, 31, 33 f. NUC
[Prompt-book]

2687. -----His official fiancee. A play founded on the novel of the same name by Berta Rucks.
n.p.: n.p., n.d. 23, 34, 11 f. NUC
[Prompt-book]

2688. -----His woman.
n.p.: n.p., n.d. 18p. NUC
[Typescript]

2689. -----Man and the world; a play.
n.p.: n.p., n.d. 1v. NUC
[Typescript]

2690. -----The turn in the road; a play in one act.
n.p.: n.p., n.d. 24 l. NUC
[Typescript. Title changed in MSS from: The mills of the gods.]

2691. -----A wolf in sheep's clothing.

n.p.: n.p., 18--? NUC OCLC H
[Typescript, prompt-book. 56, 38, 47
l.]

2692. WHARTON, Anne Lee, Lady [Br.
1632/59-1685] ALT: Wharton, Mrs.
Thomas
Love's martyr, or, Witt above crowns.
1685. Har S
[Tragedy in MSS. Entered S.R. but
not perf. Bio.D.]

WHARTON, Mrs. Thomas see WHARTON,
Anne (Lee), Lady

2693. WHEELER, Esther Gracie
(Lawrence), Mrs. William Lamont
Wheeler [Am. 19c]
A cup of tea, drawn from 1773.
Cambridge, MA: Riverside press, 1875.
21p. NUC OCLC
[3 acts]

2694. -----A doctor in spite of
herself.
n.p.: n.p., n.d. 15p. NUC OCLC
[1 act]

2695. WHEELER, H. G., Mrs. [Am. 19c]
ALT: W., H. G.
Cupid's little game. A Newport drama
in three acts. By H.G.W.
Providence, RI: E.L. Freeman & co.,
1881. 64p. NUC

WHEELER, Mrs. William Lamont see
WHEELER, Esther Gracie (Lawrence)

2696. WHEILDON, Alice Walker [Am.
19c]
Zoe Mou. An original Greek comedy.
Concord, MA: n.p., 1890. 34p. NUC
[Burlesque]

WHISHAW, Mrs. Bernard see WISHAW,
Mrs. Bernard

2697. WHITAKER, Lily C. [Am. b. 1850]
Young American Progressive Hobby
Club. Farce in one scene.
NY: E.S. Werner, 1896. 20p. NUC OCLC
H

WHITBREAD, J.W., co-author see
FORBES, Hon. Mrs.

2698. WHITE, E., Miss [Br. 19c]
Ambitious Mrs. Moresby.
1898. N
[Drama, 1 act. Prod. Comedy, 1898.]

WHITE, Mrs. LeGrand see FISKE, Minnie
Maddern (Davey)

2699. WHITEHEAD, Lucy [Br. 19c]
Aunt Jane. A little comedy.
Manchester: A. Heywood & sons, c1899.
BL
[1 male, 3 female]

2700. -----Before the bazaar.
Duologue.
Manchester: A. Heywood & sons, c1899.
BL
[1 male, 2 females]

2701. WHITEHEAD, Lucy [Br. 19c]
A block on the line. A comedietta.
Manchester: A. Heywood & sons series
of original dramas, no. 163, 1896.
11p. BL

2702. -----Granny. A little comedy.
Manchester: A. Heywood & sons, c1899.
BL
[2 males, 2 females]

2703. -----An imp of mischief. A
little comedy.
Manchester: A. Heywood & sons, c1899.
BL
[1 male, 2 female]

2704. -----An important omission.
Manchester: A. Heywood & sons, c1899.
BL
[2 males, 2 females]

2705. -----A mistaken idea. A little
comedy.
Manchester: Heywood & son series of
copyright plays, no. 5., 1898. 16p.
BL

2706. WHITEHEAD, Lucy P., Mrs. [Am.
19c]
The call of Rebekah; a scripture
drama for Sunday school concerts and
church entertainments.
Cincinnati, OH: Fillmore bros., 1895.
15p. NUC

WHITING, Evelyn Gray see CARD, Evelyn
Gray (Whiting)

2707. WIDMER, Kate Mayhew [Am. 19c]
A chase for a widow. A comedy in
three acts.
NY: n.p., 1883. 36, 37, 31 l. NUC
[Adapt. & arr.]

2708. -----"The waif of Smith's
pocket" a drama in four acts, founded
on Bret Harte's sketch M'liss.
San Francisco: Francis & Valentine,
pr., 1878. 32p. NUC

WILDE, Mrs. Harry see WILDE, Mrs.
Henry

2709. WILDE, Mrs. Henry [Br. 19c]
ALT: Wilde, Mrs. Harry
Her oath.
1891. M N
[Drama, 5 acts. Prod. Princess's,
1891.]

2710. WILDE, Lilla [Br. b. 1865]
East Lynne.
1898. N
[Drama. Prod. Cradley Heath, 1898.
OCLC: 1894 adaptation of Ellen
(Price) Wood, Mrs. Henry Wood's novel
in 5 acts. No author other than Wood
named in Sergel's acting drama.]

2711. WILDRICK, Marion White, Mrs.
[Am. 19c]
Jealousy. A comedietta in one act.
Philadelphia: L.R. Hamersly, 1889.
16p. NUC

2712. WILEY, Sara King [Am. 1871-
1909]
Poems lyrical and dramatic, to which
is added Cromwell, an historical
play.
L: Chapman & Hall, 1900. p. 97-214
NUC BL OCLC H R
[5 acts.]

WILKINS, Mary E. see FREEMAN, Mary
Eleanor (Wilkins)

WILKINS, Mary Eleanor see FREEMAN,
Mary Eleanor (Wilkins)

2713. WILLARD, Catherine McCoy
(White), Mrs. Eugene S. Willard [Am.
1853-1915] ALT: Willard, Mrs. E. S.
PSEUD: Penn, Rachel
The lucky bag.
1893. N
[Comic opera. Prod. Savoy, 1895.]

2714. -----Tommy.
1891. M N
[Comedy. Prod. Olympic, 1891.]

WILLARD, Mrs. E.S. see WILLARD,
Catherine McCoy (White)

WILLARD, Mrs. Eugene S. see WILLARD,
Catherine McCoy (White)

2715. WILLIAMS, Anna [Br. 1706-1783]
Miscellanies in verse and prose.
L: T. Davies, 1766. 184p. NUC BL OCLC
B N
[Incl.: The uninhabited island. A
trans. of Pietro Trapassi Metastasio,
"L'isola disabitata." Also attr. to
Mr. Hoole. Bio.D..]

2716. WILLIAMS, Mrs. Barney [Br. 19c]
Irish assurance and Yankee modesty.
1856. M N
[Comedy, 2 acts. Prod. Adelphi,
1856.]

WILLIAMS, Henry T., co-author see
SHIELDS, Sarah Annie (Frost)

2717. WILLIAMS, Marie Josephine [Am.
1846-1919] ALT: W., M. J.
A brown paper parcel. By M.J.W.
NY: S. French, 1899. 9p. NUC BL OCLC
H
[French's Intl. copyrighted ... ed.
of the works of the best authors. no.
26. French's acting ed., no. 2158.]

2718. -----A helpless couple. By
M.J.W.
L & NY: S. French, 1905. 8p. NUC BL E
[Lacy's Acting Ed., v. 153, no.
2284.]

2719. -----A nice quiet chat. By
M.J.W.
NY & L: S.French, 1899. 8p. NUC BL
OCLC H
[French's intl. copyrighted ... ed.
of the works of the best authors. no.
25.]

2720. WILLIAMS, Mary Elizabeth [Br.
19c]
The flower of Holywell. A drama in
five acts. Founded on the life of
St. Winefride, the virgin-martyr of
North Wales.
Dublin: M.H. Gill & son, 1886. 70p.
BL

WILLS, William Gorman, co-author see
GREENE, Louisa Lilias Plunket,
Baroness

2721. WILMOT, Barbarina, Baroness
Dacre [Br. 1767-1854] ALT: Brand,
Barbarina Ogle Wilmot, Baroness
Dacre; Dacre, Barbarina Ogle) Brand,
Baroness; Wilmot, Mrs. Thomas
Dramas, translations and occasional
poems.
L: John Murray, 1821. 2v. NUC BL OCLC
N

2722. -----Frogs and bulls. A
Liliputian piece. In three acts.
L: Ridgways, 1838. 36p. NUC OCLC

2723. -----Gonzalvo of Cordova, a
romance dramatized.
In: Dramas ... .
[5 acts, verse]

2724. -----Ina: a tragedy in five
acts. By Mrs. Wilmot.
L: J. Murray, 1815. 68p. NUC BL OCLC
N
[In verse, based on story of Inez de
Castro. Prod. Drury Lane, 1815.
Also in: Dramas ..., where a fuller
version of the catastrophe is given.
Longe, v. 320, no. 4.]

2725. -----Pedrarias, a tragic drama.
In: Dramas ... .
[5 acts, verse]

2726. -----Xarifa, a tragic drama.
In: Dramas ... .
[5 acts, verse. On the siege of
Granada.]

WILMOT, Mrs. Thomas see WILMOT,
Barbarina, Baroness Dacre

WILMOT, Olivia see SERRES, Olivia
(Wilmot)

2727. WILSON, Ann, Mrs. [Br. 18/19c]
ALT: W., A. Mrs
Jephthah's daughter, a dramatic poem.
L: W. Flexney, 1783. 55p. NUC BL OCLC
B N
[5 acts, verse. An angel intervenes
to prevent sacrifice. Author's note:
"My intentions were to have made it a
tragedy; but this my feelings would
not suffer."]

2728. WILSON, Bertha M. [Am. 19/20c]
A Chinese wedding ... arr. as a
costume pantomime in seven scenes.
Philadelphia: Penn pub. co., 1895.
23p. NUC H
[Keystone ed. of pop. plays]

2729. -----"Indian sketches," an
entertainment for home talent.
NY: H. Roorbach, c1894. 23p. NUC
[Roorbach's American ed. of acting
plays, 69.]

2730. WILSON, Bertha M. [Am. 19/20c]
Playing the society belle; or, the
tragedy of a slipper.
NY: E.S. Werner, c1894. 8p. NUC OCLC
[Monologue. Werner's original
productions]

2731. -----"Seniors," a three act
play ... .
Spearfish, SD: Register book & job
off., 1895. 39p. NUC

2732. -----The show at Wilkins' Hall;
or, A leaf from the life of Maria
Jane.

NY: Dick & Fitzgerald, c1895. 8p. NUC
H
[Monologue. Satire on the
Delsarteans.]

2733. -----Spring garlands, a "Pose"
-y drill and march ..
NY: Fitzgerald pub. corp., c1895.
11p. NUC

2734. -----The tragedy of blind
Margaret (adapted from [Henry
Wadsworth] Longfellow).
Philadelphia: Penn pub. co., 1895.
12p. NUC OCLC
[Monologue in 3 scenes. Keystone
edition of popular plays]

WILSON, Mrs. Cornwell Baron see
WILSON, Margaret (Harries) Baron

2735. WILSON, Ella Calista (Hardy)
[Am. 1851-] ALT: W., E. C.
The bachelor's Christmas; a Christmas
entertainment, by E.C.W.
Boston: G.M. Baker & co., c1884. 31p.
NUC BL OCLC
[The globe drama. Baker's edition of
plays]

2736. WILSON, Louise Latham [Am. 19c]
A case of suspension. Comedietta in
one act.
Philadelphia: Penn pub. co., c1899.
20p. NUC OCLC H

2737. -----The old maids'
association. A farcical
entertainment.
Philadelphia: Penn pub. co., c1900.
17p. NUC OCLC H
[Earlier copyright: 1900. 1 act.]

2738. -----The scientific country
school. A farcical entertainment.
Philadelphia: Penn pub. co., 1916.
28p. H
[Earlier copyright: 1899]

2739. -----The Smith mystery. Comedy
in one act.
Chicago: Dramatic pub. co., 1899.
12p. H
[Sergel's acting drama, no. 503]

2740. -----The trouble at
Satterlee's. Farce in one act.
Philadelphia: Penn pub. co., 1911.
16p. H
[Earlier copyright: 1899]

2741. -----Two of a kind. Comedy.
Chicago: T.S. Denison, 1899. 20p. H
[Amateur series]

2742. -----The wreck of Stebbin's
pride: a comedy in two acts.
Philadelphia: Penn pub., c1899. 27p.
NUC OCLC

2743. WILSON, Margaret (Harries)
Baron, Mrs. Cornwell Baron Wilson
[Br. 1797-1846] ALT: Baron-Wilson,
Mrs. Cornwell; Harries, Margaret
The maid of Switzerland: a romantic
drama in one act.
L: n.p., 1830? NUC BL E M N
[Prod. English Opera House, 1834;
Victoria, 1837. Also as: "Genevieve,
The maid of Switzerland." L: n.p.,
1834. NUC]

2744. -----The petticoat colonel; or,
All right at last. A comic interlude
(adapted from the French) with
original songs.
L: T. & J. Wallis, 1831. 46p. BL
[Farce, 1 act]

2745. -----Venus in arms, or, the
petticoat colonel.
L: F.J. Cumberland, 1837. 34p. NUC BL
OCLC E M
[A revision of the Petticoat Colonel.
Also pub.: L: J. Duncombe & co.,
1836? 26p. Prod. Sadler's Wells,
1844.]

2746. -----Venus, a vestal. A
mythological musical drama.
L: n.p., 1840. BL
[2 acts]

2747. -----What won't a woman do?
In: Venus in arms, or, The petticoat
colonel.

2748. WILSON, Olivia Lovell [Am.
19/20c]
Parlor varieties. Part three: Plays,
pantomimes, and charades.
Boston: Lee & Shepard, 1887. 234p.
NUC OCLC
[NUC title: Plays, pantomimes &
charades. Also includes 3 plays for
children. Parts 1 & 2 by Emma E.
Brewster with Lizzie B. Scribner.]

2749. -----The baker's wooing.
In: Parlor varieties ... .
[Comedy, 2 acts]

2750. -----Christmas.
In: Parlor varieties ... .
[2 scenes.]

2751. -----The cobbler's bargain.
In: Parlor varieties ... .
[Musical comedy, 1 act.]

2752. -----The family feud.
In: Parlor varieties ... .
[Tragedy, 2 acts.]

2753. -----The Irish washerwoman.
In: Parlor varieties ... .
[Comedy, 1 act, with 2 songs.]

2754. -----John Anderson, my Jo.
In: Parlor varieties ... .
[Musical, 2 scenes. All lyrics are
to the title song.]

2755. -----Left. A railroad episode.
In: Parlor varieties ... .
[Comedy, 1 act]

2756. -----Love's stratagem.
In: Parlor varieties ... .
[Romance, 1 scene.]

2757. -----The maids of Savoy.
In: Parlor varieties ... . [Musical
comedy, 2 acts.]

2758. -----The marriage of Prince
Flutterby.
In: Parlor varieties ... .
[Comedy, 1 act, with songs.]

2759. -----Miggs' revenge.
In: Parlor varieties ... .
[Scene adapted from Charles Dickens'
"Barnaby Rudge"]

2760. -----Mother Michel and her cat.
In: Parlor varieties ... .
[4 act musical comedy.]

2761. -----Nancy Lee.
In: Parlor varieties ... .
[Comedy, 2 acts.]

2762. -----Pat's excuse.
In: Parlor varieties ... .
[Comedy, 1 act.]

2763. -----The postman's knock.
In: Parlor varieties ... .
[Musical comedy, 1 act.]

2764. -----The power of song. A
musical farce in 2 acts.
In: Parlor varieties ... .

2765. WILTON, Mrs. [Br. 19c]
A study of two women.
1898. N
[Dramatic sketch. Prod. Brompton
Hospital, 1898.]

WILTON, Mrs. Frank <u>see</u> WILTON, Kate

2766. WILTON, J. H., Miss [Br. 19c]

Mrs. Brown.
1874. M N
[Comedietta. Prod. Britannia, 1874.]

2767. WILTON, Kate, Mrs. Frank Wilton
[Br. d. 1888]
Pearl Darrell.
1883. N
[Drama. Prod. in Liverpool, 1883.]

WILTON, Marie see BANCROFT, Marie
Effie (Wilton), Lady

2768. WINCHELSEA, Anne (Kingsmill)
Finch, Countess of [Br. 1661-1720]
ALT: Finch, Anne Kingsmill), Countess
of Winchelsea PSEUD: Lady, A
Miscellany poems on several
occasions, written by a lady.
L: Pr. for John Barber & sold by John
Morphen, 1713. 390p. NUC BL OCLC B N
[Incl.: Aristomenes; or, The royal
shepherd. Chetwood.]

2769. WINN, Edith Lynwood [Am. 1868-
1933]
A vision of fair women. A dramatic
paraphrase based upon [Alfred, Baron]
Tennyson's "Dream of fair women.".
Boston: W.H. Baker & co., 1891. 15p.
BL NUC
[1 act, verse. Baker's edition of
plays]

2770. WINSLOW, Catherine Mary
(Reignolds) [Am. d. 1911]
Broken trust.
Boston: n.p., c1886. NUC H
[5 acts. Typescript prompt book, 21
l.]

2771. WINSTON, Mary A. [Am. 19c]
A rural ruse; a comedy in one act.
Boston: W.H. Baker & co., c1893. 14p.
NUC OCLC
[Baker's edition of plays]

WINTER, JOHN STRANGE, pseud. see
STANNARD, Henrietta Eliza Vaughan
(Palmer)

2772. WINTER, Mary [Br. 19c] ALT: W.,
M.
A fair exchange is no robbery. A
drama or charade for drawing room
acting.
Dublin: Gill & son, 1881. 12p. BL

2773. -----Where there's a will
there's a way; or, the old family
name. An old fashioned Irish comedy
in three acts ... written in ...
1853.
Dublin: Hodges, Figgis & co., 1886.
47p. NUC BL OCLC

2774. WINTERS, Elizabeth [Am. 19c]
Columbia, the gem of the ocean.
Dialogue.
Chicago: A. Flanagan, 1899. 12p. NUC
OCLC H T

WISEMAN, Jane see HOLT, Jane
(Wiseman)

2775. WISHAW, Mrs. Bernard [Br. 19c]
ALT: Whishaw, Mrs. Bernard
The statue of Albemarle. Music by F.
Whishaw.
1892. N
[Farce. Prod. Trafalgar Sq., 1892.]

2776. -----Two or one.
1891. M N
[Comedietta. Prod. as: Will he come
home again? Avenue, 1891; &
Princess's, 1892.]

2777. -----Zephyr.
1891. M N
[Comedy, 4 acts. Prod. Avenue,
1891.]

WOGAN, Joan (Philips) see PHILIPS,
Joan

2778. WOOD, Abbey [Br. 19c] Our
tutor.
1890. N
[Farce. Prod. at Leytonstone, 1890.]

2779. WOOD, Ellen (Price), Mrs. Henry
Wood [Am. 1814-1887]
East Lynne; a drama in five acts,
adapted from her novel.
L: Dick, 1883. Philadelphia: Penn
pub. co., 1894. 52p. NUC BL T
[Numerous other adaptations prod.
See Wilde, Lilla for another version.
Dick's standard plays; Keystone ed.
of popular plays.]

2780. Duplicate entry removed.

2781.   Duplicate entry removed.

2782. WOOD, Frances Hariot [Br. 19c]
An odd fish. A play in three acts.
Beckenham: Miss Wood, 1888. 15p. BL
[Verse]

WOOD, Mrs. Henry see WOOD, Ellen
(Price)

2783. WOODBURY, Alice Gale [Am. 19c]
The match-box, an original comedy in
two acts.
Chicago: Dramatic pub. co., 1894.
15p. NUC H
[Sergel's acting drama, no. 400.
American acting drama]

2784. WOODHULL, Mary Gould [Am. b.
1861]
For old love's sake, a comedy in two
acts.
Philadelphia: Penn pub. co., 1896.
12p. NUC OCLC
[Keystone edition of popular plays]

2785. WOODHULL, Zula Maud [Am. 19c]
Affinities, a play.
n.p.: n.p., 1899. 46p. NUC OCLC

2786. -----The proposal. A dialogue.
L: n.p., 1889. NUC BL
[Dialogue. Woman convinces a suitor
of the evils women suffer in
marriage.]

2787. WOODROOFFE, Sophia [Br. 19c]
Buondelmonte, the Zingari, Cleanthes,
and the court of Flora: four dramatic
poems [with a few additional
miscellaneous poems]. Posthumously
Ed. Rev. G.S. Faber, B.D.
L: Seeley, Burnside & Seeley, 1846.
173p. BL E N
[Not intended for performance.]

2788. -----Buondelmonte.
[Tragedy, 5 acts, set in 14c
Florence.]
2789. -----Cleanthes.
[Masque, 1 scene.]

2790. -----The court of flora.
[Masque. Editor grouped 6
allegorical poems on flowers and
added connecting lines.]

2791. -----A sovereign remedy.
1847. N
[Farce. Prod. Princess, 1847. Attr.
to Adelaide Woodruffe, 1872, by
OCLC.]

2792. -----The Zingari.
[An unfinished romance, 3 acts
completed.]

WOODRUFFE, Adelaide see WOODROOFFE,
Sophia

2793. WOODRUFFE, Adelaide [Br. 19c]
Bound by an oath: a drama.
n.p.: n.p., n.d. 3 v. in 1. NUC

2794. -----Braving the storm.
L: Hastings, 1871. 13p. NUC OCLC M N
[Farce, 1 act. Prod. Drury Lane,
1871; & Sadler's Wells, 1871.]

2795. -----A sovereign remedy. A
farce. In one act.
L: E. Hastings, 18--? 13p. NUC OCLC
[Hastings' acting plays]

2796. WOODS, Margaret Louisa
(Bradley) [Br. 1856-1945] ALT:
Bradley, Margaret Louisa
Wild justice.
L: Smith, Elder & co., 1896. 87p. NUC
BL OCLC
[A dramatic poem]

2797. WOODS, Virna [Am. 1864-1903]
The Amazons. A lyrical drama.
Meadville, PA: Flood & Vincent, 1891.
73p. NUC BL OCLC

2798. WOOLSON, Constance Fenimore
[Am. 1838/40-1894]
Two women: 1862. A poem.
NY: D. Appleton, 1877. 92p. NUC OCLC
H R
[Dramatic poem. Repr. from
Appleton's Journal.]

2799. WORDSWORTH, Dame Elizabeth [Br.
1840-1932]
The apple of discord.
Oxford: Bridge & co. pr., 1892. 16p.
NUC

2800. -----One eye, two eyes, and
three eyes.
Oxford: Budge & co., prs., 1898. 24p.
NUC

WORTLEY, Lady Emmeline Charlotte
Elizabeth (Manners) Stuart- see
STUART-WORTLEY, Lady Emmeline
Charlotte Elizabeth (Manners)

WRENCH, Margaret see HOLFORD,
Margaret (Wrench)

2801. WRIGHT, Mrs. Dr. M. [Am. 19c]
Satan in Columbia's dominions; or,
America as it was, and America as it
is, in three parts.
St. Louis, MO: n.p., 1863. 19p. NUC
[Dramatic sketch]

WRIGHT, Fanny see D'ARUSMONT, Frances
(Wright)

WRIGHT, Frances see D'ARUSMONT,
Frances (Wright)

2802. WRIGHT, May [Br. 19c]

The sceptre and the cross.
1898. N
[Drama. Prod. at Oswaldtwistle,
1898.]

2803. WURM, Josephine [Br. 19c]
Princess Liza's fairy. Music by
Marie Wurm.
1893. N
[Operetta. Prod. at Southampton,
1893.]

2804. WYCOMBE, Magdeline [Br. 19c]
Cloris; or, plots and plans. With
Vernon Shael. Music by C.F. Hayward.
Wolverhampton: A. Hinde, 1885. 19p.
BL N
[operetta]

2805. WYLDE, Mrs. Henry [Br. 19c]
Her oath.
1891. N
[Drama. Prod. Princess, 1891.]

2806. -----Little sunbeam.
1892. M N
[Comedy. Prod. Lyric, 1892.]

2807. -----Le Macon. Also: The mason
and the locksmith. Translated from
[Augustin] Eugene Scribe, & [Jean
Francois] Casimir Delavigne. Music
by Auber.
L: A.S. Mallett, pr., 1879. 38p. OCLC
E
[Libretti]

X., G.E., pseud. see PAINTER, Lydia
Ethel (Hoyt) Farmer

Y., A. see YEARSLEY, Ann (Cromartie)

2808. YABSLEY, Ada [Br. 19c]
Lively Hal. Music by Mrs. Brooks.
1893. N
[comic opera]

YARNOLD, Mrs. Edwin see YARNOLD, Emma

2809. YARNOLD, Emma, Mrs. Edwin
Yarnold [Br. d. 1867]
Marie Antoinette; or, the queen's
lover.
1835. N
[Drama. Prod. Victoria, 1835.]

2810. YEARSLEY, Ann (Cromartie) [Br.
1756-1806] ALT: Y., A.; Yearsley,
Anne (Cromartie)

Earl Goodwin, an historical play.
L: G.G.J. & J. Robinson, 1791. 89p.
NUC BL OCLC B N
[Tragedy; 5 acts, verse. Prod. Bath,
1789. MS. Larpent Coll., 1789.]

YEARSLEY, Anne (Cromartie) see
YEARSLEY, Ann (Cromartie)

YORKE, Elizabeth (Lindsay), Countess
of Hardwicke see HARDWICKE, Elizabeth
(Lindsay) Yorke, Countess of

YOUNG LADY, A, pseud. see ARIADNE,
pseud.

YOUNG LADY, A, pseud. see COCKBURN,
Catherine (Trotter)

YOUNG LADY, A, pseud. see MORE,
Hannah

YOUNG LADY, A, pseud. see N., M.

2811. YOUNG LADY, A. pseud [Br. 18c]
The village maid; an opera in three
acts. By a young lady.
L: The authoress, 1792. NUC BL OCLC
[In prose & verse]

2812. YOUNG, Mrs. Henry [Br. 19c]
Bertha Gray, the pauper child; or,
The death fetch.
1845. M
[Drama. Prod. Victoria, 1854.]

2813. -----Jonathan Wild; or, The
storm on the Thames.
1868. N [Drama, 4 acts. Prod. East.
London, 1868.]

2814. -----The light of love; or, The
diamond and the snowdrop.
1867. N
[Drama. Prod. Effingham Saloon,
1867.]

YOUNG, Sir Charles Lawrence, Bart.,
co-author see LEAN, Florence
(Marryat) Church

2815. YOUNG, Margaret [Am. 19/20c]
Honesty -- A cottage flower.
1897. M
[Play, 1 act. Prod. Avenue, 1897.]

2816. -----Kitty. Dramatic sketch
for two female characters.
NY: Roxbury pub. co., 1899? 11p. NUC
OCLC
[The wizard series. Sergel's acting
drama. no. 563]

2817. YOUNG, Mary Julia [Br. 1760-
1821] PSEUD: Lady, A

Genius and fancy; or, Dramatic
sketches. By a lady.
L: H.D. Symonds, W. Lee & J. Gray,
1791. 48p. NUC BL
[Title poem a dialogue between Genius
& Fancy, praising famous actresses,
actors & dramatists]

2818. YOUNGS, Ella Sharpe [Br. 19c]
Kartoum. A lyrical drama in five
acts.
San Remo: n.p., 1892. 90p. BL

2819. -----Osman and Emineh; an
oriental story, etc.
L: Spottiswoode & co., 1879. 85p. NUC
[Contents: Osman and Emineh: a
lyrical tragedy. The Doseh; familiar
epistle to a friend. The revenge of
Michael Angelo.]

2820. ZALESKA, Wanda [Br. 19c]
Marishka.
1890. M
[Drama, 5 acts. Prod. Sadler's
Wells, 1891; Great Grimsby, 1896.]

2821. ZECH, Marie [Br. 19c] ALT:
Robinson, Mrs. C.
It is justice.
1890. N
[Drama. Prod. at Bury St. Edmunds,
1890.]

2822. ZGLINITZKA, Marie von [Br. 19c]
Harold. Translated from Ernst von
Wildenbruch. Hanover: Carl Schussler,
1884. 174p. E

2823. ZIMMERN, Helen [Br. 19c]
The beneficent bear. Translated from
Carlo Goldoni.
In: Comedies of Carlo Goldoni. Ed.
Helen Zimmern.
L: David Stott, 1892. pp. 95-145. BL
OCLC E

2824. -----A curious mishap.
Translated from Carlo Goldoni.
In: Comedies of Carlo Goldoni.

2825. -----The fan. Translated from
Goldoni.
In: Comedies of Carlo Goldoni.

2826. -----The spendthrift miser.
Translated from Goldoni.
In: Comedies of Carlo Goldoni.

2827. ZOBLINSKY, Mme. [Br. 19c]
Alessandro Stradella. A romantic
opera ... From the German of

Friedrich von Flotow, by C.
Zoblinsky.
n.p.: n.p., 1878. BL

2828. -----Annie of Tharau.
1880. N
[Operetta. Prod. at Edinburgh, 1880.

APPENDICES

CHRONOLOGICAL LISTING

1350-1599

Elizabeth I, Queen of England

Katherine of Sutton;

Lumley, Lady J.F.

Pembroke, M.S.H.

1600-1699

Ariadne

Behn; Boothby

Cavendish, Lady J.; Cockburn, C.T.

Falkland, E.T.

Henrietta Maria, Queen of England

Killigrew

Manley

Newcastle, M.L.C.

Philips, J.; Philips, K.; Philips,
K.F.; Pix; Polwhele

Wharton, A.L.

1700-1749

Aubert; Aubin

Boyd, E.

Centlivre, S.F.; Charke; Cockburn,
C.T.; Cooper, E.

Davys, M.

Egleton

Haywood, E.F.; Holt, J.W.; Hoper

Lady, A; Lady of Quality, A; Leapor

Manley; Montagu

N., M.

Pilkington, L.V.L.; Pix

Robe, J.

Weddell; Winchelsea

1750-1799

Arblay, F.B.D.

Baillie, J.; Barrell; Booth; Brand,
H.; Brooke, F.; Brunton; Burgess;
Burke; Burrell, S.R.; Buxton, I.M.;
Byron, M.C.G.

Celesia; Chezy; Childe-Pemberton,
H.L.; Cibber; Clive; Cornelys;
Cowley, H.P.; Crane, E.M.; Craven,
Baroness; Cullum; Cuthbertson

D'Aguilar; Deverell; Doremus; Dubois,
Lady

Ebsworth; Edmead; Edwards; Edwards,
A.M.; Ele

Faugeres; Forsyth, E.; Francis, A.G.;
Fry, B.

Gardner, C.; Geisweiler; Gibbs, P.G.;
Goddard, K.; Gore, C.G.F.; Graves,
C.I.M.; Griffith, E.G.

Harlow; Harrison, E.; Hatton, A.J.K.;
Henry; Hill, P.B.; Hook, H.H.M.;
Houston; Hughes, A.

I., P.

Keating, E.H.; Kemble, M.T.D.

Lady, A.; Lady in Connecticut, A;
Latter; Lee, H.; Lee, S.; Lennox,
C.R.

MacCarthy, C.; Marishall; Marriott;
Masters, J.M., Metcalfe; More, H.;
Murray, J.S.S.

O'Brien, M.; Opie

Palmer, B.E.; Parsons, E.P.; Peard;
Penny; Plumptre, A.; Plumptre, Anne;
Pope; Pye, J.H.M.

Richardson, E.; Roberts, R.;
Robertson, T.; Robins, M.E.;
Robinson, M.D.; Rowson, S.H.; Ryves,
E.

Sanford, A.; Schmall; Seymour, M.S.;
Sheridan; Sheridan, F.C.; Short, C.;
Smith, C.T.; Starke; Strathmore

Thomas, E.; Tollett; Trimmer; Turner,
M.

V., M.V.

Wallace, E.M.; Warren, M.O.; West,
J.I.; Weston, E.E.; Williams, A.;
Wilson, A.; Woodruffe, A.

Yearsley; Young lady, a; Young, M.J.

1800-1825

Arblay, F.B.D.; Attersoll

Baillie; Balfour, M.D.; Barrymore;
Berry, M.; Boaden; Brooke, F.; Brown,
C.; Burney, F.; Burrell, S.R.;
Buxton, I.M.; Byron, M.C.G.

Caulfeild, F.S.; Chambers, M.; Chezy;
Child, L.M.F.; Childe-Pemberton,
H.L.; Clarke, M.C.; Clarke, O.;
Cobbold, E.K.; Cowley, H.P.; Crane,
E.M.; Craven, E.B.B.

Darusmont; De Humboldt; Doremus

Ebsworth; Edgar; Edgeworth; Ele

Faucit; Fletcher; Fraser, S.; Fry, B.

Gibbs, P.G.; Goddard, K.; Godwin,
C.G.G.; Goldsmith, M.; Gore, C.G.F.;
Graves, C.I.M.

H____, E.; Harvey, M.; Helme, E.;
Hemans; Henry; Hill, I.; Holcroft;
Holford; Hornby

Inchbald; Isdell

Jamieson; Jordan, D.B.

Keating, E.H.; Kemble, M.T.D.;
Kennedy, G.

Lady, A; Laurent; Lawrence, S.;
Leadbeater; Lee, S.; Lefanu; Lewis,
M.G.; Liddiard

Macaulay, E.W.; McTaggart; Martin;
Masters, J.M.; Minton; Mitford; More;
Morgan, S.O.

Nooth

Palmer, B.E.; Peard; Pinckney, M.H.;
Plowden; Plunkett, E.G.; Polack;
Porter, A.M.; Porter, J.

Richardson, S.K.; Robertson; Robins,
M.E.; Rowson

Sanford, A.; Schmall; Scott, J.M.;
Selden; Serres, O.; Seymour, M.S.;
Sharp, I.O.; Siddons; Smith, S.P.;
Starke, M.; Symmons

Vaughan; Vernier

West, J.I.; Weston, E.E.; Wilmot,
Baroness; Woodruffe, A.

1826-1850

Adams, S.F.F.

Bacon, D.S.; Baillie; Barnes, C.M.S.;
Bartholomew, A.C.F.; Bloomfield;
Boaden; Boyle; Browning, E.B.;
Bullock; Byron, M.G.

Campbell, H.; Chapman, J.F.; Clarke,
M.C.; Cooper, E.; Corbet; Crowe,
C.S.; Cunningham, V.; Cushing, E.L.F.

Davidson, F.A.; Davies, B.; Dodge,
H.M.; Downing, H.

Ebsworth; Ellet, E.F.L.

Florance

Garnett, C.C.B.; Gilman, C.H.; Gore,
C.G.F.

Hale, S.J.B.; Hall, A.M.F.M.; Hall,
L.J.P.; Hallett; Hamilton, S.;
Hardwicke; Hastings, Lady F.; Hentz;
Herring; Hervey, E.L.M.; Hill, I.;
Holcroft; Holmes, A.M.M.; Howitt,
M.B.

Jameson, A.B.M.; Jones, M.E.M.

Kelly, F.M.; Kemble, F.A.; Keteltas;
Kitching

Lady, A; Landon; Leckie; Lee, E.B.;
Lee, H.; Leslie, E.F.; Lewis, E.G.;
Little, S.L.R.; Lovell; Lowe, H.

Maberley; McFie; McTaggart; Martyn; Mayo; Medina; Mitford; Molini; Morgan, S.O.

Norton, E.B.S.E.

Osgood, F.S.L.

Packard, H.J.; Pardoe; Park, E.; Phillips, E.; Pickering, E.; Planche; Polack; Poyas

Read, H.F.; Ricord; Ritchie; Ritter; Roberts, E.; Robinson, E.; Rouse

Sandbach; Sargant, J.A.; Shannon; Smith, E.O.P.; Smith, S.M.; Stewart, H.W.; Stoepel; Strettle; Stuart, M.; Stuart-Wortley, Lady; Swanwick

Tallant; Thompson, A.C.; Thompson, M.A.; Trelawney; Trotter, E.H.

Walker, A.; Ward; Wells, A.M.F.; Wilmot, Baroness; Wilson, M.H.B.; Woodrooffe, S.

Yarnold; Young

1851-1875

Additon

Baker, D.P.; Barstow, E.M.; Bateman, S.F.C.; Bennett, A.R.G.; Bernard; Berrie, E.; Bidalles; Bigot; Bowers; Bowman, A.; Bradbury, S.L.A.; Bradley, N.H.; Bridges, E.; Browne, F.E.; Brunner; Bull

Calvert, A.H.B.; Campbell, A.M.L.; Carey, H.M.; Cavendish, Lady; Chatterton; Child, L.M.F.; Childe-Pemberton, H.L.; Clayton, E.; Cleaver; Clephane; Cobb, M.L.; Coleman; Colquhoun; Conkling; Cook, E.; Corder; Corwin; Cresswell; Crosby, F.J.; Crowe, C.J.; Cunningham; Curtis, A.R.W.

Daly; Dana; Delesdernier; Denvil; De Vere; Dewitt, J.D.; Dickens, F.; Dietz; Dufferin and Clandeboye

Edwards, A.; Ellet; Evans, M.; Evans, R.; Evelyn, J.

Fiddes; Field, M.K.K.; Fielding; Fitch; Fitz-Simon; Frances; Fraser, J.A.; French, L.V.S.; Frere; Frothingham; Fullerton

Garthwaite; Gibson, C.; Glazebrook; Gowing, E.J.B.A.; Graves, A.C.S.;

Greene, L.L.P.; Greer, M.; Gregory, H.S.

Hall, C.; Hart; Harwood, I.; Hazlewood; Henry, S.M.I.; Hervey; Hosmer; Howarth; Howe, J.W.; Howell, S.; Hume-Rothery

Irvine; Irving, E.

Jones, L.

Keating, E.H.; Keeble; Keene; Kellogg, C.L.; Kemble, F.A.; Kemble, M.T.D.; Kidder; Kinney; Knox, I.C.

Lacy, K.; Lambert, M.H.P.; Lambla; Lane, S.; Lazarus; Lean, F.M.C.; Leslie, M.E.; Leslie, M.F.F.; Lewis, E.A.B.R.; Lindsay, C.B.E.; Logan, O.L.; Lovell, M.A.L.; Ludlow

MacConaughy; McCord; MacFarren; Mackarness; Maxwell, M.E.B.; Medina; Miles, S.E.H.; Mitford; Moore, A.; Munson

Norton; Novello

Ogilvie

Peel; Phibbs; Phillips, E.; Prideaux; Pritchard, J.; Putnam, M.T.S.L.; Pyer

Raymond, K.; Ringwalt; Ritchie, A.C.O.M.; Ritchie, M.K.; Ritter, C.F.M.; Roberts, S.L.; Rowsell

Sadlier; Sanderson, M.; Sandford; Schiff; Seymour, M.S.; Shields, S.A.F.; Shore, A.; Shore, L.C.; Skelton; Smedley; Smith, A.; Smith, A.M.; Smith, E.O.P.; Spencer, B.Z.; Steele, A.C.W.; Stevenson, K.C.C.; Stoepel; Stowe, H.E.B.; Sturrock; Swanwick; Swayze, K.L.E.

Thomas, J.H.P.; Thomson, A.; Thomson, K.B.; Townsend, E.

Vandenhoff; Varrie; Vaughn; Victor, F.A.F.

Walcot; Wallace, B.; Webster, J.A.D.; Wheeler, E.G.L.; Williams, Mrs. B.; Wilton; Woodruffe, A.; Wright

Young

1876-1899

Achurch; Ackerman; Adams, C.; Adams, E.; Adams, Mrs. E.; Adams-Acton;

Alcott; Aldrich; Allen, A.M.; Allen, Annie; Allen, C.H.; Allen, L.; Allen, M.T.; Allen, M.; Alleyn; Alma-Tadema; Amory; Andrews, F.H.; Anstruther; Archer, Miss; Archer, F.E.; Aria; Armitage; Armstrong, L.M.C.; Arnold, L.C.; Ascher; Ashley, E.U.; Attenborough; Avery-Stuttle; Ayer, H.H.; Aylmer; Ayres, L.L.

Bancroft, M.E.W.; Bannan; Baring; Barker, A.E.; Barrett, G.F.; Barrow; Barry, C.E.; Barry, H.; Bateman, I.E.; Bateman, L.M.B.; Bateman, S.F.C.; Bates, M.H.E.; Bates, R.; Bayliff; Beauchamps; Beckett; Beerbohm; Bell, F.E.E.; Bell, L.C.; Bell, M.; Bennett, E.; Beresford; Beringer, A.D.; Bernhardt-Fisher; Bessle; Bevington; Bigg; Binns; Blandin; Blevin; Bloede; Booth, Mrs. O.V.; Boynton, M.M.; Bradbury, L.A.; Bradbury, S.L.A.; Bradley, K.H.; Bradley, N.H.; Bradshaw, A.M.T.; Brewster, E.E.; Bright, E.; Bright, F.; Bright, K.C.; Brown, A.F.; Brown, M.F.; Browning, E.B.; Brunton; Burnett, F.E.H.; Burney, E.; Burton; Burton, Mrs. H.S.; Buxton; Byron, M.C.G.

Cadogan; Calvert, A.H.B.; Cameron, K.; Campbell, A.P.; Campbell, A.M.; Campbell, G.E.; Campbell, J.S.C.; Campbell, J.M.; Campbell, J.E.; Campbell, M.D.; Carlyle, R.; Carr, A.V.S.; Carroll, M.T.; Case, L.V.; Cassilis; Chandler; Chandos; Chapin; Childe-Pemberton; Chippendale; Clark, J.R.; Clarke, C.S.; Clay, Mrs. R.; Clayton, E.; Clevedon; Clifford, L.L.; Clifton, M.A.D.; Cockburn; Coffin; Colburn, C.W.; Colclough, E.S.; Collet, R.; Collette; Colman, J.; Compton; Connelly; Connelly, C.L.; Cook, M.C.; Corbett, E.B.M.; Corder, H.L.W.; Costello; Cote; Courtenay; Cowen; Cowen, H.; Cox, E.R.; Cox, Mrs. D.; Crackanthorpe; Craigie; Crane, E.M.; Crane, E.G.; Creighton, B.; Crewe, A.; Crosby, F.J.; Crumpton; Culbreth; Cummings, M.; Currie, M.M.L.; Curtis, A.; Curzon; Cusack; Cuthell

Dallas; Dalrymple; Darling, I.F.; Davenport, F.L.G.; Davis, H.; Davis, L.; Davis, M.E.M.; Davis, Mrs. M.; Dawes, S.E.; Delafield; De La Pasture; De Navarro; Dening; De Nottbeck; Denton, C.J.F.; De Retan; De Witt, E.; Dickinson, A.; Dickinson, E.L.; Diehl; Dietz; Dillaye; Dillon; Dix; Dixey; Dixie;

Dixon, M.H.; Dolaro; Don; Donnell, F.T.; Doran; Dorisi; Douglas, J.; Douglass, A.S.; Dowling, M.T.; Downing, L.C.; Downshire; Duckworth; Duer; Dugan; Duncan; Dunne; Duquette; Durant, H.; Duval, M.V.; Dyer, E.

Edouin; Ehrlich; Eldredge; Elliot, S.F.; Elliott, C.; Ellis, R.; Elwyn

Fairbairn; Fairfax; Fairgrave; Farjeon; Fawcett, M.G.; Fenton, S.; Field, M.K.K.; Fields, A.A.; Fields, L.M.; Filippi; Fiske; Fletcher, E.; Fletcher, J.C.; Flewellyn; Flint, M.M.; Fogerty; Forbes; Ford, E.S.; Ford, H.; Forrest, A.; Forrester, E.; Forrester, S.; Franklin, J.; Fraser, J.A.; Freake; Freeman, M.E.W.; Freiligrath-Kroeker; French, A.W.; Frey; Friedlieb; Frothingham; Frothingham, M.S.; Fuller, A.C.; Fullerton, Lady G.C.; Furniss

Gaddess, M.L.; Gailey; Gale, R.E.B.; Ganthony; Gaskell; Gathercole; Gay, M.M.; Gaylord; Gaynor, L.; Georgia, N.; Gibbs, B.V.; Gibbs, J.D.; Gilbert-Gilmer; Giraud; Glazebrook; Glen, I.; Goddard, Mrs. E.; Goldschmidt; Goodfellow; Goodloe; Goodrich, F.M.; Gorton, M.J.; Gowing, E.J.B.A.; Graham, M.; Gratienne; Graves, C.I.M.; Gray, L.; Gray, M.C.; Green, K.; Greer, M.A.; Greet; Greville; Griffith, H.S.; Griffiths, J.C.; Groenevelt; Grove, F.C.; Guernsey; Guion; Guthrie

Hale; Hamilton, C.J.; Harkness, M.L.; Harrison, C.C.; Harrison, E.; Harrison, M.S.L.K.; Hart, F.; Harvey, A.M.; Harwood, I.; Hatton, B.; Haughwout; Hawkins, P.L.; Hawthorn, M.; Hayes, M.X.; Hayes, M.B.; Hazard, E.; Helmore; Hemenway; Hendershot; Henderson, E.; Henderson, F.L.; Henderson, H.L.; Henderson, L.M.; Henry; Herbert; Hernaman; Herzog; Heyne; Heywood, D.A.; Higgins, G.W.; Hill, G.L.; Hills, H.; Hilton, H.; Hingeston-Randolph; Hinkson, K.T.; Hoare, F.; Hodgson, A.H.; Hodson; Holford, M.A.; Holley; Holt, S.B.; Holton; Hooper, L.; Hope, K.; Hope, N.; Hope, V.; Hopkins, L.P.S.; Horne, M.B.; Howard; Howell, A.R.; Howie; Howlett; Hughes, A.; Hughes, L.M.; Humphreys, M.G.; Hunt, A.; Hunt, M.R.; Hunt, V.; Hunter, G.L.; Hunter, Mrs. T.; Hyde, E.A.

Ingelow; Ingraham; Irish; Ives, A.E.;

Jackson, B.; James, A.; James, F.A.P.; Jameson; Jaquith; Jay, H.; Jenner, A.; Jervey; Johnson, A.L.; Johnson, E.; Johnson, F.M.; Johnson, M.; Johnson, S.A.; Johnstone; Jones, C.A.; Jones, G.P.; Jonson, D.F.; Josephine;

Karadja; Kavanaugh; Kendal; Kennerley; Kennion; Kenyon; Kimball, H.P.; Kingston, G.; Kitchel; Knapp, L.M.; Kummer

Lake, B.; Lambert, M.H.P.; Lancaster-Wallis; Lane, S.; Lane-Fox; Lanner; Latham, G.; Latimer, K.M.; Lawrence, E.; Lazarus, E.; Lean, F.M.C.; Lee, M.C.; Leete; Leigh, A.; Leigh, N.; Leterrier; Leverson; Lewis, A.G.D.; Lewis, C.; Lewis, C.M.; Libby, L.J.; Liljencrantz; Lindley; Lippmann; Lipthwaite; Littleton, M.L.; Livingston, M.V.F.; Lloyd, M.F.; Lochlan; Locke, B.M.; Locke, N.M.; Logan, O.L.; Lonergan; Long, L.A.; Lord, A.E.S.; Lord, H.F.; Lowther; Lutkenhaus; Lutz; Lynch, H.

McCollum; McCray; MacDonnell; McFall; MacFarren; McGrath; McIntyre; McKay; McKean; Mackenzie; McNamara; Maddison; Magin; Maguire; Malloy; Manning; Marean; Marriott, F.; Marx; Masters; Mather; Mathews, F.A.; Matthews, E.V.B.; Maxwell, M.E.B.; Meadows; Medd; Meller; Mercedes; Merington; Merivale; Meriwether; Merriman; Merritt; Merron; Miller, Mrs. T.; Milner; Monckton; Monroe, H.; Montgomery, E.E.; Montgomery, M.; Morgan, C.A.; Morgan, G.W.; Morison, C.W.; Morison, M.; Morland, C.E.; Morse, E.L.B.; Morse, M.; Morton, M.W.; Morton, M.; Moses, A.J.; Moubrey; Munday, L.A.H.; Murray, E.; Musgrave

Naucaze; Neal, M.; Nicholson; Nightingale; Niles; Nordon; Norton, J.

O'Brien, C.G.; O'Brien, C.; O'Connell, A.; Orne; Overbeck

Pacheco; Painter; Palmer, Mrs. B.; Parker, C.B.; Parker, M.S.; Parker, N.; Parsons, L.M.S.; Patry; Payn; Payson; Peattie; Peck, E.W.; Pelham, N.H.; Pendleton, C.; Perkins, M.R.; Perry; Pfeiffer; Phelan; Phelps, J.A.C.; Phelps, P.; Phelps, S.; Phillips, Mrs. N.; Pierce, S.E.; Pinckney; Pineo; Pittman, H.D.; Plumb; Pollard, J.; Pollock, E.;

Polson; Porter, C.E.; Potter, M.; Praed; Praeger; Pratt, S.H.; Prentiss, E.P.; Prevost; Prideaux; Pullen; Purvis

Rae; Ramsay, A.; Rand, K.E.; Randford; Ray, E.; Raynor, V.M.; Reade, G.; Reid, B.; Reynartz; Richardson, A.S.; Richardson, A.S.S.; Richey, O.; Righton; Riley, C.; Ritchie, F.; Rittenhouse; Rivers, F.; Robbins, C.A.; Roberts, C.L.; Robertson, J.; Robinson, H.J.H.; Rogers, M.M.; Rohlfs; Rose, A.M.; Ross, R.S.; Rosse; Rover; Rowley, M.S.; Rowsell; Runcie; Ryley, M.L.; Ryley, M.;

St. Aubyn; St. Ruth; Saker; Sanford, A.; Sanford, M.W.; Santley; Saull; Savorgnan; Scott, M.A.; Scotti; Scudder; Seaton, R.; Seawell; Selous; Serle; Seymour, M.S.; Sharp, E.; Shears; Shedlock; Sheridan, F.C.; Sherwood, C.H.; Shields, S.A.F.; Short, M.; Silsbee; Simpson, E.G.; Simpson, K.; Sinclair, K.; Skidmore; Smale; Smart; Smith, A.C.; Smith, L.; Smith, L.A.J.; Smith, M.C.K.; Smith, S.J.; Speed; Stannard; Staples; Steer; Stewart, K.; Stockton, E.; Stone, A.A.; Stuart, A.; Stuart, M.; Sturm; Swan, M.; Swanwick, A.; Swanwick, C.; Sylvester, C.A.

Talladay; Tammie; Tawney; Taylor, A.H.; Temple, G.; Terrot; Thayer, J.M.; Thomas, E.M.; Thompson, A.; Thompson, E.J.S.; Thompson, H.; Thorne; Tiffany, E.B.; Tinsley; Toler; Tollemache; Townsend, G.M.; Tretbar; Troubetzkoy; Trumbull; Tucker, C.M.; Tudor, C.; Tullock

Ulmer

Valentine, L.J.; Van de Velde; Vaughan, V.; Vaughn; Vincent, L.B.; Vokes; Votieri; Vox; Vynne

Wade, F.; Walker, A.M.A.; Walker, J.E.; Wall, A.R.; Wallace, M.; Wallberg; Walton, K.A.; Washington, L.H.W.; Webb, M.G.; Webster, J.A.D.; Webster, R.D.; Weed; Weldon; West, A.L.; Wheeler, H.G.; Wheildon; Whitaker, L.C.; White, E.; Whitehead, L.; Whitehead, L.P.; Widmer; Wilde; Wilde, L.; Wildrick; Willard, C.M.W.; Williams, M.J.; Williams, M.E.; Wilson, B.M.; Wilson, L.L.; Wilson, O.L.; Wilton; Wilton, K.; Winn; Winter, M.; Winters, E.; Wishaw; Wood, A.; Wood, E.P.; Wood, F.H.;

Woodbury, A.G.; Woodhull, M.G.;
Woodhull, Z.M.; Woods, M.L.B.; Woods,
V.; Woolson, C.F.; Wordsworth;
Wright, M.; Wurm; Wycombe; Wylde,
Mrs. H.

Yabsley; Young, M.; Youngs, E.S.

Zaleska; Zech; Zglinitzka; Zimmern;
Zoblinsky

LIST OF ACTRESSES

Achurch, Janet; Ackerman, Irene; Allen, Annie; Alleyn, Annie

Bancroft, Marie Effie (Wilton), Lady; Barry, Helen; Barrymore, Mrs. William; Bateman, Isabel Emilie; Behn, A.; Bessle, Elizabeth; Booth, Mrs.; Bowers, Elizabeth Crocker; Brand, Hannah; Bridges, Eloise; Brunton, Anna (Ross); Burney, Estelle

Carey, Miss; Centlivre, Susanna (Freeman); Chapin, Alice; Charke, Charlotte (Cibber); Chippendale, Mary Jane (Snowden); Cibber, Susanna Maria (Arne); Clayton, Estelle; Clive, Catherine (Raftor); Collette, Mary; Cornelys, Teresa (Imer); Cowen, Henrietta; Cummings, Minnie

Daly, Julia; Davenport, Fanny Lily Gypsy; De La Pasture, Elizabeth Lydia Rosabelle (Bonham); Delesdernier, Emily Pierpont; De Navarro, Mary (Anderson); Derwent, Elfrida; Dickens, Fanny; Dickinson, Anna; Dietz, Linda; Dillon, Clara; Dix, Beulah Marie; Dolaro, Selina; Don, Laura

Evans, Rose

Faucit, Harriett Elizabeth (Diddear); Fiddes, Josephine; Filippi, Rosina; Fiske, Minnie Maddern (Davey); Fogerty, Elsie; Furniss, Grace Livingston

Ganthony, Nellie; Gardner, (Cheney); Gibbs, P. Graddon; Griffith, Elizabeth (Griffith); Grove, Florence Craufurd

Hatton, Ann Julia (Kemble); Hatton, Bessie; Haywood, Eliza (Fowler); Henderson, Henrietta; Hill, Philippina (Burton); Hilton, Hilda; Hook, Harriet Horncastle (Madden); Hughes, Annie

Inchbald, Elizabeth (Simpson); Irish, Annie

Jordan, Dorothy Bland

Keene, Laura; Kelly, Frances Maria; Kemble, Frances Anne; Kemble, Marie-Therese (DeCamp); Kidder, Kathryn

Lancaster-Wallis, Ellen; Lewis, Catharine; Lindley, Henrietta; Logan, Olive

Monckton, Lady; Moubrey, Lilian

Pope, Miss; Pritchard, Johanna

Richardson, Sarah (Watts); Ritchie, Anna Cora (Ogden) Mowatt; Roberts, Sara (Lacy); Robertson, Mrs.; Robinson, Mary (Darby); Rowson, Susanna (Haswell)

Saker, Marie (O'Brien); Sandford, Edith; Santley, Kate; Siddons, Sarah (Kemble); Stoepel, Matilda Agnes (Heron); Scott, J.M.

Thomson, Augusta

Ulmer, Lizzie May

Vandenhoff, Charlotte Elizabeth; Vokes, Victoria

Wade, Florence; Wilde, Lilla; Wilton, Kate; Winslow, Catherine Mary

Yarnold, Emma

SUBJECT INDEX

Abolition, 501, 877, 912, 1484, 1670, 2150, 2151, 2189, 2202, 2252, 2469, 2510

Adaptations and Translations (see also Appendix), 106, 148-149, 257, 259, 664, 1138, 1367, 1577, 1764, 1831, 1905, 1933, 2174, 2575, 2630, 2744

Allegory, 1991, 2412, 2580

Amateur, 131, 556, 571, 654, 674-676, 711-714, 718, 719, 830, 915, 1138, 1139, 1167, 1181, 1299, 1303, 1342, 1346, 1378, 1435-1453, 1638-1641, 1643, 1644, 1677, 1736-1744, 1765, 1836, 1838, 1924, 1962, 1968-1970, 1972, 2015, 2029, 2031, 2032, 2163, 2226-2229, 2356-2358, 2360, 2373, 2386, 2387, 2392, 2393, 2440, 2441, 2511, 2522, 2575, 2706, 2741

American Indian, 113, 345, 700, 767, 779, 1166, 1672, 2729

Ballad opera, 274, 864, 1178, 1760

Ballet, 967, 1017, 1584

Biblical heroines, 348, 691, 897, 1117, 1743, 1965, 2118, 2239, 2306, 2529, 2573, 2582, 2727

Biblical themes, 348, 456, 691, 897, 1002, 1117, 1127, 1632, 1743, 1884-1886, 1890, 1891, 1922, 1965, 2118, 2239, 2306, 2408, 2529, 2582, 2607, 2706, 2727

Burlesque, 65, 605, 614, 968, 1178, 1179, 1295, 1405, 1470, 1475, 1836, 1957, 2021, 2101, 2196, 2238, 2270, 2316, 2343, 2417, 2460, 2475, 2696

Canadian history, 688, 939, 1842

Cantata, 385, 670, 985, 1639, 1642, 2627

Charade, 38, 67, 216, 273, 314, 317, 941, 1144, 1186, 1238, 1419, 1454, 1455, 1459, 1733, 1999, 2075, 2357, 2358, 2362, 2364, 2365, 2367-2380, 2383, 2385, 2653, 2772

Christmas, 132, 226, 319, 414, 721, 722, 858, 1056, 1145, 1345, 1455, 1464, 1637, 1638, 1641, 1677, 1737, 1738, 1741, 1928, 2029, 2552, 2735, 2750

Classical themes and myths, 131, 220, 286, 288, 342, 343, 672, 674-676, 817, 820, 823, 826, 908-910, 1077, 1161, 1162, 1316, 1317, 1448, 1453, 1594, 1702, 1708, 1811, 2141, 2170, 2199, 2234, 2300, 2465, 2466, 2609

Comedietta, 55, 58-60, 110, 138, 139, 147, 148, 180, 182, 187, 190, 192, 194, 195, 197, 199, 205, 206, 208-210, 214, 215, 218, 239, 245, 249, 250, 265-268, 281, 324, 326, 333, 334, 353, 386, 398, 400-403, 411, 412, 485, 492, 508, 513, 518, 530, 567, 568, 608, 619, 623, 640, 697, 698, 710, 711, 713, 718, 719, 726, 760, 777, 828, 829, 832, 836, 854, 892, 893, 904, 944, 1000, 1001, 1003, 1028, 1034, 1081, 1082, 1087, 1088, 1102, 1121, 1135, 1139, 1141, 1197, 1199, 1200, 1205, 1207, 1234, 1263, 1266, 1290, 1308, 1332, 1387, 1418, 1423, 1435, 1440, 1442, 1444, 1445, 1447, 1449, 1472, 1473, 1483, 1523, 1526, 1528, 1529, 1530, 1533, 1538, 1539, 1540, 1542, 1543, 1560, 1565, 1567, 1570, 1571, 1587, 1621, 1622, 1660, 1663, 1664, 1674, 1690, 1723, 1776, 1780, 1781, 1782, 1784, 1787, 1788, 1790, 1791, 1793-1800, 1806, 1813, 1839, 1840, 1905, 1906, 1994, 2003-2006, 2008, 2009, 2011, 2024, 2054, 2059, 2061, 2065, 2069, 2070, 2071, 2140, 2143, 2162, 2186, 2187, 2226-2228, 2232, 2247, 2276, 2280, 2290, 2301, 2317, 2320, 2324, 2358, 2359, 2364, 2366, 2368-2373, 2377, 2379, 2383, 2386, 2401, 2403, 2416, 2418, 2422, 2431, 2437, 2438, 2448, 2450, 2463, 2478, 2484, 2489, 2496, 2498, 2549, 2564, 2568, 2570-2572, 2583, 2584, 2589, 2595, 2602, 2640, 2677, 2701, 2711, 2736, 2766, 2776

Comedy, 7, 14, 30, 40, 45, 53, 66, 69, 78, 83, 86, 87, 93, 98, 100, 102, 116, 126, 129, 130, 140, 141, 150, 151, 153-156, 160, 165, 169-174, 177,

189, 203, 207, 210, 214, 219, 221,
222, 229, 232, 236, 237, 248, 252,
257, 261, 311, 312, 323, 327, 329,
338, 339, 344, 354, 355, 361, 366,
370, 377, 380, 397, 399, 404, 423,
428, 434, 458, 462-464, 466, 467,
469, 470, 472-475, 477-479, 481-483,
496, 514, 519, 526, 527, 529, 532,
533, 542, 554, 555, 563, 569, 570,
593, 594, 615, 616, 620, 622, 624,
627-629, 631-636, 638, 642, 643, 648-
650, 654, 656, 659, 664-666, 673,
684, 685, 689, 692, 693, 695, 703,
706, 720, 724, 725, 730, 731, 745,
750, 753, 762, 765, 781, 782, 786,
789, 792-794, 799, 848, 853, 855,
857, 859, 863, 873, 875, 894, 905,
917, 918, 922, 923, 925, 927, 938,
947, 949, 954, 957, 961-963, 972,
989-993, 997, 1014, 1015, 1032, 1033,
1041-1043, 1045, 1047, 1048, 1061,
1062, 1085, 1086, 1090, 1091, 1093,
1095-1100, 1113, 1123-1125, 1131,
1132, 1136-1138, 1152, 1153, 1155,
1171, 1176, 1180, 1202, 1211, 1216,
1235, 1245, 1246, 1248, 1250, 1252,
1253, 1262, 1264, 1265, 1267, 1268,
1279, 1280, 1298, 1312, 1319, 1320,
1325, 1333, 1346, 1356, 1361, 1363,
1366, 1370, 1373, 1377-1379, 1385,
1388, 1400, 1407, 1410, 1411, 1413,
1414, 1421, 1476, 1479, 1500, 1501,
1504, 1518, 1521, 1532, 1536, 1546,
1547, 1551, 1553, 1592, 1593, 1611,
1615, 1616, 1618, 1626-1628, 1630,
1633, 1645, 1665, 1666, 1668, 1675,
1678, 1679, 1688, 1706, 1710, 1745,
1750, 1761, 1766, 1774, 1776-1779,
1808, 1810, 1827, 1829-1831, 1835,
1837, 1838, 1850, 1879, 1910, 1914,
1916, 1924, 1926, 1927, 1929, 1937,
1939-1953, 1955, 1969-1973, 1978,
1980, 1981, 1983, 1993, 2039, 2040,
2056, 2064, 2084, 2086, 2087, 2090,
2091, 2095, 2116, 2124, 2126, 2138,
2149, 2157, 2158, 2165, 2168, 2174-
2176, 2179, 2180, 2188, 2191, 2194,
2220, 2224, 2243, 2249, 2257, 2258,
2261, 2263, 2271, 2289, 2291, 2295,
2296, 2302, 2320-2322, 2325, 2331,
2334, 2336, 2338, 2339, 2340, 2346,
2347, 2353, 2359, 2361, 2394, 2395,
2419, 2423, 2425, 2440-2442, 2453,
2464, 2481, 2515, 2528, 2544, 2546-
2548, 2550, 2551, 2553-2556, 2563,
2575, 2586, 2588, 2599, 2610-2612,
2620, 2626, 2630, 2631, 2634-2636,
2670, 2681, 2699, 2702, 2703, 2705,
2707, 2716, 2739, 2741, 2742, 2749,
2753, 2755, 2761, 2762, 2771, 2773,
2777, 2783, 2784, 2824-2826

Comic opera, 71, 340, 341, 352, 358,
359, 534, 610, 663, 809, 1031, 1218,
1288, 1384, 1508, 1525, 1550, 1897,
1898, 2085, 2107, 2171, 2223, 2253,
2265, 2282, 2283, 2332, 2462, 2808

Comic sketch, 1220-1223, 1227-1229,
1233, 1235-1238, 1240-1244, 1322,
1446, 2569, 2625

Dialect, 547, 758, 848, 1226, 1402-
1404, 1439, 1597, 2020, 2048, 2486,
2493

Dialogue, 125, 132, 241, 300, 302-
305, 307, 343, 459, 522-524, 641,
701, 715, 717, 769, 784, 813, 861,
872, 1022, 1214, 1225, 1232, 1338-
1341, 1381, 1397, 1513, 1515, 1597,
1631, 1635, 1636, 1638, 1717, 1718,
1892, 1893, 1922, 1923, 2141, 2153,
2329, 2330, 2518, 2600, 2675, 2774,
2786

Domestic drama, 29, 104, 123, 406,
528, 572, 586, 956, 1026, 1386, 1512,
1699, 1802, 1807, 2010, 2163

Drama, 1, 3, 5, 9, 24, 25, 33, 39,
49, 57, 70, 79, 80, 92, 95, 106, 109,
111, 115, 118, 127, 133, 179, 193,
224, 231, 238, 242, 243, 246, 253,
254, 258, 259, 272, 284-286, 295,
309, 335-337, 345, 348, 350, 362,
363, 381, 405, 415, 419, 424, 427,
429, 433, 437, 445, 453, 457, 489,
491, 494, 498, 500, 531, 579, 580,
583, 585, 591, 592, 595, 596, 600-
602, 606, 609, 645, 646, 647, 651,
668, 677-679, 681, 683, 686, 691,
709, 732, 736, 744, 749, 751, 770,
772, 773, 778, 779, 788, 790, 802,
805, 833, 846, 871, 876, 877, 880,
884-886, 888, 889, 891, 926, 933-936,
946, 948, 950, 952, 988, 1002, 1005,
1007-1011, 1018, 1044, 1049, 1058,
1060, 1064, 1066, 1068, 1079, 1089,
1092, 1104, 1107-1110, 1112, 1114,
1115, 1116, 1126, 1158, 1160, 1175,
1183, 1191, 1194, 1195, 1208, 1212,
1217, 1251, 1281, 1282, 1285-1287,
1289, 1291, 1311, 1314, 1318, 1324,
1326, 1344, 1364, 1371, 1372, 1376,
1389, 1391, 1392, 1406, 1408, 1424,
1480, 1494, 1495, 1497, 1505, 1509,
1510, 1535, 1555, 1557, 1566, 1573,
1575-1583, 1590, 1591, 1598, 1600,
1601, 1612, 1625, 1646, 1653, 1656-
1658, 1669, 1676, 1694, 1696, 1700,
1720, 1731, 1732, 1752, 1753, 1764,
1765, 1773, 1804, 1805, 1809, 1815,
1817, 1832, 1841, 1842, 1846, 1849,
1873, 1878, 1915, 1968, 1982, 1988,
1992, 1995, 1996, 2026, 2043, 2055,
2063, 2073, 2078, 2102, 2104, 2108-
2113, 2115, 2118, 2121, 2122, 2125,

2137, 2139, 2145, 2147, 2160, 2161,
2164, 2166, 2167, 2169, 2172, 2173,
2177, 2183, 2189, 2197, 2202, 2215,
2221, 2222, 2231, 2241, 2242, 2244,
2266, 2272, 2273, 2277, 2288, 2298,
2319, 2333, 2335, 2390, 2392, 2393,
2396, 2406, 2435, 2444, 2445, 2447,
2449, 2456, 2457, 2458, 2461, 2469,
2471, 2473, 2474, 2476, 2477, 2487,
2505, 2508, 2510, 2519, 2520, 2521,
2526, 2527, 2531-2538, 2541, 2557,
2558, 2562, 2596, 2603, 2616, 2623,
2624, 2637, 2654, 2656, 2658, 2659,
2665, 2685, 2695, 2698, 2706, 2708,
2709, 2720, 2723, 2743, 2767, 2792,
2793, 2797, 2802, 2809, 2812-2814,
2818, 2820, 2821

Dramatic poem, 8, 357, 376, 416, 430,
431, 456, 502, 687, 734, 739, 766,
803, 804, 831, 838, 883, 965, 1019,
1029, 1037, 1050, 1094, 1117, 1118,
1127, 1190, 1192, 1209, 1215, 1283,
1323, 1334, 1347, 1382, 1383, 1431,
1514, 1524, 1594, 1595, 1596, 1604-
1607, 1629, 1632, 1702, 1703, 1758,
1985, 1997, 2042, 2136, 2142, 2146,
2170, 2184, 2218, 2239, 2243, 2256,
2274, 2300, 2304, 2389, 2407, 2408,
2413, 2420, 2480, 2504, 2506, 2543,
2573, 2580, 2608, 2609, 2622, 2641,
2647, 2727, 2787, 2796, 2798

Dramatic sketch, 181, 230, 251, 712,
920, 1020, 1067, 1078, 1172, 1304,
1436, 1439, 1441, 1648, 1691, 1692,
1770, 1818, 1819, 1853-1855, 1857-
1859, 1896, 1986, 1987, 2154, 2155,
2159, 2206-2210, 2303, 2405, 2432,
2485, 2530, 2657, 2660, 2662, 2663,
2666-2669, 2765, 2801, 2816

Duologue, 4, 137, 144-146, 183, 184,
240, 368, 369, 418, 425, 435, 436,
438, 440, 441, 446-450, 452, 490,
505-507, 509, 510, 515, 525, 530,
582, 743, 747, 847, 849, 913, 922,
929, 1059, 1074, 1129, 1135, 1213,
1296, 1425, 1518, 1564, 1571, 1620,
1623, 1682, 1693, 1722, 1792, 1814,
1961, 2002, 2007, 2012, 2135, 2229,
2308, 2310, 2312, 2314, 2315, 2488,
2490, 2491, 2517, 2567, 2621, 2700,
2817

Early Christians, 92, 1118, 1212,
1997

Easter, 1640, 1642

English Civil War, 170-172, 668, 781,
895, 2712

English history, 42, 88, 291, 298,
379, 429, 588, 843, 896, 899, 920,

972, 1053, 1055, 1078, 1126, 1212,
1294, 1297, 1511, 1709, 1762, 1845,
1856, 1859, 1887, 1992, 2005, 2181,
2489, 2495, 2507, 2508, 2810

Entertainment, 11, 301, 317, 319,
347, 414, 455, 571, 576, 577, 808,
810, 830, 835, 862, 967, 969, 970,
1016, 1036, 1073, 1181, 1299, 1303,
1305, 1307, 1309, 1310, 1337, 1342,
1404, 1416, 1463, 1493, 1736, 1738-
1740, 1742, 1744, 1962, 1979, 2018,
2019, 2029, 2030, 2036, 2128, 2217,
2279, 2316, 2545, 2735, 2737, 2738

Extravaganza, 488, 1460-1463, 1475,
1478, 1705, 1816, 2615

Fairy, 121, 517, 536, 811, 818, 825,
858, 940, 1128, 1155, 1167, 1197,
1198, 1214, 1261, 1313, 1337, 1427,
1437, 1438, 1460-1463, 1465, 1470,
1474, 1475, 1478, 1481, 1617, 1644,
1655, 1756, 1757, 2035, 2246, 2248,
2327, 2356, 2357, 2360, 2516, 2560,
2601

Farce, 10, 12, 13, 15, 28, 52, 56,
119, 134-136, 157, 159, 200, 235,
256, 260, 262-264, 315, 316, 320,
322, 325, 328, 330, 346, 351, 387,
388, 390, 393, 413, 420-422, 454,
465, 471, 480, 484, 495, 521, 547-
553, 578, 581, 637, 657, 669, 699,
733, 754, 756, 800, 801, 807, 814,
878, 881, 951, 973, 976, 977, 981,
998, 1040, 1063, 1065, 1069, 1101,
1103, 1119, 1120, 1196, 1269, 1270,
1321, 1327, 1357, 1358, 1362, 1368,
1369, 1374, 1375, 1412, 1430, 1432,
1468, 1498, 1516, 1544, 1548, 1561,
1563, 1667, 1673, 1681, 1754, 1767,
1768, 1785, 1786, 1789, 1881, 1901,
1907, 1909, 1931, 1974, 1989, 2013,
2014, 2028, 2047, 2066, 2067, 2068,
2072, 2077, 2097, 2100, 2103, 2106,
2127, 2152, 2201, 2216, 2240, 2250,
2251, 2287, 2297, 2337, 2341, 2342,
2344, 2387, 2415, 2424, 2429, 2430,
2433, 2483, 2539, 2542, 2559, 2561,
2587, 2613, 2617-2619, 2649, 2671,
2673, 2697, 2740, 2764, 2775, 2778,
2791, 2794, 2795

Female characters, 18, 56, 131, 143,
145, 148, 213, 276, 277, 315, 320,
322, 420, 421, 425, 435, 448, 505,
555, 712, 714, 716, 758, 829, 878,
921, 964, 985, 986, 990, 992, 1034,
1073, 1102, 1134, 1214, 1304, 1435,
1436, 1440, 1441, 1445, 1448, 1453,
1464, 1466, 1467, 1523, 1526-1533,
1535-1544, 1567, 1570, 1620, 1621,
1623, 1663, 1678, 1716, 1739, 1742,

1785, 1814, 1907, 1909, 1924, 1959, 1964, 2016, 2018, 2020, 2028, 2045, 2046, 2051-2053, 2141, 2175-2177, 2196, 2308, 2314, 2329, 2346, 2347, 2388, 2392, 2393, 2397, 2445, 2515, 2517, 2542, 2544, 2547, 2566, 2588, 2677, 2816

French history, 258, 1281, 1283, 1495, 1545, 2043, 2104, 2136, 2220, 2526, 2443

French Revolution, 133, 1367

Greek history, 20, 680, 734, 1140, 1284, 2082

Heroines, 18, 113, 114, 118, 220, 291, 343, 378, 429, 460, 561, 595, 626, 682, 688, 704, 708, 748, 764, 772, 773, 785, 869, 870, 958, 1002, 1009, 1044, 1053, 1058, 1078, 1118, 1150, 1157, 1165, 1194, 1209, 1210, 1315, 1329-1331, 1347, 1494, 1517, 1524, 1549, 1632, 1708, 1747, 1749, 1751, 1844, 1859, 1864, 1918, 1992, 1995-1997, 2043, 2096, 2098, 2099, 2108, 2141, 2142, 2170, 2182, 2221, 2231, 2234, 2300, 2443, 2454, 2465-2467, 2514, 2573, 2679, 2720, 2724, 2726

Historical drama, 64, 72, 288, 289, 313, 379, 571, 595, 682, 688, 732, 739, 841, 870, 886, 987, 1150-1152, 1156, 1160, 1164, 1188, 1214, 1347, 1383, 1494, 1520, 1557, 1588, 1596, 1652, 1720, 1842, 1924, 2006, 2009, 2034, 2044, 2110, 2206-2210, 2219, 2274, 2386, 2407, 2410, 2413, 2444, 2471, 2540, 2574, 2723, 2724, 2726, 2781

Holidays, 347, 774, 865, 914, 969, 970, 1036, 1337, 1443, 1643, 2529

Home performance, 137, 245-250, 314, 319, 321-329, 398, 400-403, 521, 588-590, 684-686, 769, 835, 913, 922, 956, 973, 1022, 1056, 1076, 1077, 1101, 1123-1125, 1145, 1197-1200, 1300, 1454, 1455, 1460-1462, 1464-1468, 1470, 1472-1475, 1478, 1480-1482, 1526-1533, 1535-1544, 1617, 2001-2005, 2007-2012, 2075, 2076, 2246, 2248, 2308, 2311-2315, 2359, 2361, 2364, 2366, 2368, 2369-2372, 2377, 2379, 2383, 2567-2571, 2572, 2601, 2749-2760

Interlude, 122, 383, 535, 536, 633, 653, 658, 1369, 1499, 1503, 2060, 2062, 2382, 2744, 2745

Irish life and culture, 105, 275, 529, 927, 946, 949, 952, 1016, 1041, 1114, 1597, 1618, 1848, 1988, 2044, 2305, 2496, 2580, 2773

Jewish life and culture, 27, 865, 1595

Joan of Arc, 1703, 2284, 2502, 2660

Juvenile Author, 113, 352, 356, 561, 2276, 2780, 2787

Lady Jane Grey, 117, 1078, 1159, 2146, 2304

Legends and legendary figures, 34, 275, 1153, 1156, 1158, 1192, 2490, 2514

Libretto, 31, 233, 391, 603, 604, 607, 611, 613, 671, 945, 1174, 1316, 1485-1492, 1724-1729, 1895, 2199, 2285, 2292, 2326, 2332, 2530, 2578, 2638, 2807

Literary figures, 47, 831, 1072, 2148, 2343, 2460

Mary, Queen of Scots, 297, 538, 766, 1496, 2576

Masque, 108, 131, 274, 392, 520, 674, 676, 722, 909, 985, 986, 1146, 1443, 1453, 1647, 1654, 1695, 1730, 1811, 1866, 1958, 1991, 2027, 2523, 2585, 2652, 2746, 2769, 2789, 2790, 2817

Melodrama, 105, 439, 573, 746, 780, 837, 928, 1025, 1038, 1046, 1084, 1147, 1230, 1292, 1422, 1522, 1589, 1714, 1803, 2037, 2081, 2117, 2119, 2214, 2269, 2294

Memorial volume, 537, 814, 2787

Military drama, 952, 1379

Minstrel, 501, 1181, 1301, 1307, 2028, 2397

Monologue, 143, 185, 188, 201, 202, 204, 211-213, 276-280, 511, 512, 516, 530, 716, 752, 755, 757, 758, 775, 874, 921, 1083, 1134, 1142, 1143, 1585, 1680, 1683, 1684, 1716, 1783, 1845, 2015, 2016, 2020, 2045, 2046, 2049, 2051-2053, 2566, 2730, 2732, 2734

Musical, 4, 79, 95, 317, 392, 393, 394, 760, 808, 810, 816, 862, 949, 994, 995, 996, 1016, 1115, 1146, 1212, 1415, 1416, 1516, 1605-1607,

1638, 1640, 1695, 2128, 2217, 2246,
2248, 2417, 2286, 2537, 2539, 2744,
2746, 2764,

Musical comedy, 797, 943, 945, 1206,
2001, 2041, 2472, 2751, 2757, 2758,
2760, 2763

Musical sketch, 1812, 2185

Mystery and morality plays, 68, 416,
1254-1260, 1296, 1323, 1928, 2411,
2543, 2607

Opera, 18, 31, 283, 499, 587, 652,
660, 898, 998, 1166, 1261, 1426,
1427, 1448, 1485, 1586, 1870, 1895,
2025, 2252, 2318, 2326, 2615, 2811,
2827

Operetta, 6, 16, 63, 306, 379, 395,
566, 612, 671, 798, 806, 964, 1030,
1070, 1071, 1182, 1302, 1345, 1420,
1637, 1641, 1644, 1713, 1746, 1828,
1875, 1919, 2022, 2212, 2213, 2236,
2285, 2398, 2399, 2400, 2421, 2434,
2803, 2804, 2828

Pageant, 1073, 1549, 1671, 2031, 2733

Pantomime, 382, 661, 916, 1168, 1169,
1313, 1469, 2728,

Pastoral, 108, 294, 343, 430, 459,
653, 655, 812, 959, 1203, 1204, 1415,
1513, 1552, 1629, 1892, 1959, 1998,
2525, 2529, 2597

Patriotic, 527, 576, 969, 1146, 2251,
2468, 2774

Proverb plays, 356, 426, 644, 2076,
2355, 2356, 2366, 2381, 2384, 2511

Recitation, 68, 125, 308, 502, 503,
575, 696, 776, 921, 1021-1024, 1053,
1402, 1403, 1613, 1707, 1732, 1775,
1904, 2048

Roman history, 81, 118, 559, 1035,
1343, 1719, 1816, 1997, 2650, 2390

Sappho, 966, 1029, 1609, 1651, 1964

Satire, 47, 191, 495, 631, 637, 686,
765, 827, 982, 983, 1633, 1687, 1689,
1715, 2148, 2622, 2628, 2643, 2644,
2645, 2646, 2732

Scottish history, 540, 599, 785, 824,
1714, 2119, 2211,

Sketch, 196, 217, 247, 275, 384, 389,
394, 409, 543, 574, 714, 841-845,

850, 851, 856, 908, 914, 915, 994-
996, 1081, 1226, 1531, 1556, 1558,
1559, 1568, 1572, 1652, 1660, 1662,
1670, 1871, 1872, 2311, 2313, 2486,
2492-2494, 2497, 2750, 2756, 2759,

Spectacle, 2293, 2468,

Suffrage, 686, 701, 1683, 2221, 2521,
2786

Tableaux, 27, 125, 577, 668, 984,
1055, 1317, 1319, 2017, 2078, 2120,
2349, 2350, 2375, 2428

Temperance, 57, 58, 125, 300-307,
385, 575-577, 876, 881, 1021, 1023,
1024, 1236, 1613, 1707, 1717, 1718,
1775, 1833, 1904, 1920, 1923, 2153,
2196, 2335, 2518, 2522

Tragedy, 18, 19, 20, 22, 23, 64, 81,
82, 84, 85, 88-91, 94, 95, 97, 99,
101, 103, 104, 113, 117, 128, 151,
220, 287, 292, 297, 313, 342, 343,
375, 378, 460, 468, 476, 538, 539,
540, 561, 562, 564, 565, 626, 630,
639, 662, 672, 682, 700, 702, 704,
708, 734, 748, 764, 766, 783, 785,
816, 866, 869, 870, 896, 897, 900,
939, 955, 958, 966, 987, 1012, 1035,
1053, 1080, 1094, 1105, 1111, 1140,
1149, 1150, 1159, 1161, 1165, 1176,
1177, 1188, 1193, 1210, 1215, 1247,
1249, 1284, 1294, 1297, 1315, 1328,
1329, 1330, 1331, 1343, 1367, 1401,
1428, 1496, 1511, 1517, 1520, 1545,
1548, 1574, 1588, 1595, 1596, 1603,
1614, 1649, 1650, 1651, 1708, 1719,
1747, 1749, 1751, 1759, 1762, 1763,
1844, 1856, 1861, 1864, 1865, 1869,
1876, 1887-1889, 1918, 1938, 1954,
1956, 1963, 1990, 2033, 2079, 2082,
2088, 2089, 2092-2094, 2096, 2114,
2126, 2129, 2146, 2150, 2151, 2170,
2181, 2182, 2211, 2219, 2225, 2233,
2234, 2275, 2284, 2300, 2407, 2420,
2426, 2427, 2443, 2451, 2454, 2455,
2466, 2467, 2470, 2482, 2502, 2505,
2512, 2540, 2574, 2581, 2582, 2606,
2614, 2633, 2648, 2650, 2679, 2680,
2682, 2724-2726, 2752, 2780, 2781,
2788, 2810, 2819

Tragi-comedy, 161, 175, 271, 2117

U.S. Civil War, 331, 1080, 1240,
2017, 2388, 2510, 2632

U.S. History, 113, 253, 254, 527,
528, 667, 955, 1079, 1107, 1146,
1194, 1231, 1670, 1671, 1672, 2253

U.S. Revolution, 73, 1510, 2643

Vaudeville, 108, 2198, 2200

Verse (see also Dramatic poem), 64,
65, 68, 80, 82, 84, 88-92, 94, 99,
108, 112, 113, 117, 150, 160, 275,
283, 284, 286-292, 294, 297, 299,
312, 313, 343, 347, 348, 350, 356,
359, 375, 378, 381, 476, 494, 498,
503, 538, 539, 540, 556, 562-565,
578, 652, 672, 683, 691, 700-702,
708, 764, 783, 785, 870, 897, 900,
931, 958, 1021-1024, 1029, 1038,
1053, 1055, 1064, 1109, 1147, 1149,
1150, 1152, 1153, 1156, 1158-1162,
1165, 1177, 1178, 1188, 1191, 1193,
1197, 1198, 1210, 1212, 1214, 1247,
1249, 1284, 1295, 1296, 1316, 1328,
1330, 1331, 1343, 1378, 1426, 1443,
1460-1463, 1465, 1470, 1475, 1478,
1481, 1482, 1496, 1497, 1508, 1517,
1545, 1574, 1603, 1610, 1614, 1650,
1651, 1654, 1716, 1719, 1736, 1739,
1742, 1744, 1747, 1749, 1751-1753,
1759, 1761-1763, 1811, 1821-1825,
1845, 1853-1857, 1861, 1865, 1869,
1884-1892, 1957, 1960, 1963, 1968,
1990, 2015, 2016, 2027, 2035, 2036,
2056, 2092-2094, 2096, 2098, 2126,
2145, 2150, 2151, 2153, 2181, 2182,
2190, 2202, 2211, 2213, 2222, 2225,
2233, 2234, 2235, 2246, 2248, 2275,
2284, 2306, 2390, 2410-2412, 2428,
2444, 2452, 2454, 2455, 2471, 2476,
2477, 2479, 2504, 2505, 2507, 2508,
2514, 2516, 2520, 2523-2526, 2540,
2581, 2582, 2600, 2601, 2606, 2607,
2614, 2656-2660, 2662, 2663, 2665-
2668, 2669, 2675, 2679, 2680, 2723-
2726, 2769, 2782, 2797, 2810, 2811,
2818, 2819

INDEX OF ADAPTATIONS AND TRANSLATIONS

Aeschylus

Browning, E.B.

Swanwick, A.

Webster, J.A.D.

Agrell, Alfhild

Bell, F.E.

Alexander, Mrs., pseud. [Annie (French) Hector]

Lindley, H.

Alcott, Louisa May

Gould, E.L.

Alfieri, Vittorio, Count

Holford, F.

Amalie of Saxony, Princess

Jameson, A.B.M.

Ameen, Elin

Bell, F.E.

Anderson, Hans Christian

Jones, L.

Arnaud, Francois Thomas Marie de Baculard d'

M'Taggart, A.

Augier, [Guillaume Victor] Émile

Greville, B.V.G., Baroness

Austen, Jane

Fillipi, R.

Barrière, Théodore

Glazebrook, H.

Beaumarchais, Pierre Augustin Caron de

Griffith, E.G.

Beaumont, Francis

Booth, Mrs.

N., M.

Behn, Aphra

Cowley, H.

Benedix, Julius Roderich

Wall, A.R.

Bennett, John

Lütkenhaus, A.M.I.

Bible, The

Francis, A.G.

Bird, Robert Montgomery

Medina, L.

Bisson, Alexandre

Riley, C.

Bizet, Georges

Doran, M.

Black, William

Merivale, Mrs.

Stockton, E.

Boccaccio, Giovanni

Pix, M.

Bourlin, Antoine Jean [Dumaniant]

Inchbald, E.S.

Wallace, E.M.

Boutet de Monvel, Jacques Marie
[Monvel, Jacques Marie Boutet de]

H_____, E.

Bremond, Sébastien

Pix, M.

Brome, Richard

Behn, A.

Bunn, Alfred

Kellogg, C.L.

Bunyan, John

Siddons, S.K.

Burnett, Frances Eliza (Hodgson)

Burnett, F.E.H.

Calderón de la Barca, Pedro

Holcroft, F.

Cameron, Caroline Emily, Mrs. Lovett
Cameron

Morland, C.E.

Campe, Joachim Heinrich

Helme, E.

Cané, Miguel

Denvil, Mrs.

Carroll, Lewis, pseud. [Charles
Dodgson]

Delafield, E.

Celenio [Moratin], Inarco

Holcroft, F.
Cervantes, Miguel de

Burton, Mrs. H.S.

Stewart, H.W.

Chapman, George

Lennox, C.R.

Cittin, Mme.

Burney, Frances

Clifford, Lucy (Lane)

Clifford, L.L.

Collins, Wilkie

Bateman, S.

Logan, O.

Connelly, Michael

Lindley, H.

Cook, Mabel Collins

Cook, M.C.

Corneille, Pierre

Brand, H.; Burrell, S.R.

Philips, K.F.

Cosenza, Giovanni Carlo, Baron

Field, M.K.

Cromie, Robert

Lindley, H.

Dahn, Friedrich

Tretbar, H.D.

Daly, [John] Augustin

Hazlewood, Miss
Dancourt, Ernest Grenet-

Beerbohm, C.

Davis, Helen

Davis, H.

Defoe, Daniel

Colman, J.

Delavigne, Jean Francois Casimir

Gore, C.G.F.M.

Wylde, Mrs. H.

Dennery, Adolphe Philippart

Davidson, F.A.

Stevenson, K.

D'Epinay, C.

Beerbohm, C.

Destouches, Philippe [Nericault]

Brand, H.

Inchbald, E.S.

Lady, A

D'Hervilly, Ernest

Beerbohm, C.

Diaz, Abby (Morton)

Chaney, Mrs. G.L.

Dickens, Charles

Bates, R.; Bell, L.C.; Beringer, A.

Johnson, F.M.

Shattuck, H.

Thorne, E.

Wilson, O.L.

Dieulafoy, Joseph Marie Armand Michel

Kemble, M.T.D.

Dreyfus, Abraham

Beerbohm, C.

Dubry, Louis-Emile

Bradbury, L.

Dumanoir, Philippe Francois Pinel

Davidson, F.A.

Dumas, Alexandre, the elder

Kemble, F.A.

Dumas, Alexandre, the younger

Leslie, M.F.F.S.

Stoepel, M.H.

Echegaray, José

Lynch, H.

Edwards, Annie

Edwards, A.

Egan, Pierce, the younger

Pierce, S.E.

Etheredge, Sir George

Pix, M.

Euripedes

Elizabeth I

Lumley, J.

Webster, J.A.D.

Feuillet, Octave

Bell, M.

Fielding, Henry

Haywood, E.

Fletcher, John

Booth, Mrs.

N., M.

Flotow, Friedrich Von

Zoblinsky, C.

Garnier, Robert

Pembroke, M.S.H., Countess

Gaskell, Elizabeth (Cleghorn)

Horne, M.B.

Genlis, Stéphanie Felicité Ducrest de St. Aubin, Comtess de

Inchbald, E.S.

M'Taggart, A.H.

Goethe, Johann Wolfgang Von

Bannan, M.R.; Bennett, A.R.

D'Aguilar, R.

Kellogg, C.

Swanwick, A.

Goldoni, Carlo

Griffith, E.G.

Zimmern, H.

Goldsmith, Oliver

Davenport, F.

Greville, Henry, pseud. [Alice (Fleury) Durand]

Greville, B.V.G.

Grey, Maxwell, pseud. [Mary Gleed Tuttiet]

Garrard, L.

Grillparzar, Frans

Frottingham, E.

Lee, E.B.

Guarini, Battista

Lennox, C.R.

Haggard, H. Rider

Lawrence, E.

Halévy, Ludovic

Ayer, H.H.

Halm, Friedrich

Lovell, M.A.L.

Harte, Bret

Widmer, K.

Hauptmann, Gerhart

Morison, Mary

Hawthorne, Nathaniel

Peck, E.W.

Haywood, Eliza (Fowler)

Minton, A.

Hertz, Henrick

Chapman, J.F.

Heseltine, William

Keteltas, C.M.

Heywood, Thomas

Walker, J.E.

Holberg, Ludvig, Baron

Corbet, Miss

Hugo, Victor

Chapin, A.

Ibsen, Henrik

Archer, F.

Lord, H.F.

Marx, E.

Iffland, August Wilhelm

Geisweiler, M.

Plumptre, A.

Jackson, Helen Hunt

Dillaye, I.

James, Florence Alice (Price)
[Florence Warden, pseud.]

James, F.A.P.

Jarosy, Rudolf

Morse, M.

Jolly, Antoine Francois

Gibbs, J.D.

Jonson, Ben

Lennox, C.R.

Kingsley, Charles

Bowers, E.

Körner, [Karl] Theodore

Tollemache, B.

Kotzebue, August Friedrich Ferdinand
von

Geisweiler, M.

Inchbald, E.S.

Plumptre, A.

Labiche, Eugene Marin

Gibbs, J.D.

Lake, Barbara

Lake, B.

L'Aronge, A.

Morton, M.

Lean, Florence (Marryat) Church

Lean, F.M.C.

Lee, Harriet

Lee, H.

Legouvé, [Gabriel Jean Baptiste]
Ernest Wilfred

Stoepel, M.H.

Le Mierre, Antoine Marin

Starke, M.

Lennox, Charlotte Ramsay

Lennox, C.R.

Lessing, Gotthold Ephraim

Frothingham, E.

Holcroft, F.

Lipmann, Julia Mathilde

Lipmann, J.M.

Longfellow, Henry Wadsworth

DeVine, A.

Furniss, G.L.

Mackean, M.F.

Thompson, C.

Wilson, B.M.

Lytton, Edward Bulwer Lytton, Baron

Medina, L.

Morton, M.

Maeterlinck, Maurice, Count

Porter, C.E.

Manni, Domenico Maria

Ward, Miss

Marivaux, Pierre Carlet de Chamblain de

Clive, C.R.

Marmontel, Jean Francois

Griffith, E.G.

Lady, A

Marston, John

Behn, A.

Lennox, C.R.

Mason, Alfred Edward Woodley

Bateman, I.

Maxwell, Mary Elizabeth (Braddon)

Fairbairn, M.H.

Steer, J.

May, Thomas

Centlivre, S.F.

Meilhac, Henri
Ayer, H.H.

Mercier, Louis Sebastien

Inchbald, E.S.

Mérimée, Prosper

Doran, M.

Metastasio, Pietro Trapassi

Williams, A.

Mills, Elvira L.

Coleman, Mrs. W.

Molière [Jean Baptiste Poquelin]

Centilivre, S.F.

Parsons, E.P.

Monti, Vincenzo

Burney, Frances

More, Hannah

Lady in Connecticut, A

Mornay, Philippe de

Pembroke, M.S.H., Countess

Mosenthal, Salomon

Garthwaite, F.

Moser, Gustav von

Barry, H.

Garraway, A.

Lawrence, E.

Scotti, S.

Münch-Bellinghausen, Eligius Franz
Joseph, Baron [Halm, Fredrich]

Prentiss, I.P.

Ochlenschlager, Adam

Lee, E.B.

Opie, Amelia (Alderson)

Kemble, M.T.D.

Ossian

Fraser, S.

Ouida, pseud. [Louise De la Ramée]

Sandford, E.

Webb, M.G.

Pailleron, Édwourd

Bessle, E.

Pallico, Silvio

Ellet, E.F.

Panton, Jane Ellen

Lindley, H.

Patrat, Joseph

Inchbald, E.S.

Pfahl

Bright, F.

Piestre, Pierre Étienne

Stevenson, K.C.

Pixérécourt, René Charles Guilbert de

Plunkett, E.G.

Plato

Harrison, E.

Pollock, Ellen [Harley St. John,
pseud.]

Pollock, E.

Poullain de St. Foix, Germain
Francois

Cibber, S.A.

Praed, Rosa Caroline (Murray-Prior),
Mrs. Campbell Praed

Praed, R.C.M.

Randolph, Thomas

Behn, A.

Ramsay, Allan

Turner, M.

Reade, Charles

Aldrich, M.

Ellet, E.F.

Reynard, Jean Francois

Centlivre, S.F.

Roberts, Morley

Beringer, A.

Roseux, Armand des
Cadogan, A.

Rowley, William
Pix, M.
Walker, J.E.

Rowson, Susanna
Plumb, H.P.

Rucks, Berta
Weston, E.E.

Rueda, Lupe de
Tollemache, B.

Saint-Pierre, Bernardin de
Ringwalt, J.

Sand, George, pseud. [Amandine Aurore
Lucie Dupin]
Bateman, S.

Sandeau, Jules
Greville, B.V.G.

Sardou, Victorien
Davenport, F.
Richardson, A.S.

Scheffel, Joseph Victor Von
Ross, R.S.

Schiller, Johann Christoph Friedrich
von
Craven, E.
Kemble, F.A.
Molini, Miss

Swanwick, A.
Trelawney, A.

Schmithof, E.
Matthews, E.V.B.

Scott, Walter
Macaulay, E.W.

Scribe, Augustin Eugene
Davidson, Mrs.
Gore, C.
Harrison, C.C.
Wylde, Mrs. H.

Seneca, Lucius Annaeus, the younger
Elizabeth I

Settle, Elkanah
Ariadne

Shakespeare, William
De Navarro, M.; De Nottbeck, G.
Hughes, A.
Siddons, S.K.; Sterling, S.H.
West, A.L.

Sheridan, Frances (Chamberlaine)
Pope, Miss

Siraudin, Paul
Harrison, C.C.

Souvestre, Emile
Keating, E. H.

Stepaniak, R. Sergius

Garnett, C.

Stevenson, Robert Louis

Forepaugh, L.

Stowe, Harriet Elizabeth (Beecher)

Stowe, H.E.B.

Sudermann, Hermann

Lowe, H.T.P.

Swan, Annie [Annie (Swan) Burnett-Smith]

Irish, A.

Swift, Jonathan

Horne, M.B.

Tennyson, Alfred, Baron Tennyson

Haughwout, L.M.

Winn, E.L.

Thanet, Octave, pseud. [Alice French]

Gray, M.C.

Thiboust, Lambert

Glazebrook, H.

Harrison, C.C.

Torring-Gutenzell, Joseph August [Torring und Kronsfeld, J.A. Von]

Starke, M.

Twain, Mark, pseud. [Samuel L. Clemens]

Beringer, A.

Valnay, E.

Hayes, M.X.

Vanlyon, Elizabeth

Richey, O.

Villetard, Edmond

Walcot, M.

Villetard de Pruniers, Adolphe Belot Charles Edmond

Walcot, M.

Voltaire, Francois Marie Arouet de

Celesia, D.

Weisse, Christian Felix

Holcroft, F.

Whittier, John Greenleaf

Little, S.L.R.

Whyte-Melville, George John

Forrester, S.

Wilenbrugh, Ernst von

Zglinitzka, M. von

Wilford, [Florence] Miss

Prevost, C.M.

Wills, William Gorman

Davenport, F.

Wood, Ellen Price

Wilde, L.

Wood, E.P.

Zschokke, Johann Heinrich

Farjeon, E.